LANSDOWNE

The Last Great Whig

LANSDOWNE

The Last Great Whig

SIMON KERRY

Published in 2017 by Unicorn,
an imprint of Unicorn Publishing Group LLP
101 Wardour Street
London
W1F 0UG

www.unicornpublishing.org

A catalogue record for this book is available from the British Library

Every effort has been made to trace copyright holders and to obtain
their permission for the use of copyrighted material. The publisher
apologises for any errors or omissions and would be grateful to be
notified of any corrections that should be incorporated in future
reprints or editions of this book.

ISBN 978-1-910787-95-3

Edited by Johanna Stephenson
Proofread by Ramona Lamport
Designed by Ocky Murray
Printed in Slovenia

CONTENTS

ACKNOWLEDGEMENTS

DOREEN SLATER FIRST introduced me to the Bowood Archives and the 5th Marquess of Lansdowne's papers in the late 1970s. Kate Fielden and Jo Johnston have subsequently spoilt me with their knowledge and expertise on the subject. To Lord Lansdowne and the Trustees of the Bowood Collection I am very grateful to have been given free access to the archive and permission to use material.

Since the 5th Marquess's papers have been housed in the British Library they have been painstakingly catalogued by Dr Robert Smith, Dr Christopher Wright, Dr William Frame and more recently Dr Alexander Lock.

I would especially like to thank Christopher and William for all their help.

To the all those members of the British Library staff at the Western Manuscripts Reading Room that I encountered during my research I would like to express my thanks.

I should like to acknowledge the gracious permission of Her Majesty the Queen to quote from material in the Royal Archives.

The standard and condition of documents that I have researched in both private and public collections has been exceptional and in all but one case access to the papers has been made easily available. I would like to recognise the generosity and friendliness of all the archivists and staff that I have encountered. In particular, I would like to mention Colin Harris at the Bodleian, James Towe and Aidan Haley at Chatsworth, Robin Harcourt Williams and Vicki Perry at Hatfield, Mark Blunt at Hove, Tony Pilmer at the Royal United Services Institute, and Pam Clarke at the Royal Archives at Windsor.

I would like to thank Anne de Courcy, Dr Laurence Guymer,

Professor Jane Ridley, Professor John Rogister, Mary Rycroft and Dr Kamini Vellodi, for reading draft chapters of the book. As exceptionally busy individuals it was extremely generous of them to spare the time to do this. The work has benefitted and been improved enormously from their suggestions and advice.

I owe a huge debt to Professor Thomas Otte who supervised my PhD. He was and continues to be a great inspirer, enthusiast and original thinker.

Over the years that I have researched Lansdowne, I have met and been introduced to many individuals interested in him and his world. Among those with whom I have had some fascinating and insightful discussions and correspondence on the subject I would like to thank The Duke of Abercorn, Dr Lana Asfour, Lord Astor of Hever, Philip Astor, Lord Baker of Dorking, Nicholas Baring, David Bigham, Jamie Bigham, Charles Cator, Dr Hugh Cecil, Dr Jonathan Conlin, Lord Dalmeny, Dr Jenny Davy, The Duke of Devonshire, The Lord Digby, Lord Egremont, Dr Peter Frankopan, Dr Andrew Gailey, Dr Jayne Gifford, Dr Thomas Goldsmith, Peter Hardy, The Lord Heseltine, Bea Hemming, Dr Geoff Hicks, Gerard Hill, Lady Diana Holderness, Professor Anthony Howe, The Marquis of Huntly, Lord King of Bridgwater, Ramona Lamport, Andrew Lownie, Imogen Lycett Green, Professor Ranald Macdonald, Diana Makgill, Lord Robert Mercer-Nairne, Joanna, Viscountess Mersey, Geoffrey Morley, Ocky Murray, Cathy St Germans, Gaia Servadio Myddelton-Biddulph, Peter Sinclair, Professor Sir Hew Strachan, Lady Emma Tenant, Dr Ralph Townsend, The Late Marquess of Waterford and Suzanne Williams.

It is pleasant to acknowledge the substantial assistance I have received from Unicorn. I very much appreciate the support Ian Strathcarron gave my work. I would also like to thank Lucy Duckworth, Ryan Gearing and Simon Perks. In helping with editing and providing a critical eye I am especially grateful to Johanna Stephenson.

Finally, my deepest thanks are to my loving and supportive wife, Nadine, to whom this book is dedicated.

A NOTE ON THE NAMES

Many names and terms that were used by Lansdowne and his contemporaries have since changed: Bombay/Mumbai; Burma/Myanmar, etc. In order to tell Lansdowne's story and the world that he lived in I have preserved many of the original names and terms then in use while also recognising their modern equivalents.

Because of the rules of succession to British and Irish peerage titles, the eldest son and heir succeeds to the rank and titles of his father. The Petty-Fitzmaurice family has numerous courtesy titles under the peerage title of the Marquess of Lansdowne. Rather than jumping from one name and title to another, as he succeeded towards the peerage, I have chosen to refer to the 5th Marquess of Lansdowne as 'Clan', his family nickname, up until he became Marquess and from then on call him 'Lansdowne'. Clan was short for 'Clanmaurice'.

The Conservative Party, which was founded in 1834 from the Tory Party, was unofficially called the Unionists when in 1895 the party was in active coalition with the Liberal Unionists against Home Rule. In 1912 the Unionist Party formally merged with the Liberal Unionists as the Conservative and Unionist Party. In 1922, after the creation of the Irish Free State, the name Conservative was used more than Unionist. Between the years 1895 and 1922 I have referred to the party as the Unionists.

INTRODUCTION

HENRY CHARLES KEITH Petty-Fitzmaurice, 5th Marquess of Lansdowne was affectionately known to friends and family as 'Clan'. Before I became his biographer, I knew him as my great-great-grandfather. I was brought up at Bowood, his country house in Wiltshire, and spent my holidays at Meikleour, his Scottish home. As a child, my grandfather knew Lansdowne and could remember, aged six, climbing over the garden wall of Lansdowne House in Berkeley Square into his aunt's garden of Devonshire House which extended to Piccadilly Street. It must have been an extraordinary time to be alive.

When I was a child, the 5th Marquess of Lansdowne fascinated me. He was one of the most significant political figures of the declining years of the British Empire, holding the offices of Governor-General of Canada, Viceroy of India, Secretary of War, Foreign Secretary and Leader of the House of Lords, but he was all but forgotten by history. Bowood was filled with his mementoes from Canada and India. They stirred my imagination and made him appear very approachable to me, but it was his 'Peace Letter' written at the height of the First World War that gave me a sense of his voice and values: honest, courageous and open. Sacrificing his reputation for what he regarded as a matter of honour filled me with admiration. He was, as Harold Macmillan, the British Prime Minister, noted, the last great Whig to make a striking impact.

Years later I visited Derreen, his Irish home that still belonged to relatives of mine and his. This house and its garden on the west coast of Ireland, bordered by the Atlantic on one side and the Caha Mountains on the other, which he created and nurtured over a lifetime, were where I felt his presence most clearly. It was here that I first felt the urge to draw Lansdowne out of the shadows of history and place him in his own social, political and intellectual milieu.

When I started this work, part time, I had no specific organising idea in mind beyond doing my research as thoroughly as possible and adding to our knowledge of this subject. My first proper step was a PhD in History on Lansdowne's period at the War Office. Then, when I began to look into Lansdowne's archive of unpublished private papers at Bowood, it became clear that he not only epitomised the challenges that his class had to face from the late Victorian period through to the interwar years but that his life and career profoundly affected the course of modern history. I experienced a real sense of enthusiasm for this project and the opportunity to correct the complicated received wisdom on him. It was a real delight to handle these papers, and his handwriting was easy to decipher, unlike many of his correspondents.

Until 1995, when part of the collection moved to the British Library, Lansdowne's papers were kept at Bowood, where they were partly catalogued in their original hardboard filing boxes. They were (and are) in excellent condition, but access was by arrangement with the Bowood archivist and it was not unusual for researchers to find that the papers were unavailable. Many historians have lamented that they were unable to see this major collection.

When I began working on Lansdowne's official papers in the Western Manuscripts Room at the British Library, they were arranged in much the same way as at Bowood. I got to know the Keeper of the archive and the staff very well, as I had to personally request each volume from the Keeper and then have it issued to me, normally in an unbound tray, by the staff. Today the collection is formally catalogued and can be requested through the Library's online catalogue, but the staff still issue the papers in the same manner. The collection comprises approximately 28,000 documents in 432 bound and unbound volumes.

I have been fortunate to be the first person to work right through this enormous archive. Lansdowne's 1929 biographer, Lord Newton, had overlooked important papers and later regretted not making a stronger case for him. My own view is that Newton's work is a product of its time, researched and written in haste. All the key facts of Lansdowne's career are there and in the right order but little light is thrown on the man himself or his world. Although Newton was a close political acquaintance he fiercely disagreed with Lansdowne's 'Peace Letter' at a time when it was still fresh in the public imagination. Thorough enquiry of the sources, I found, revealed a quite different picture and approach to bring it to life. I decided to attempt the work from the standpoint of what actually interested the man himself: to get Lansdowne to answer some of the great questions of the day and to give account of what he thought was happening around him. He was after all a man of his time operating in a contemporary system that he both shaped and by which he was moulded.

Structurally the narrative falls into four chronological and thematic parts divided by the key arguments and controversies. First, he builds a brilliant career at home and overseas; second, he becomes a cabinet minister and Leader of the House of Lords; then comes the Great War and, in 1917, the 'Peace Letter'; and the consequences of that haunt Lansdowne to the end.

Until he was aged fifty, Lansdowne was heavily influenced by his intimate relationship with his mother. Through his schooldays and the years abroad, until her death in 1895, he corresponded with her almost weekly. The letters read like a diary, with health and weather reports, social gossip, financial and family concerns laced with political insight and description of his work. He speaks as if she is sitting next to him. Strongly visual, with humorous descriptions of people and places, these letters offer a glimpse of a very human person dealing with the trials of everyday life, the challenges facing his class and the strain on Britain and its place in the world. They also shed light on Lansdowne's Whig belief that as a champion of civil liberty, it was his duty to improve the world around him, leaving it better than he found it. Unfortunately, Lansdowne destroyed the replies from his mother, making it somewhat complicated to interpret the entire conversation.

A further difficulty was how to categorise my material and decide what mattered. Newton made full use of Lansdowne's letters to his mother, quoting them at length but rarely explaining Lansdowne's intention or the consequences. Aiming to be more objective, I had to be selective, balancing this rich and colourful source with drier official correspondence. This is extensive, notably the 11,000 documents relating to Lansdowne as Viceroy of India in the British Library's India Office Records.

As I got to know Lansdowne, I became somewhat possessive and very ready to defend him. However, the many letters I read from his time at Eton showed that he was not always very friendly and I found it hard to empathise with someone who preferred his own company. At Oxford, under Benjamin Jowett, his tutor, though, he matured. No doubt his father's death and his weighty inheritance were factors in this, but his determination to work hard and make himself a better person was inspiring and my empathy returned. I was further impressed that, after his early marriage to Maud Hamilton, daughter of the Duke of Abercorn, he did not become a spoilt society man. Instead he chose to devote his working life to politics and a strict observance of duty and rectitude. Even with all his connections, this was not easy. With his profound dislike of speech-making, and a large balding head and pointed nose atop a short body, he had to work much harder than many of his political contemporaries to establish his credibility. But he succeeded with unfailing courtesy.

Lansdowne was only thirty-eight when he was appointed Governor-General of Canada. By then, he had been active in Parliament for seventeen years, steered bills, chaired committees of inquiry and worked hard as a junior minister, showing insight, tact and discretion beyond his years. He had laid a solid political foundation. In Canada, and later in India, he was a well-respected and successful leader, encouraging self-government while handling international and personal pressure. A lover of wilderness and open spaces, he travelled extensively in both countries, meeting Indigenous Americans in Canada and tribesmen and princes in India. He was the first governor-general to travel by train all the way west to British Columbia. In India he brought the Government of India closer to the princely states, secured agreement with the Amir of Afghanistan to protect India from foreign attack and left the local institutions more liberal than he found them. He returned to England aged forty-nine, a much wiser and balder man.

In the second phase, up to 1914, his cabinet positions at the War Office and Foreign Office and his leadership of the House of Lords lacked a rich source of human interest such as that of his letters to his mother. For me, this was particularly challenging. Lansdowne was a modest and cautious man, never his own hero. He did not keep a diary and in public rarely mentioned personal achievements. He did not give press interviews and seldom posed for photographs. Few letters survive from or to his family. His eldest son, my great-great-uncle, an amateur archivist, destroyed many of Lansdowne's personal papers. This phase reminded me of G.M. Young's quip, that 'what passes for diplomatic history is little more than the record of what one clerk said to another'. Fortunately, Lansdowne's clerks left many revealing and amusing anecdotes.

Lansdowne's success as a diplomat depended on how he managed and interacted with those around him, from his clerks to the monarch. His story has an excellent cast: Queen Victoria, Edward VII, Gladstone, Salisbury, Balfour, Chamberlain, Lloyd George and Asquith. As I read through their papers I began to make some sense of the jigsaw puzzle of his life at this time. Creating a database of all the documents I found, including dates and addresses, gave a clearer picture of where Lansdowne was and what he was dealing with at any given moment. But peeling away layers of his personality presented enormous difficulties. Fortunately, I found some gems, such as an unpublished pamphlet written by Lansdowne to his grandson in 1914, which enabled me to see the genuine human being behind the mask.

Lansdowne was the last great Whig magnate to govern Britain. Although his political allegiance shifted gradually from Liberal to Liberal Unionist to Unionist, his intellectual thinking remained grounded in Whig aristocratic paternalism, with respect for the establishment and individual virtue. By the time he wrote the 'Peace Letter' these virtues no longer appealed to – or were even understood by – many members of the establishment. Intellectually and emotionally apart, he was regarded as detached, stuffy, an impassive aristocrat. Such labels stuck.

I formed a different picture. I see him as courageous, skilled and fair-minded. With no experience of the cut and thrust of debating in the House of Commons, his style was courteous and refined. This served him well as Foreign Secretary in the Anglo-Japanese agreement, the Entente Cordiale and the special relationship with the USA. As a gentleman politician, he did not have the hearty contempt for his opponents that was expected. His restraint made it easy for the press to make him a scapegoat for military blunders in the Boer War, though the decision to go to war had been made with full cabinet agreement.

Lansdowne was not a weak War Minister, but I cannot say the same for his time as Unionist Leader of the Lords during the constitutional crisis. Misunderstanding the temper of the country and his party, his decision to defend the Lords and reject the People's Budget of 1909 was disastrous. The price that he and Balfour paid was costly, and the direction and leadership of the Unionist Party were irrevocably altered. It puzzled many people that Lansdowne, aged sixty-six, decided to stay on as party leader in the Lords and work with Bonar Law for another five years, after Balfour resigned as party leader in the Commons. As I wrote this chapter, the answer became clear. Lansdowne's work was unfinished. He lived and breathed politics, believed in the House's continued significance, and his position as opposition leader of the Unionists in a chamber dominated by his own party was too good to abandon.

This sense that his work was unfinished continued to drive Lansdowne in the next phase of his life, 1914–17. Reading through the files of July and August 1914, it became clear to me that he was unjustly labelled a traitor as a result of the 'Peace Letter'. In those critical hours in 1914, while Asquith hesitated, Lansdowne was adamant that Britain should support her Allies. His important part in convincing Asquith and Grey that they must declare war against Germany has only recently been established by historians. Lansdowne's experience of Ireland, Canada and India had impressed on him the need for a strong and secure Empire, protecting her interests and the balance of power. After three years of human suffering and wastage he could keep quiet no longer and published the 'Peace Letter'.

When I came to the aftermath of the 'Peace Letter' and Lansdowne's final years, I continued to be impressed by his responsibility and determination. He continued his duties – speaking in the Lords on issues that mattered to him, such as Ireland and reform of the Lords, managing his estates, and doing his duty as Lord Lieutenant of Wiltshire and a trustee of the National Gallery. Up until his early eighties he gardened and fished and socialised. He was devoted to his family, and much loved by them in return.

As Lansdowne's biographer, I have tried to avoid applying my own standards and prejudices to his past. That does not mean I have not judged his past but, although over many years I have immersed myself in his life and world, and done my utmost to accurately interpret the sources I have found, the entire picture still remains elusive to me.

Nonetheless, from my research I am certain that the appalling criticism he received as War Minister and following the 'Peace Letter' unjustly ruined his reputation and threw him into obscurity. I have come to respect Lansdowne and the values he lived by, and believe that a century later they are never more important. In researching and writing this book, I hope I have gone some way to recovering his damaged character, by demonstrating that Lansdowne was not just singularly modest and morally courageous, but a man who was trusted, and that his life and career can act as a prism through which the transition of Britain from a dominant great power to a much reduced power can be examined.

SECTION I

AT HOME AND ABROAD

1

EARLY LIFE
AND SCHOOL

THE WINTER OF 1844–45 was unusually cold and London was frequently shrouded in dense fog. At Lansdowne House in Berkeley Square, Emily, second wife of Henry Shelburne, was healthy and active and not at all oppressed by her pregnancy. On 14 January 1845, Henry Petty-Fitzmaurice, Viscount Clanmaurice, was born. Doctor Locock, the Royal obstetrician, who delivered the boy, was satisfied in all regards. 'Clan', as he was nicknamed, was strong and hearty and slept as soundly as his mother. Three days later the family left London for the fresher air of Bowood, the 12,000-acre family estate in Wiltshire with its Robert Adam designed house at the centre of the Capability Brown landscaped park.

Assisted by her mother, Margaret Mercer Elphinstone de Flahaut, Baroness Keith, Emily made a rapid recovery although her move downstairs was delayed because of the cold. Henry, a loving and generous husband, was also a hardworking MP for Calne and largely absent during Emily's recovery. She bore no resentment, the birth of her child the only thing wanting to make her completely happy. With no competition for affection, Clan developed a very close bond with Emily, one that lasted all their lives. Neither of his siblings, Edmond (b. 1846) and Emmy (b. 1855), shared as intense a relationship – or correspondence – with their mother as did Clan. Up until her death in 1895, Clan and Emily corresponded almost weekly in lengthy letters, often written late at night or at the weekend. Clan would comment on her remarks and add his own news as if they were discussing the situation in two armchairs. Her love and aspirations for her eldest son were enormous. After Henry's early death, of paralysis in 1866, she took neither husband nor lover but devoted herself to Clan, who became more than a son and more of a patriarch and guardian of his family's welfare.

Undoubtedly Emily's relations with her husband were affected by Clan's arrival. Henry made no attempt to compete for his wife's affections, but his relations with Clan were somewhat formal, while Clan – delighting in his father's political successes – was sensitive to the price he paid in his absence from home. Clan's arrival pleased Henry's father, the 3rd Marquess. He and Emily were fond of each other, and a strong bond also developed between grandfather and grandson, until the former's death in 1863 of a head injury. Their respectful friendship had a significant influence on Clan's life and career.

Clan's forebears were landowners and Whig politicians: Anglo-Irish on his father's side, French and Scottish on his mother's.[1] His paternal family were a branch of the Geraldines.[2] The Fitzmaurices settled in Ireland in the twelfth century, married into native Irish families and remained Catholics until the seventeenth century. Their lands were called Clanmaurice and the family castle was at Lixnaw. The first twenty Lords of Kerry were a law unto themselves.[3] Thomas, the 21st Lord, married Anne, only daughter of Sir William Petty, anatomist, inventor and physician-in-chief (1652–59) to the Commonwealth Army in Ireland.[4] Petty, who had left home with 4s. 6d., was paid £18,532 8s. 4½d. in 1658 for producing the Down Survey, the basis of land title for over half of Ireland. As one of the committee allocating land, he bought claims at a quarter of their true value and amassed 270,000 acres in south Kerry alone. He was accused in Parliament of dishonesty, but no vote was taken and charges were never pressed. Anne, who was egregiously ugly, although able and intelligent,[5] and Thomas, honoured by an earldom in 1723, had two sons. The younger son, John, inherited the Petty estates and became a Whig MP. Living mainly in England after 1751, he purchased Bowood, which became the family seat. In 1753 he was made Earl of Shelburne.

John's eldest son, William, was the first Lansdowne. Born in Dublin and brought up in Kerry, he joined the army, rapidly reaching the rank of colonel and aide-de-camp to George III. Succeeding his father in 1761, he took his seat in the Lords as a Whig. A far-sighted man, he agreed to become a Minister for the third time, in March 1782, if the King accepted American Independence. In July he became Prime Minister, negotiating peace with the United States, France and Spain. He resigned in March 1783 and was created 1st Marquess of Lansdowne in 1784. Although he was widely distrusted by his contemporaries and accused of being a Tory because of his respect for George III, his unpopularity and reputation for deceit were undeserved.

After the 2nd Marquess died in 1809, the title passed to his dashing half-brother Henry. He was MP for Calne and Chancellor of the Exchequer at the age of twenty-six. Serving in eight Ministries, he was like his father a moderate Whig with strong natural judgement. Queen Victoria trusted his advice and offered him a dukedom, which he refused. *Punch* approved:

> Lord Lansdowne won't be Duke of Kerry.
> Lord Lansdowne is a wise man, very.
> Punch drinks his health in port and sherry.[6]

Emily's family were of Scottish and French origin. Her grandfather, George Elphinstone, was sent to sea with a £5 note and told to make his way in the world. He rose to become Whig MP for Dumbartonshire and later Stirlingshire, commanded the Channel Fleet, supervised Napoleon's removal to Saint Helena and was ennobled as Viscount Keith in 1814. His wife was Jean Mercer of Aldie, whose family owned large Scottish estates. In 1817 the marriage of their daughter, Margaret, to Charles de Flahaut, an illegitimate son of Adelaide de Flahaut and Charles de Talleyrand-Périgord, delighted the London gossips, as Lord Keith was known to dislike all Frenchmen, especially Bonapartists.

Margaret and Charles had five daughters. Emily Mercer-Elphinstone de Flahaut was the first, born at Edinburgh in 1819. She was lively and determined. With an interfering nature and strong will, she did not care for apologetic speeches or profusions of thanks. Chopin dedicated his Bolero Op. 19 to her when she was fifteen. A confirmed Orléaniste, she dreaded in a very British way the possible misunderstandings between her father-in-law and father.[7] At twenty-four she married Henry Shelburne, born at Lansdowne House in 1816 and educated at Westminster and Cambridge. When his elder brother died in 1836, Henry became the only surviving son of the 3rd Marquess, who was passionate about politics. Henry was less driven. As an MP, Under-Secretary of State for Foreign Affairs and member of the Adullamites, he was a competent administrator but lacked the charisma and flair that made his father the 'Nestor of the Whigs'. Widowed after six months in 1841, he remarried and found Emily a loyal companion.

At three months, Clan was baptised at St George's, Hanover Square, London. He was a quiet baby. His mother believed the best proof of his kindness was that he never cried.[8] She needed no wet-nurse but employed a French-speaking nanny, Mlle Steinbauer, nicknamed 'Mussy', who encouraged him to speak and write in both English and French. Nurturing their son's abilities through a conventional upbringing and education was of great importance to both parents. Unlike many, they were keen to see as much of their child as they could. Clan was not brought up in the nursery and kept at a distance from adults, but in the company of his parents and their peers. Among them, Lady Grey, the former Prime Minister's wife, noted 'I travelled years on in my fancy to make him as celebrated as any amongst them. He really is a very remarkable baby.'[9]

Aged eight, Clan was studying with a private tutor at Bowood. James Laurie thought him amiable and his interest in Latin surprising, but criticised what the Germans term the state of *Starrsinn* (stubbornness) into which he frequently lapsed. In spring 1855 his tranquil life was radically disrupted when Emily's third child was born and Clan left for boarding school near Henley-on-Thames.

Woodcote, run by the Reverend Philip Nind and his wife Agnes, had about forty boys aged from eight to fourteen, many with a similar background to Clan. He started in the lower 4th class but in his first term was moved to the upper 4th, where the other boys were all two years older although Nind believed that he would keep pace with them.[10] Having to make new friends did not come naturally. This was partly the result of his upbringing. Clan had spent very little time with boys of his own age but, with only seventeen months between them, he and his brother Edmond were very close and their parents wished them to share experiences equally. Fortunately, they developed a lasting affection and rarely competed with each other. This is all the more remarkable given Clan's greater inheritance, both material and physical. Clan inherited his mother's French looks: white pale skin, dark black hair and narrow face, with a prominent shaped nose and bluey grey eyes that twinkled kindly below a high forehead.

One reason for their close relationship was Edmond's strength of character and intellect, which enabled him to pursue his own career as a successful Liberal minister and life peer. Another was Clan's generosity and patience towards his brother, even in their later careers when they sat on opposing political benches. It was not in Clan's nature to impose on or judge others, but to respect individual differences. After Edmond's arrival at Woodcote in 1857, Nind noted that Edmond surpassed his elder brother in steady work, but Clan would attain high distinction in the future.[11] School suited Clan and did him a great deal of good. He became Head of School in his final year.

Clan started at Eton on 24 April 1858, the first of his family to go there; his father and grandfather had been to Westminster. Under the Headmaster, Dr Charles Old Goodford, Eton was a school of 820 boys. With its 'houses' and prefectural hierarchies, Eton replicated Victorian social reality. Goodford, gravely dignified, was both a thinker and a man of action, a teacher and a gentleman. Clan entered the strongly aristocratic house of the Reverend Augustus Birch, who nonetheless was reputedly indifferent to class and loathed stupid people. Birch acted the languid swell. He kept his wife in his own part of the house, so that no one had anything to do with her.[12] The house itself, home to Clan for four years, was uncomfortable, with a narrow, dark and awkward staircase.

Education at Eton in the 1850s was equally physical and academic. While Clan's academic career flourished and his interest in imperial and foreign policy was stimulated, it was his fondness for the outdoors that really developed, although Birch had no interest in sport. Clan's passion for exercise included cricket, football, swimming, running, shooting and rowing.

Clan made many lifelong friends in Birch's – Arthur Balfour,[13] who was his fag,[14] was one – yet he was slow to make friends in other houses. Eton's size and house system meant over half the school boys did not know one another. While he never sought the approval of others, he also tried to avoid trouble for others, often complete strangers. In his first term he concealed the loss of some money, causing Birch great distress. He was caned when he prompted a friend in class who had not done his work and could not recite his lines by heart.[15]

Birch thought Clan was peculiar in disposition and unlike his contemporaries. He found him interesting to deal with,[16] talented without imagination and clear headed but rather uncertain, not a worker, nor ambitious to stand high at Eton and get a first at Oxford.[17] He criticised Clan's want of consideration and gentleness, wishing he would be more thoughtful of others.[18] He thought Clan was too prickly and was concerned about his impulsive and sharp retorts or provocations in dealing with fellow men. Clan preferred his own company, although his mother was surprised that he preferred 'messing' alone. He explained that his wish to eat tea by himself allowed him greater flexibility with his time and that his 'mess' colleagues were rowdy and had got him into trouble with Birch.[19]

Although Clan lacked a role model at home and school, he found a mentor in his father's closest friend. Earl Granville, Liberal statesman and Leader of the House of Lords, was suave in manner, intimate with men and matters at home and abroad, schooled in diplomacy, practised in administration, universally liked everywhere, an able and ready speaker.[20] Granville saw in Clan the son he never had and spoke of him with great regard and enthusiasm.[21] Paying visits to Eton and Lansdowne House, his influence on Clan was stronger and more lasting than any other family friend: there was no one more loyal to his friends or more ready to help when the chance presented itself. Clan could not recall a single instance when Granville let him down.[22] On 16 March 1861, Clan was confirmed into the Anglican faith at the school chapel at Eton. Aged sixteen, he took this rite of passage into adulthood seriously. Shortly afterwards, he was torn between rowing and books; rowing won.

Rowing had its own social life. On 'check nights' in June and July the Upper Boats would row their eights to Surly Hall and dine on duck and green peas, while the Lower Boats consumed champagne and cake back at the boathouses.[23] A place in the 'Boats' was a move Clan would have given his ears to get. After he got his place, Birch warned his parents that if they wished Clan to become a scholar they should remove him from Eton and the single pursuit of pleasure, which ruled his boating set. He feared that in the critical months leading up to taking the Oxford examination, if he did not learn to work, which the Eton system could not enforce on an Upper boy, he would never learn to work at all.[24] While neither Emily nor Henry enforced discipline on their children, they removed Clan from Eton and placed him in a crammer to prepare for Oxford.

This proved to be a blessing, although Clan had some regrets about leaving Eton early, having built up plenty of confidence in his own ability while there. However, he never recognised his own intellectual capacity. He later remarked that an imperfect knowledge of Horace is always supposed to be the only intellectual equipment of an Eton boy.[25]

Unlike many schoolboys his age, Clan did not thrive on taking exams and learning by rote, which was exactly what crammers did. Living with the Revd Lewis Campbell – a protégé of Benjamin Jowett – and his wife at the Vicarage, Milford on Sea, Hampshire, Clan believed that he would learn a great deal.[26] Sensing his strong desire to make himself a better person, Campbell advised sending him to Balliol to study Classics (*Literae Humaniores*) under Jowett rather than to Christ Church. Clan was not unrealistic as to the difficulty of the scholarship but considered an attempt worthwhile, especially if he passed and 'won' his rooms; an inducement offered by Balliol to any scholar whom they thought was likely to do the college credit.

Jowett, twenty-seven years older than Clan, and a theologian and translator of Plato, believed that Balliol existed for the benefit of its students and was a great picker, trainer and placer of able young men. Over the course of his career he guided into positions of influence hundreds of men, including three viceroys and a prime minister. He used his position to host distinguished parties at Balliol. He once told Clan, one of the best things that can be done in this world is to introduce literary men to statesmen and clever struggling young men to persons of rank and position.[27]

Clan took the entrance exam in November 1862 and passed. Campbell was pleased for his student but rather like Nind and Birch before him noted that the only obstacle to Clan's future success was a want of imagination.[28]

2

OXFORD

THE DEATH OF his grandfather, the 3rd Marquess, in January 1863, shocked Clan although having lived a full life and reached the age of eighty-two he felt there was no cause for complaint.[1] Clan's everyday life was largely unaltered but for his change of name. Clan chose the courtesy family title, Kerry, whereas his father had become Earl of Shelburne. As he told his mother, 'I do not at all approve of changing names, it takes away all ones [*sic*] notion of identity, it is a slight consolation that I shall always be called Clan by you & all righteous persons'.[2] Clan also entered the Royal Wiltshire Regiment of Yeomanry Cavalry. His father thought it did young men 'good and they learn a little of their neighbours'.[3] He received his commission as Captain on 24 April.

In October 1863, Clan arrived at Oxford, a slim young man of five foot six, paying £8 to become a member of the university and £23 to enter Balliol College.[4] He was immaculately dressed with high collar and tie; indeed, he remained dapper all his life, without any peculiarity of attire. He had a little ground-floor sitting room and bedroom, and his scout was an imposing personage. He met many Etonians, but none that he was friendly with.[5] Invitations poured in: 'a breakfast to go to somewhere every morning and sometimes two or three to refuse'.[6] Unlike many contemporaries, Clan was not politically active at Oxford. He joined the Union for its reading rooms, not for its debates.

Jowett took him as a student, setting him large and challenging amounts of work.[7] Along with Granville, Jowett had a critical influence on Clan. He articulated the link between a classical education and public life. His political philosophy strongly influenced Clan: his Whig virtues, his training for imperialism and his unemotional view of the world. Jowett instilled in him the virtues of hard work and a career in politics. But for him, Clan's life might have turned out quite differently.[8] Clan got on very well with Jowett, who wished to govern the world through his pupils.[9] Years later Jowett remarked that Clan had never really done justice to his talent for scholarship. Clan spent his summer holiday reading with Jowett at Askrigg in Yorkshire. However, Jowett's strict demands left him quite 'savage' and he vowed never to repeat the experience. Still he realised that he would never get a First without hard work.[10]

Clan rowed at Stroke for the Torpids boat[11] and disproved of students who took no exercise as a First was not worth having if achieved at the expense of fresh air and good health.[12] He joined the university 'drag', which was a 'pack of mongrels that hunted a red herring twice a week'.[13] Ensured of a good gallop he found it great fun and capital exercise.[14] He avoided fox hunting as it overlapped with his lectures, but bought a small terrier that killed rats efficiently and enjoyed going shooting for pheasants and woodcock. He was a keen theatregoer, as was the rage then for men of his class, and was elected to the Bullingdon Club. His only misdemeanours were occasional ventures to seize a few door knockers as trophies from placid front doors.[15]

Early in 1865, under Jowett's auspices, Clan employed a coach for the study of Aristotle. He was a four-foot black man called Green. Clan thought him 'hideous to a degree but as his knowledge of philosophy is as great as his countenance is distorted' he hoped the arrangement would succeed.[16] Next term he hired a coach for logic, who he noted was a very clever Glasgow professor, with wild eyes and dishevelled hair redolent of tobacco smoke, who was altogether frowzy. They got on well.

Jowett proposed reading with him for two months that summer. Although Clan had vowed the previous summer never to spend another holiday reading with the demanding Jowett, he liked him and agreed to go. While they were studying at Pitlochry, in Perthshire, Jowett reported to Clan's father, 'I have rarely known anyone quicker at apprehending a new or difficult subject. He sees the point of a thing in a moment. Also I find him a most amiable companion. Indeed he is universally liked.' However, Jowett also found Clan wanting in interest in political and general subjects and such indolence prevented him from doing justice to his abilities.[17] Jowett's success with Clan was assured when Edmond decided in 1864 to go to Cambridge and not cramp his brother's way of life at Oxford.

In March 1866 Clan was 'very pleased' to become a member of White's Club in London.[18] White's was the unofficial headquarters of the Conservative Party, although Whigs could also belong. He had not known that his father had nominated him. Subsequently he joined and acted as a trustee of Brooks (the headquarters of the Whig party and his favourite club), and became a member of the Travellers, Reform and Turf clubs. He enjoyed the convivial atmosphere and the gossip of clubland but he was restrained in eating and drinking, which then was not only unusual but (according to Ernest Hamilton, his brother-in-law) came very near to including reproach.[19] On occasions when the House of Lords sat late into the night he stayed at Brooks, which was closer to work than Lansdowne House. While gentlemen's clubs reinforced the male bonding created at schools such as Eton, they also served as a refuge for the upper classes in a changing world. Clan hankered little for such sentiment. He was quite realistic about his class: 'Many of us are poor, a good few disreputable, pretty idle and without sense of responsibility. It is not much of an army.'[20]

At the end of his third year at Oxford, Clan's father died and he became the 5th Marquess of Lansdowne, aged twenty-one. He inherited Bowood and its extensive estate, estates in Ireland of approximately 138,000 acres (accounts differ), Lansdowne House in London with its 4-acre garden, and notable works of art. He was entailed through his mother to her Scottish estates of 10,418 acres.[21] He also inherited an enormous debt, although sources differ as to the amount.

Four days after his father's death, Lansdowne received an invitation from Jowett to join him on another reading holiday, this time at Tummel Bridge, Perthshire. Offering his support, Jowett remarked, 'life must seem very strange and sad at first when you suddenly become your own master in this unexpected manner'.[22] Lansdowne and a fellow student went and over the course of six weeks found themselves writing an essay every other day for Jowett, who was halfway through translating 2,100 pages of Plato.

In October 1866, Lansdowne returned to Balliol and found a new coach, Williams, who was, Lansdowne thought, a 'horrid little blackguard, but very clever'.[23] He took rooms outside College at 88 High Street. Soon new responsibility was forced on him. He was required to divide his time between his studies, his estates and local politics. He relied for advice on his mother, Charles Gore (his father's executor and married to his aunt) and his agents in Ireland and at Bowood. Lansdowne learned early never to act without advice.

Such wealth and status when so young might have been disastrous. That he avoided this was commented on by Jowett:

> When I pass by your splendid house in London I feel a sort of wonder that the owner should be reading quietly at Oxford. But you could not do a wiser or better thing for besides the value of the distinction and the knowledge plus increased power which is thus gained, you show the world that you are not going to be at the mercy of them and of their fashions and do not mean to live surrounded by hangers on, having already learned

the value of independence and knowing that there are higher things than wealth or rank, which are means and not ends and may be the greatest evil or the greatest good as they are used.[24]

During the summer before his final exams, Lansdowne joined Jowett in Scotland for the last time. He found it hard work and felt that none of the serious business of life could ever be as tedious as grinding on for ever at the same dreary books.[25] Jowett told Florence Nightingale:

I am very doubtful about Lord Lansdowne's success. He has a good deal of ability and works well. But his mind is French and superficial and runs away from speculation and philosophy.[26]

Examinations began on 21 November 1867 and ended a week later. Lansdowne was very disappointed with his performance and imagined he had missed a great prize.[27] Within a few days he had brushed aside his disappointment and was working with Jowett and his coach Williams, in preparation for his *viva voce* on 10 December. He longed for the day to come as the state of half-emancipation that he felt he was in was 'positively intolerable'.[28]

Narrowly missing the First he so wanted, Lansdowne received a Second in *Literae Humaniores*. He did not question the result but both Williams and Jowett thought the examiners had made an egregious mistake. Jowett was disappointed, believing that Lansdowne had failed,

not from want of ability but from a certain want of interest and from the cares of the world coming upon you too soon; and I failed to make you understand the amount of interest and hard work that was required. It does not do for a young man to begin where an old man leaves off. Knowledge of the world and of political subjects; reticence, self-control, freedom from personal feeling, are the qualities to be aimed at. I don't object to a touch of idealism or speculation also if kept in its proper place. But how few statesmen have these qualities in any degree?[29]

3

A YEAR OFF

IN 1868 LANSDOWNE was relieved to leave the demanding academic environment of Oxford. He decided not to rush into employment but to take a few months off in order to take stock of his inheritance and broaden his horizons. It was in the management of his estates that his early life found its best expression. He had different feelings for each of them and his instinct was often correct, although he generally based his decisions on what was expected of him.

Only at Derreen, his home in County Kerry, was Lansdowne free of others' expectations, and it was his favourite property. Over 15 miles from the railway and telegraph office at Kenmare, it was like another world with its own climate and time. Due to the warming effects of the Gulf Stream he was able to create a luxuriant garden with vast ferns and rare rhododendrons. All the fires in the house burned peat. He had 'an almost diseased affection' for Derreen[1] and on arrival sometimes lay on the grass and rolled about with his legs in the air 'like a disembarked donkey'.[2]

Whether gardening at Derreen, walking on the Scottish moors or riding across the North Wessex Downs at Bowood, his love for his properties was immense. Passionate about conserving the landscape, he regularly spoke at agricultural society events and was outspoken in the Lords on the land question in Ireland and England. He understood these issues, not only because of his close observation of nature, but also because he listened to the concerns of his estate tenants and employees.

Bowood was home, the place Lansdowne returned to after the week's grind in London. The estate was tenanted – he disliked directly overseeing farms – and managed by a resident land agent; Lansdowne did not interfere but dictated policy and principle. Lansdowne House in London was the family's *baraque héréditaire*. Its fine Adam rooms with pastel walls, carpeted marble floors, intricate plasterwork and magnificent staircase were ideal for entertaining. Dance's library served as a ballroom and Wyatt's corridor was used for sitting out. Smirke's gallery contained one of Europe's finest collections of classical sculpture. It embodied all the peculiar qualities of a Whig house; a monument to their liberal tradition. Lansdowne did not like London with its dirt and smog, but that was where his work was. He had a love/hate relationship with Lansdowne House. It was one of the grandest family houses in London but it cost him thousands of pounds per year to run.[3] He did not miss it when it was let and happily stayed at his mother's house in Grosvenor Square, at Mackellar's Hotel in Dover Street or at Brooks Club.

On Emily's death, the five Scottish estates passed to Lansdowne, although he and the Scottish land agent had managed them since 1870. Emily had had Meikleour rebuilt in the 1870s to resemble a French château and filled it with Louis XV furniture and tapestries, which ate into the income generated by the farmland and grouse-shooting. By 1895 the estates just broke even. Lansdowne associated them with his mother and 'having a good time'.[4] He was sad that his busy schedule did not enable him to spend more than a few weeks each year in Scotland.

Landownership was costly; Lansdowne's Irish holdings were also volatile. Unlike many Irish landlords, though, Lansdowne did not yield to threats. The challenges of his lands in Ireland strongly influenced his entire career. His Irish holdings, all tenanted, were the second largest in private hands, covering parts of Dublin, Meath, King's County (Offaly), Queen's County (Laois), Limerick and Kerry. Lansdowne was a modest man, but he could not escape his prominence in Ireland. It bewitched him. He thought that no one who 'has not seen it can have any idea of the charm of the country when it is at its best'.[5] To better understand it, Lansdowne made three or four visits a year, a few months in all, based mainly at Derreen.

Lansdowne imagined that to the public he was 'a Croesus'. In reality he was encumbered with debt left by his father and spent £20,000 annually on his estates. Bowood, he accepted, 'is not a poor man's residence'[6] – it never yielded a surplus and always required support from Coutts, his bankers, and the cost of holding onto Lansdowne House meant 'family pride is an expensive luxury'.[7] Lansdowne's only dependable revenue came from a small dividend in stocks and his Irish estates – £18,000 in a very good year – but, following the Land Commissioners' reduction of rents in the 1890s, that too was to disappear completely. Lansdowne thought it nothing less than sheer confiscation.[8] The expense of reclaiming unpaid rents swallowed up every shilling. No wonder he was suspicious of lawyers.[9]

Reducing his overdraft was a constant concern. Occasionally financial anxiety overtook him and he would discuss with his family selling his Irish estates or letting Lansdowne House or Bowood; he once joked that unless his eldest son married a Rothschild the family would 'probably migrate permanently to South Kensington'.[10]

His most often repeated threat was to sell Lansdowne House. Doing so would allow him to clear his huge debt and to live comfortably in a smaller London home instead of starving in a palace. It would also enable him to keep a better house at Bowood and to deal more liberally with local claims.[11] Lansdowne disliked the humiliation of living shabbily in a large house and receiving hospitality that he could not return, worrying about paltry retrenchments that 'after all leave one little better off than if they had never been made'.[12]

Lansdowne's mother thought his concerns ridiculous. She fancied that he was addicted to croaking without sufficient cause[13] and that he was overly anxious as to the future.[14] He understood long before the rest of his class the plight they were facing and the erosion of their power base – the land. This foresight was largely a result of managing his estates in Ireland and his knowledge of the situation there and in England.

Until 1874 British agriculture had seen two decades of prosperity. Lansdowne's tenants were well-housed and there was no shortage of employment for farm labourers. Then a run of bad seasons, poor harvests, foreign competition and 'unjust and foolish legislation'[15] irrevocably damaged farming. Lansdowne had disagreeable interviews with 'despairing farmers'[16] and his agents were gloomy. In consultation with them he reduced rents at Bowood by 20 per cent and in Ireland by 45 per cent. His Irish difficulties were exacerbated by the Land War, Fenian disturbances and the Plan of Campaign, whose leaders targeted the Lansdowne estates. Lansdowne believed that what happened in Ireland would affect the rest of the United Kingdom: 'the owners of the great houses may hold out for one or two or three generations but the crisis will come',[17] and 'all we can do is to be prepared and not to carry too much deck cargo in the shape of debts and mortgages'.[18]

Lansdowne saw his ownership of estates and titles in terms of temporary stewardship; he aimed to hand them over to the next generation for their enjoyment. While he accepted primogeniture, he also carried out his mother's wish that the Scottish properties were not commingled with the Lansdowne properties, which is why he passed them to his younger son. Lansdowne knew not only the terrain of his estates but also their history, and how and why his forebears collected their possessions. Unlike his brother Edmond, he did not write about his family's history or politics, but he read widely on both and was influenced by them. Lansdowne was not a businessman. He could read the warning signs facing his class but could not avoid the crisis without eroding his capital. During his lifetime he had to sell his most valuable paintings and sculptures, all his Irish estates except for Derreen and Sheen Falls estates, and most outlying land around Bowood. Even after settling his inherited debts, outgoings still exceeded income. His English and Scottish estates never produced a surplus and his prediction of a serious fall in value of landed estates[19] was realised.[20] Lansdowne was realistic: he could not afford to extend his estates, purchase works of art or be a patron of artists and intellectuals as his predecessors had. In conserving the family fortune, he took some pleasure knowing that it was not for racing and gambling.

Lansdowne's anxiety for the future of his inheritance mirrored his anxiety for Britain and her place in the world. That anxiety propelled him into politics as the first member of his family to take issue over imperial and Irish affairs. In February 1868, during his 'year off', Lansdowne took his seat in the House of Lords.[21] He then travelled to Paris to be a guest of his grandfather, Charles de Flahaut, at the Chancellerie. He visited the Louvre, the Luxembourg Palace and the Senate, where he was especially struck with Jules Favre's eloquence. He noted that in French politics not a day seemed to pass without a disgraceful row of some kind generally ending in a personnel shake-up.[22]

Lansdowne plunged wildly into the dissipation of Paris society and attended many concerts and dances. Anticipating an introduction to an American girl with a dowry of £6 million, he considered the mortgages as good as paid. He visited the salons in the Faubourg Saint-Germain, the haunts of the literary world and the *hôtels* of the aristocracy on the opposite bank. Meeting girls for the first time outside London, he enjoyed a few flirtations. Alice Miles was English and eighteen, and there was talk that they were engaged. Alice noted:

> What on earth would the busy bodies say if they heard of his three visits this week and some little Parisian details! – It is a great bore because I shall have to avoid the poor young man in public, for though he pleases me immensely, and the envious glances cast on me by young ladies 'on their promotion' amuse me still more, I cannot afford to have it said I am his lordship's property.[23]

A few months later she confided to her diary:

> If I continued a certain demure little flirtation with him, it was merely from force of habit. I studied him closely during the fortnight he was in Paris, beginning at his pretty hands and feet a lady might be proud of and ending with his keen grey eyes, that have so little weakness about them:

and came to the conclusion that he would be very lovable indeed, if – he were not a Marquis and owner of £70,000 a year. For as to being in love with a man in that position, you might as well talk of the tender passion in conjunction with Napoleon III, and how Mme de Castiglione and the rest of his favourites would laugh if accused of such an enormity.[24]

In November Lansdowne was invited to the Château de Compiègne. He expected to find the 'affair a great bore'.[25] Emperor Napoleon III and Empress Eugénie hosted three house parties a year: one for statesmen and senior officials, one for leaders of fashion, and one for soldiers, diplomats and artists.[26] Lansdowne was impressed by the 1,300 rooms; his manservant Price was 'flabbergasted at the scarcity' of imperial bath tubs.[27]

Napoleon and Eugénie welcomed their 120 guests formally at 7 o'clock in the Grande Salle des Fêtes, after which they behaved as hosts rather than sovereigns.[28] Lansdowne disliked eating dinner at such a time as it made the evenings so long.[29] Among the other guests he was struck by General Bazaine and the great many other French Marshals all with grey hair and red ribbons.[30]

Although he was determined to be shy and bored,[31] Lansdowne stayed at Compiègne for a week. Amusing himself, with all his heart,[32] he joined a paper chase in the forest to catch the Empress. Out hunting, he rode next to the Prince of Wales when a stag made a tremendous leap that failed to clear the future monarch and sent him and his horse flying five or six yards off the road into the heather.[33] He also went on an imperial shoot as one of ten guns. The total bag was 1,460; the Prince of Wales shot 270 head and Lansdowne 260, owing to the enormous quantity of rabbits that he killed.[34]

4

GETTING STARTED

In AUTUMN 1868 Lansdowne visited his Irish estates and witnessed the backwardness of the countryside. It impressed on him his responsibilities as a landlord and moulded his imperialist values. When Lansdowne inherited in 1866, Ireland was gripped by what came to be known as a Land War. In Kerry, nationalist politics were strong despite the restraining influence of the Trench family (Lansdowne's agents) and local priests. William Steuart Trench was principal agent. Lansdowne valued his knowledge of Irish matters (Trench was author of the *Realities of Irish Life*) but did not like him or his fixed opinions.[1] He was especially irritated at Trench's high living: he 'has got everything very comfortable, regardless of expense, which three words he might well adopt for his motto'.[2]

His son, John 'Towny' Townsend Trench, was assistant agent with *de facto* control of the estate. He and his family lived at Lansdowne Lodge in Kenmare in, like his father, considerable comfort. He kept a yacht in the harbour ready to carry his family down the bay, or if the wind made that impossible a whale-boat with a picked crew of stalwart oarsmen was always at their service.[3] Lansdowne thought he was a bad negotiator, inaccurate in thought and language, prone to act hastily and as difficult to manage as his father. But Lansdowne was reluctant to get rid of John Trench, as he feared he would be very sore and vindictive, and would probably make running the estates in Ireland even more difficult.[4]

On 16 September 1868 Lansdowne arrived in Dublin. During his stay at the new Shelbourne Hotel,[5] a nearby fire caused huge damage, prompting his ironic comment 'what incendiaries we are when we get into this country'.[6] After a month visiting his properties in Dublin, Meath, Queen's County and Limerick, he reached Kerry. Although his visit to Kenmare was a success it was marked by sectarian divisions between

Catholics and Protestants, and demands from his tenants for fixity of tenure and improved tenant rights. Travelling by boat down the Kenmare estuary he arrived at Derreen on 12 October, in the dark and landing on the boatman's shoulders.[7] The tour taught Lansdowne important lessons about land tenure, tenant and landlord rights, sectarianism, poverty and employment. In time, he made the Irish Question his own and strongly influenced thinking on it.

Before leaving Ireland he stayed at the Viceregal Lodge in Dublin as guest of the 1st Duke of Abercorn, a friend of Lansdowne's parents. He met Maud Hamilton, Abercorn's seventh daughter, and began a friendship that led to marriage. She was five years younger than Lansdowne and a few inches taller, with thick brown hair, a thin graceful figure and slender arms. The Abercorns were firm Tories and politically active at Baronscourt, their Ulster home, and in Parliament, whereas the lively, spontaneous Maud was more of a Radical supporter. She was less intellectual than Lansdowne and rarely opened a book, but was socially accomplished and good company. The Abercorns are the Duke and Duchess in Benjamin Disraeli's novel *Lothair* (published in 1870), and one of their daughters, Maud or Bertha, is 'Corisande'.[8]

If 1868 initiated Lansdowne into his inheritance, 1869 was an initiation into life itself. Jowett was eager for Lansdowne to get into political life as soon as possible: 'A man of energy and character ought to find some real work to do.'[9] He recommended him to see Granville. Lansdowne, understanding the importance of patronage, did so, not expecting immediate results.

Although Lansdowne belonged to the Liberal Party, he regarded himself as a Whig. From the Glorious Revolution of 1688 until the fall of Shelburne's government in 1783 the Whigs broadly dominated English parliamentary life.[10] But between 1783 and 1830 their power faltered with the rise of the younger Pitt and the recovery of the Tory Party, the Napoleonic Wars and splits among the Whigs themselves. However, by the First Reform Act of 1832, Whiggery was again the dominant force in politics.[11] The gradual move of the Peelites from the Tories towards alliance with the Whigs ensured their political power remained strong up until 1859 when they merged with the newly established Liberals. Whiggism did not cease at that point but continued to influence political thinking.

Although Whiggery took root with the overthrow of King James II, in defiance of royal despotism and as a populist ethos that understood political authority as stemming from the people, as it developed over the succeeding centuries its very disposition was distorted and eventually destroyed by its own success. During the nineteenth century many prominent Whigs, including Melbourne and Grey, were notably wary of change but, burdened by their own self-identity and history, were moved to act on the wants and wishes of the people. Duty bound to prevent any collision between the King and the people, they were the orchestrators of reform.[12] Such action led many to argue that the Whig association with the people was nothing but ambition mounted on popularity.[13] Whereas in the seventeenth and eighteenth century the patrician, landowning Whigs had been in advance of the people and leading them cautiously along the path of reform and progress, by the end of the nineteenth century the three Reform Bills of 1832, 1867 and 1885 had shifted their authority and placed it firmly in the hands of a mass electorate.

To make matters more complicated, while the Whigs were defenders of liberty, they were not paragons of equality. While they zealously guarded their special relationship with the people, it was largely on their own terms and these did not go to extremes. Arguing for progress in public and urging caution in private they were forced to adopt double standards.[14] Supressing their true feelings over their intellectual and historical self-identification, they were both in denial and discomfort. As the people were seduced away from them by the allure of ever greater democracy, so they were reduced to being mere aristocrats.[15] By 1886 political Whiggism was essentially redundant. In the years that followed the Liberal schism, the principal political parties and their public officials were no longer leading the people but following public opinion and caught up between assuaging that and their own party needs. In such an environment, individuals promoted ever more sensational and vote-winning programmes.[16] Caught between their Liberalism and their landlordism, many former Whigs opted for the latter.[17] But while modern politics drove Whiggism closer to extinction, the Whig tradition and its principles did not altogether disappear from politics.

Whig principles were fundamentally associated with political, religious and social reform, and the recognition of individual liberty. By contrast, Tory principles recognised the Crown and the Church as guarantors of political and social order, and opposed any unwarranted interference with the well-established British constitution. In governing with such principles, the Whigs appeared to enjoy the best of all worlds; serving the interests of the nation and its people and the interests of their own order. Both were mutually reinforcing.[18] To the Whigs, self-identification was inseparable from political allegiance. As noted by the essayist Walter Bagehot:

> Whiggism is not a creed, it is a character. Perhaps as long as there has been
> a political history in this country there have been certain men of a cool,
> moderate resolute firmness, not gifted with high imagination, little prone

to enthusiastic sentiment, heedless of large theories and speculations, careless of dreamy scepticism; with a clear view of the next step, and a wise intention to act on it; with a strong conviction that the elements of knowledge are true, and a steady belief that the present world can, and should be, quietly improved. These are the Whigs.[19]

Whiggery really meant the great landowning families; the most exclusive group of the aristocracy, including the Grosvenors, Spencers, Cavendishes, Bentincks, Russells, Pelhams, and Petty-Fitzmaurices.[20] Resting their power in such a consortium moulded by blood and breeding, Whiggery influenced Lansdowne's predecessors in their upbringing, marriages, intellectual traditions and social standing. Convinced they were the chosen people, they also saw themselves as the guardians of the country's liberties.[21] Lansdowne grew up with this thinking. Despite the merger of the Whigs and Liberals he never fully embraced Gladstonian Liberalism. Gladstone's zeal for religious and political causes sat uncomfortably with the moderate Liberalism for which Whigs like himself and his political colleagues, including Granville and Hartington, were spokesmen. Gladstone's power rested in moral opinion; for the Whigs it lay in educated opinion.[22]

Following the Liberal victory in 1868, Granville put forward Lansdowne's name for a position in Gladstone's ministry. Lansdowne was appointed to the dormant position of Junior Lord of the Treasury, working under the Chancellor of the Exchequer, his local MP, Robert Lowe. Although the work was unpaid, the role interested Lansdowne, who was pleased to begin where his father had started twenty-one years before.[23] Lansdowne thought Lowe tended to put everything in the most lively, most exciting, and the most startling form,[24] and the role offered Lansdowne considerable freedom, his duties being to decide on superannuations and give support to his colleagues from the Lords.[25]

Lansdowne started work on 8 January 1869 at the House of Lords. Owing to its gentlemanly nature, he had a less demanding task than his opposite number in the House of Commons, and also did not experience the hard, political world of the Commons. Surrounded by gentlemen politicians, he adopted their courteous, refined speech and manners. This was admired and respected at that time, whereas in later years it counted for little among machine politicians weaving and dealing to defeat the opposition. Lansdowne also adopted a non-partisan line, whereas the public and his party valued more combative figures. He simply did not have the hearty contempt for his opponents that was expected. Lansdowne was nonetheless a highly skilful, proficient and prescient politician. Early in his career he recognised how the power of the Commons had risen, would continue to rise and would increasingly produce political leaders. He looked to the establishment and the Lords for inspiration and resistance to populism.

Lansdowne proved a conscientious Junior Lord.[26] However, he disliked making speeches, sensing a tendency to speak too fast, which he found difficult to correct and was the result of shyness.[27] He offered to resign when MPs criticised his unsalaried role; like a modern internship, such a position eliminated anyone who had to earn their living. Gladstone, who thought it was commendable to have a token honourable susceptibility, altogether deprecated his decision. He advised Lansdowne to at least wait until financial work for the year was complete.[28] Lansdowne did not resign, but his threat did no harm; it showed he was a man of moral fibre.

In July Lansdowne attended Goodwood Races, and among his house party was Maud Hamilton. A love affair blossomed that lasted all their lives. That Lansdowne loved her very much is evident in his few surviving letters to her. In one he wrote, 'I have loved you because of the complete sincerity of your nature. I am conscious that your influence upon me has throughout been one which has strengthened that which was good and just in my nature, and weakened that which was narrow and selfish.'[29] In August they became engaged, followed on 8 November 1869 by a double wedding with Maud's sister Albertha and the Marquess of Blandford at Westminster Abbey, with 250 guests at Chesterfield House for the wedding breakfast; the Prince of Wales proposed the toast. Lansdowne would have preferred a quieter and more unassuming affair.[30] Setting off to honeymoon at Bowood, they left for Paddington Station at 1.40 p.m. to catch the 2 p.m. train. In the rush he never saw his best man, Kenneth Howard, or his brother; he had to fight his way through the crowd and dispose rapidly of the Waleses.[31] Arriving at Chippenham at 4.50 p.m., they were met by Lansdowne's colleagues in the Royal Wiltshire Yeomanry Cavalry.[32] A tremendous crowd cheered the couple into their open carriage. The lodge at Bowood

> was illuminated with limelights and floral devices, and a huge set piece of fireworks with an inscription or some device of the kind had been put up, and was fired as the advanced guard of the escort reached the gates. The effect was disastrous & ludicrous.[33]

The device discharged thousands of rockets and shells, making the advanced guard of the cavalry unmanageable. One rider, Lansdowne was later informed, drew his sword and swearing nothing would stop him, charged the gates as if they had been an enemy's battery.[34] The chargers turned sharply. Many threw their riders and then bolted. The terrified horses harnessed to the open carriage plunged uncontrollably, upsetting it. After it was righted, dismounted members of the Yeomanry presented arms as the carriage and its shaken passengers arrived at the house.

Sharing the responsibilities of running the household with her husband, Maud brought a new warmth and lightness to Bowood. She was also to free Lansdowne from his mother's apron strings, though his mother remained a powerful influence. Shortly after his wedding he wrote to her:

> I wish I did not feel that amidst so much happiness, you have so small a share of it. I shall be happy here, and no one has more to make him so, but I shall miss you all nevertheless.[35]

The relationship between Maud and Emily was always tense but, although Lansdowne often bemoaned that his mother did not appreciate Maud, Emily was secretly much pleased by her.[36] One can only wonder if anyone would have been good enough for her son. The rest of the family were keen on her. Lansdowne was very fond of Maud's family, his only criticism being that they were Tories and her six brothers talked endlessly of politics, a subject he avoided in dining rooms, smoking rooms or anywhere outside work.

Lansdowne's political career was also prospering but he remained cautious about his prospects. By March 1870, seeing bills through the House had become routine: 'I have been doing several odd jobs in the House & looking after one or two uninteresting Treasury bills, otherwise things have been slack.'[37] When Northbrook left the War Office to become Viceroy of India in 1872, there was delay in replacing him as Under-Secretary of State for War and several names were mentioned. Jowett wrote to Florence Nightingale questioning, 'am I to have an under-secretary at war? Lord Lansdowne is a very good man for the post.'[38]

The idea was not new to Lansdowne, but there seemed to be so many reasons for not deciding without careful reflection[39] – notably his health and ignorance. He discussed it with Granville and Edmond. In those days, when death came to people quite easily, it was common to discuss health issues. Although he was not a hypochondriac, Lansdowne spoke often about his health. Having suffered from sciatica for some years after Oxford, he consulted his doctor, who was confident of his health. Lansdowne told Gladstone that if Cardwell did not consider his complete ignorance of War Office matters an obstacle he would accept the post.[40] Cardwell assured him that when he came to the office he did not know a gun from a sword.

Lansdowne accepted on 24 April. Lord Cardwell, Secretary of State for War since December 1868, was a man of proven administrative competence. A former Peelite and Chancellor of the Exchequer, he handled financial problems with considerable expertise.[41] Although never inspiring as a spokesman in the Commons, he did engender enthusiasm among his colleagues at Pall Mall, particularly Lansdowne. Army reform had not figured prominently in the election campaign of 1868, but after the Franco-Prussian War Cardwell recognised that it was impossible to send an expeditionary force to the Continent while the army remained on a peace footing.[42] When Lansdowne became Under-Secretary of State, Cardwell's principal army and War Office reforms were complete but some changes were still taking shape.

Lansdowne's office had doors into Cardwell's office and into that of his private secretary, Digby Pigott, 'a capital fellow and not the least formidable or pretentious'.[43] 'I do not think that you have got the pleasantest place under government,' Jowett wrote, 'but you have got one of the most interesting and important posts at this time.'[44] Maud viewed it with 'doubtful approbation' and consoled herself by the reflection that there was a strong possibility the government would not last.[45] Lansdowne was criticised as an unfit civilian, who only knew French society; Cardwell thought otherwise. In June he appointed him to chair a committee on the Royal Engineers. When Britain sent General Wolseley to war against the Ashanti Kingdom, Lansdowne assisted with mobilisation. Cardwell's reforms met strong resistance and Lansdowne was given the task of appeasing the critics, for which he was well prepared by his experiences in Kerry.

While still dealing with the Anglo-Ashanti War, Lansdowne chaired a committee on points of friction between the Control Department, which oversaw finance, and the various military departments.[46] He was surprised to find how 'few and trivial' the problems were.[47] Civil-military relations were never smooth at the War Office and were still creating tension when Lansdowne became Secretary of State for War in 1895. He completed his report just before the government fell in February 1874. He was disappointed to leave office, but he needed a rest. Despite his doctor's earlier diagnosis, while at the War Office he suffered from sciatica and a form of rheumatism that attacked a joint in his lower back, causing him severe discomfort.[48] After leaving office he made a rapid recovery.

That summer, Jowett visited Bowood: 'I found a very high opinion of Lord Lansdowne. His house is conducted admirably both by him & his wife. There is an enormous maturity about him & although he will never be a great liberal he will always be an able & eminent statesman, possibly Prime Minister. The manners of both of them are charming for their simplicity.'[49] At the year's end Jowett remarked that 'his mind like that of his brother [Edmond] is in politics, whether he has sufficient force &

imagination I am not certain but he has the right ideas about things &
an ambition to be something more than Lord Granville whom in some
respects he resembles'.[50] Maud thought Lansdowne's whole soul was in
politics; like Jowett, she hoped he would some day be Prime Minister.
Lansdowne was an ambitious man, but his ambition was under the
control of his judgement. Jowett urged him that the real time for making
a reputation in politics was upon him now that he was out of office,
commenting, 'one can have independence and can act for yourself and
you have leisure and can make a carefully prepared speech'.[51] Lansdowne
had made several good speeches but, as yet, nothing considerable such as
might be remembered and talked about.

At this time the former Whig peers were disappointing in both
numbers and enthusiasm. Similarly, most Liberal MPs were neither
Whigs nor Radicals but ordinary, prosperous Britons whose political
ideologies were bound neither by association to great houses nor by
theoretical intransigence.[52] By the 1870s Gladstone had reshaped the
party and former Whigs were further marginalised. Lansdowne's
brother, Edmond, encouraged displacement of the Whigs and in time
the rise of the Radicals; Lansdowne, whose politics were neither radical
nor partisan, did not. He believed in liberal progress, based upon
moderate concessions to responsible opinion. He supported some of
Gladstone's social or moral reforms and attempts to facilitate individual
advancement, although like the old Whigs before him, he questioned the
urgency of empowering the masses and attaining democracy. However,
he saw it coming and, by the early 1890s he was convinced Britain was at
the beginning of the triumph of democratic principles.[53] As a pragmatist
he did not mean to resist, but rather to support stability and the status
quo while it lasted.

During Lansdowne's six years out of office he honed his understanding
of his political responsibilities and obligations, and devoted his other
energies to supporting his wife and young family. Maud gave birth to
four children: Evelyn, nicknamed 'Evie', was born on 27 August 1870;
Henry, always known by his title, 'Kerry', arrived on the morning of
Lansdowne's twenty-seventh birthday, 14 January 1872; Charles, called
'Charlie', was born on 12 February 1874; Beatrix, nicknamed 'Bertie',
followed on 25 March 1877. Both parents were besotted with them.
The children lacked for nothing and had a happy childhood. Unlike his
father, Lansdowne was playful with his children. Like most children of
their class they had a nanny; a schoolroom was created at Bowood and a
tutor was employed. The boys were sent off to school at the age of eight;
the girls were educated at home.

Following the April 1880 election, Lansdowne expected to be offered
a post by Gladstone:

Up to the present I have not the slightest idea what it is likely to be, but I see that most of the papers send me to Ireland, and I am already receiving applications for court appointments at which to use old Spencer's favourite expression 'my stomach rises'. I would not mind Irish work, or living in Ireland, but the flunkeydom & parade would be insupportable. Besides this there are some Irish measures which nothing will induce me to have anything to say to. I shall not be sorry to have office as I like having regular work to do, and fret less over it than if I have to provide work for myself. £.s.d. is another consideration and I am half afraid that Ireland would be a losing affair. I could not do it shabbily and the traditions of the office are horribly extravagant. Altogether I confess to being a little worried.[54]

Gladstone, following 'Peel's rule' that ministers must serve in junior posts before entering cabinet, offered him India or Ireland.[55] Lansdowne decided 'the real work in the India Office was preferable to the sham in the Phoenix',[56] so, on 13 May 1880, the Marquess of Hartington appointed him Under-Secretary of State for India.

5

A MATTER OF PRINCIPLE

FOLLOWING HIS APPOINTMENT as Under-Secretary of State for India, Lansdowne should have been absorbed with affairs in India, but his attention was on the Irish Land War, which had gained prominence and was a threat to landlords in Ireland and Britain. Many Irish farmers and labourers endured conditions little different from the famine years. Some lived in simple one- or two-storey cottages, with walls often built of mud, and others in one-bedroom cabins. During the late 1870s butter prices fell, fewer cattle and pigs were kept, tenant farmers – often in arrears – were evicted and labourers were laid off. As distress worsened, Fenian agitators gained influence. As one of Ireland's largest landowners, Lansdowne was in the line of fire.

The Liberal government responded by introducing a Compensation for Disturbance Bill to stem the rise in evictions. Lansdowne strongly disapproved of the principle of the measure, which he believed would create immense mischief. He feared that the consequence would be to permanently weaken the position of Irish landlords. He told Gladstone that he could make no secret of his opinions. His position as both an Irish landlord and a member of the government rendered it impossible for him to avoid the discussion. As such, it would have been disloyal of him to remain in office under an administration whose Irish policy he condemned.[1]

On 2 July 1880 Gladstone asked Lansdowne to delay his resignation owing to the serious nature of the subject matter, while letting him know that he was in no way responsible for what the government did outside his department and the House of Lords. Granville thought Gladstone managed Lansdowne very cleverly but was all too aware of the latter's very strong will.[2] Next day, Hartington – from a similar Whig heritage

– informed Lansdowne that the cabinet refused to drop the bill in the middle of the second reading. He hoped Lansdowne would wait until the course of the government's bill was more settled.[3] Lansdowne agreed that his immediate responsibility to the government did not begin until the bill reached the Lords. Nonetheless he would incur considerable responsibility by allowing it to be inferred that he was a consenting party to the bill.[4] Beyond his immediate anger with the measure, he worried that the Liberal Party would be history if things continued on the same course.[5] On 7 July Lansdowne offered his resignation again. Gladstone attempted to dissuade him, but no limitation of the bill would satisfy him – only its withdrawal. Having resigned, he felt very low.[6]

Queen Victoria read of Lansdowne's resignation in the newspapers and asked Granville if it was true.[7] He confirmed it was and that Lansdowne's decision was a blow to the government.[8] The Queen, who thoroughly disliked Gladstone, thought the Irish Land Bill was 'a great misfortune and what is worse, people believe Mr Gladstone intends it as a prelude to a similar measure in England'.[9] Lansdowne's resignation was the first distinguished step of a career in which the defence of the landowning class against a threat from the left was to be a principal theme.[10] To Lansdowne the issue was one of principle, not class: as a Whig, he regarded the threat of government intervention in private property as a threat to liberty.

On 2 August the Irish Land Bill was debated in the Lords.[11] No one foresaw that it would trigger one of the greatest changes in parliamentary history. 'Lansdowne seems to have spoken well,' Gladstone's private secretary noted.[12] The Lords rejected the Bill by 282 to 51, a larger majority than expected. The rebels included Granville, 60 Liberal Whigs and 20 Irish landowners. The vote foreshadowed the Whigs' final exit from Liberal ranks and, as Asquith remarked forty-six years later, was the starting point of the standing quarrel between the Liberal Party and the Upper House, which culminated in the passing of the Parliament Act of 1911,[13] depriving the Lords of their veto.

Lansdowne's opposition to the Land Bill was exploited by his enemies, who attacked the administration of his Irish estates.[14] At the end of September Charles Russell, an Irish-born Catholic lawyer and MP for Dundalk, was sent by the *Daily Telegraph* to collect evidence. With two friends and a shorthand writer, he arrived in Kerry to uncover the worst. Lansdowne was amused that he began by going to the wrong man, who gave him a very good report.[15] Russell was deeply annoyed, particularly as his Irish affairs were already under scrutiny from the Bessborough and Richmond Commissions.[16] Previously, reluctant to embroil himself in press controversy, Lansdowne had allowed falsehoods about his estates to pass unchallenged.[17] However, this was different, and he was glad that his brother Edmond was watching the case.[18] On 11 November Russell attacked with a letter to the *Daily Telegraph*, with further letters appearing in December. He alleged that Lansdowne was unknown to his tenants, that his agent had visited the Iveragh properties only once in five years, the tenants there were literally afraid to call their souls their own,[19] they lived in poverty and children had gone about naked in the winter of 1879.[20] Lansdowne was advised to take no notice, but wrote to the *Daily Telegraph* on 21 November and answered every charge. His refutation was supported by Edmond and by the Senior Fellows of Trinity College Dublin, who also owned property in Kerry. Russell published his letters in a book, *New Views on Ireland, or Irish Land: Grievances: Remedies*, aiming to present the public with 'the full means of judgment'.[21] Lansdowne in turn, published, in a pamphlet, the letters Russell had suppressed. Russell then dropped the matter. Lansdowne was a fair landlord who contributed to public works – roads, bridges, piers, schools – and provided work for those wanting employment. Lansdowne took a pragmatic view of the situation in Ireland. He believed that no amount of tenant rights would ever turn his Kerry tenants into solvent farmers. Their insufficient landholdings resulted in their living upon the verge of insolvency in even prosperous seasons. He felt the only remedy was in the gradual consolidation of these infinitesimally small farms.[22]

The agrarian insurrection, the strongest for two centuries, continued through the winter; the government turned to coercion as strict as any Conservative's.[23] Lansdowne fiercely defended property rights and deplored Gladstone's methods of 'pacifying' Ireland. In August 1881 he openly criticised Gladstone's Second Irish Land Bill, seeing it as simply a repudiation of the 1870 Land Act by the ministers who drafted it. Attempting to subdue an agrarian rebellion by conceding proprietary rights to the Irish peasantry would, he believed, rob the landlord of two of the principle attributes of ownership: namely, the right of determining whether to let or not let one's land, and the right of selecting the person to whom one wishes to let it.[24] Lansdowne gathered support among Whig colleagues to amend the bill at committee stage. Gladstone conceded their main points on 15 August and the Act received the royal assent a week later. Lansdowne believed its terms 'were as good as we could possibly have looked for. Fortunate are those who have not, as I have now, to deal with its practical application.'[25] With limits on rent-fixing and eviction, maintaining his Irish estates was no longer feasible; Lansdowne accepted it was better to sell them. The 1881 Irish Land Act effectively destroyed his property rights and the doctrine of free contract in rents.

Although the bill did something to pacify agitation in Ireland, the murders of Frederick Cavendish, Hartington's brother and Under-Secretary for Ireland, and Thomas Burke, his secretary, broke the spell.

Lansdowne was deeply shocked: 'we are at last face to face with the forces from which Irish agitation derives its fatal strength. Poor Fred Cavendish will have died quite in vain if his tragical end has not served to tear the scales off the eyes of the fatuous idiots who believed so readily in the new millennium.'[26] Lansdowne blamed Gladstone for his Irish troubles, for Gladstone's 'recklessness is something quite appalling'.[27] Jowett thought the same:

> I feel very strongly the mischief that – [Gladstone] is doing, and that he probably will do, as long as he lives, for the future. But whatever we might wish I do not see that his hold on the middle & lower classes is shaken therefore he is the master 'until this tyranny be overpast.' Had Dizzy been alive or had the Tory party been stronger or better led, the result might have been different.[28]

In April 1883, qualified by his French connection, Lansdowne was asked to chair a select committee on plans for a Channel tunnel.[29] Lansdowne strongly favoured this but the majority of his committee opposed it and the cabinet dropped it. Gladstone's secretary, Edward Hamilton, noted, 'the Cabinet are probably right, as there is no denying that the mass of public opinion is adverse to the project'.[30] Lansdowne was disappointed by their decision but was later able to joke:

> A friend, usually very calm in his judgement but I am told the acute sufferer of sea sickness, met me in the street: 'If you stop this tunnel – look out for yourself.' I took refuge in my club and met another very old friend of the military persuasion. He put his fist inconveniently near my face and said 'Old fellow, if you allow this *** tunnel none of us will ever speak to you again.' Bedlam was the mildest form of punishment with which we were threatened, whether we went for or against.[31]

As well as Gladstone's Irish policy, Lansdowne denounced Liberal foreign policy, which was based on patience, peace and mid-Victorian restraint. Lansdowne quickly realised that, with the Empire expanding in the 1870s and early 80s, the climate had changed: imperial unity did not require uniformity in language or race, and imperial pressures required strength, not suavity. Although Lansdowne was neither jingoistic nor expansionist, on 28 January 1881 he had denounced the government's proposed abandonment of Kandahar. Taking this controversial line 'was very hard work, our people didn't much like what I said, and altogether the effort was a painful one'.[32] As his career developed, he became indifferent to being unpopular or controversial if he felt his judgement was sound.

In May 1883, despite their quarrels over the Land Bills and their increasingly strained relations, Gladstone recommended Lansdowne, over the Duke of Albany, to be Governor-General of Canada. Active in Parliament for seventeen years, fluent in French and a nobleman, Lansdowne was well qualified. It would be naive, however, to see Gladstone's offer as altruistic. As a prominent Anglo-Irish landlord and critic of government policy, Lansdowne was a threat to Gladstone. While no one in government or the opposition objected to the appointment, nationalist sentiment at home and abroad was inflamed. Lansdowne was threatened by the Irish in Canada and forced to complete a short memorandum containing references to one or two supporting documents by which he could defend himself.[33] Far from welcoming the opportunity to leave England, Lansdowne accepted it largely because he was heavily in debt. He told his Liberal colleague, Rosebery:

> I had a good deal of difficulty in deciding but many reasons seemed to point in the direction of assent – I have never been further from home than Paris except on two occasions when my rheumatic ailments drove me as far as Aix-les-Bains & Wiesbaden. To flanner [*sic*] on the Boulevard and to be douched with hot water are both in their way good things, but a man who went down to the grave with no experience beyond this of the world outside England would leave a great part of his education incomplete. Besides this I am glad to be once more united by official ties to my party & I do not very much regret relinquishing the role of the candid friend of H.M. Government which I have been playing for some time past.[34]

Shortly before taking leave Lansdowne wrote to Edmond, 'If any misfortune should happen to me – and Fenian bullets are not the only contingencies of which one has to think – I know that Maud and the children will find a faithful friend in you.'[35]

6

CANADA - SETTLING IN

AFTER TEN DAYS of seasickness while making the crossing on the *Circassian*, from Lough Foyle, on the north coast of Ireland, to Quebec, Lansdowne, along with his family and staff, reached his destination two days later than expected, at 8 p.m. on 22 October 1883. Anticipating unrest from Irish residents, the Canadian government took special precautions to protect him and his family, and to ensure the safety of the Queen's ships in Canadian waters. That night, while the Lansdownes stayed on board the *Circassian*, Sir John Macdonald, Canada's Prime Minister, and his cabinet met at the Hotel St Louis, Quebec, to discuss arrangements. Disguising possible threats with suitable fanfare, they planned a warm welcome, even though the temperature was 0 °C.

Next morning, the government steamer *Druid* drew alongside the *Circassian*. On board were Lord Lorne, the outgoing Governor-General, Macdonald and some of the cabinet. Taken ashore to a hearty welcome, the Lansdownes were immediately driven in an open carriage, with a cavalry escort, to the provincial government's buildings. In the library, Lansdowne, dressed in a Windsor uniform, dark blue with scarlet collar and cuffs, was sworn in as Governor-General:

> The ceremony was not particularly pompous – Lorne on a sort of dias [*sic*], I on a chair below – magnificoes, justices and provincial authorities distributed over different rows of chairs. Melgund reads my commission, I recite a long declaration of fidelity to the Crown, take several impressive oaths administered by the Chief Justice, take Lorne's place on the dais & then deliver the great seal to the Secretary of State. This over, we drove off, still with our escort, to the theatre where the civic address of welcome was delivered by the Mayor, a cheery little Frenchman, M. Langelier –

This he read first in French & then in English, making a bold attempt to grapple with my numerous English & Irish titles, all of which were recited in the preamble – I made a short reply, first in English & then in French, the audience – almost all French Canadians listened respectfully to the first & cheered some of the passages, but before I had got one half a dozen words of the French reply the whole audience burst into rapturous applause which continued more or less until I had finished. I suppose my French was less bad than some to which they have been used, at any rate it pleased the good folk of Quebec.

From the theatre we drove to the station, where we found a special with several most comfortable cars – in one of which we had a most comfortable hot luncheon, cooked on board & well served up. Nothing can exceed the comfort of these cars & particularly of the little bed rooms provided for the passengers – I had much sooner spend 10 days in one than in a state room on board the *Circassian*.

At Ottawa we found a great crowd & a very friendly reception all along our route through the town, which looks very new & uninteresting by gaslight.

Both in Ottawa & Quebec the people seemed well disposed and I did not hear a single Irish groan, altho' it would not have surprised me if our friends had made a little counter demonstration. I am told that there is nothing whatever to fear from that quarter, and that the bad feeling which was got up at first against my appointment has very much subsided, if it has not been instrumental in provoking a reaction.[1]

Lansdowne took over two official residences and one unofficial. Most of the time he, his family and staff lived at Rideau Hall, about 2 miles outside the federal capital of Ottawa. Close to an ugly suburb and almost 3 miles from Parliament Hill, along rutted and muddy tracks, it was a long, low, unpretentious, two-storey building, built in 1838 by a stonemason from Perth as his home. Acquired by the British government in 1868 and enlarged with a forty-nine-room wing,[2] it looked 'singularly like a suburban private lunatic asylum'[3] with 'the entrance front as ugly as anything can be'.[4] Lansdowne found fault with the furniture and decoration too, although 'the general effect is bright and cheerful – with a little papering and rearrangement and some pictures and prints on the walls we shall get on very well'.[5]

The Lansdownes created a cheerful household. Lansdowne inherited some staff from Lorne and brought others with him. His military secretary was the Scottish-born Gilbert John Elliot-Murray-Kynynmound, Lord Melgund (later the 4th Earl of Minto). Small, tough, competitive and with a passion for sports, games and outdoor life, Melgund was a natural choice. Melgund's wife Mary – daughter of General Sir Charles Grey,

Queen Victoria's private secretary – possessed charm and grace and was a good athlete. Melgund was an orthodox Whig of the Palmerston vintage and shared Lansdowne's contempt for Gladstone.[6] Lansdowne had known Melgund since they were at Eton and had tried for years to find him an administrative post. It was Lansdowne's view that Lady Melgund would be a great success with the local inhabitants and that her husband was 'indefatigable and always cheery and pleasant'.[7] Melgund's duties ranged from arranging official visits to organising Government House entertainment, but none required daily attention; a chief clerk and several assistants did most routine work. Working from offices at Rideau Hall and the Parliament Building, Lansdowne did most of his own paperwork. To Lansdowne it was 'child's play' compared to the work of an English department.[8] Melgund was not prepared for so little activity and, frustrated, soon left Canada.

Lansdowne's aides-de-camp (ADCs) were two army officers, Henry Anson, aged twenty-five, and Henry Streatfeild, aged twenty-six. Most evenings, 'Streaty' played picquet with Lansdowne, who thought he was about as good or as bad as he was, as well as being charming and popular.[9] Anson's father was the Earl of Lichfield and his mother, Harriet, was Maud's sister. Lansdowne thought he had 'a capital head on his shoulders and was painstaking and accurate',[10] and 'quite the best of A.D.C.'s'.[11] Anson had brought his sister Florence, aged twenty-three, and the fate of Streatfeild seemed inevitable. 'I do not see how he and little Florence are to avoid falling in love with each other and as neither of them have a sixpence it will be disastrous if they do. She is a nice little thing and a pleasant companion for Maud'.[12] In December Florence and Streatfeild announced their intention to marry. Lansdowne felt they had behaved well and that on the whole it was perhaps better that they should know '*ce qui en est*' than that their flirtation should be indefinitely prolonged.[13] Lansdowne's staff were very popular; on tours around the country they were dragged off at all hours of the day and night to drink champagne with all and sundry. They would reappear after such events, a little bleary-eyed, and Lansdowne would joke how he meant to keep them on toast and water the following week.[14]

Although Lansdowne's involvement with Irish matters was cutoff by distance, he could not relax; the threats against his life were very real. Plots for his removal were organised by Fenians in the United States, where the American-Irish press constantly attacked him. On one occasion he received what appeared to be a bomb, which was fortunately discovered because the packing was faulty and it arrived partly unwrapped. On another, a Fenian assassin from Chicago hid in the woods at Rideau Hall waiting for Lansdowne. All he saw was Kerry, then twelve years old, skating on the ice. Reportedly, the Fenian's heart failed him and he resisted killing the boy.

The family was guarded by members of the Dominion Police who, Lansdowne believed, were not so infallible as their reputation made out. Newspapers regularly featured exaggerated stories that Lansdowne was the target of threatening letters, but the Canadian authorities often received information of Fenian plots for his removal directed from the United States.[15] While Lansdowne ignored these attacks, his concern for his family – particularly Maud, who he perceived did not realise the position quite so clearly as he did – caused him to write a letter for preparations in event of his death. He made suggestions for their children's education, his burial, souvenirs to be given to friends and Maud's remarriage.[16]

These threats made mixing in Canadian society harder. Lansdowne found among the upper echelons 'some people of whom I should like to see more and the worst of them are not, I think so tiresome as a political dinner in the London season'.[17] Except for Macdonald, he did not believe Canadian ministers were of the same intellectual mould as the best politicians in England, but they were remarkable people in their way. The women he found less laudable, 'but we contrive to have a small population of these, so Maud escapes pretty easily – Sometimes I am overwhelmed with fear lest her sense of the ridiculous should become too strong & get the whole of us into disgrace.'[18]

Lansdowne's success depended not just on his relations with Canadians, but also with London. In 1883 the Colonial Secretary was Edward Stanley, 15th Earl of Derby. A former Conservative Foreign Secretary, he became a Liberal in 1880 and, soon after, a political colleague of Lansdowne's and instrumental in his Canadian appointment. A cordial and informative correspondence with the Queen was also essential. Like his predecessor, every three months Lansdowne wrote long letters explaining the principal issues facing Canada. Even though she never visited Canada, Queen Victoria was keenly aware of the Dominion and strongly in favour of Confederation, which her father had proposed in 1814.

By 1883 Canada was a vast territory stretching from the Atlantic to the Pacific, north of the 49th parallel.[19] In 1867 the country had become a federation, its colonies and territories constitutionally subject to Westminster. Anglophone and francophone areas lived in an enforced marriage, but most Canadians supported their position as an independent Dominion within the Empire. The country was sparsely settled by four million people, drawn together by the promise of the railways opening up the country. Indigenous Americans still possessed much of the prairies and buffalo roamed the plains. Beyond the grasslands, 40 per cent of the country was covered by forests of spruce, poplar and pine; another 9 per cent was freshwater lakes and rivers. Summer temperatures could rise above 35 °C, while lows of

-25 °C were not uncommon in winter; spring and autumn were more temperate.

Establishing an immigrant population, expanding agriculture and trade and a strong manufacturing base were keys to the successful National Policy introduced by Macdonald. Now aged sixty-eight, the first Prime Minister of the Dominion had served under four Governor-Generals.[20] A Scot trained as a lawyer, he believed Canada could be a powerful auxiliary to the Empire. He possessed a forceful personality, glib tongue and marvellous memory for names and faces. There seemed little in common between Macdonald and Lansdowne, except both men disliked Gladstone. Macdonald considered Lansdowne the ablest chief under whom he had ever served.[21]

Canada had come to expect a nobleman as Governor-General.[22] Many scholars have tended to view the post-Confederation Governor-General as a figurehead, a glorified postman. Yet its legal instrument gave the office wide powers, notably to ensure that Canada had a prime minister and a government. Lansdowne usually exercised his powers on the explicit advice of the Canadian Prime Minister but, as the Queen's representative, he worked under instructions from the British government, conveyed through the Colonial Office. It was his duty to defend the rights and interests of the imperial government. So he had to reconcile within himself the conflicting interests and demands of two governments. His task was also ceremonial, strengthening ties between Britain and Canada.

Travelling across the country, Lansdowne participated in community activities and festivals, visited hospitals, schools and workplaces, gave speeches and supported various organisations. In hosting dinners, receptions and skating parties he created a good impression. On any given day he might make three or four speeches, receive an address, hold a reception and attend a dinner or ball, always aware that the Fenians might assassinate him. Before he came, Macdonald had anticipated that Lord Lansdowne would have an unpleasant time in office.[23]

Lansdowne immediately faced problems: the Canadian Pacific Railway (CPR) financial crisis, provincial discontent, Indigenous American unrest and strained relations with the United States of America (USA) over fisheries. The CPR was a government-supported private enterprise of enormous importance to Canada, so Lansdowne believed.[24] But, as Governor-General, he felt he should remain an impartial observer of the political and financial intrigues that it created. The project began in 1868, but negotiations lasted until 1881 when Macdonald signed a contract with the CPR syndicate to complete the line within ten years. Shortly after Lansdowne's arrival the syndicate ran out of money and in one of his first letters to Queen Victoria Lansdowne reported the excitement over the financial transaction between the government and the CPR. While he thought it was undesirable for the government to be mixed up in the matter he informed the Queen that the CPR was regarded as a national undertaking and had been supported as such.[25] In early 1884 the Canadian public and Liberal opposition began to question the government's involvement with the CPR and its financial difficulty. The trigger was a relief bill with a government guarantee; although the Liberal Party in Canada exploited the issue, the Bill passed the Commons on 28 February and received the royal assent (from the Senate) on 5 March. The CPR was rescued with a loan of $22 million.

While interesting himself in the internal affairs of Canada, Lansdowne also developed strong views on external policy, particularly in regard to dealing with the USA. Lansdowne was pro-American and believed Britain should work harmoniously with the United States. Arriving with minimal knowledge of American politics and politicians, he learned quickly. A cautious policy was vital to Lansdowne's negotiations with the Americans. 'Any incident which might imperil these relations would be regretted here', he told the British ambassador in Washington.[26] Interestingly the incident occurred at sea and not on land.

The main cause of tension between the two countries was the question of fishing and boundary rights, regulated by the Treaty of 1818 and eased by the Reciprocity Treaty of 1854, which removed duty on many products, allowed US fishermen into Canada's Atlantic coast fisheries and let British subjects fish in equivalent US waters north of the 36th parallel. US protectionists campaigned against this and, during the American Civil War, Britain's allegedly pro-southern sympathies increased northern opposition. The Reciprocity Treaty was abrogated by the USA in March 1866. After Canadian Confederation in July 1867, US fishermen were relegated to the terms of 1818, which permitted their vessels to enter bays and harbours in Nova Scotia, New Brunswick and Prince Edward Island, but only for the purpose of shelter, repairs and purchasing wood and water. The 1871 Treaty of Washington gave US fishermen access to Canadian inshore fisheries, in return for a payment, and gave free entry of Canadian fish into the USA. In 1883 the US Senate resolved to abrogate the fishery clauses of the 1871 agreement. Canada had to protect her rights under the Treaty of 1818.[27] In May 1883, although the expiry of the 1871 fisheries clauses was two years away,[28] the British initiated negotiations. With no response by December 1883, Lansdowne realised nothing would happen without fresh steps. He suspected that Downing Street's view differed greatly from Ottawa's.[29]

When not undertaking his formal duties, Lansdowne unwound with another type of fishing. Like his predecessors, he wrote to the Lieutenant Governor of Quebec, successfully asking to lease a stretch of the Cascapedia River, which contained some of the best salmon fishing in North America. In 1884, on the river bank a few miles north of New Richmond, among dense woods with few birds but overrun with deer, bear, skunk, mosquitoes, black flies and sandflies, Lansdowne built a 'rough house',[30] which he named 'New Derreen' after the house he adored in Kerry. Only fly fishing was permitted, from canoes because the river banks were so overgrown. While New Derreen was being built, Lansdowne visited his other official residence at Quebec. The Citadel had been converted into a residence by Lord Dufferin, Governor-General in 1872–78. Lansdowne thought the rooms were

cozy and have a homely look about them. There is a nice drawing room and dining room below, a ball room beyond, and a platform outside long enough for a before-breakfast quarterdeck walk, with a view which words cannot describe. I have got a nice little study with windows out of which I can look down on to the top masts of Messrs. Allan's steamers.[31]

Lansdowne was delighted with the platform and the good air, but the complete absence of garden was an 'immense drawback'.[32]

That summer, the Lansdownes spent nearly three weeks in Quebec City. Lansdowne visited Laval University and the Legislative Council of Quebec, where he received an address from both houses. He replied in French and English, noting later:

I find it almost impossible to concoct a speech in English and then translate it into French, and whenever I have to do anything of the sort in two languages I write the original in French and render it into English afterwards.[33]

Meanwhile, the wooden house went up rapidly, and was ready for use by 6 July. Although he took a break, Lansdowne continued working on various matters – honours, US–Canada relations, and the arrival of Riel.

On 10 July Macdonald informed Lansdowne that Louis Riel, leader of the Red River Rebellion of 1870, had returned to Canada at the invitation of about 600 Métis near Prince Albert on the North Saskatchewan River. The Métis, who were as wild as the full-blood Indians and much more fierce,[34] were descendants of intermarriage between Cree, Ojibway, Saulteaux or Menominee aboriginals, and French Canadian, Scots or English colonists. They were aggrieved and starving. Riel's arrival created panic. He intended to help Métis obtain their legal rights in the Saskatchewan Valley, where many Métis had moved from Manitoba. Extermination of the buffalo had left them without food, while lake steamers and railways had almost ended the need for porters and thus their earnings as human freighters.

The Métis believed they shared with Indigenous Americans in the original title of the land and claimed compensation. The Manitoba Act of 12 May 1870 had given them a land grant of 1,400,000 acres. They could choose to plead their Indigenous American blood and receive their share of the reserve or they could choose to be independent farmers, acquire homesteads and preemption to another quarter-section of land like anyone else. Most did not take to farming. Many émigré Métis who were prominent in the agitation had received grants and sold them to land speculators, before moving west and asking for fresh grants, which the government was unwilling to offer.

The land question, which Lansdowne fondly imagined he had left behind in Ireland, seemed to him to lie at the root of the grievances. It appeared to him that the government should endeavour to meet and discuss matters with Riel as soon as possible.[35] He suggested sending an intermediary, but police reinforcement was essential: 'Indians with empty bellies, speculators with empty pockets, horse thieves and frontier raiders, Fenians and Farmers' Unions, and all with a mere handful of men to keep the peace. It is wonderful to me that we get on so well.'[36] In December the Métis sent a petition to Ottawa, from where it was forwarded to the Colonial Office. Riel let it be known that, if he was paid off, he would persuade his followers to accept any settlement offered and he would then leave the north-west permanently. He demanded $100,000, but would accept $35,000.

Meanwhile, the Lansdownes returned to Ottawa and lived 'as quietly as mice, giving a dinner a week or perhaps three a fortnight and, save for this, keeping clear of all ceremonies'.[37] Lansdowne evidently enjoyed his first year in Canada, and thought it was a great achievement to have got through it as well as he did. He thought he had spent £7,000 more than his official income and doubted that his finances had improved. He hoped the Bowood staff had made progress with much needed estate maintenance and that Herbert Smith, the resident agent, would not want quite so much money for buildings repairs and maintenance.[38] On 14 January 1885, Lansdowne celebrated his fortieth birthday and his son Kerry's thirteenth with a servants' ball at Government House in Ottawa. The Lansdownes retired at midnight but:

> I fancy they went on till after 3 a.m. and judging by my cellar book must have had what they call a 'good time' out here. I feel very old at times and I see more and more of the top of my head, deeper lines on my face and an increasing number of grey hairs in my moustache every day. On the other hand I am well in health and can beat my A.D.C.s at tennis.[39]

On 4 March 1885, Grover Cleveland was inaugurated as President of the United States. His appointment of Thomas Bayard as Secretary of State was well received in Canada. Bayard promised to be more liberal in commercial policy and his early pronouncements on fisheries were encouraging. However, Lansdowne knew that Macdonald might have difficulty persuading Canadians to accept, even for a short time, hostile tariffs on their fish and fish products entering the USA, while US fishing vessels still had the same access to Canadian waters as before.[40] While Lansdowne and Macdonald discussed possible terms, in late August the Colonial Office sent Lansdowne a dispatch, inviting Canada and Newfoundland to specify proposals to put to the United States. After protracted negotiations, President Cleveland recommended to Congress that a fisheries commission be set up.

7

THE NORTH-WEST

DISCUSSIONS WITH RIEL failed. The government ignored his bribe and started an inquiry into the Métis petition. Frustrated, Riel formed a Provisional Government of Saskatchewan on 19 March 1885, announcing that 'he would bring Sir John Macdonald down at his feet yet'.[1] The outbreak started at the confluence of the North and South Saskatchewan Rivers, where there was a Cree reserve, 300 miles from Qu'Appelle, the nearest point on the Canadian Pacific Railway (CPR). On 26 March the Métis defeated one hundred Canadian Mounted Police and volunteers at Duck Lake. The timing could not have been worse for the government. Winter was ending, so that with rain, blizzards and high winds, trails became impassable, rivers unfordable, and as the CPR was unfinished north of Lake Superior, moving troops was difficult. The rebel victory stirred the Cree to move men on Battleford, where they were joined by Assiniboines. It seemed that the Métis uprising would be followed by a general aboriginal revolt in the North-West.

At this time, Big Bear, chief of the Plains Cree, was resisting government pressure for his people to take a reserve. While he was awaiting a better offer, his tribe starved, their rations cut off by the government. At Frog Lake on 2 April, his war chief killed nine men, including the Indian Agent, Thomas Quinn. Lansdowne thought the massacre 'very disagreeable. Every occurrence of this sort makes the whole position more difficult. These Indian Agents are many of them great knaves and are being paid for old scores now.'[2] However, some important Indian chiefs around Calgary proved loyal, saving the government's face. Among them was Crowfoot, chief of the Blackfoot, who professed his allegiance to the Queen no matter what happened.[3]

The rebellion made good newspaper copy. Bulletins from Winnipeg reported in the Canadian papers were accurate, but news in other countries showed bias, mostly caused by US reporters. *The Times* correspondent, writing from Philadelphia, did his utmost to discredit Canada, always making the worst of their misfortunes.[4] After three weeks of skirmishes, the rebels were short of ammunition. Riel surrendered on 15 May and was sent to Regina to be formally charged. Lansdowne was sorry that he was not shot in action, as his trial would cause no end of trouble, and resuscitate all the bitter feelings that had agitated Canada ten years earlier.[5] The rebels fired their last shots on 3 June at the battle of Loon Lake in what is now known as Steele Narrows Park.

On 20 July the trial of Riel for high treason began at Regina. Hardly any local supporters rallied to his cause. Even the local Catholic clergy had no sympathy, believing he had undermined their position and deprived their congregations of advantages.[6] Riel was sentenced to death, eighteen rebels were sent to prison and eleven Indigenous people were sentenced to hang, though three were reprieved. Big Bear and Poundmaker were sentenced to three years at Stony Mountain Penitentiary. Riel appealed against his conviction, but it was upheld; the Canadian cabinet decided that he should hang. Lansdowne did not intervene. On 12 November a messenger bearing the Governor-General's warrant for execution left Ottawa for Regina. Macdonald warned Lansdowne: 'we are in for lively times in Quebec, but I feel pretty confident that the excitement will die out'.[7]

The affair aroused much interest in Britain, and the Queen spoke against Riel's execution. Lansdowne was unmoved, explaining why, in his opinion, clemency could not be exercised: 'the grievances of the half-breeds were greatly exaggerated, and it was the second time Riel had caused loss of life and civil war'.[8] Riel was hanged on 16 September. An attempt was made to start a demonstration in the French quarter of Ottawa, but it came to nothing.[9]

The rebellion was more important in its results than in itself. The campaign had exposed weaknesses in Canada's military: hesitant leadership, extravagant transport, inadequate hospital service, insufficient supplies. Lansdowne resisted interfering, claiming he was no soldier, but he recognised the need to strengthen the defences of the North-West.[10] However, the Métis were destroyed politically; the Indigenous people suffered less.[11]

One indirect consequence of the Riel affair was an end to the friendly atmosphere and bonds that Lansdowne had cultivated between himself and his staff, in particular the Melgunds. Shortly after Melgund returned from the campaign in the North-West, he took a holiday in England, during which a disagreement developed with Lansdowne over his future employment, escalating into a heated row after his return.

As a result, he resigned. Lansdowne was sorry to lose him but believed 'he had not been quite as useful to himself as he might and that he never realised how much a Governor-General ought to depend on his Secretary'.[12] Lansdowne replaced Melgund with Streatfeild and as his new ADC appointed Alfred Byng, an old friend, a good creature, 'rather mad I fancy'[13] but 'preferable to some unknown masher which was the alternative'.[14]

Before Melgund's departure, Lansdowne made a tour of the North-West, accompanied by Melgund and the other staff. Travelling by CPR to Port Arthur, by steamer to Fort William, then by rail to Murillo and Kakabeka Falls, he arrived at Stony Mountain Penitentiary on the morning of 17 September and met Poundmaker, the Cree chief:

> a magnificent fellow, dignified enough to be an emperor & looking like one. I had a talk with him thro' an interpreter and am sorry for the poor wretch who was I think led astray by the half breeds.[15]

On the 21st, Lansdowne reached the Qu'Appelle Valley on horseback, spoke at the Indian School to thirty indigenous children and then to the townsfolk. After a 50-mile ride on an American Quarter Horse, he reached Troy at 9 p.m. and, after addressing a crowd, rejoined the train. He continued via Regina and Moose Jaw to Dunmore, then on a narrow-gauge railway to Lethbridge, where he declared the line open. In the evening he dined with miners and the Bishop of Saskatchewan, making another speech. Next morning, he started early on horseback for the Blood Indian Reserve:

> we rode on towards the Reserve and were met at the border of it by Red Crow and his principal chiefs all on horseback in full costume. After fraternizing with Red Crow we all galloped on together across the Prairie. On my arriving at the Reserve my formal interview or 'Pow wow' with the Indians took place. I sat in the arm chair with my little staff and the Police officers around me and an interpreter by my side. Red Crow and his Chiefs opposite in a semi-circle. The conversation lasted some time and we discussed sundry Indian grievances. At the conclusion my presents were produced – a silver medal and a pair of field glasses for Red Crow, with pipes, knives, and tobacco for the minor notables. We all parted excellent friends and in the evening we camped at a very pretty spot on the other side of the river where our tents had been pitched and where Tinson who had been indefatigable provided us with a very good supper.[16]

The ride from Fort MacLeod to Calgary was 102 miles. They broke their journey at Mosquito Creek, where Lansdowne found a little place full to overflowing with cowboys who had gathered in for a Prairie Race meeting on the following day. A hind quarter of beef was lying beside the backdoor of the house and the cook of the establishment was busily engaged in cutting chunks off this and frying them for each lot of hungry guests as they came in. We got our turn with the rest, and I must say that although you would probably not have thought the surroundings of the feast very appetizing we did thorough justice to it. After supper we made friends with the cowboys and had some songs and swallowed a great deal of bad tobacco smoke.[17]

On 30 September the party travelled east to Blackfoot Crossing to meet the Blackfoot Indians.

Their chief Crowfoot is the most influential Indian of the whole lot and we were anxious to be as civil to him as possible. Crowfoot and several hundred of his people met us at the station and followed us on horseback to the Reserve into which however they allowed us to precede them, they themselves halting about three quarters of a mile off. After half an hour's delay we saw the whole body moving down towards us at a gallop, the whole crew finally charging down upon us at a furious pace and firing their guns and rifles loaded with ball cartridge in every direction and in unpleasant proximity to our heads and those of their neighbours. One or two of them were absolutely naked with the exception of a waist belt and a few feathers, with which their long black locks hanging nearly down to their saddles were ornamented. I never saw a wilder sight. We had a very successful Pow-wow, at the conclusion of which there was the usual distribution of presents, Crowfoot receiving a large silver medal, and a silver bell something like that which the President of the French assembly uses when he wishes to call the members to order. I think the old fellow was rather taken with this. These Indians are extraordinarily eloquent, and although one cannot understand a word they say their gesticulations and the wonderfully mobile expression of their features go far towards telling you what they are driving at. The effect is however a good deal marred by the translation of their fervid declamations into Cowboy English by the interpreter.

Crowfoot came back to the cars and saw me off with many protestations of friendship. Some of the Chiefs were fine looking fellows in spite of their tawdry finery which together with the absurdity of their names rendered it a little difficult to keep one's countenance with becoming gravity. When a gentleman rejoicing in the name of 'Bad Dried Meat', 'White Pup', or 'The Louse', decorated with perhaps an old soup plate out of which the centre has been carefully cut so as to admit of its being turned into a necklace, or wearing as a coiffure a stovepipe hat brushed the wrong way with a magnum bonum steel pen mounted as an *aigrette*, comes forward and shakes you fervently by the hand for five minutes with many insufferable groanings and profane gesticulations, one's sense of the ridiculous becomes almost irresistible. I believe however that I was fairly successful in behaving myself.[18]

Lansdowne recorded that

we parted great friends. He is a clever Indian & behaved very well & I think my visit may have done good & helped to keep him straight.[19]

Travelling via Calgary, the party entered British Columbia:

On each side of the track the mountains rise sheer above us in the wildest and most beautiful shapes. The high peaks mostly covered with snow with here and there a glacier – while below our feet the Kicking Horse River is tearing away towards the Pacific. The timber too is fine. Altogether it is a grand and wonderful sight and it is the more impressing after the dreary flatness of the Prairie scenery.[20]

Continuing on horseback, they reached the CPR's western section on 4 October. Provided with a steamer by the CPR, they crossed the Shuswap Lake. In the evening they watched Indigenous people spearing salmon by torchlight in their canoes. They reached Kamloops the next day. Having crossed the Rockies, the Selkirks and the Gold Range, they entered the Coast Range. Although Lansdowne had intended to be present when the last rail of the CPR was laid, he had to give up all idea of driving the last spike. Because of bad weather the CPR was still 28 miles short of completion, so Macdonald advised him to return to Ottawa as planned.[21] On 6 October they made their way to Port Moody to board a government steamer to Victoria. British Columbia pleased Lansdowne better than anywhere. It was his view that 'If he had to live anywhere in Canada he would pitch his tent there.'[22] At a dinner in Victoria, Lansdowne spoke of the natural resources of British Columbia and the effect of the CPR and stronger links with the rest of Canada:

When once it becomes known that an emigrant can arrive here in less than three weeks from the date of his departure from Liverpool, and find on his arrival such a climate as yours, you will I think have plenty of occupants for your vacant lands.[23]

8

A TEMPTING OFFER

WHILE LANSDOWNE HAD made enormous progress in ensuring cordial relations between Britain and the Dominion states, the US Congress had done nothing to improve its relations with Britain and Canada. Lansdowne was disappointed by the inaction on fisheries and believed the chances of an agreement had evaporated.[1] The Canadians resorted to implementing their strict rights of the Treaty of 1818, which effectively excluded US fishermen from Canadian waters. Lansdowne regretted this as it would 'probably lead to a row'.[2]

In April 1886, Lionel, 2nd Baron Sackville-West, British ambassador in Washington, reported a claim by the US Consul-General at Halifax that there was nothing in the 1818 Treaty to prevent American fishermen from landing fish, if caught outside the 3-mile limit, at a Canadian port and sending them in bond to the USA; if the Canadians refused, this would violate their bonding agreement. Lansdowne thought the 1818 terms clearly gave US fishermen access to Canadian ports only for wood, water, shelter and repairs.[3] He foresaw they would have to seize one or two US fishing boats and there would be a row;[4] indeed, on 8 May the *David J. Adams* was seized in Digby harbour, Nova Scotia, by the Canadian steamer *Lansdowne*. Bayard, the US Secretary of State, warned that such indiscreet action threatened to jeopardise their amicable relations.[5] Canadian public feeling was bitter:[6] if foreign fishermen could restock with bait in Canada whenever they liked, the 1818 convention would be 'seriously impaired'.[7] With a Canadian general election approaching, Lansdowne told Granville, the new Liberal Colonial Secretary, that there would be general indignation if the British government compromised:

It was the Americans that denounced the Reciprocity treaty of 1854; that it was their fishermen who compelled the abandonment of the system of fishing licenses introduced after the expiration of that Treaty for their convenience; that it was their government that abrogated the Fisheries Clauses; that after obtaining the gratuitous use of Canadian territorial waters for nearly an entire season in 1885 their Congress has put an end to the prospect of an equitable settlement from the appointment of a commission recommended by the President.[8]

Lansdowne's argument fell on deaf ears and negotiations between Ottawa, London and Washington continued.

Early in 1886 Lansdowne's sons, at school in England, had been reunited with the family in Ottawa. After a six-week break they left New York on the *Aurania*. Lansdowne planned to follow later in the year with the rest of his family. While most Canadian girls went to public or convent schools, Evie and Bertie were supervised by a nanny and governess. Evie had been altered by life abroad. Her father thought she was 'growing into a fine specimen of a young woman, and though not a beauty I think she will be very taking – she has a splendid complexion and one of the best countenances I ever looked at.'[9]

Although the fisheries dispute brought new complications every day, Lansdowne insisted on taking summer leave. The family left on 1 August without formalities.[10] Reaching London on 16 August, Lansdowne spent just over two months in England visiting friends and his estates, and discussing Canada–US relations with the new government. He accomplished a lot of work and thought he did some good.[11] They returned to Ottawa on 8 November, the boys following in December.

For most of February 1887 the Lansdownes and staff were in Montreal for the Winter Carnival. Wishing to be indebted to no one but unable to find a house to rent, they were lent a 'bijou residence' in McTavish Street to use for their stay. Dinners nearly every night made the place stuffy.[12] Lansdowne held a ball for 800 people, visited schools, convents, colleges, McGill University, hospitals and charitable institutions, made speeches in both languages, opened the Ice Palace and toboggan slides, played in curling matches and skated every day. One Carnival evening there was a skating party in costume. Evie and Bertie went, as did Maud dressed as Mary Queen of Scots, and Lansdowne, who detested dressing up,[13] as the Duke of Brunswick. Charlie and Kerry dressed as pages, resplendent in crimson velvet and tights. The whole visit cost Lansdowne personally £1,000, but he thought it was money well spent.[14] Montreal was impressed.

While Lansdowne was in Montreal, Salisbury reshuffled the cabinet. Following Randolph Churchill's resignation from the Conservatives,

Salisbury offered Goschen, a Liberal Unionist, the position of Chancellor of the Exchequer. Goschen accepted, provided a Liberal Unionist peer joined the ministry. Salisbury invited Lansdowne to join the cabinet as Secretary of State for War or the Colonies.[15] Hartington, Lansdowne's former chief at the India Office and fellow Irish landlord, urged him to accept 'as it would be a great help to the maintenance of the Union'.[16] The twelve hours that Lansdowne spent considering his answer were filled with anxiety. Whatever choice he made had significant consequences not just for himself but for his family and staff. Finally, he refused, although 'the temptation to accept was immense'.[17] He liked Goschen and would have liked to work with him;[18] he was keen to re-enter political life and join the cabinet. But because of politics, partly home, partly Canadian, he could not accept; his Whig scruples prevailed. He also had no idea what the government's Irish policy would be and had no desire to separate from Hartington or other Liberal Unionist friends:

> The difficulty of my position is that I'm an Irish landlord and open to all the suspicions which cling to the skirts of that unfortunate class. Here in Canada we are threatened with a dissolution and may have a very serious crisis. There has not been so much bitter antagonism of race and religion in the country for many years ... A new governor-general coming now without knowledge of men and facts placed face to face with a new ministry might find himself in a great disadvantage. We have a disagreeable quarrel with the United States as to fisheries which will lead to mischief if we do not succeed in arriving at a settlement of some points before another fishing season begins. I may to some extent be influenced by the abruptness of the break with Canada.[19]

Bolting in these circumstances would have looked very bad,[20] and he believed nothing should discredit his office. Maud was strongly against leaving too, but 'her judgement is not trustworthy on such a point, first because she is a violent radical – hates the Tories, secondly because she is a violent Canadian and is thoroughly happy out here'.[21] And what might happen if Lansdowne did go home?

> What would have been my position if, after abruptly 'scuttling out' of this country, and crossing the floor of the House of Lords, probably alone, I had found that I disagreed with my heterogeneous colleagues? I might have had to choose between resignation, which would have been bad for me and not good for the Govt., or the retention of office under circumstances thoroughly distasteful to me, and perhaps detrimental to my political prospects.[22]

Lansdowne's decision did not surprise Granville, who was certain he would refuse.[23]

Lansdowne's political value was clear to both parties. Gladstone wished to recover his support, telling Granville in 1886 that, 'if they could get Lansdowne to join them, the Parnellites would now be climbing up the backstairs of Lansdowne House'.[24] But Gladstone's attempt to give Home Rule to Ireland and the break-up of the Union and integrity of the Empire that might follow, had irreparably damaged relations with Lansdowne, who felt utter disgust and contempt,[25] telling Charles Gore that 'if the GOM [Grand Old Man] would hang himself off his own shirt tails no one would be better pleased than … Clan'.[26] Although Lansdowne was distant from parliamentary intrigue, in 1886 he left the Liberals to join the Liberal Unionists. This party, formed by Hartington to defeat Home Rule and afford a basis for reconciliation of the Liberals, included many Whigs and was soon bolstered by a Radical faction led by Joseph Chamberlain and John Bright. Chamberlain had been a stalwart force of radical Liberalism against the Whigs, so it was surprising that he joined the alliance. Lansdowne suffered much anxiety. He thought Chamberlain's political speech-making, 'without exception most mischievous, dangerous and thoroughly dishonest', and feared his object was to stir up a bitter class feeling against the landed interest.[27]

With his attention focused on Canadian and British parliamentary matters, Lansdowne was distracted on 22 March 1887 by further threats from Ireland. Shortly after two evictions on his estate at Luggacurren in Queen's County, William O'Brien, leader of the Land League and editor of *United Ireland*, campaigned in *The Times* to highlight the affair. The Toronto branch of the Irish Land League seized the opportunity and invited O'Brien to Canada to speak on the matter. Lansdowne informed Queen Victoria that O'Brien probably expected to be well-received because the Canadian Parliament had voted against coercion and for Home Rule, but this was because the Irish vote was powerful, not because members were convinced or had studied the question.[28] It was his view that feeling in Canada was very anti-landlord and that the public was totally ignorant of the facts.[29]

A pragmatic politician, Lansdowne understood the importance of 'public opinion'. He believed this was another expression for 'the common sense of the country'.[30] Public popularity had little value for him. He did not give press interviews, never posed for press photographs and rarely attempted to influence an editor or inspire a personal story.[31] Most public figures had many hubristic stories to tell of themselves – not so Lansdowne. In public he seldom spoke of personal achievements, he did not keep a diary and even in forty years of letters to his mother he was never his own hero. As a result he was often misquoted or misunderstood. Maud might have feared such an outcome in this case. Before leaving Ireland on 1 May, O'Brien vowed to

> appeal to honest masses of our race and of every race in Canada to choose between Lord Lansdowne and the peaceful tenantry whom he seeks to exterminate by a system of clearances as odiously unjust and inhuman as those which filled the pesthouses of the St Lawrence with dying Irish victims in the days of the Great Famine.[32]

On 3 May Lansdowne set off for a tour of Toronto, arranged months earlier. His reception was quite remarkable and very significant.[33] He was welcomed by the mayor, members of the Provincial Government and a large crowd, with a total absence of police or troops.

> There was an unbroken line of people all the way from the N. Toronto station to Govt. House and large crowds in the principal streets and at the intersection of the thoroughfares. The windows full of people all along the route. I am told 40,000 people must have turned out. The city I believe only spent $200. As we are very unknown in Toronto and have in fact rather neglected the city considering the place which it holds, it is obvious that the whole manifestation was a protest against O'Brien's crusade rather than a personal complaint to us. Viewed in this light it has great importance.[34]

O'Brien, after an enthusiastic reception in Quebec and a very bad one in Montreal, arrived in Toronto on 17 May and attracted a large crowd of curious spectators at a meeting in the park. Lansdowne thought O'Brien's arrival was a tame affair, telling Macdonald 'the whole thing as you foretold a failure'.[35]

Lansdowne's success continued. During the rest of the visit, his party visited schools, colleges, factories, workshops, theatres, concerts, baseball matches and races, and got an excellent reception at each:

> I never heard a disloyal sound during our whole stay and at all the large gatherings the exhibitions of loyalty were extraordinary. God Save the Queen everywhere, even in the churches where the whole congregations positively roared it forth.[36]

Lansdowne was exhausted by the end, several pounds lighter and perceptibly greyer. Returning to Ottawa at the end of May, he was pleased with his welcome. It was all the more remarkable because he had refused to be dragged into a controversy with O'Brien and left the public to judge the matter for itself.[37] On this occasion the Canadian public and press valued his rectitude.

By August 1887 the fishery negotiations had made progress and Salisbury asked Chamberlain to be chief commissioner of the delegation to Washington, with plenipotentiary powers to negotiate the fishery question. Lansdowne and Chamberlain had rarely met face to face, but spoke of each other as characterising all that was worst in their party. Nonetheless, Lansdowne told Sir Henry Holland, the new Conservative Colonial Secretary, that the appointment was satisfactory to Canada.[38] There were to be three commissioners for the United States, one for Canada and two for Britain, but Lansdowne wanted more. Sackville-West was the second British commissioner and Charles Tupper, the Canadian ex-High Commissioner to London, who had previously rather irritated Lansdowne,[39] was selected for Canada.

The commission began talks in Washington on 21 November and then met two to three times a week. According to Bayard, progress was impeded by Sackville-West, who was tired, costive and indolent. In all their meetings, he opened his mouth once, to ask that a window be closed.[40] Lansdowne was kept informed but had little influence. On 10 December the conference adjourned for a break, Lansdowne noting that 'a short breathing space will do no harm'.[41]

During this Christmas break, Chamberlain arrived at Ottawa accompanied by two secretaries and two Pinkerton detectives. Lansdowne, who had previously considered Chamberlain's politics unreasonable[42] was curious to see how they would get on: 'People say that he has toned down very much & is more reasonable on all subjects than he was.'[43] On his arrival, Lansdowne hosted a dinner party, inviting several Canadian ministers, including Macdonald. During the days that followed they discussed the fishery dispute and relations with the USA. Lansdowne was satisfied by what he heard, remarking that Chamberlain was 'a pleasant member of society, light in hand, a good talker & as far as one can judge very frank and outspoken. Radical as he was, I would a 1000 times sooner have to deal with him than with Gladstone. I am very glad to know him better than I did.'[44] 'As for Maud he flirted outrageously with her.'[45]

The conference reconvened on 9 January 1888 when Bayard abandoned his previous proposals for new conditions. Lansdowne had no words for his disgust at the tortuous proceedings of the US plenipotentiaries. The fishing season was about to begin and there was deadlock. Chamberlain threatened to break off negotiations unless they were resumed on the terms agreed before Christmas. Eventually Bayard acquiesced and on 14 February agreement was reached. Next day, Ash Wednesday, the treaty was signed, giving Canada much greater territorial jurisdiction than she had in practice enforced. It fully recognised Canada's right to prevent her ports from being used as operating bases for the deep-sea fisheries, unless a fair equivalent was given for the privilege.[46] Lansdowne was generally pleased with the treaty. To Canada and Britain, it came as a surprise when, the following August, it was rejected by the US Senate with a Republican majority of three.

On 31 December 1887, while Chamberlain was staying at Rideau Hall with the Lansdownes, Salisbury had written to Lansdowne to report that Dufferin was resigning as Viceroy of India and Lansdowne's name was naturally the first that occurred to him.[47] Although Lansdowne was a Liberal Unionist, Salisbury added there was no competition from the government's point of view. The appointment was Queen Victoria's suggestion, but she had expected the changeover to happen in 1890.[48] Lansdowne took his time because he disliked the idea of a fresh term of imperial exile.[49] After two weeks in which he discussed the offer with his family, he accepted.[50] *The Times* welcomed this as a fresh guarantee of the Union. It was also a compliment to Irish loyalists.[51] Lansdowne wrote:

> I am offered a magnificent post, the most responsible and honourable in the service outside England. It is placed within my reach while I am still comparatively young, at a moment when, if ever, I ought to have some work in me. As between this appointment and the chances of office at home, I should scarcely hesitate. I am not over well pleased with either side of domestic politics, and the fact of being an Irish landlord is a terrible embarrassment whenever Irish questions are being dealt with. If I can do reasonably well in India I shall at all events have something to my credit when I have to give an account of my stewardship. I am to begin another term of banishment – but I have made up my mind to face it.[52]

On 15 May 1888, at a farewell dinner in Ottawa, Lansdowne broke with the usual custom of departing Governor-Generals by raising political disputes, including fisheries. He said that during his term of office Canada had prospered in industry, education and culture; whatever happened with the fisheries treaty, they would never see a return to previous conditions. Referring to the increasing demands upon Canada for commercial union with the United States and Imperial Federation, he expressed strong reservations to both. As a free-trader, he believed the former would be to the material advantage of Canada; but Britain would see it as a 'moral affront' if her goods were discriminated against. As to Imperial Federation, he believed public sentiment in Canada would not tolerate giving up the freedom to manage its own affairs. After just under five years in the Dominion he was convinced that Canadians valued the absolute supremacy of their own Parliament. Even if an imperial Chamber sat at Westminster:

You might send your best men to it, but before they had been there six months they would find that the real power remained where it was before, within the walls of the Parliament buildings at Ottawa.[53]

The *Montreal Gazette* – targeted at anglophone business leaders – commented favourably on his speech, but the independent Toronto *Mail* and Toronto *Globe* were less enthusiastic.[54]

Macdonald regarded Lansdowne, with the possible exception of John Young, Lord Lisgar, as the most perspicacious Governor he had known. He and his ministers were struck by Lansdowne's quick grasp of the complex, often difficult, nature of British–Canadian relations.[55] Macdonald wrote: 'I am afraid that Lady Lansdowne and you have rather spoiled both my wife and myself, and that it will be some time before we become reconciled to the newcomers.'[56] Lansdowne had fond memories of Macdonald and Canada, writing to Macdonald in 1899: 'I fancied myself back in my study at Ottawa, listening to your utterances as to the House of Commons prospects and difficulties unsuspected by the outside world, within the cabinet.'[57]

9

THE VICEROYALTY

PALMS, BOUGAINVILLEA, CROTONS, frangipani on all sides, black policemen with yellow turbans, natives of all complexions, in all manner of garbs, chocolate coloured babies with no clothes and pot bellies, dignified old gentlemen with black skins apparently walking about in their night gowns.[1]

Such were Lansdowne's first impressions of India as he drove to the Governor's residence in Bombay on 3 December 1888.

Sixteen days earlier, on a grey drizzly November morning, Lansdowne had taken leave of friends and family, empowering his brother-in-law, Everard Digby, to manage his estates. Lansdowne and Maud crossed the Channel from Dover, boarded a train at Calais and travelled to Brindisi, on the east coast of Italy, where they met their daughters Evie and Bertie. Leaving wintry Europe they sailed on the P&O steamer *Sutlej*, via the Gulf of Suez, where everyone slept on deck because the temperature below was 32 °C. The women regarded this 'as a capital joke probably because the men expected to be tucked up in warm cabins'.[2]

At 8 a.m. on 3 December, to a salute of thirty-one guns, they stepped ashore from their launch at the Apollo Bunder, the pier at Bombay. To Lansdowne's horror the launch's funnel snorted a mixture of coal dust and steam, which settled on Maud's embroidered white dress, ruining it in seconds. It was not the arrival she was hoping for, or Lansdowne for that matter. They were greeted by a great line-up of officials and notables, including Prince Arthur, Duke of Connaught, Commander-in-Chief of Bombay, and his wife Princess Louise Margaret of Prussia. Replying to the address of welcome, Lansdowne spoke of his impending challenges as an ordeal as severe as that faced by any public figure.[3] While he was aware of his situation, he took satisfaction knowing that he was well qualified to govern the Sub-continent.

At Malabar Point, the Lansdownes were assigned their own villa in the Government House compound. They met their hosts for meals in the central residence, which Lansdowne likened to a huge conservatory. 'I keep looking up for the glass roof, expecting that I shall find my way into the fresh air.'[4] In three days of sweltering heat and bright sunlight, the Lansdownes enjoyed meeting many leading Bombay men and women. Lansdowne and Maud also made official visits to some of the city's municipal institutions and principal sites. The soon-to-be Viceroy thought Bombay was really a very beautiful place of magnificent colouring.[5]

On 6 December the Lansdownes travelled to Calcutta by special train: four viceroy's saloons, six other saloons, a 2nd/3rd-class carriage for attendants, road van, horse box and two brakes. Lansdowne and Maud each had their own carriage, with bed and bath.[6] The heat was extreme and metal objects were too hot to touch. Lansdowne was captivated by the scenery: trees, crops, people, animals, birds, all new and interesting. He was almost as delighted as Bertie when they came alongside a troop of monkeys promenading.[7] At Howrah Station, in Calcutta, holy men mixed shoulders with notables and office workers to give them an enthusiastic welcome.

Calcutta was the capital of British India. It had grown up along the banks of the Hooghly River as a point of transhipment from water to land. The city was fashioned in the manner of a grand European capital by the British, who tended to live in isolation from Indians. With a population of around 750,000 people, it was the second largest city in India after Bombay. With a tropical climate and average temperature of 26 °C degrees, it was unbearably hot for much of the year and buildings needed to be well ventilated.

Lansdowne had imagined that Government House would be the size of St Peter's in Rome, with two or three Buckingham Palaces tacked onto it.[8] The real thing was indeed huge beyond description. Completed in 1803 for Lord Wellesley, Government House occupied 84,000 square feet. The main front, plastered in yellow stucco, was dominated by a grand set of stone steps leading up to a six-column classical portico. In plan it was a central core with four radiating wings, with the state rooms in the centre and the wings accommodating the offices and residential quarters. The rear portico was crowned with a dome. Lansdowne and Maud were rather overwhelmed by the vastness of the rooms.[9] As with all British residences in India, Government House was as much a political statement as a home for the Viceroy.[10] Every bit of the palace was a reminder of British imperial power. Maud liked the place but Lansdowne missed the sweet simplicity of Ottawa and Quebec.[11]

My study is tolerable – businesslike and fairly cheerful, but oh! the bedroom with its height and cold distempered walls and colossal bed large enough for half a dozen couples and enveloped in a vast tent of mosquito netting running all the way up to the ceiling, which is so far up that one can scarcely see it. Then the crowd of black servants oppresses me. I told them to go to bed (if they ever do such a thing) an hour ago, but I know I shall find the whole gang outside my door including a six-foot-four specimen who is always there standing at attention, and who I am beginning to think is stuffed, for he never moves or changes his position, whereas Gholam something or other (who is my personal attendant) and his myrmidons think it necessary to salaam and play other heathenish antics every time I go by. I have come across the remains of a corkscrew stair (now disused) from this floor to that above, which was I am convinced contrived by one of my predecessors with the sole object of escaping from Gholam the all pervading.[12]

The Lansdownes redecorated their apartments with some pictures and furniture they brought from England. They also rehung the blue damask walls of the Throne Room, which had not been touched since the late 1870s, with green silk.

Such a vast palace required a staff of over five hundred. Breaking with tradition, Lansdowne put his *kitmagars* (waiters) into white uniforms instead of scarlet and gold.[13] He also had the nine different types of olive green coaches used by the Viceroy repainted with his emblem of two crossed Ls. To superintend his household and ceremonial matters he appointed Lord William Beresford. Lansdowne knew him socially and thought he was the most delightful of companions, but apart from that he had a very fine and chivalrous character. He had extraordinary tact, and knew how to handle people of all sorts.[14]

Having selected the person to keep his household in order for the next five years, Lansdowne turned his attention to other household staff, from surgeon to stablemen. Four British ADCs and two Indian ADCs were recruited.[15] They attended upon the Viceroy, communicating his orders for the day, and accompanying him and also the Vicereine.[16]

As Viceroy, Lansdowne was superficially an autocrat, but subject to the control of Whitehall and the majority view of his Executive or Supreme Council. British India – which comprised present-day India, Sri Lanka, Pakistan, Bangladesh, Myanmar, Nepal and Iran – had a population of 287 million in 1891. The British ruled two-thirds of India directly, with suzerainty over the other third, which consisted of six hundred princely states in whose affairs the Viceroy was supposed to interfere only if necessary. Although Lansdowne, then aged forty-three, was the first of his family to go to India, the first Lord Lansdowne had held shares in the East India Company and had showed more knowledge of Indian affairs than all the Ministers at Westminster.[17]

When Lansdowne arrived, change was in the air. India was the Empire's most valued possession and it was Britain's responsibility to safeguard the territories.[18] By the Government of India Act of 1858, direct rule of India was transferred from the British East India Company to the Crown in the person of Queen Victoria, with the Viceroy representing the Crown. India was transformed by good government and economic development, with the cooperation of princes, local leaders and large numbers of Indian troops, police officers and civil servants.

This period, known as 'the Raj', also saw the emergence of nationalism and demands for self-rule in India. This threat was checked by divisions in Indian society, so that it was unable to unite against the British, who played off these divisions. The underlying political unrest and tension convinced Lansdowne that the British could not ignore Indian aspirations; the British government continued to think otherwise. They governed with Enlightenment views based on a Western concept of progress, reason, justice and equality. Lansdowne, as a Whig, an imperialist and believer that Britain by virtue of its military and financial power was superior to India, thought similarly, but he also realised that it was impossible to understand India's legitimate aspirations from a purely European standpoint.[19] What both Lansdowne and the British government overlooked was the notion of advancement that already existed in India and had done for three thousand years, namely a spiritual progress linked to democracy. Battling with his own conservatism while wanting to do the right thing but not free to do it made Lansdowne's position difficult. It is surprising that he achieved as much as he did.

Beforehand, Lansdowne had spoken with Jowett, whose two brothers had served and died in India. Jowett saw India's difficulty as social, rather than political: if the British could be regarded as friends, not masters, threats would reduce.[20] In this he was supported by Florence Nightingale, who made the education of Viceroys a favourite occupation. To every Viceroy from Canning to Elgin, she spoke at length of the need for sanitation reform. Nightingale had met Lansdowne twice before he left, telling him that he had the greatest position in the world for doing good[21] and that principles of sanitation were the same whether in India or Britain.[22] Lansdowne agreed and made public health conditions an important policy of his term of office, enhancing the provincial sanitary boards.

One of the best pieces of advice Lansdowne received shortly after his arrival in India came from Sir John Eldon Gorst, Under-Secretary of State for India, on the growing interference of the House of

Commons in India matters. Pulling no punches, he told Lansdowne that the Government of India (GOI) 'cannot retain the confidence of the House of Commons unless it keeps up its character as a progressive and reforming Government'. 'Nothing,' he wrote, 'could be more mischievous than the crude application of British democratic maxims to India…'. But between Scylla and Charybdis there is a safe passage, avoiding on the one side stupid resistance to all change, and on the other weak surrender to fantastic theories. 'The House of Commons,' he warned, 'when it finally pronounces, is irresistible … You can no more free yourself from it, than from war, famine, pestilence … or any of the other evils with which you have to cope. If the Secretary of State is left uninstructed or misinformed, the administration of the Government of India is at the mercy of any ignorant impulse which might seize upon the House of Commons at any moment, and your policy is liable to be interrupted and reversed when you least expect it.'[23]

Although Lansdowne's predecessor, Lord Dufferin, had smugly declared that India was in a satisfactory condition, this was overly optimistic. Lansdowne knew that the Viceroy's task would not be easy.[24] India faced financial crisis, border problems with Afghanistan, China and Siam, food insecurity, poor sanitation, inadequate railways and failing education. There was growing controversy over Indian-European relations, civil service recruitment, taxation and political representation.[25] Some of these issues appear in Rudyard Kipling's 'One Viceroy Resigns', his poem about the changeover from Lord Dufferin to Lord Lansdowne: the poet's portrait of disillusion provoked Dufferin's anger but it was not without truth.

Dufferin, a Whig grandee and Irish landlord, told Lansdowne that 'an hour's conversation when we meet will be sufficient to let you know all that is necessary about the men with whom you will have to work or the questions left for you to settle'.[26] He advised Lansdowne to recruit a good private secretary for all official business. 'Do not let him be a young relation or a pleasant "society man".'[27] Lieutenant Colonel John Ardagh, who had proved himself in both civilian and military work, accepted Lansdowne's offer of the post. Lansdowne was delighted. He believed that Ardagh would not get himself or the Viceroy into difficulties with the Indian military, who were a powerful section of society.

Lansdowne's arrival marked a new practice by which he spent a few days as guest of the outgoing Viceroy before assuming office, thus ensuring a smooth handover. Lansdowne and Maud made an excellent impression on the British community, many of the Indian princes and other conservative-thinking Indians. Everyone regarded them as the epitome of a British aristocratic couple, with their ranks and social skills complementing each other. They acted their viceregal roles quite naturally, without being overawed by their privileged position. They were as comfortable among the locals as among the notables. Even with his aversion to formality, Lansdowne performed his duties with unfailing dignity and polished grace.

At 9 a.m. on 10 December 1888, dressed in full splendour, Lansdowne proceeded to the Throne Room for his investiture. In the corridor he passed Canning's portrait and wondered what Canning would have said 'if he had been told the urchin after whom he used to enquire so affectionately was one day to fill his place'.[28] In a ceremony lasting a few hours, accompanied by ceremonial music and attended by important British officials and local notables, the commission from the Queen Empress was read and Lansdowne took his seat as the 9th Viceroy and 33rd Governor-General of India. He became Grand Master of the Order of the Star of India, Knight Grand Commander (GCSI) and bearer of the Order of the Indian Empire (GCIE). Queen Victoria had authorised him to confer the Order of the Crown of India (CI) on Maud.[29] After Lansdowne had been sworn in, the Dufferins left Calcutta.

Soon Lansdowne formed a routine and found his thorough preparation paid dividends. He got up at around 8 a.m. and, after a short turn in the garden and breakfast, he would see Beresford and the day's ADC, then work until lunch. He would continue with work from 3 p.m. until 4.30 p.m., go out for an hour and a half, then work until dinner at 7 p.m. A typical week would include a ball for perhaps 150, a small dinner for 12 and a large dinner for 80 followed by a dance. There might also be a state dinner or state ball for 500, a garden party or a levee (a reception for a large assembly), or a dinner given in their honour. At levees Lansdowne had to bow to each of the 1,800 or so guests, so that his neck became quite stiff. Sunday was his only quiet day. His week mapped itself out almost automatically:

> Monday and Tuesday getting ready for the mail. Wednesday and Thursday receiving the secretaries of the different departments who bring me on those days all the papers about which they wish to talk to me – Friday Council meeting – Saturday clear up arrears as far as one can and off to this place [Barrackpore] in the evening for Sunday. The above represents the inevitable minimum, but there are continual excrescences and interruptions and I find it hard enough to make room for the work which reaches me every day through my own secretary who comes in with a barrow full of files at 10 every morning.[30]

Lansdowne took regular exercise by walking, riding, playing tennis, pigsticking, shooting, game hunting and fishing, although the fishing, he joked, was not fit for a Viceroy[31] since salmon was completely absent from its rivers.[32] He was abstemious with food and alcohol but an intrepid pioneer in gastronomic matters, sampling as much local food as he could, although he was fastidious to the point of hypochondria about his health.[33] At various times in India he was assailed by new illnesses: lumbago, influenza, neuralgia, constipation and diarrhoea were frequent, 'or it is a headache, or a sore throat, or irritation in the eyes, or something else to remind one that this climate was not designed for Europeans'.[34] The heat was incinerating, he abhorred dust storms and disliked intensely the rainy season.

But Lansdowne was in India to govern, and this came first. As in Canada, he had to keep Queen Victoria informed. Adept in the language and manners of the Royal Household, Lansdowne wrote long letters in a prosaic and formal style about every six weeks. Her monthly letters to Lansdowne demonstrate an almost maternal concern. The Viceroy reported to the Secretary of State for India, who in 1888 was Lord Cross, and through him to the cabinet. By temperament and age, Cross[35] was a mid-Victorian politician, reputedly with a strong dislike of responsibility.[36] He and Lansdowne corresponded by weekly letter and often by daily telegram. Lansdowne's letters are cogent, calm and authoritative, revealing how quick he was to settle in and grasp his duties.

The India Office was largely funded by Indian revenue. Its object was to maintain the nexus between British politics, administration and commerce, and the GOI. The India Office reported to the Secretary of State through a Council, mainly elderly men who had had distinguished careers in India. The Council were strongly against loosening the ties binding India to Britain. They believed that India should be held at all costs, and Indians were unfit to manage their own affairs. All this made Lansdowne's position uncomfortable. He knew many of the Council, having briefly served in 1880 as Under-Secretary of State. The incumbent in 1888 was John Eldon Gorst. Reputedly competent but caring only (as one Indian administrator wrote) for his 'bloody career',[37] Gorst harboured unconcealed contempt for Lord Cross, who was intellectually inferior and rather afraid of him.

Lansdowne was advised by his Executive or Supreme Council, which met every Friday. Its five members represented defence, home affairs, legal, public works and finance, each serving for up to five years. The Viceroy could not reshuffle or dismiss this Council. Fortunately, Lansdowne liked what he saw; there was not a really big man among them, but they were mostly sensible and well informed about their own departments.[38]

Sir Frederick Roberts, Commander-in-Chief (C-in-C) India, sat as an extraordinary member.[39] He did not have to attend regularly, except in March for budget discussions.[40] Roberts, known as 'Little Bobs' because he was so short, was older than Lansdowne. Anglo-Irish by birth and educated at Eton, he had distinguished himself in the Second Anglo-Afghan War and the relief of Kabul. He, Lady Nora and their children, Aileen, Ada and Freddy, became close friends of the Lansdownes. Lansdowne wrote after his death, 'I loved him as I have loved few people in the world. Of all the men I have ever met he seemed to me the most absolutely genuine and sincere. If at any moment and in any circumstances one could have unrolled the scroll of his mind, I am convinced there would not be found on it a single mean or ungenerous thought.'[41] As such he was a perfect ally for Lansdowne.

The Legislative Council comprised the Viceroy's Executive Council plus twelve additional members, whom he could appoint, and forty-five Indians nominated as non-official members, although their participation was almost negligible. Dufferin's private secretary likened this Council to a moribund jellyfish. Indian government was operated by an obstinately conservative and staunchly imperialist collective. But Lansdowne was not powerless, for the framing of laws was solely the responsibility of the Governor-General in Council. He initiated, formulated and shaped each enactment.

Aside from these central bodies, the Presidencies and Provinces of India were administered by Governors, Lieutenant Governors, Chief Commissioners and Political Agents, each with their own Councils. Lansdowne made it a priority to meet these men, and he favourably impressed many of them. As Viceroy he could select Lieutenant Governors, but the Governors of Bombay and Madras were appointed from London. Lansdowne found not only London officials obstructive to his Indian vision, but also many within the Anglo-Indian bureaucracy. Most Lieutenant Governors did not want to jeopardise their prospects by acting contrarily to their colleagues in London. Across India many thousands of Indians were employed by Provincial Governments, but the administrative cadre, the Indian Civil Service (ICS), numbered fewer than a thousand. Lansdowne believed the ICS *were* the British government in the eyes of most Indians.

Although India was administered by civilians, the army played a crucial role. Without the control of the War Office in London over its development and movements, the army in India was very powerful. Numbering 180,000 Indian troops, including Reserves and Imperial Service forces, and 100,000 British troops and volunteers, the India Command was headed by the C-in-C India. He ensured the efficiency of troops, conducted operations, advised the Viceroy on military matters and determined military campaign strategy. The Viceroy decided whether a campaign should take place and exercised supreme authority over troops in India. Lansdowne, who formed a close relationship with Roberts, was influenced by his views on reforming the army and his Forward Policy for defending India. The Viceroy's role was people management on the largest scale, and here Lansdowne excelled. He was courteous, accommodating, open-minded and tolerant, but also assertive, courageous and principled. His letters show his genuine delight in discovering other cultures. It was said at the time that any foreign power willing to trouble India would find in Lansdowne a fighting Viceroy.[42]

10

A FIGHTING VICEROY

ENCOUNTERING THE SMALL but growing class of educated Indians, Lansdowne recognised the need to give Indians a greater share in administration, through reform and expansion of the Legislative Councils, an idea first suggested by Dufferin and the Indian National Congress, a political party formed in 1885. As a Whig, it was natural for Lansdowne to act as a broker between the Indian nationalists and a Conservative government that balked at such reform. By offering timely concessions he could forestall radical nationalist demands and isolate the extremists.[1] Moreover, with Anglo-Indian leaders and allies in London, Congress was fundamentally loyal to the British; Lansdowne saw them as unthreatening. He thought it ridiculous that these individuals, well-educated in India at English schools, should be unable to criticise their government[2] and he was prepared to go further than Dufferin. The consensus of Congress was that the Indian Councils Act of 1861 needed amendment, to admit a considerable proportion of elected members, refer all budgets to these Councils, and allow the right to interpellate (interrupt and ask a question) and discuss the government's annual financial statement.[3]

Lansdowne supported these ideas, believing they would greatly improve the public image of the Government of India (GOI),[4] although he expected they would trouble GOI officials. He also believed these concessions would take momentum away from the Congress movement.[5] Cross was willing to endorse interpellation and discussion of the budget, because they did not need legislation,[6] but neither he nor Salisbury would approve the principle of election,[7] which they saw as incompatible with Eastern ideas. Salisbury feared it would undermine British rule, leaving the Indian peasantry at the mercy of a westernised Indian oligarchy.

London's opposition to change was shared by many senior Indian administrators. Lord Reay, Governor of Bombay, thought a Legislative Council, partly nominated and partly elected, would needlessly weaken government;[8] Lord Connemara, Governor of Madras, did not think India ready for representative government in any shape or form.[9] Lansdowne feared that the word 'election' acted as a red flag.[10] He had to explain that his scheme was not anything like popular election in the English sense of the term.[11]

The backlash reinforced Gorst's warning that the difficulty in governing India was not his Council nor the GOI, but the interference of Whitehall and the House of Commons now that the British public was taking more interest. Congress had many supporters in Parliament, and the princely states had permanent envoys in London, promoting parliamentary action. Popularity, not policy, could decide India's future.

On 22 June 1889 the cabinet discussed Lansdowne's proposals and approved the rights to interpellate and discuss the budget, along with the increase in members – but not elections. It was less than Lansdowne hoped for, but he was extremely glad that the government was willing to introduce a bill; not to do so, after so much talk, would have created a bad impression.[12]

Decisions made elsewhere also affected military policy. Defending India was costly, but not to the British exchequer, for the GOI paid for the army. From 1860 to 1914 there was barely a year without military activity on India's thousands of miles of frontier. On the north-west border, the GOI feared Russian expansion; on the east, it was treading on the toes of China and Siam. At any point, they might have to deal with crimes committed by people on the frontier, against their neighbours or against British India.[13] The problem was that India's frontier was so ill-defined and the neighbours so barbarous and unmanageable that small wars, which cost money and often led to larger uprisings, were unavoidable.[14]

No part of Lansdowne's work interested him more than frontier affairs.[15] He believed British India should have a good working frontier, one that would fit with the physical features of the country, as well as the liabilities of which the British could not divest themselves. 'With Russia, encroaching on one side and France on the other, to say nothing of the Chinese, our hands are forced.'[16]

Three days after becoming Viceroy, Lansdowne sent an expedition against lawless tribes on the frontier between Chittagong and western Burma. He favoured gradual subjugation of the lawless tracts between Assam, Chittagong and Burma. Little could be done at that late season, but a road was begun with the aim of supplying a forward post before the rainy season.[17] Simultaneous trouble in the North-West Frontier region provoked greater concern. Rapid Russian advances into

Afghanistan and Kashmir, Chinese interference in the small states south of the Hindu Kush and Afghan suspicion of Britain indicated the need for a new frontier strategy, based on intelligence, military strength and political control.

In spring 1889 Abdur Rahman Khan, the Amir of Afghanistan, stirred up a political fuss about a new British railway project that was to run across half a dozen miles of unimportant desert, the line being as useful to Afghanistan as it was to India.[18] The Amir's interests, apart from intense avarice, lay in keeping his powerful neighbours outside his borders. Lansdowne disliked what he heard about the Amir, but he took the attitude of 'Better the devil one knows'. He doubted that the GOI would be better off dealing with a more humane but less manageable ruler.[19] Lansdowne believed the GOI had a perfect right to the land in question, but had no wish to irritate the Amir. A strong, friendly Afghanistan was essential to restrain Russia, but impossible if the British could not even enter the country.[20]

In April, as it began to get hot in Calcutta and Barrackpore, where Lansdowne had a weekend retreat on the eastern bank of the Ganges, he and his staff travelled to Simla, 7,000 ft up in the Himalayan foothills, and part of Nepal when the British discovered it in 1819. The hill station grew rapidly, becoming in 1864 the summer capital of India. Simla was the smartest of Indian hill stations,[21] with its Tudor-style houses, gothic church and cottage gardens clinging perilously close to cliffs thousands of feet up, yet looking as if they had been transplanted from Surrey. The climate was subtropical, although in spring the dust storms in the plains below left the air thick with dust. When the rainy season arrived in June, the air became steamy and lifeless, and clammy fogs ceaselessly rolled against the hilltops, producing anything from mist to a deluge. Although Lansdowne was not fond of India's horse racing, there was a pretty little course at Simla that also hosted dog shows, flower shows, picnic parties, polo matches, cricket matches and gymkhanas. As in Calcutta, the British lived apart from the local people, and government officials objected to Indian princes acquiring property at Simla. Lansdowne thought their presence was distinctly undesirable.[22] One of many concerns was that, by fraternising with such people, British officers would become targets of bribery.[23]

From Calcutta to Simla was nearly 1,200 miles and it was customary for the Viceroy to make this journey into a spring tour, giving him an opportunity to see more of the country and meet Anglo-Indian officials and Indian princes. The Lansdownes spent eight days visiting Allahabad, Cawnpore and Lucknow before arriving on 10 April at Viceregal Lodge, completed by the Dufferins the previous year. This handsome house, almost new, was on a palatial scale. Maud was astonished to find her boudoir had three fireplaces.[24] They were delighted to have electric light, which produced 'no smoke, no dirt, no stink, no trouble'.[25]

Lansdowne settled in quickly but found the following six months monotonous, and the mists and cool mountain air increased his homesickness. The woods of deodar and cedar were carpeted with maidenhair fern and full of strange shrubs and flowers. Although the scenery was magnificent, he complained there were no valleys, only narrow ravines with dry torrent beds and not a lake or river to be seen.[26] In June the rains were unusually bad and the stifling fog was worse. It reminded him of the worst of the west of Ireland's climate.[27]

Lansdowne found escape from monotony in the extraordinary variety of work he had to get through: frontiers, honours, Council reforms, forestry and farming prospects, military matters, corrupt officials, railways and sanitation.[28] He had a charming room to work in, was much less interrupted than at Calcutta and got through the backlog of work.[29] But while at Simla he also rode, walked, gardened and played tennis. He was offered sport by local landowners and rajas: hunting tiger, leopard, rhinoceros, bear, elephant and buffalo, and shooting pheasant, partridge, duck and quail. Entertaining was vital in making a successful impression; once the season began in late May there were dinners, dances, balls and garden parties, sometimes several in a week.[30] Lansdowne found this formidable and costly, since everything had to be done *en grand*.[31] Guests arrived by rickshaw, often with two drivers in front and two behind, ringing their bells to warn pedestrians on the narrow roads. Fewer Europeans visited than in Calcutta, but governors, lieutenant governors, chief commissioners and other high officials made it to Simla during the season. The formality and lack of privacy that oppressed Lansdowne in Calcutta did so too in Simla, where even a picnic was spoilt:

> you would have laughed if you had seen the number of tents & retainers of all sorts – I longed for my one old soldier and two canoe men of the Cascapedia, and felt inclined to get in a passion when I found a silver candelabra ... & cut flowers on the dinner table, but it is no use to rebel & I don't know that it makes much difference whether one has six redcoated retainers or 16 or 60 – I consoled myself by giving the slip next day to the military secretary, the ADC in waiting, the head policeman, my jemadar, the rank & file of inferior myrmidons, and fanfiler-ing myself unobserved through the deodars & down the steep hillside, which I descended some 3000 ft.[32]

It was fortunate that Lansdowne's adventurous spirit never got him into trouble in India.

Leaving Simla on 22 October Lansdowne toured the North-West

Frontier to see at first hand the political problems created by geography and clash of cultures. He was at different times accompanied by Maud, their staff, military advisers and Roberts. Lansdowne found the history of British frontier operations unpleasant to read. He believed the traditional policy of keeping aloof from frontier tribes was shortsighted and, with Russia at the doors of Herat (in Afghanistan), out of date. However, unlike Roberts and Mortimer Durand, Foreign Secretary of India, Lansdowne discouraged a Forward Policy to control Afghanistan and check any Russian threat to India, at least in the wider sense of the term.[33] Although he was labelled an annexationist, nothing was further from the truth. Lansdowne was strongly averse to gratuitous extensions of British territory.[34]

On 30 November Lansdowne returned to Calcutta. During the five-week tour he had learned all he could about the frontier peoples and the region's military and commercial routes. He was struck by the frontier's natural strength and by the native troops and tribesmen, particularly the Punjab regiments. To Lansdowne, they were magnificent when their physique and general appearance were compared with those of an ordinary European. It was a wonder to him how the British came to be in possession of the country.[35] That was largely because men from martial races and warrior castes respected British officers, who in turn respected their traditions and welfare. Moreover, British rule was preferable to Russian.

11

PEOPLE AND POLICY
IN INDIA

WHILE LANSDOWNE AND his advisers drafted a new policy for the North-West Frontier region, on 3 January 1890 'Eddy' Albert Victor, Prince of Wales arrived at Calcutta. A mass of notables greeted him at Prinsep Ghat and crowds cheered him to Government House. Lansdowne, who was well acquainted with the young Prince, thought he looked more robust than at any time previously.[1] He also realised that Indian civilities bored him horribly.[2] Civilities also bored Lansdowne. He did not relish entertaining as Dufferin had done, judging that Calcutta society was very well-dressed but that its individuals were far from lovely. In his view, the many globetrotters who arrived at Government House expecting hospitality had left their country for their country's good.[3] Maud smoothed Lansdowne's temper and took full advantage of the architecture and treasures in the Viceroy's residence to recreate the elegance of Lansdowne House and Bowood. They used the Lansdowne plate for formal dinners, the family's silver candelabra gleaming on the huge dining table, with massive silver bowls of fragrant flowers. Few in India had seen such a display of aristocratic wealth, which seemed to impress. In reality, Lansdowne was heavily indebted, even after sales of land and works of art.

While Lansdowne successfully masked his own financial difficulties, he could not hide those facing India. The problem was the fluctuating rupee–sterling exchange rate: the pound sterling was tied to the gold price, but the Indian rupee (over 90 per cent silver) was tied to the price of silver. After 1873 as the price of silver fell, currencies based on silver depreciated relative to those based on gold, so anything paid for in sterling became more expensive in India.[4] The effect on India was catastrophic. Apart from the hardship caused by the falling rupee, it also slowed railway construction. Developing the network was a policy Lansdowne cherished. He saw it as the GOI's most important duty, for railways would expose and release India's latent wealth.[5] Also, in a crisis, troops could be moved easily and famine could be mitigated quickly. Railway decisions, however, were often made in London by officials favouring private enterprise. Pushy promoters obtained guarantees which, Lansdowne believed, greatly harmed the GOI.[6] Some of Lansdowne's closest advisers supported the view from London, fearful that left to operate it alone would be unwieldy and costly.[7]

Lansdowne was against depending on private enterprise, which did not really exist in India. Private companies, he believed, only backed railway projects on unfavourable terms to the general public.[8] In Canada he had seen the harm done by concessions that enriched speculators and gave promoters mischievous influence in public life,[9] but he reluctantly accepted that it was not quite the same in India and the GOI would be glad if companies took on some railway work. Nonetheless, he fought against giving private enterprise the most profitable railway lines. In April 1890, when he passed the Indian Railways Act, numerous projects were struggling with rapid expansion, new routes, competing lines and different gauges.

In May newspapers in India reported the death of Phool Mani, a eleven-year-old child bride married to a man twenty-four years older. Consummating the marriage had caused her death. The husband was sent to prison. There was a storm of indignation and newspapers blamed the women who forced girls to consummate marriage.[10] Andrew Scoble, legal member of the Viceroy's Council, suggested raising the age of consent from ten to twelve. Lansdowne noted that the press were in favour, and surely this was a case where state interference was justified. He believed that the class in question was quite unable to protect itself and without government protection the result would be continued grievous suffering and permanent injury.[11]

One outspoken critic of child marriage was Behramji Merwanji Malabari, Parsi poet, author and editor of the *Indian Spectator* and *Voice of India*. He deplored the 'social evil' of 'baby marriage' as a cause of racial deterioration, poverty and overpopulation, and demanded legislation. Lansdowne liked Malabari and wished he would convert public opinion. Some of his advisers were apprehensive about Malabari's comments, but Lansdowne was not.[12] So long as the GOI were merely protecting children from ill treatment, and not interfering in social or domestic customs, they were unassailable.[13] Introducing the Age of Consent Bill, Lansdowne saw an opportunity to take the public into his confidence and show how far he was willing to go.[14] The issue divided the Congress movement: those in London were in favour while those in India were against, fearing the bill would weaken their influence over orthodox Hindus but also over Muslims, who were sensitive to any violation of marriage customs. Protestors argued it would lead to prosecutions motivated by vindictiveness and criminal investigations into family matters of the most private kind.[15] Protests failed to prevent the Age of Consent Bill becoming law in March 1891, when Lansdowne spoke perceptively of Hinduism, demonstrating his awareness of the religion and respect for its traditions. However, he also hinted that in the interests of humanity and progress the bill should be passed.[16]

While moderate social reform had begun, military reform was largely ignored. The East India Company's forces had been divided into three Presidency Armies, based in Bombay, Madras and Bengal. Lansdowne aimed to get rid of the Presidency system in its existing shape and divide the Armies into districts of suitable shape and size in accordance with need.[17] Aiming to remove the friction between the GOI and the provincial governments, and the resulting inefficiencies, in July 1890 he proposed placing the different departments of the Presidency Armies under the control of the GOI. However, Cross and his Council in London saw no reason for change and the Duke of Cambridge, Commander-in-Chief of the British army, was 'most concerned' about Lansdowne's proposal of one army with one Commander-in-Chief.[18]

This did not discourage Lansdowne from pressing for better fighting material in the ranks of the Indian armies. Having seen for himself the fine physique and admirable qualities of the men of the North-West Frontier and discussed with Roberts having the right stamp of men, Lansdowne believed that a shake-up was necessary because the GOI faced a real threat of war and the reliability of the whole Indian army to prosecute it was uncertain. Roberts agreed, but the Duke of Cambridge, at the Horse Guards in London, did not.[19] During 1890 Lansdowne had some success strengthening regiments in all three Presidencies with hardy Sikhs, warriors who were at the top of their caste system.

In April the Indian Councils Bill passed the Lords, even though Salisbury voted against it. In the Commons, obstruction was rife. Lansdowne feared the bill would go to the wall.[20] In August, without a clear lead from the Tories, his fear was realised, when the bill met its death after the first reading. Breathing a sigh of relief, Cross thought that it had gone as far as was wise and prudent to go.[21] However, Lansdowne was not finished, and put the matter aside until the next session.

Attention in India soon turned to a visit from Nikolai Alexandrovich Romanov, the Tsarevich and future Nicholas II, who had finished his schooling in May. His father, Tsar Alexander III, decided to send him on a foreign tour to India. Lansdowne was glad as he believed even the people of India would see it this as a sign of British strength.[22] Cross, who disliked any Russian entering India,[23] told Lansdowne that the visit was unofficial and advised that the GOI should follow the practice adopted on the Prince of Wales's visit the previous January.

Arriving in Bombay in December, the Tsarevich was met on board his frigate by the eccentric new Governor-General, Lord Harris,[24] who wore plain clothes and yellow boots with an air of informality. M. Onou, a Russian diplomat accompanying the Tsarevich, suspected the British had deliberately withheld the usual honours to influence Indian opinion.[25] Their suspicions deepened when they heard that Lansdowne was not to welcome them formally at Howrah Station in Calcutta. Believing that they were to be met by the Lieutenant Governor of Bengal instead, the Russians threatened to avoid Calcutta altogether or visit incognito.[26] After Salisbury heard about this, Lansdowne was ordered to meet the Tsarevich at the station and place him at his right hand in the carriage. Lansdowne consented under pressure, feeling completely over-ruled on ceremonial by London at the last moment.[27] This annoyed Lansdowne, who believed that in India, as a matter of principle, the Queen's representative should always rank before anyone else.[28]

On 26 January 1891 the Tsarevich's entourage reached Calcutta. Lansdowne found him to be a good-humoured, easy-going lad, much easier than the Prince of Wales.[29] The Russians were extraordinarily pleased with their reception at Calcutta.[30] The visit made no great impression in India, despite a rumour that the Tsarevich had been sent as a hostage, a pledge of Russia's peaceful intentions, and was being paraded by order of the Queen.[31]

12

MANIPUR AND
MAHARAJAS

WHILE CALCUTTA SOCIETY prepared for the Tsarevich's visit in January 1891, Lansdowne and his Council were considering a disturbing report on factory workers. India's cotton industry had been expanding while exports of cotton yarn from England had declined in markets where they competed. British manufacturers had demanded that British factory laws should apply to India to reduce the advantage of Indian capitalists, who benefitted from cheap labour and longer hours of work. Pressed by Cross to amend the Indian Factory Act of 1881, Lansdowne was reluctant. He did not believe the Indian labour system should replicate Britain's. He supported the view held in India that they were being forced into the measure in order to enable British manufacturers to compete with them on better terms.[1]

After an international conference in Berlin in March 1890 recommended a minimum age of ten and one rest day per week for all workers,[2] Lansdowne was forced to amend the Indian system. However, in early 1891 an internal report, commissioned by him and his advisers, found that the existing limit of eleven hours per day for women adequate, that child workers should be legally at least nine and at most fourteen, and their work hours should follow a half-time system. To Lansdowne, the proposals were sensible but Cross wanted India to follow exactly the Berlin recommendations.[3] Lansdowne replied that this was unreasonable – 'we will be taken to task by the millowners for what will be represented as an undue concession to Lancashire'[4] – and quoted a past remark by Cross himself: 'due regard must be had to the circumstances of India which are in many respects different from that of any European nation'.[5] That was the basis of the GOI's proposal.

Cross was in a dilemma. He could either succumb to pressure

from MPs and Lancashire manufacturers or defend Indian interests. Succumbing, he decided the Factory Bill must pass into law that session.[6] The GOI had little choice. Cross accepted one adjustment, a 30-minute break for half-timers, so arranged that machinery need not be stopped. On 19 March 1891 the Viceroy's Legislative Council passed the bill. The Act covered all factories employing fifty or more people. It gave much more protection to child workers and regulated the welfare of female labour for the first time.[7] In debate, Lansdowne stated that the GOI had given due consideration to the difference between Indian and British working conditions and that Indian manufacturing was quite strong enough to survive the new restrictions. Privately he felt the timidity shown by some was not very creditable.[8] The Act failed to impress workers and political leaders in India. To protect British interests, one of India's greatest artistic traditions was compromised. For many villagers, their spiritual and economic welfare was bound to the manufacture of cotton.

On 28 March Lansdowne learned of an uprising in Manipur, situated between Assam and Burma. It became a major news story, provoking excitement and much criticism, especially of Lansdowne. Postponing the Viceregal spring tour he was undertaking, he travelled to Simla to manage the situation. The GOI attempted to assert its authority, planning to arrest Tikendrajit Singh, commander of the Manipuri armed forces, and restore the Maharaja. It had disastrous consequences, with the murder of the Chief Commissioner of Assam, the Political Agent of Manipur and a number of British officers. A large British force descended on Manipur and on 27 April won the twenty-eight-day war. Newspapers spoke wildly of the GOI taking vengeance. Lansdowne thought few Britons would mind making an example of Manipuris, but he was afraid the real culprits would flee to the hills and the soldiers' wrath would lead to over-severe reprisals.[9] He believed Gurkhas were 'the most desperate little savages when their blood was up'.[10]

Cross was glad to hear that Lansdowne was against annexation.[11] The Viceroy believed it would be wiser to recognise a native ruler, perhaps a junior prince, and place him under British protection with a selected Political Agent to control the state.[12] In Cross's opinion, great blame rested somewhere, but since the chief actors were all dead he declined to say a word.[13] Queen Victoria was very much distressed and was thirsty for information.[14] She warned Lansdowne against wholesale punishment of the innocent or incitement to revenge: 'this only, too easily encouraged, would not redound to our honour or add to our power for the future'.[15] In her view the British Commissioners and Political Agents in India were much inferior to what they had been: 'if we do *not take care* and employ people of a higher calibre socially and more conciliatory we shall suffer for it'.[16] Lansdowne, who had appointed the Chief Commissioner of Assam, disagreed and offered to meet the charge.[17]

The event caused a greater stir in England than in India, where there was never any real doubt of the GOI's ability to restore order. Politically it demonstrated the fragility of Britain's indirect rule in India and the strength of native loyalty to princely rule. Rewards were offered for capture of the principal agitators and courts of inquiry were established, one for ordinary cases and another for members of the ruling family.

Cross insisted that no one should be tried for murder except the leaders[18] and all ordinary cases be referred to him. Lansdowne saw this as a withdrawal of confidence that would permanently impair his authority. He was willing to submit to London sentences passed on the main culprits but if Cross made him submit the other cases, he could draw only one conclusion.[19] Cross relented. The trial of Tikendrajit and the other leaders began on 11 May. The Queen wanted Tikendrajit to be banished, interned or imprisoned for life, but not executed.[20] Lansdowne disagreed, maintaining that all subjects of a princely state who rebelled against the paramount power were worthy of death, although the GOI had discretion to inflict a lesser penalty. They could not allow subjects of a princely state to rebel and then plead that they were only obeying orders.[21] He believed that Tikendrajit, having led the revolution, had directly caused the hostilities in March and the British officers could not have been killed without his knowledge and consent.[22]

Lansdowne was unfairly attacked in the British and Indian press.[23] A society paper printed a false rumour that he was threatening to resign and Indian newspapers repeated it on the highest authority.[24] During June the matter was hotly debated in Parliament. Lansdowne was personally abused in the Commons; in the Lords the GOI was strongly criticised. Despite this the government wisely supported Lansdowne. The crisis was apparently over.[25]

In reality, it was not quite over. To Lansdowne the question of annexation was closely linked to the decision on sentence; he could not be responsible if there was not adequate punishment of the state of Manipur or the leading criminals.[26] He and the GOI were adamant that the leading culprits were guilty of waging war against the Queen and should be sentenced to death or exiled for life with forfeiture of property. He was surprised when the cabinet decided that Tikendrajit's guilt should be judged by English law; the criminal law that applied was surely the law of the Indian Empire.[27] Lansdowne's demand was met and on 13 August Tikendrajit was publicly hanged, as were the other principal culprits. Lansdowne commuted the death sentence on the regent, who was exiled along with twenty-one others. Curzon wrote that he never read a telegram with greater pleasure (bloodthirsty as it sounded) than that announcing the decision to execute Tikendrajit. 'The amount of rot talked about Manipur over here was enough to make one despair.'[28] The events demonstrated Lansdowne's willingness to take a tough stance, as he had done in Canada during the Métis uprising. Perhaps that experience had hardened him to expect repercussions.

On 7 August Lansdowne led the first sedition case against an Indian newspaper. The nationalist *Bangabasi* was owned and edited by a strongly orthodox Bengali patriot called Krishna Chandra Banerjee, who vehemently attacked British imperialism. During the agitation about the Age of Consent Act, the *Bangabasi* stirred up trouble by claiming that the GOI had interfered in the Hindu religion. Lansdowne had no sympathy and believed that the GOI should test the law by prosecuting the paper: the 'license of the press is producing disastrous consequences and it should if possible be checked'.[29] He was not confident that a Calcutta jury would find them guilty, if only because the law was not very clear;[30] but, 'if we succeed, a very salutary impression will be produced on the Press, which is already funking: if we fail, we shall have demonstrated the insufficiency of the law as it stands'.[31]

Lansdowne and the GOI believed that Cross did not fully appreciate the serious danger, in a country like India, of the growing licence of the press. In fact, Cross was dreading a debate on the subject in Parliament,[32] especially as some British newspapers naturally disliked the idea of press prosecutions.[33] On 22 August the jury were discharged without reaching a unanimous verdict.[34] When a retrial was ordered, the defendants expressed their willingness to publish an apology and never again cause disaffection. Lansdowne withdrew the prosecution,[35] believing it had had very good results and that the GOI's critics in the press had been thoroughly frightened. In accepting the apology good humouredly, the GOI would 'free itself from vindictiveness'.[36]

With Manipur and the *Bangabasi* case having dominated his six months in Simla, Lansdowne left on 15 October for his autumn tour. As in the previous year, a visit to some princely states was planned, to allow their princes the opportunity of 'opening their hearts' to Lansdowne.[37] The GOI, closely watching events in the North-West Frontier, naturally looked to Kashmir for cooperation. Lansdowne considered Pratap Singh, the Maharaja of Kashmir and Jammu, a despot, whose people had been cruelly ground down. As a Hindu ruler in a state with a Muslim majority, he was also as much a foreigner in his state as the British were.[38] In 1889 he had voluntarily retired and Lansdowne placed administration of the state in the hands of a Council of five, led by Amar Singh, the Maharaja's youngest brother, and assisted by the British Resident and British officers. The Indian press abused Lansdowne freely for his alleged disrespect of the Maharaja.

In October 1891 Lansdowne met William Prideaux, the British Resident, at Srinagar and proposed restoring some of the Maharaja's former powers, without imperilling the work of the Council.[39] On meeting the Maharaja, Lansdowne was impressed. He found him weak and superstitious, but with simple habits and no expensive tastes, unlike his followers.[40] The difficulty was to restore his dignity without undermining Amar Singh. After full discussion, Pratap Singh agreed to reduce his annual spending from 9 to 6 lakhs and was reinstated as President of the Council with Amar Singh as Vice President.[41] Otherwise the Council was unchanged.[42] Lansdowne believed they had ended the worst abuses; he was as hopeful as one could be for a princely state.[43] By prioritising the interests of the state and dealing positively with Pratap Singh, he retained the confidence of other Indian princes and their subjects.

Leaving Kashmir on 8 November, Lansdowne visited the rulers of Gwalior, Bhopal and Indore before reaching Calcutta on 28 November. Even in so short a time, he was sure his meetings had done some good. His description of his visits to Bhopal and Indore are both amusing and important. Bhopal was the only Indian state ruled by a woman. The Begum of Bhopal received Lansdowne, on 20 November,

at the station completely enveloped in a pale 'greenery yallery' kind of domino, and moreover concealed from the public gaze by a sort of hoarding covered with brilliant textures. When she had paid her respects she slipped off to her carriage window, in which glass was replaced by the thinnest gauze, and oh! rapture! behind this was the royal countenance, uncovered & plainly visible. She is a determined looking little lady, not disagreeable to look at & young for her age (52). She is in great good humour, as this is the first time that a Viceroy has been to Bhopal in her reign. On 21st she paid me her visit … then I had visits from no less than five minor chiefs, followed by a bouquet of 10 or a dozen local magnates who came in a bunch.

In the afternoon (6.30) I drove to the Palace to return H.H's visit. The city was brilliantly illuminated & the Court D'Honneur at the Palace was really a fine sight – at the foot of the steps was my hostess, more like a green chrysalis than ever – we toiled up the stair case, & through long corridors, hand in hand, to the durbar room which was bright & pretty – gorgeous gold embroidered carpets, the finest I have seen yet – we had a very friendly conversation, & then came the usual anointment with nauseous attar of roses, followed by garlands, very splendid – Then 'she' & I waddled down stairs again, I holding tight to her tiny little hand, lest she should trip up over her draperies, & roll down to the bottom in a bunch – the little hand in question was encased in a green silk glove, with the fingers much too long.

In the evening we had the state banquet here in the big tent – 60 Europeans in all – at dessert in came the Begum her face still invisible – stood up boldly at the head of the table, &, quite unabashed, proposed the Queen's health & then mine in a very loyal little speech which was translated for us by the Resident. It was really a very courageous performance on the little lady's part, & there was in spite of the grotesqueness of the costume, a certain pathos and dignity about the whole proceeding. The worst thing about her is her voice which is shrill and unpleasing – I forgot to tell you that she paid Maud a private visit after hers to me in the morning – I also did not say that I began the day (like an idiot) by getting up at 6.30 to shoot snipe – there were no snipe to shoot & I should have been better in bed … We start tonight for Indore, & shall reach Calcutta on Saty. to begin our <u>fourth</u> season there.[44]

On 25 November Lansdowne recorded his impressions of Indore:

Our Indore visit has gone off well. Holkar [Shivaji Rao, Maharaja Holkar XII] has a bad reputation, and is at times very eccentric & hard to manage – I suspect however that those entrusted with the task have not always set about it quite in the right way. Nothing could have been better than his behaviour on this occasion. He is a huge creature, tall, & weighing I should think 20 stone, tho' still quite young: talks English fluently & on the whole well, but not always with an exact appreciation of the value of words. He has been worried by his relations, a man here may have any number of stepmothers, and by the low native press. He came to me this morning & poured all his grief into my ear, & I think I comforted him a little, & convinced him that if he would run straight, we would support him loyally – we had a terrible day yesty – visits and return visits from 11 AM till dusk….[45]

For the return visits the minor Rajas had established themselves each in his own durbar tent on the open ground behind the Residency and looked like a huge circus – I drove in a carriage & four from tent to tent 'touched & remitted' little bags full of gold mohurs in cash, was presented all over again to the retainers who had already been presented to me in the morning, was garlanded & smeared with their horrible attar of roses some ½ a dozen times – all this while each Raja's band was playing what purported to be 'God save the Queen' in a different key, and the salutes overlapped one another and completed the confusion. After all this we had a mild little garden party at the Residency –

Then we drove off (nearly 4 miles) to dine at the Maharajas Palace – where a motley collection of 170 *convives* were gathered – after dinner came the usual speeches, & after the verbal fireworks, a good *feu d'artifice*, the only drawback of which was to be found in the fact that the rockets

& other aerial pieces were directed towards us, and burned holes in the ladies frocks. Holkar assured Maud that it was all right, *ce qui n'empecha pas* her gown from having several holes burned in it – By the way he told me that Maud's pearl necklace was one of the best he had seen, not on account of the size of the pearls, but because of their 'light' – I thought this rather discriminating, as most of the chiefs affect huge yellow things like turnip radishes – to bed well tired out.[46]

13

A YEAR OF CHANGE

WHETHER NEGOTIATING WITH princes or maintaining the frontier, Lansdowne took a pragmatic attitude to each situation. But in all cases he had to balance politics, morals and economics.

In early 1892 a frontier dispute with Siam escalated and political expediency led Lansdowne to entertain Prince Damrong of Siam at Calcutta. Relations with Siam had become strained in 1888, after they made territorial claims to land east of the Salween River in Burma. The GOI was wary of the Siamese giving the French a pretext to expand.[1] The area between the Salween and the French colonies was politically no man's land; to Lansdowne, accepting the Siamese as neighbours was not a question of right or wrong, but expediency. They were friendly and strong, but scarcely honest. However, beyond the Salween, unless they were careful, they might become coterminous with China or France. Lansdowne thought France the worst neighbour of all, owing to her practice of territorial confiscation; a clash with the French was eventually inevitable, but meanwhile they should safeguard British interests, with Siam as a buffer. 'What we need in regard to Siam is to make her will in our favour and remain under our influence during her life. If this is attained, the longer she lives the better.'[2]

Salisbury, who also wanted to keep Siam as a buffer, blamed the GOI for being swayed by local officials, with little heed to imperial interests. Lansdowne blamed Edward Gould, the British Consul at Bangkok, who, he believed, 'far from giving the British credit for the leniency with which they have treated Siam[,] has apparently represented us as having been exacting and dictatorial in our conduct towards that power'.[3] Assuring Cross he would bear Salisbury's wishes in mind, Lansdowne promised to respect the shadowy Siamese claims while not letting down the feudatory

Shan states in their territorial disputes with Siam.[4]

The problem for Lansdowne was not really that local officials were unprofessional (they seldom were) but that decisions taken in India were controlled to the utmost degree by Whitehall. The need to get permission before the GOI could order its own officers to act against encroachment, for example, was especially irksome.[5] He was also concerned that the Indian Empire was spreading, but its defences were not increasing accordingly.[6] He showered attention on Prince Damrong, reiterating British willingness to transfer to Siam the Shan state of Keng Cheng, but months later nothing was settled. Despite Siamese fear of France, Lansdowne believed they would reach agreement.[7]

After the Calcutta season, the Lansdownes and their staff journeyed west to Bombay as part of their spring tour. Harris, the Governor-General, assigned them a charming seafront bungalow. Lansdowne had not seen the sea for over three years; the sight and smell of it did him good, although it stirred up wild longings in him.[8] In Bombay he opened a new waterworks at the Tansa River, visited a leper asylum and inspected a steamer carrying pilgrims to Mecca. His account of the pilgrims shows his humanity and his awareness of the reality of life for others.

> There were over 1100 on board, and the space allowed is 6 ft × 1½ feet or 9 sq. ft per head – not a very liberal allowance, but I am afraid that owing to the manner in which the ship is measured, & owing to the fact that every pilgrim carries his own baggage & provisions with him (or her), the actual space available is considerably less. The whole ship, on deck and between decks, was packed with the poor creatures – men and women, old & young – coming from all parts of the country – there they lay with their bags, bundles & bones, so mixed up, & so close together that I had to pick my way on tip toe, putting my foot wherever I could find room for it among the confusion of limbs & bodies. It was a blazing hot day, and altho' the ports were open, the smell was enough to make one sneeze. I tried to picture to myself the scene below in a gale of wind with everything battened down – I asked the officer who shewed us round what happened when there was a row – he said there never was a row, and I dare say he told the truth. The patience & gentleness of these people is beyond belief. As for their faith – Well, shew me 1100 Englishmen who would brave the journey across India, and the horrors of that emigrant ship in order to save their souls alive – we have done something to protect the poor wretches who used to be ill used & robbed at every stage – but I fear not enough.[9]

This story is as relevant today as it was over a century ago.

On 2 April 1892, Maud sailed for England and organised the wedding of her daughter Evie to Victor Cavendish, heir of the Duke of Devonshire.[10] Lansdowne thought he and Maud had been very lucky. It made all the difference to him that Evie chose to marry 'a man of impeccable repute rather than a good-looking idiot with tall collars and a taste for gambling and fast society'.[11] Lansdowne was rather unhappy to feel that this was happening while he was at a distance.[12] It seemed strange that he was giving her away to a man whom he had never seen and would probably not see until long after they were married.[13] Bertie was disgusted at finding she could not attend the wedding on 30 July.[14] Maud and her sons went, Kerry playing the role of the bride's father.[15]

During the summer, while they were away, Lansdowne rented a cottage in Mahasu, near Simla, where, with Bertie and one or two staff and guests, he would usually 'Sunday out'. He discovered some fine forest walks and felt he was really in the country.[16] These long hikes gave him ample opportunity to reflect.

One issue that concerned him was India's relations with the Amir of Afghanistan, which had significantly deteriorated. The problem, Lansdowne realised, was not with the GOI but with the Amir, who spoke of Lansdowne as an enemy and regularly blamed Mortimer Durand for the trouble between their countries.[17] Determined to dominate the frontier tribes himself, the Amir took umbrage at the GOI's influence and methods. He refused to cooperate and report the strength of his forces, which Britain needed to know in case of a Russian invasion. All this was not unreasonable had Afghanistan been an independent sovereign power, but their relations with the Amir belied that. Lansdowne believed the Amir owed his position to the British; he took a close interest in his behaviour and when necessary used strong words to him, as a father might to a mischievous child. But he doubted whether these letters had much effect.[18]

Since the India-Afghanistan border was undefined, the Amir felt free to occupy advanced positions such as Asmar, Bajaur, Kurram, Chageh and Wano. The GOI maintained he had no claim to these places, but the Amir's unofficial warfare forced Lansdowne to apply diplomatic pressure. In August he informed the Amir he was sending Roberts to Kabul, thinking the C-in-C India was the most likely man to secure his confidence.[19] The Amir was warned that, if he refused to meet Roberts, they would force him to evacuate his territorial claims. Lansdowne would instruct the GOI to demarcate the frontier and enforce withdrawal of any Afghan troops or officials found beyond it.[20] If the Amir met the British in a moderate spirit, Lansdowne would deal generously with him.[21] The Amir thought of Roberts as a soldier urging the Forward Policy. Kabul maintained a stony silence, waiting to see what action the British would take.

On 11 August 1892, Salisbury's government lost a vote of confidence and resigned the following day. Gladstone travelled to Osborne House, Isle of Wight, and accepted the seals of office for his fourth Liberal administration. Queen Victoria informed Lansdowne that

> apart from the pain of parting from some great personal friends and people whom she can trust and rely on, the danger to the country, to Europe, to her vast Empire, which is involved in having all these great interests entrusted to the shaking hand of an old, wild and incomprehensible man of 82½ [Gladstone] is very great! It is a terrible trial, but, thank God the country is sound, and it cannot last.[22]

Lansdowne also learned that

> it is pretty clear that no Indian business nor anything else except Home Rule will receive any attention from the new Parliament. The Radicals call the new Ministry 'The G.O.M's G.O.G.' – Grand Old Gang.[23]

Since a large section of the Liberal Party kept in touch with Congress and voiced strong opinions on how India should be governed, Lansdowne's position became more difficult.

Lansdowne was anxious about who would succeed Cross. Hearing it was Lord Kimberley, a former prominent Whig, he was relieved. He knew him well and, but for his views on Ireland, thought him sound enough.[24] His training and experience made him far more suitable as Secretary of State for India than Cross. The Queen disagreed: 'Lord Kimberley is not so courageous nor so conciliatory as her excellent friend Lord Cross.'[25] Lansdowne was advised by Arthur Godley, the Permanent Under-Secretary of State at the India Office, 'you should be very careful to keep him thoroughly posted up as to what you are doing and what you intend to do – I do not for a moment mean to say that you have not done this under the reign of Lord Cross; but merely that Lord Kimberley would be far more exacting on the point than Lord Cross, who was, on the whole, decidedly easy going. This Lord Kimberley certainly is not.'.[26] Cogently and authoritatively, Lansdowne continued his weekly correspondence with the Secretary of State but the style was now more prosaic.

Kimberley's attitude to Afghanistan had a sobering effect on Lansdowne's policy. Kimberley was confident that Russian pressure would draw the Amir closer to the British. He encouraged Lansdowne to keep him in good humour and to desist from advance movements. He believed Lansdowne and the GOI underestimated the importance of keeping the Amir on good terms.[27] In fact Lansdowne knew exactly the value of good relations but was less willing to make sacrifices than Kimberley and London were to achieve it.[28] At the end of the year, with still no reply from Kabul, Lansdowne accepted that abandoning Roberts' visit would not be an unmixed misfortune.[29] This a response to Gladstone's view that Russian expansion in Central Asia was natural and, for India, benign.

During 1892, Lansdowne had obtained royal assent to the Indian Councils Act. Aware that time was running out for them, the Tories reintroduced the bill in the Lords in February. It was then steered through the Commons by George Curzon, the Under-Secretary of State. Jowett was very glad: 'it will do something to conciliate the natives. I wish that you would some-day give the English a good lecture on the ways of behaving to them'.[30] The bill was passed 'quietly' on 26 May.[31]

It increased the Viceroy's Legislative Council and the Legislative Councils of Bombay, Madras, Bengal and the North-West Provinces. It increased nominated, but omitted elective, Indian representation, and introduced the right of discussing the annual Financial Statement.[32] The Queen, watching the Bill's passing with great interest, impressed on Lansdowne the great importance of securing adequate representation for Muslims, whom she considered 'undoubtedly by far the most loyal of the India people'.[33]

Congress was dissatisfied, primarily because the bill maintained the imperial character of the Councils and left the Executive untouched. Lansdowne's flirtation with Congress was over; he rapidly fell out of favour with Octavian Allan Hume, its founding father. Owing to the change of government it was the task of the Liberal government to implement the Act. Kimberley – whose views did not differ greatly from Lansdowne's – was more supportive of the elective principle than Cross had been. In framing the regulations, he and George Russell, the new Under-Secretary of State ensured the elective principle was, with reservations, introduced into the Councils. This went some way to appease critics in India but not as far as Congress wanted.[34] Although Lansdowne's Whig principles achieved a moderate success it was too little too late. It did, however, provide a useful inducement for Congress to achieve its aims by moderate and constitutional ends.[35]

That Kimberley was a more demanding chief to Lansdowne than Cross became apparent in the matter of trial by jury in cases of murder and culpable homicide. In India it was often noted that, whatever the weight of evidence in cases involving capital punishment, juries tended to release criminals. Although some members of Lansdowne's Council were keen to legislate, Lansdowne was against it. By leaving the conditions of trial by jury to local governments, the GOI would be less open to attack. Public opinion on certain crimes was so variable that it was better to let local governments adjust practice to local requirements.[36]

In capital cases where trial by jury had been introduced in Bengal, Bombay and Assam, it had proved a failure. Lansdowne realised that the GOI would have to step in to end the frustration. But in October, before he could act, the Bengal government issued a notification to this effect. The result was outcry from the press and the public; local Indians denounced it as a monstrous abuse of power. In England there was a feeling that it would have been wiser to have left the jury system alone.[37] Kimberley warned Lansdowne to expect a sharp attack and proceed no further without his approval.[38] He advised cancelling the notification.[39] Owing to the agitation it was impossible for Lansdowne to carry out Kimberley's order and remain Viceroy; his position in India would be untenable after a public reprimand by the British government. He threatened resignation.

Kimberley realised that Lansdowne's resignation would give enormous importance to the agitation and do proportionate injury to public interests,[40] but he was not willing to protect the notification as there was not enough support for it in Parliament. Not wishing to lose Lansdowne or votes in Parliament, Kimberley pressed the GOI to accept a commission to examine the jury question. He insisted, however, on the immediate cancellation of the notification. Lansdowne, knowing that retreat was inevitable, accepted but he was bitterly disappointed and his irritation was heightened by the fact that people in England were unable to realise that the noisy agitation in Calcutta had nothing to do with the feeling of Bengal or India generally.[41] As the Bengali press and Congress boasted of their success, Lansdowne appealed to Kimberley to postpone cancellation until after the commission's report, or 'you are ordering us to throw its corpse to the dogs'.[42] The commissioners reported in April 1893, the notification was withdrawn quietly and there was no discussion in Parliament. The measure was never revived.

14

THE END IN SIGHT

AS LANSDOWNE AND the GOI were recovering from the 'trial by jury' bruising, in February 1893 a deputation from the Indian Currency Association warned Lansdowne that India's economy was in great trouble and that because of the rupee's weakness, foreign investors were no longer putting their money in India.[1] Lansdowne, who had made every effort to maintain a stable currency since arriving in India was alarmed. With the GOI at the mercy of financial markets, decisions on projects ranging from agriculture to railways had become risky, and government intervention was critical.

The crisis was hurting not only the GOI and foreign investment but also British officials and servicemen in India, who received their salaries in rupees. As the rate fell, so the money they sent home was worth less and less. Their discontent threatened to paralyse the civil service. In January 1893 Lansdowne had received a 'harrowing' deputation of their members whom he was desperate to help before he left India.[2] Traders were badly affected too and the Hooghly River was full of idle ships; there was a general feeling of despair, notably evident by the number of petitions pressing the GOI to act.[3]

The Indian Currency Association had been established in 1892 by businesspeople based in India wishing to press the GOI to stop the fall in the silver rupee and move to a gold standard.[4] Lansdowne hardly needed convincing but he knew the difficulties of persuading London that change was needed. In June 1892 he had recommended moving to a gold standard, fixing the exchange rate at 1s. 4d. (15 rupees to the sovereign)[5] and closing the Indian mints to free coinage of silver, in order to reduce the number of rupees in circulation.[6] He hoped that Indian interests would be protected by an international agreement. This was not to be; even the International Monetary Conference in Brussels the following December failed to bring change.[7]

After melancholy budget discussions in February and March 1893, Lansdowne wondered how it was possible for India to manage its finances creditably under an exchange system that in just two years had added 4,200,000 rupees to India's liabilities. He was no more responsible than the man in the moon for the drop in the silver price, but it was nonetheless unpleasant for him to find his finances in disorder.[8]

The British government appointed a committee under Lord Herschell to examine the practicality of amending the India Currency Act of 1870 and adopting the gold standard. Despite all the predictions, the committee's report of 31 May was unanimous and supported Lansdowne's essential measures. To prevent a further fall of the rupee, Indian mints were to be closed to free coinage of silver.[9]

Lansdowne was pleased by the findings of the report, noting that its plans would cause fewer fears and difficulties than the scheme it was based on. But his relief was temporary as the crisis deepened. The proposal, he insisted, should be implemented immediately or it would be shipwrecked, with very serious consequences in India.[10] London agreed. The day before he introduced the Currency Bill, he wrote to his mother:

> I hope, for your sake, that your mind is a blank on the currency problem but you have heard enough about it to know that it is one of life and death to us, and that we are resorting to a very violent remedy for our disease – I hope our measure may succeed – we are sure to be abused whether it turns out well or ill, if it fails I shall never hear the end of it. Ld K [Kimberley] has, as usual, known his own mind and acted promptly & vigorously as soon as the Herschell report was before him.[11]

Herschell's report was published in India on 26 June 1893 and enacted by the Indian Coinage and Paper Currency Bill on the same day. It could not have come soon enough. For over two years no debates in the Viceroy's Council had been so exhaustive as to the currency question.

This 'financial coup d'état', as Ardagh, Lansdowne's private secretary, called it,[12] prevented speculators using the period before enactment to import silver. The silver standard, which had been in force since 1835, was abandoned, although the GOI retained the right to coin silver rupees on its own account. A gold standard for India was authorised, but gold was not made legal tender immediately,[13] and currency notes could be issued in exchange for gold coins. The rupee no longer depended on the market value of its silver content, so there was an immediate fall in the price of silver and dislocation of trade with silver-using countries. Lansdowne thought the GOI was not out of trouble altogether but, if the measure succeeded, it would be the best thing that had been done for India in many years.[14] Some Indian newspapers and leaders of Congress criticised Lansdowne's action as a crime because of its suddenness and also because no additional members of the Legislative Council were at Simla when the Act passed. Lansdowne was unrepentant. His currency measures fulfilled the GOI's object: the rupee stabilised and later rose. Discontent among the Indian Civil Service, local business and traders was reduced.

During 1893, social agitation was a very real problem for the GOI. An anti-cow-killing movement founded in the 1880s had gathered pace, and riots in Ballia and Gorakhpur, in the North-West Provinces, triggered further riots at Gya in Bengal. On 26 June Muslims were attacked at the Bakra-Eid festival at Azamgarh: women's nose rings and ear jewels were violently torn away, men were murdered and the police lost control. In August rioters in Bombay killed sixty people and injured five hundred.[15] On Lansdowne's very first day in India he had seen bunting put up by the Bombay Society for the Preservation of Cows, preaching 'No happiness for India's people without the cow', 'The cow is India's foster-mother' and 'God bless the cow'.[16]

To Hindus, killing a cow was sinful, but many Muslims ate beef and participated in their slaughter. Hindus formed the Gaurakhsha Sabha (cow protection society) to save cattle from those who would slaughter them. The advanced wing of Congress found in the movement a way to connect with the great mass of Hindus,[17] and one of their members, Bal Gangadhar Tilak, argued in the *Kesari*, a Marathi newspaper, that Muslims were the aggressors in the anti-cow-killing riots. Through the Central Special Branch of the Thuggee and Dacoity Department, the GOI closely followed the increasing tension between Hindus and Muslims.

In India, religion was a matter of public ritual and display based around annual festivals. It was GOI policy not to interfere with local customs but, where religions competed over limited sacred space, disputes occurred, and British officials then had to decide whose festival should have precedence.[18] The Indian press accused the GOI of *divide et impera*, fomenting animosity between Muslims and Hindus.[19] Lansdowne and his Executive Council discussed legislation, but thought it too risky. Protection of the cow united Hindus, of whatever sect; for them it was the question of all questions and the war cry of the discontented.[20] Although the movement was ostensibly aimed against Muslims, it also targeted the British.[21]

By late August the movement was becoming dangerous. Lansdowne believed the British were so weak all over India, in terms of officials, soldiers and police, that it was near impossible to cope promptly with any collision between factions.[22] He saw the connection between Congress and cow protection as rather like that between Parnell and Home Rule.[23] To Indian nationalists the Irish agitation provided a model and Gladstone's policy towards it an encouragement.[24] Two months after the Bombay riots, unrest receded.[25] Lansdowne opposed coercion, which would revive the agitation. He favoured strict neutrality, although he felt the GOI should legislate against newspaper editors who printed incendiary statements that they did not in good faith believe to be true and should amend legislation to give police powers at assemblies and processions.[26] This pragmatic approach suppressed the worst abuses.

About the same time, Afghanistan's military threatened to destabilise the frontier, so the GOI detained some guns and military stores imported by the Amir. In March 1893 the Amir's secretary visited Calcutta to discuss the matter. This was Thomas Pyne, an engineer and rather a busybody, who revelled in his position as diplomatist[27] but was very useful to the GOI.[28] Negotiating for the guns and stores, he mentioned that the Amir had been unable to see Roberts because of illness, the Hazara rebellion and the severe winter. Kimberley suggested it might be politic to let the Amir have his guns and stores, but Lansdowne insisted on first having a report of Pyne's visit and the Amir's behaviour. Meanwhile, the British government hastened to revive Lansdowne's scheme of a mission to Kabul. The reason was Russian claims in the Pamir Mountains, where the Amir had an interest. To prevent a serious quarrel with Russia, Rosebery, the Foreign Secretary, advised the GOI to tell the Amir to leave trans-Oxus Shignan and Roshan, in present-day north-east Afghanistan.

Lansdowne did so, seeing an opportunity to relieve Britain of a major international difficulty while also settling Indian affairs; he trusted that, meanwhile, London would ensure that the Russians did not move into Roshan and Shignan.[29] Instead of Roberts, he sent Durand, his own Foreign Secretary, as he was better informed, could speak Persian and had a good relationship with Pyne. Although the Amir was known to dislike Durand, he agreed to meet him. Durand knew why: the Amir had been shocked at having his consignment of arms and military stores stopped. On 2 October Durand reached Kabul, noting: 'The Amir of today is a quiet gentlemanly man, his manner and voice is so softened and refined that I could hardly believe it was really Abdur Rahman.'[30]

The Amir, who made decisions only on Sundays, discussed matters with Durand over a period of six weeks. On 12 November they settled what became known as the Durand Line Agreement. Lansdowne believed Durand deserved great credit for his achievement.[31] The agreement was also a coup for Lansdowne's patience and tact. Queen Victoria was particularly glad it happened while Lansdowne was still in

India.[32] Maud described it as 'a feather in his cap'.[33] Durand was made a Knight Commander of the Order of the Star of India (KCSI) and the Amir, who was fond of honours, became a Knight Grand Cross of the Order of the Bath (GCB). By demarcating the border and spheres of influence, the agreement brought the Afridis, Mahsuds, Wazirs, Swatis and other tribes under British control or nominal rule, and the GOI increased the Amir's annual subsidy from 12 to 18 lakhs. The 800-mile Durand Line was demarcated in 1894–96.

At this time, Lansdowne was preoccupied with his final departure from Simla. Six months earlier he had optimistically written that he was planning to leave India on 8 December.[34] But his optimism turned to frustration during the summer, because the British government refused to name his replacement. Lansdowne wondered if they were not sure of still being in office by December.[35] On 5 September he learned that Sir Henry Norman, aged sixty-seven, would replace him. Lansdowne had known him at the India Office in 1880, liked him[36] and did not think he would truckle to agitators in India or London.[37] The appointment took everyone else by surprise and was much criticised in India, where many officials saw Norman as one of themselves;[38] local Indians, attaching great importance to ancestry and social rank, did not understand how 'secretary Saheb' could represent the Queen.[39] Two weeks later, Norman changed his mind because he believed he would not last the five-year term. Lansdowne's irritation was palpable. Eventually, on 12 October, Kimberley announced Lord Elgin as the new Viceroy. Lansdowne, who knew him only slightly, thought him very shy and retiring.[40] He was said to be insignificant in appearance,[41] but his name was more welcome in India than Norman's.[42]

15

FAREWELL TO INDIA

THE LANSDOWNES' FINAL viceregal tour was in Burma. Sailing back to Calcutta on the *Warren Hastings*,[1] Lansdowne wrote to Evie about Burma, whose 'people are so cheery and good humoured':

> The Burmese ladies would have amused you with their bright dresses, their great top knots of black hair (not always their own I am afraid, for you see them buying it openly in the stalls all-round the big Pagodas) their huge cigarettes as big as an office ruler and their intense appreciation of a joke – Rangoon and Mandalay are full of ex queens and princesses, the belongings of King Theebaw, and his predecessor Mindon Min. We have had perfectly calm weather … Yesterday we picked up a big Burmese boat which had lost his way and was drifting out to the South. There were 5 men on board. Very thirsty poor things, for they had got to their last quart or so of water. We have taken them with us after scuttling their wretched craft, a miserable thing of rough planks tied together with strips of bamboo.[2]

They reached Calcutta on 14 December 1893. There followed a series of farewells. Calcutta merchants gave Lansdowne a banquet, Calcutta society put on a ball and the Muslims presented addresses. The educated Hindus held aloof, having never forgiven Lansdowne for various 'more or less imaginary affronts'.[3] While excited to be taking leave and counting the days to it, he was quite worn out.[4] Nevertheless, dutiful to the end, he had some important matters to clear up, not least the currency question.

On 27 January 1894, Lord Elgin assumed office as Viceroy and Governor-General of India. Lansdowne liked what he saw of him: Elgin struck him as quiet, cautious and businesslike. He felt very sorry for Lady Elgin, whom he thought pitiably weak and quite unfit for what awaited her.[5] As for Lansdowne himself, after five years in India he still felt '*vera souple*' [very supple], as they said at Meikleour

> but the top of my skull is as bare & shiny as a billiard ball, and the few remaining hairs on either side are growing very grey – as for my moustache it is badger pied with more white than black in it. The family nose stands out in bolder relief than ever, and the last five years have worn many and deep lines on my forehead & temples – the only other infirmity … (I omit temper) is my increasing deafness.[6]

On 27 January Lansdowne, Maud, Bertie and the household staff had a tremendous leave-taking and sailed from Prinsep Ghat aboard the *Warren Hastings*.[7] Maud's cabin was like a little drawing room.[8] They stopped at Ceylon's Trincomalee for three hours to take on coal before berthing at Colombo for three days. They encountered a severe gale off Sicily and were lucky to get through safely.[9] On 21 February, because of the weather, they landed at Naples rather than Marseilles, and travelled on over land, arriving in London four days later.

Rosebery asked the Queen's apothecary, James Reid, why Lansdowne was so successful in India. Reid explained with an example involving Abdul Karim, Victoria's *munshi*:

> a short time ago he conferred on Munshi's father (an old Hospital Sergeant, whom *we* however call 'Doctor') the honour of appending to his name the letters K.B., which stand for Khan Bahadan or 'great chief'. This is the solution of the conundrum you put to me, and explains the real secret – of *our* wish to honour a Viceroy who has shown such laudable discrimination of native merit![10]

Lansdowne was later honoured with an equestrian statue, which cost the subscribers 80,000 rupees, although thirty-five Indian rulers met three-quarters of the cost. Lansdowne rather regretted it, feeling the Maidan (Calcutta's huge park) was already disfigured by far too many statues, which the crows imagined were perches for their benefit.[11] He advised the fund-raising committee that he would have preferred some other memento.[12] The statue[13] was unveiled with great ceremony in January 1901 by Lord Curzon, who reported:

> The sculptor has hoisted it to an enormous distance from the ground, where it is scarcely possible to see him at all. He has shrouded his features under a gigantic pith helmet, and, in so far as one can see them at all from below, they seem to me to present about as much resemblance to Lansdowne as they do to Campbell-Bannerman or Jesse Collings.[14]

Lansdowne's term of office was a success both for its achievements and for the foundations it laid for his successors. By pursuing the Forward Policy, he strengthened British influence in Afghanistan and Persia against the gradual advance of Russia. In defining boundaries, he reduced the risk of future misunderstandings and costly small wars. Being against annexation and needless interference, he induced tribal chiefs in the North-West Frontier to take greater responsibility for managing their territory, which avoided locking up troops in remote areas. Lansdowne was not alarmist but he recognised that in the event of a war India should be well prepared. His reorganisation of the army aimed to improve its fighting efficiency without exhausting the Exchequer. Restricting recruitment from certain castes while encouraging enlistment from warlike tribes served this end. Lansdowne's efforts were however, subject to London, and his attempt at localising army commands was dismissed. His view that the government's intransigent attitude was a 'fatal mistake'[15] was a defining feature of his term of office.

Lansdowne protested against interference in Indian affairs by the Secretary of State and Parliament on numerous issues, including the currency question, the Factory Act, the Indian Councils Act and trial by jury, over which he threatened to resign. Even under a Liberal government that tried to reconcile the condition of affairs at home with the government of an Indian Empire, Lansdowne did not get his own way. His hope was to give India a progressive administration and to satisfy Indian aspirations for a greater say in ruling the country. Having been a hero of Congress in 1890, Lansdowne was by 1893 denounced by the extreme press as an enemy of the people and a mere puppet in the hands of civil servants.

In the circumstances, that Lansdowne achieved as much as he did is significant. He was willing to go much further than his predecessors or colleagues in reforming the Legislative Councils, proposing to introduce elections because he genuinely believed in the merit of indigenous candidates, giving a voice to local knowledge, and in the benefits to the GOI. If the constitutional structure of the GOI was such that attempted reforms were slow and halting, Lansdowne's vigour in piloting the Age of Consent Bill is noteworthy. Faced with widespread agitation against it, he displayed firmness and sense. He recognised that India was not and never could be anything but itself. Considering the Indian Factory Act, he accepted that Indian and British working conditions differed. Even if India was not ready for representative government, he foresaw that the Indian Councils Act would demonstrate British willingness to increase Indian participation in local government.

Likewise, he wanted the princely states to be administered by enlightened local rulers with a keen interest in the people's welfare. He believed Indian states were an integral part of the Empire and their administration should not be inferior. In dealings with their leaders, he displayed courtesy and firmness. Against the wishes of Queen Victoria, he insisted on executing rebel leaders at the court of Manipur. He expected the Indian Civil Service and his subordinates to show diplomacy and common sense. He allowed subordinates a free hand, rarely interfering directly. Those he befriended in India, such as Roberts, became lifelong friends.

If there was a weakness to his viceroyalty, it can be said that Lansdowne was not always clear-sighted. As he himself realised, he was quite often out of his depth in the changing political environment at home and abroad. This was notably the case at the height of the currency crisis, when the GOI resorted to an aggressive remedy that eventually led to India establishing a gold exchange standard.

Except for six months between Canada and India, Lansdowne had been away from home for over ten years. As his departure from India approached, he was counting off the days before relinquishing office, and the lack of privacy, the formality and hard work that went with it. Although Lansdowne found the climate and some of the customs of India difficult, he never shirked his duty. Indeed, owing to his values and his devotion to duty he performed many tasks from which others might have recoiled, such as visiting the sick, afflicted and poor, and improving sanitation. If Lansdowne's administration was steady, it certainly did not lack glamour. The entertainments that he and Maud put on were on a grand scale. Contrary to his hopes of saving money while abroad, Lansdowne spent much more than his salary while in India. He did more than was asked of him and through his moderate changes left India in a more stable and efficient state than he found it.

SECTION 2

IN OFFICE

16

THE WAR OFFICE

ON 2 JANUARY 1894, Queen Victoria informed Gladstone that she wished to ennoble Lansdowne further; if he declined the dukedom, she would give him the Garter. Arguing that Lansdowne's record in India had been 'very chequered', Gladstone challenged this.[1] Some at court believed he was blinded by political animosity. The Queen told Lansdowne that Gladstone was not ready to reward a Unionist.[2] With insufficient income to live like a Duke, Lansdowne was secretly relieved to not have to refuse the offer. He told the Queen that the Garter was 'more than sufficient recompense' for his service.[3]

Two months later, Lansdowne was appointed a trustee of the National Gallery – as his grandfather had been in 1834 – and remained so until he died in 1927. Over those years the Gallery bought 250 works and received 1,465 more. The trustees in the 1890s had wide powers in acquisition, cleaning, access and hanging. Most were leisured amateurs, and experts were beginning to question this. Lansdowne had no illusions about his expertise. 'My own artistic career began and ended with the production of some execrable pencil drawings which I produced at school, and which, indifferent as they were, would have been even worse, if they had not been liberally touched up by the drawing master.'[4] He expressed his opinions with diffidence. By this time he had also received Honorary Doctorates of Law from McGill University in Montreal and from Oxford University.

Settling back into life in Britain, Lansdowne divided his time between London and Bowood. He loved being back and revelled in the British scenery more than ever.[5] Nothing seemed much different. Writing from Bowood, he told his mother:

I can scarcely believe that I have been away more than 5 years – I might have walked out of this room a fortnight ago, so little have its contents been disturbed.[6]

In Wiltshire, he started work each day at 8 a.m. and found he had no spare time until the dressing bell rang; there was much to do on the estate.[7] Amid the confusion of their Indian unpacking, he wished he had not accumulated so many finely made caskets, carpets and decorative objects. He did not know where it was all to go.[8]

Lansdowne was thinner than before and had some bilious attacks; he was treated with medicinal external applications and Turkish baths for his bones. Maud was diagnosed with whooping cough, although she refused to believe it. In 1895 Lansdowne's mother fell ill and, at midnight on 25 June, to his great sorrow, she died, surrounded by her family. As he told Charles Gore, his paternal aunt's second husband, 'our relations were not only those of mother and son but of two old friends telling one another everything'.[9]

As Lansdowne re-entered British politics, Gladstone relinquished the leadership of the Liberal Party. Lansdowne thought the Grand Old Man's departure and Rosebery's accession would strengthen the Radical party, but how long would they hold together?[10] On 31 January 1895, at a Unionist demonstration in Calne Town Hall, he appeared in public supporting the Unionist Party for the first time.[11]

I have been told that my presence on this platform requires explanation. I have nothing to explain. It is not the platform, it is not the party designation, it is the principles which signify. I am not conscious of having changed mine; some of those with whom I used to act have changed theirs and I have refused to follow. It is the betrayal of 1886 which has brought me here.

The Radicals and other factions in the Liberal Party held together for only fifteen months, falling in June 1895 over a vote of censure on military supplies. After the cabinet agreed to resign, Rosebery travelled to Windsor to inform Queen Victoria. Hours later she invited Salisbury to form an administration. On 24 June he met Devonshire (as Hartington had now become) and Chamberlain at his London house in Arlington Street to discover whether the Liberal Unionists would enter a coalition government. Devonshire agreed, provided they received assurances on policy. Salisbury promised any four cabinet places to them. After Chamberlain refused the War Office, he informed Devonshire that he was giving the post to Lansdowne because 'he is a devoted follower of yours and would work with you very well on Army matters'.[12] Lansdowne's appointment to the War Office was well received.

On 25 June Salisbury kissed hands with Queen Victoria. In July, with no formal manifesto, Salisbury won a landslide victory against a divided Liberal Party. His third administration was dominated by foreign and imperial issues.[13] His nineteen cabinet ministers had an average age of fifty-six, which some thought too old. Salisbury, sixty-five years old, was showing signs of old age. Eight ministers were upper-class and eleven middle-class. The cabinet contained four Liberal Unionists (five if one counts Goschen): Devonshire, Chamberlain, Lansdowne and Lord Henry James of Hereford, previously a strong party Liberal. Ten years earlier it would have seemed unbelievable that Liberals and Conservatives could be members of one cabinet.

The War Office was the nerve centre for military policy and government of the Army. It was a highly complex department and continually in the eye of a political storm raging around its operation and organisation. The main offices, at 80–91 Pall Mall, were 'a tiresome jumble of rambling passages, sudden stairs and confusing turns',[14] its rooms permeated by the odours of colza oil lamps and leather fire buckets. The department had eleven other sites in London and outposts at Enfield Lock, Birmingham and Waltham Abbey. It was probably the largest administrative establishment in the world,[15] and 'most unsatisfactory, partly owing to the fact that the different departments were so scattered and partly to the unsuitability of the main structure'.[16] Lansdowne thought it was 'an intolerable situation which interfered with the efficient conduct of business'.[17] The buildings were so poor and the ill-health of the 1,140 staff so well known that within days of starting work Lansdowne proposed a new War Office building, bringing all the principal officials under one roof.[18]

The separation between buildings was reflected in staff divisions between the civilians and the military. As head of department and cabinet minister, Lansdowne was responsible to Parliament for the whole conduct of Army policy and administration, including the financial estimates. As well as attending debates, meetings, committees and the War Office Council, he oversaw Army supplies, equipment and preparation for war and military expeditions. Unlike his predecessor, Henry Campbell-Bannerman, who was distinctly lazy, hated detail[19] and left his civil servants to run the department, Lansdowne took a personal interest in administration and staffing.[20] There is no record of the hours he kept, although as a 'non-Saturdayite' in Salisbury's cabinet he did almost all his work at the office from Monday to Friday, snatching the weekend away.[21] The post was one of the toughest in government and many had struggled with it. The path of a Secretary of State for War, according to Crewe, was 'not strewn with roses but rather resembles one of those caravan routes across the African desert, strewn with whitened bones which show the disasters of those who have passed that way before'.[22]

Lansdowne employed a private secretary at the War Office alongside the two assistant private secretaries, who were civil servants. Because Lansdowne sat in the Lords, his Parliamentary Under-Secretary for War was in the Commons. On 30 June Salisbury offered St John Brodrick this post. Queen Victoria had wanted someone who had not taken sides in army affairs and could work with soldiers.[23] She favoured a pre-Cardwellian Army with limited civilian authority over it.[24] Being obliged constitutionally to accept the advice of her minister,[25] she finally agreed to Brodrick's appointment.

Younger than Lansdowne and a graduate of Eton and Balliol, Brodrick had remarkable brain power, knowledge of military history and belief in himself.[26] They had long known each other socially and Lansdowne was sure that they would work well together.[27] As Financial Secretary to the War Office from 1886 to 1892, Brodrick was unpopular with senior officers. Field Marshal Wolseley thought he dominated Lansdowne.[28]

Below the Parliamentary Under-Secretary in the hierarchy was the Permanent Under-Secretary, principal policy adviser to the Secretary of State, a career civilian and non-political. He maintained the office's traditional practice from one ministry to another[29] and regarded all governments as much the same.[30] As the link between Lansdowne and the various departments, and responsible for managing the Central Office, the smooth running of the War Office depended on his knowledge and skill. Sir Arthur Haliburton, who started as Permanent Under-Secretary when Lansdowne entered the office, was a 'permanent official of the old style, but more broad-minded than some of his class, and with a considerable gift of lucid literary expression';[31] he developed a close working relationship with Lansdowne, who valued his knowledge. Haliburton believed that civil power should administer the great departments of state.[32]

The Financial Secretary of the War Office was an MP who ran the civil department of the office. Salisbury appointed Joseph Powell Williams, a Liberal Unionist, a Chamberlainite and a businessman. Lansdowne knew him only very slightly,[33] and we do not know how they got on.

In contrast to the central and civil departments, the military departments in July 1895 were under the office of the Commander-in-Chief, at that time the Duke of Cambridge. One month before Lansdowne came into office the Duke announced his intention to retire,[34] and Salisbury wished Wolseley to succeed him rather than Redvers Buller, the choice of the Liberals. Prince George, 2nd Duke of Cambridge, was Queen Victoria's first cousin. Naturally conservative, he distrusted political interference in the Army, which he feared would make promotions dependent on party politics. During July and August Lansdowne arranged for his replacement. Wolseley was born and educated in Dublin, joining the Army in 1852 and rising rapidly to become Viscount Wolseley and Field Marshal in May 1894. An advocate of reform, he used political initiatives to achieve his aims, although he was by temperament strongly opposed to politicians, whom he disliked for 'conforming to the democratic system of the day'.[35] He had publicly stated that 'our system of military administration has been growing more and more civilian in character since the days of Wellington. Soldiers don't think the arrangement a good one.'[36] The military department was based in Pall Mall and oversaw ten divisions: the Military Secretary, Military Intelligence, Adjutant-General, Quartermaster-General, Works, Armaments, Medical, Military Education, Chaplain-General and Veterinary.[37]

Almost every aspect of the senior officers' activities had political implications and cost money for which the civilians demanded explanations. This invariably caused friction which, as Lansdowne had prior experience of, was of long standing.[38] Shortly after becoming minister, he remarked that the friction was less acute than when he was there in 1872 during Cardwell's time,[39] but naturally 'there will be differences between the civil officials at the War Office and military officials. It will be so to the end of time.'[40]

A further aspect of this problem was how to decide questions of a professional or technical nature. The soldiers complained 'The difficulty at the War Office is that the heads of it are civilians who are constantly changing.'[41] Lansdowne took a practical approach: although the politician's hand could not be forced by senior officers, neither should a more or less ignorant Secretary of State pretend to expertise but should 'gather the best information he can from the experts'.[42] Whether soldiers or civilians, 'we are all of us animated by a common desire to make the Army efficient and to study its requirements'.[43] But, as the Crown's representative to Parliament, he objected to senior officers intruding in politics; 'the Secretary of State and the Secretary of State alone is responsible to Parliament, and the Commander-in-Chief is responsible to the Secretary of State as his principal military adviser'.[44] In his experience, 'the soldier who is also a politician is apt not to be very much trusted in the Army'.[45] The right mode of conducting business in the War Office was that 'the soldiers and civilians should, as far as possible, sit side by side, and not occupy different branches of the office and occupy their time in controversies with one another'.[46] To Lansdowne, whatever military measures the senior officers thought advisable, they had to reckon with the Secretary of State and he had to convince the cabinet and the Chancellor. Inevitably the senior officers received 'something notoriously a great deal less than they would have liked to have and they had to make the best of it'.[47] In his view, the Army could only be organised on financial lines.[48]

Running the War Office was further complicated by petty jealousies and rivalries among the senior officers themselves. While they were united in wishing to transfer financial and supply functions to their side of the War Office, they disagreed on broader issues of Army reform. Different views on regimental organisation, education, training and staff planning divided traditionalist soldiers and reforming soldiers to such a degree that the possibility of a cohesive senior officer corps lay dormant. Moreover, military life conditioned officers to accept the status quo and not question regulations. Even among the reformers there were notable differences of opinion on military policy and the purpose of the Army. Whereas Roberts and his clique advocated reforms and strategic priorities informed by service in India, Wolseley and his clique modelled their ideas on experience in Africa and Britain.[49] The difficulties of climate and terrain in colonial outposts influenced their thinking about diet, clothing, weaponry, drill, composition and tactics. Without a General Staff laying down textbook methods, campaigning became highly personalised, which invariably appeared to favour certain officers over others. The top brass in the War Office were at the pinnacle of their careers and Lansdowne suspected he was 'less alarming to them as one military officer was to another'.[50] However, by 1895 such patronage had diminished and Wolseley's 'ring' and Roberts's clique had less influence. Moreover, with age and ill health, Wolseley harboured petty animosities against many of his 'ring' colleagues, undermining their ability to work together to reform the War Office and the Army.

In taking on the War Office, Lansdowne had to contend not only with its inefficiency and internal frictions but also with the dynamics of cabinet, the Liberal opposition, parliamentarians with services backgrounds, civilian reformers and the press.

The cabinet's inner circle comprised Salisbury, Balfour, Devonshire, Chamberlain, Goschen, Hicks Beach, Hamilton and Lansdowne. The Prime Minister and also Foreign Secretary, Salisbury was, like Lansdowne, cautious and reserved, disliking insincerity and public praise. Lansdowne, who knew him both personally and professionally, could not imagine a kinder or more indulgent chief.[51] Salisbury's principle was that all final policy decisions lay with the cabinet. Like Lansdowne, he opposed military interference in politics; it was not the place of senior officers to comment on government policy[52] and 'any attempt to take the opinion of the expert above the opinion of the politician must, in view of all the circumstances of our constitution, inevitably fail'.[53] Salisbury encouraged increasing civilian authority.

Salisbury's belief that the cabinet was at the core of Britain's constitutional arrangements was shared by his nephew Arthur Balfour, who had known Lansdowne since Eton. He was deeply interested in defence, later establishing the Committee of Imperial Defence, and one of the few politicians to understand the need for military–naval cooperation in a comprehensive policy of defence. Among other cabinet ministers supportive of Lansdowne was Spencer Compton, 8th Duke of Devonshire, who was self-contained, unemotional and prone to self-doubt.[54] Lansdowne had served under him as Under-Secretary of State for India in 1880, and Lansdowne's daughter Evie had married Devonshire's heir, Victor Cavendish, in 1892. Devonshire's formidable prestige and seniority profoundly reinforced the importance of imperial defence, warning that 'we take our Imperial position so much for granted that sometimes we almost forget that we have an Imperial position at all'.[55] One colleague with a broader view of imperial considerations was Joseph Chamberlain, whom Lansdowne had got to know while Governor-General of Canada. Chamberlain had little interest in the mechanics of defence. He thought of armed force as an intimidating tool in negotiation rather than for deployment in warfare,[56] and the War Office and Admiralty were 'mostly occupied in preparations for the defence of our markets and for the protection of our commerce'.[57]

In contrast, Michael Hicks Beach, Chancellor of the Exchequer, took an intense interest in Lansdowne's management of the War Office. Nicknamed 'Black Michael' due to his temper,[58] Hicks Beach indulged in sharp verbal attacks on colleagues. He was determined to limit rising demands for defence expenditure, since 'we were not, we never had been, and we never should be, a great Military Power. Our first line of defence, our first line of attack, if attack be necessary was the Navy.'[59] His preferential treatment of the Admiralty pleased George Goschen, First Lord of the Admiralty. One of the 'very cleverest men'[60] in the cabinet, he was admired for his honesty and personal integrity. Lansdowne had known him professionally since he was Under-Secretary of State for War in 1872, and their relations were amicable. Goschen managed the Admiralty on 'what were called business principles' – personal responsibility, promotion by merit and rigid control of costs.[61] For the British Empire to prosper, it had to be well organised and exploit its strengths. In attempting to be strong everywhere, it was in danger of collapsing under the weight of its defences.[62] The Royal Navy did not 'defend' the Empire; it applied pressure wherever a potential enemy was most exposed.[63]

Applying pressure against any threat from Russia was a task for the India Office and George Hamilton, Secretary of State for India. Hamilton had a strong sense of duty and loyalty to the Tories but limited political skills; he had rejected the War Office post in 1887, believing it was 'the most difficult and invidious post in the cabinet'.[64] Hamilton was among the few cabinet ministers with military experience. Owing to tradition, economics and a collective complacency in the invincibility of the Army, the cabinet all agreed that civilian authority should dominate the military.

Having never sat in the cabinet, Lansdowne first had to be sworn in as Privy Councillor. The Council met on 1 July so that he could be sworn in as Secretary of State; then he took the 1 p.m. train to Windsor to receive the seals of the War Office from Queen Victoria. The delay was tiresome as he was 'really wanted at the War Office' but without his seals he could not appoint an Under-Secretary in the Commons in order to see the Army vote passed before Parliament was dissolved on 8 July.[65] There is no evidence to suggest the Queen had pressed for his appointment as she had done for the viceroyalty in 1889,[66] but she welcomed it.

With little threat, foreign or domestic, to Britain, there was natural antipathy to Army reform among politicians in 1895. In the Commons, military debates were often held at the 'extreme end of the session and in a jaded House'[67] or to 'empty benches'.[68] Lansdowne saw this neglect as 'due mainly to the comparative indifference of the public in the affairs of the Army and to the absence of that interest which is taken in the sister service'.[69] This complacency extended to the Liberal opposition, who were uninterested in Army reform. They aimed to severely limit Britain's military responsibility,[70] on the basis that improving Army efficiency would undermine industrial capacity and spark off riotous spirits.[71] Without an alternative policy, the opposition largely resorted to destructive criticism, which Lansdowne with his command of the subject and polite language in the Lords, and Brodrick with his confident manner in the Commons, easily deflected.[72]

Former Army and Navy officers were in Parliament to challenge civilian power and advance their self-interests, and many of them knew senior officers in the War Office.[73] They could offer alternative policies but were often reluctant; they could not give a coordinated lead in the Commons and failed to motivate debate in the Lords. With their individual expertise restricted very often to their knowledge of regimental life, they lacked cohesion and leadership. Lansdowne did not see them as a threat.

Lansdowne also had to reckon with civilian reformers. This small clique of men, including the MPs Charles Dilke and Hugh Arnold-Forster and the military historian and journalist Henry Spenser Wilkinson, were more prominent than services parliamentarians in shaping public discussion. They believed that imperial defence transcended party politics and that defence should be coordinated under one minister advised by an officer from each service. In their view, the Army suffered because civilians had power without knowledge; and not until the senior officers had real authority could they be accountable for the condition of Britain's defences.[74] Committed to the primacy of the Navy and the command of the seas, they worked in and out of Parliament to remove barriers between political and military affairs.

Outside Parliament, the press – in particular, *The Times* – pushed its own doctrinaire views on the War Office and Army reform. Its constant attacks on Lansdowne prompted Campbell-Bannerman to ask, 'what has happened to *The Times*? It used to be so reasonable and willing to support the present system in the main.'[75] Although we cannot measure the influence of the press on public opinion, its effect on politicians was always important. In the 1890s, newspapers were intimately bound to political organisations and individuals. They served those interests, often to their commercial detriment. Newspapers proudly labelled themselves Unionist, Liberal or Irish Nationalist, and modified their loyalties as new stars and party constellations appeared. Hungry for 'information', a literate working class transformed the press. Politics neither sold newspapers nor followed them.[76] Although the lack of public interest in military matters limited the potential of the press to push the reform discourse and the question of civilian supremacy further, Lansdowne could not ignore them. That he was willing to listen to and occasionally act on their reasoned recommendations was indicative of his broad-minded approach to operating at the War Office.

17

REFORM OF THE WAR OFFICE

ALTHOUGH LANSDOWNE HAD no preconceived vision of reform, within weeks of taking office, having consulted his colleagues, he had a strategy. Reforming the War Office had to be attacked first, before the problem of Army reform.[1] Before appointing Wolseley, Lansdowne telegraphed him: 'you must clearly understand that changes in the position of the Commander-in-Chief are inevitable. The precise extent is not yet decided, but I think they will be on the lines indicated by the late Secretary of State.'[2] Campbell-Bannerman's scheme, partly based on the Hartington Commission report of 1890, made the Commander-in-Chief 'principal adviser of the Secretary of State'. With him were the four other military heads of department, each 'directly responsible' to the Secretary of State, forming a 'deliberative council' (Army Board), with the Adjutant-General responsible for Army discipline.[3] Wolseley accepted the appointment as Lansdowne described it,[4] but it was soon apparent that he had other ideas.

On 26 August 1895, Lansdowne outlined the government's scheme for reorganising the War Office.[5] He deflected criticism from the opposition Liberals while validating the report by Hartington (now his cabinet colleague, Devonshire) as a 'sufficient and authoritative exposition' of the three main defects in military administration: 'an excessive centralization of responsibility in the Commander-in-Chief';[6] 'in the distribution of work amongst the heads of the great military departments no sufficient provision had been made for the consideration of the plans for the military defence of the Empire as a whole, or for the examination of larger questions of military policy'; and an insufficient representation of a consultative element.[7]

The Hartington Commission had recommended a central organising department under a Chief of Staff and the abolition of the Commander-in-Chief's office, but Lansdowne, like Campbell-Bannerman before him, was against this. He believed that public opinion would not support the abolition of Commander-in-Chief,[8] a post closely associated with the Crown, and that a Chief of Staff 'entirely dissociated from executive work, would be out of touch with the Army and would, in all probability, not secure its confidence'.[9] Moreover, such an officer would 'inevitably become the real Commander-in-Chief'.[10] Under Lansdowne's scheme the department of the Commander-in-Chief would substitute for a General Staff.[11] He would hold his office under the usual rules for Staff appointments, would exercise general command over the British Army at home and abroad, issue Army orders and hold periodic inspections of troops; he would be responsible for commissions, promotions, appointments, honours and rewards, for the departments of military information and mobilisation, and for the general distribution of the Army; he would be the principal adviser to the Secretary of State, giving him general, as distinguished from departmental, advice upon all important questions of military policy.[12]

The Adjutant-General would be charged with the discipline, education and training of the Army, together with returns, statistics, enlistments and discharges. The Quartermaster-General would deal with supplies, transport, Army quarters, movement of troops, the pay department and the Army Service Corps. The Inspector-General of Fortifications would be responsible for barracks, fortifications and War Office lands, and the supply and inspection of warlike stores. The Inspector-General of Ordnance would oversee equipment for armaments and inventions.[13] Lansdowne foresaw that military opinion would emerge more distinctly in a military board without his presence,[14] so he retained Campbell-Bannerman's Army Board. Salisbury wanted Lansdowne to preside over it, but Queen Victoria approved his non-participation.[15] Comprising the Commander-in-Chief and the other heads of department, it reported on selections for promotion, certain staff appointments, proposals for estimates[16] and 'such questions as may be from time to time referred to them by the Secretary of State'.[17]

To improve understanding among civilians and senior officers of the cost of proposals and the long-term objectives that justified the annual estimates, Lansdowne decided that Ralph Knox, the Accountant-General, should attend the Army Board. Within a few months, Knox noted 'that the soldiers did not like the change, because they have to face one another and argue out their ideas instead of attempting to push them through independently, and they don't like my presence, because it makes them consider the financial aspects of affairs and also lets me know the differences of opinion'.[18]

While the Army Board provided a consultative element as recommended by Hartington, there was also a War Office Council, presided over by the Secretary of State and comprising the Parliamentary Under-Secretary, the Permanent Under-Secretary, the Financial Secretary, the Commander-in-Chief and the four heads of the military departments, with other experts summoned as required.[19] This Council was similar to those of 1890 and 1892. The Secretary of State determined the agenda and all decisions were in his name, not that of the Council. Purely consultative, its purpose was to help the minister reach a consensus with his senior officers and civilian advisers. As the Secretary of State alone was responsible to Parliament, he took the final decisions on any matter under discussion.[20]

Lansdowne's scheme was repeatedly criticised in and out of Parliament.[21] The persistence of the attacks during August and September compelled minute consideration of the wording of the new Order in Council. As one of the fiercest critics, Wolseley was determined to force Lansdowne to redraft it. Producing his own draft Order in Council, 'as a sort of compromise between the extremely civilian views embodied in the Hartington Commission report, and the purely military view of the Army-men who have experience in Army administration', Wolseley reiterated that the Commander-in-Chief must be responsible for the discipline of the Army, or he could not be responsible for its fighting efficiency.[22] Military opinion was unanimous that dissociating the Commander-in-Chief from controlling the discipline of the Army, or even appearing to, would be 'fraught with danger', and 'no scheme would work, or be understood by the Army which does not give the Commander-in-Chief an undoubted right of interference in questions of discipline'.[23] Lansdowne understood Wolseley's argument, but was unmoved.

The Commander-in-Chief's pre-eminence was not in question; Lansdowne's scheme made that officer the principal adviser to the Secretary of State, with unlimited right to advise.[24] He informed the cabinet that 'the Commander-in-Chief would certainly have his say' on Army discipline and would clearly have command, which 'in the eyes of the public most contributes to the dignity of his position'. The Order in Council would 'unmistakeably show' that 'the Commander-in-Chief is in a position different from that of the other Heads of Departments, a position giving him a general power of supervising and directing the whole of the military work of the office'.[25]

Lansdowne's reorganisation was confirmed by Order in Council on 21 November 1895, and the Commander-in-Chief became 'the principal adviser of the Secretary of State on all military questions', and 'charged with the general supervision of the Military Departments of the War Office'.[26] It was also announced[27] that 'all important questions would be referred to the Commander-in-Chief before submission to the Secretary of State'.[28] As Lansdowne later explained, he 'never contemplated that the Commander-in-Chief should be kept in the dark'[29] nor be sidelined by discussions with heads of department behind his back.[30] What he wanted was to get 'the actual mind of a man who was an expert in a manner in which I should not get it if I was only to see him in the presence of the Commander-in-Chief'[31] because 'when you have a number of these high officers sitting round a table they will not give you the same absolutely frank, unreserved opinion that they will when you get them quietly in your room'.[32] The new 'regulations reserved to the Commander-in-Chief a far larger measure of control and authority than was contemplated by the Hartington Commission, by the late government, or by the advocates of decentralization in the press'.[33] Lansdowne voiced the same opinion in evidence to the Royal Commission on the War in South Africa in 1903.[34]

Following the Hartington commissioners' recommendation of a Naval and Military Council, Lansdowne created the Cabinet Defence Committee,[35] with Devonshire as its chairman. Although two interdepartmental committees existed, they were subordinate to the cabinet and met infrequently. The Colonial Defence Committee, revived by the Salisbury government in 1885, offered suggestions on broad imperial defence principles.[36] The Joint Naval and Military Committee, also based on the Hartington recommendations, 'met infrequently to consider the service estimates in relation to each other and to make recommendations to the cabinet where the final decision would be taken and to consider and authoritatively decide upon unsettled questions between the two departments, or any matters of Joint Naval and Military policy'.[37] In this part of the War Office reform, Lansdowne demonstrated the government's appreciation of the need for Empire-wide planning. In doing this, he garnered support from many services parliamentarians, and even Arnold-Forster.[38]

Unfortunately, the principal architects of this committee, which included Salisbury, Balfour, Devonshire, Goschen, Hicks Beach and Lansdowne, disagreed on its composition and functions. This divergence of opinion, matched by a lack of enthusiasm for making them a reality, condemned the Cabinet Defence Committee from the start. If defining its duties had been difficult to achieve in the autumn of 1895, getting it to meet was harder.[39]

Between 1895 and 1900 the committee failed to meet the expectations of the Hartington Commission report;[40] it became merely an informal committee of the cabinet, largely because those responsible ignored it. Balfour was leading the Commons, Salisbury after 1897 suffered from poor health and Hicks Beach doubted it could do the work suggested for it.[41] Its duties remained vague and it lacked real power. Professional members attended for only part of the proceedings, with no formal part in discussions. To Wolseley, 'their meetings are always interesting, sometimes to a soldier amusing and always illustrate how absolutely unfit civilians are to manage a war or indeed to lay down rules or orders for the conduct of any military operations'.[42] It had no agenda,[43] met infrequently and 'rarely at a time of year when it was possible for ministers to concentrate their attention upon questions requiring careful study'.[44] Lansdowne felt 'discussions were not always sufficiently "focussed" and became consequently somewhat desultory'.[45] No minutes were kept, which convinced Arnold-Forster it was 'a fiction'.[46] Its ineffectiveness reveals the lack of interest at cabinet level (and of popular pressure) for reform of defence matters.

Unsurprisingly, the new Defence Committee and the regulations in the Order in Council were criticised in and out of Parliament. Wolseley was appalled:[47] with 'neither the supreme control exercised by the Secretary of State, nor the administrative functions now conferred on those below him', he argued that he had 'become a fifth wheel to a coach'.[48] 'Between the ministerial head on the one hand and the departmental heads on the other, he has been crushed out, and the Secretary of State has become the actual Commander-in-Chief of the Army.'[49] Wolseley quickly made senior officers aware of his views on precedence and authority.[50] He ordered Evelyn Wood, the Quartermaster-General, to communicate with him before putting any matter to Lansdowne.[51] As a result, Lansdowne 'minuted' papers to Wood, but received them back through Wolseley.[52] Lansdowne disliked this practice but accepted that 'it comes well within the Commander-in-Chief's powers of supervision'.[53] Wolseley continued it because it reinforced his position and because he believed that Lansdowne could not understand the complexities of military affairs.[54]

Although Lansdowne was a close friend and admirer of Wolseley's rival, Lord Roberts, this did not influence Lansdowne's willingness to work with Wolseley or maintain cordial relations. They worked in adjoining rooms at the War Office and constantly communicated. He often invited him to dine at Lansdowne House or to stay at Bowood, and Wolseley regularly accepted, but judged his host harshly in private. In letters between 1895 and 1900 to his wife, Louisa, he refers to Lansdowne as 'an ass',[55] 'my little French Jew',[56] 'the smallest minded man and least capable of all the War Ministers I have known',[57] 'a whipper-snapper of a War Office clerk',[58] 'a man who in any of his dealings with me would ruthlessly turn on me'[59] and a 'poor little creature not worth fighting over'.[60] That Louisa and Maud were close friends who established and managed the Officers' Families Fund only increases speculation that Wolseley's frequent illnesses while at the War Office corrupted his mind.

That Lansdowne did not react to such criticisms may have increased Wolseley's frustration.

Wolseley was not the only one disappointed. Lansdowne's new organisation of Army Board, War Office Council and Defence Committee, the 'three storied arrangement of Council', seemed to *The Saturday Review* 'to promise nothing but confusion, and to testify to nothing but timorous fear of unpractical men who try to dissipate responsibility instead of concentrating it'.[61]

To its critics, the reorganisation of 1895 created an unworkable system. Lansdowne disagreed, and 'never yielded to the temptation of saying that it was no fault of mine, and that I was acting on the advice of others'.[62] He believed it was 'in principle a perfectly sound system'.[63] Only once did he impute blame to Wolseley for mismanagement of the system established in 1895 and this was on 4 March 1901, four months after leaving the War Office, during the 'War Office Administration' debate in the House of Lords. Lansdowne was well aware of the pressures on him during his reorganisation:

> I have no doubt that there are imperfections in our scheme, but we cannot, I fear, please: The Queen, who wishes to keep the Army under the Crown, and who would like to clip Wolseley's wings, providing the reversion of an extra pair for the Duke of Connaught. Devonshire, who harkens after his own headless Army and Chief of Staff. Goschen, who thinks there is nothing like the leather of the Admiralty. Wolseley and Buller, who want the military discipline to prevail and the Commander-in-Chief to be the real master. Balfour, who wants a logical and self-consistent scheme which he can defend in argument against Dilke's fire on one side and that of *The Times* on the other.[64]

The War Office system was neither unworkable nor, as Balfour predicted, did it 'break down under serious strain'.[65] Hostile to any changes at the War Office, Lansdowne's ideas were never given a fair trial and failed to heal the mutual suspicions between soldiers and civilians. It was not until constraints on British power and changes in the international environment in the early 1900s were fully felt that collaboration and the priority of efficient defence planning became possible.[66]

On 29 December 1895, while Lansdowne was busy defending his scheme, some 10,000 miles away Leander Jameson – with five hundred mounted police under Major Sir John Willoughby – rode into the South African Republic, often referred to as the Transvaal, to trigger an uprising by Uitlanders (British expatriate workers) at Johannesburg. The Uitlanders did not rise and three days later, finding his position against 1,500 Boers hopeless, Jameson surrendered. The raiders, including some British officers, were imprisoned in Pretoria. Lansdowne thought 1896 had got off to a bad start.[67] The failure of the Jameson Raid to empower the Uitlanders and overthrow Kruger's state polarised the two white races in South Africa, and Lansdowne believed that it 'certainly had the effect of creating deep-seated mistrust of us in the mind of the South African Republic'.[68] Suspecting British government involvement, President Kruger began preparing for war with Britain.

While the jingoist supporters focused attention on the political rights of Uitlanders, many of these Uitlanders and their financial supporters were not model agents of the state. Some, like Alfred Beit and Julius Wernher, were not even British and others were adventurers. Nor was the British claim to have no interest above suspicion. Critics noted that Hercules Robinson (Lord Rosemead), the British High Commissioner in Cape Colony since 1880, was a friend of Cecil Rhodes, the mining magnate and Prime Minister of the Cape Colony, and had been a director of his De Beers Company. Such ties led some people to assume that British policy in South Africa was, if only indirectly, driven by a 'kind of buccaneering capitalist, working for his own private agenda'.[69] Public opinion in Britain would not support a war started on these grounds and any cabinet desire for a preemptive strike needed careful consideration. Strongly in favour of 'wait and see', Lansdowne believed the Boers had got wind that the British could afford to wait longer than Kruger could.[70]

18

REFORM OF THE ARMY

HAVING 'ATTACKED' THE War Office during 1895, Lansdowne turned to Army reform in 1896. Although, in operations around the world since 1870 the Army had got through 'not only without disgrace but with considerable credit',[1] it was 'out of joint',[2] 'wanting in elasticity'[3] and needing simplification.[4] He recognised the difficulty of Army reform[5] and, as a supporter of modern, practical military thinking, had much in common with the senior officers, 'who cared little for names and phrases if a fighting line worth the money spent could be produced'.[6]

With a reputation for frugal administration, Lansdowne was considered capable of 'repairing the main defects of the existing machine',[7] whereas his critics urged 'total' reform. Lansdowne's objective was the sound defence of Britain at home and abroad. Undertaking moderate changes to achieve this, he could justly claim that in his term of office 'not a year has passed in which they [the government] had not done something to make the Army stronger and more efficient'.[8] Before 1899 he successfully defended a military system that many soldiers, parliamentarians, civilian reformers, many newspapers, some of the opposition and the Royal Family were 'all clamouring to abandon'.[9]

Military opinion was particularly influenced by two models: war in Europe, and war in India and the Colonies. Parallel to these crosscurrents was the assumption that Britain was 'secure behind the sturdy hulls of the Royal Navy, and with most of its wars on land against poorly armed and often badly led inhabitants' could afford to be very cautious about military development.[10] Small colonial wars did not prepare the Army for war with modern armaments. Many generals and commanding officers, blinkered by their past success, refused to accept that technology was changing the nature of war. If the Army was successful, most politicians saw no need for reform.

Lansdowne believed in the objects of military organisation and administration laid down by Cardwell and the role of the Army as defined by Stanhope's 1888 memorandum.[11] Under Cardwell the power of the War Office was centralised, purchase of officers' commissions was abolished and a home reserve force was created with short terms of service for enlisted men. Stanhope had set out the strategic aims of the Empire, and how the Army supported these aims. Lansdowne had no overall vision for reforming the Army, but he did think it singularly complicated. 'It has, in the first place, been the outcome, not of any deliberate plan of construction, but of gradual and spontaneous growth; our Regular Army, our Militia, our Volunteers have grown up side by side, at first with scarcely any connexion, upon no definite plan.'[12] Also, Britain was the only European country that relied on voluntary enlistment.[13] To Lansdowne the basis of the military system was threefold: 'for a great part of the Army the term of service should be of moderate length so as to yield an efficient reserve'; 'infantry battalions which were abroad should be supported by an adequate number of properly organised battalions at home capable of supplying the necessary drafts'; and 'there should be a connection between the country and the Army'.[14]

This view was partly shared by Wolseley, who was a devoted follower of Cardwell's system[15] and had strongly influenced Stanhope.[16] Lansdowne and Wolseley assumed war in Europe was unlikely, although Wolseley took the threat of French invasion more seriously than Lansdowne.[17] They were not followers of the Blue Water School,[18] but Lansdowne saw the Navy as 'our first line of defence'.[19] However, naval and military defences must be considered together: 'partners the two services are, partners they must remain'.[20] Although Wolseley wanted to improve the state of the Army, he believed that wholesale reform was unnecessary.[21] Lansdowne partly shared this view. They both wanted to make the Army a profession and administer it on 'sound and simple business principles'.[22]

They recognised the 'inestimable value' of regimental feeling – *esprit de corps* – and were determined 'to foster it in all ranks of the Army'.[23] Lansdowne admired Britain's ability to produce 'men to lead, and to inspire with their courage troops belonging to races less civilised than our own'.[24] He had a 'sincere hope that we should frequently see native troops taking the field by the side of our own'.[25] Wolseley thought otherwise, harbouring an intense dislike of using Indian troops in battle. While their views differed in certain respects, both men recognised that the size of the Army had not kept pace with the expanding Empire. Lansdowne freely admitted that 'we are finding great and increasing difficulty in providing both for the normal wants of the Empire and for the special calls which come upon us with growing frequency'.[26]

Where they differed greatly was in finance. Lansdowne was also far more aware of the cost of reform than Wolseley: 'Financial and military considerations are inextricably intermixed. We cannot emancipate ourselves from the financial limits which the state of the National Exchequer imposes upon us.'[27] Lansdowne administered with financial caution, yet he also defended the Army estimates wherever he saw parsimony undermining efficiency. Between 1895 and 1899 the annual estimates increased by 14.2 per cent, and Parliament voted in £9,458,000 for military loans for the defence of Britain and the Empire.[28]

With military and financial considerations in mind, Lansdowne's four military bills of 1896 were chosen to allow the 'machine to run on in the old grooves' while getting the War Office and headquarters into order.[29] These 'innocents', essential to the Army's efficiency, were 'ruthlessly massacred' by the opposition and service parliamentarians.[30] They were 'muddled out of existence'[31] largely because of the government's other commitments – notably the Irish Land Bill. Devonshire's Cabinet Defence Committee managed a few desultory discussions about naval and military policy in the Mediterranean. Lansdowne admitted that as 'we all became busier & busier with Land Bills & such like rubbish, this really big question slid into the background'.[32] In contrast with the lack of appetite in Parliament to improve the Army and in cabinet to reform defence, the War Office was a department of 'exceptional activity'.[33] Pressing matters in Egypt, Abyssinia and South Africa, alongside the move for the existence of a short-service system, occupied most of Lansdowne's time.

While the government waited to see what President Kruger would do next, the War Office began to redirect its policy in South Africa, from imperial defence to, as Lansdowne told the Royal Commission in 1903, maintaining 'the safety of the Colonies'.[34] This change intensified the divisions between civilians and soldiers about questions of reinforcements and military strategy. Wolseley essentially equated Army reform with Army increase.[35] In February and July 1896 he drew Lansdowne's attention to reinforcing the garrisons in South Africa. Lansdowne was against spending more until a need was demonstrated, and he saw no need yet.[36] Salisbury agreed, suggesting that with the present tension any troop movement would be taken as hostile to the Boers and 'If the Jingo party in the Transvaal contrived some act of aggression it would generally be said that our agitating policy had driven them into it.'[37]

Meanwhile, Lansdowne recognised the need to increase the home army and fix the Cardwell system, accepted by 'successive governments',[38] which was based on the principle that each double-battalion regiment would always have one battalion abroad and another at home to support it. With the growing Empire, that equilibrium had not been maintained since 1872, and no government had done anything about it.[39] Lansdowne now aimed to redress the imbalance. Wolseley, in suggesting reinforcing South Africa, also proposed using the Guards as a means of balancing the infantry or 'line', which was split between seventy-five battalions abroad and sixty-five at home. Lansdowne approved: sending the Guards battalions abroad was cheaper than raising new line battalions and, by bringing the Guards into the system and making them into a kind of infantry of the line, they would be better utilised and Guardsmen would see overseas duty.[40] Most of the service parliamentarians accepted the proposal, although a concern was voiced that they were about to alter the conditions of a 'Guardsman's amusement'.[41] The critics tried to stop it, but the Queen, although she made some enquiries, accepted the proposal,[42] and the Duke of Cambridge and some senior ex-Guardsmen supported it. In February 1897, with this backing, Lansdowne and Brodrick got the measure through Parliament. By this means, Lansdowne enabled three line battalions to return to Britain, which allowed three others abroad to have a home battalion to support them. To establish parity, the Cameron Highlanders would be given a second battalion, the 142 infantry regiments thus forming 71 linked battalions.

As Lansdowne was proposing a role for the Guards in the Mediterranean, tensions in South Africa escalated. Fearing another attempt to subvert the Transvaal, the Volksraad (the Transvaal parliament) legislated against publications that endangered the peace, and introduced an Aliens Expulsion Act and Aliens Immigration Act.[43] On 8 April 1897 Lansdowne, Chamberlain, Balfour, Goschen and Hicks Beach met to discuss the South African situation; Salisbury was absent owing to illness, which began to happen increasingly often. Chamberlain advised that the small Cape garrison and the loyal colonists' lack of confidence in British action made his position weak. Urging reinforcements of 3,500 men, he concluded, if 'they see we are in earnest. They will give way as they have always done.'[44] Lansdowne believed they should wait and then send an ultimatum followed by an overwhelming force when the time came.[45] He was outnumbered. Hicks Beach thought a force should be sent for political reasons alone; Balfour and Goschen agreed.[46]

The soldiers were equally divided. Wolseley agreed with Chamberlain; Buller and Wood were with Lansdowne. After further discussion, on 12 April Lansdowne proposed sending 'three battalions of field artillery and another battalion of infantry. The field artillery without loss of time'[47] and 'Rather than send troops to the Northern Frontier of the Cape, they should strengthen the garrison of Natal and occupy in force Laing's Nek.'[48] His colleagues approved. It was not only economical, but avoided crossing the Orange Free State. Salisbury valued the Laing's

Nek plan 'both for its intrinsic merits and for its effect upon English opinion. It is essentially and on the face of it a defensive measure. It is the natural reply to the excessive armaments of the Boers and implies no aggressive tendencies whatsoever.'[49] At the same time the government started diplomatic moves to avert the growing crisis. Alfred Milner was sent to South Africa to replace Hercules Robinson (Lord Rosemead), who was suffering from dropsy, and a British naval force was dispatched for Delagoa Bay (present-day Maputo Bay). In light of this, the Transvaal revoked the Immigration Act on 6 May and amended the Expulsion Act on 14 July to allow an appeal to the courts.[50]

With the crisis averted, Lansdowne's political position was strengthened. In June the reinforcements reached South Africa; the force in Natal was increased by 2,460 to 4,347 men and in the Cape by 279 to 3,807 men, bringing the total in South Africa to 8,154 men. Although the effect was positive and did not trigger a hostile reaction from the Transvaal, Milner believed the Cape garrison should be nearer 10,000,[51] as did Wolseley and Ardagh. But Lansdowne differed, telling the cabinet, 'the responsibility of the Imperial Government should be limited to the defensive requirements of the naval stations and that Imperial troops should not be called upon for the defence of colonial land frontiers'.[52] Privately he told Hicks Beach that the South Africans were not doing enough for their own security. He doubted they ever would while they had a large British garrison.[53]

Shortly before Lansdowne set out his position on South Africa, Wolseley returned to work after nine months' absence due to jaundice, although his memory and ability to recognise people were impaired.[54] During his absence the readiness of the British army was questioned. In May a memorandum by the sixty-five service MPs noted that the existing system, although they did not wish to change it, had reached its 'full development' and was unsatisfactory.[55] To the military press, 'the whole subject bristles with difficulties in a country where enlistment is voluntary and in which general prosperity is diametrically opposed to recruiting'.[56] Lansdowne knew that the quality of recruits was unsatisfactory,[57] but 'although many specials [immature youths below the required physical standard] were enlisted most reached the standard within a few months'.[58] Wolseley and the Army Board wanted to offer a significant increase in pay. Lansdowne disagreed. In September Wolseley publicly announced 'our military machinery is overstrained and is out of gear' and 'no longer able to meet effectively the demands now made upon it'.[59]

As public opinion digested Wolseley's comments, Brodrick wrote to Lansdowne with an idea: 'to put a certain number of facts before the public as a grave problem for the government and the country to discuss.

This will rouse people and get the mind of the Cabinet into a channel which will prepare them for any proposal you may make.'[60] Brodrick outlined these 'facts' at Guildford on 13 October. Echoing Wolseley, he described the incessant calls on the Army: 50,000 men on the Indian frontier, two battalions in Crete, two battalions and artillery in South Africa and troops in Egypt; the Cardwell system of linked battalions was unhinged.[61] As public concern increased, the Queen noted that the Army was in a bad state.[62] Seizing the opportunity, Arnold-Forster attacked the War Office just as the Army Board and cabinet were discussing the Army estimates. In seven letters, he set out to show that organisation of the Army was against common sense: 'The system has broken down at every point, the linked battalions do not perform their mutual offices, the depôts do not fill up their gaps, the required recruits are not forthcoming, those who are obtained are not of the right stamp or quality.'[63] His case was that 'the Army system has broken down'.[64] Initially, Lansdowne did not refute this, possibly because Roberts informed him 'that although Mr Arnold-Forster's facts and figures in his letters to *The Times* may not be strictly accurate in all their details, his statements are substantially correct. It will be difficult to reply to his indictment.'[65]

After Arnold-Forster's third letter, Lansdowne wrote to Haliburton, by then retired from the War Office, that 'Arnold-Forster's "facts" are so damaging that it will scarcely do to leave them unchallenged'.[66] He suggested that Haliburton take up the 'cudgels for us' and write to *The Times*, although not too uncompromisingly.[67] Not since the Crimean War had the public shown such anxiety about the Army not being what it ought to be. As events developed, Lansdowne used the situation and public anxiety as negotiating tools in cabinet to obtain new measures, set out in his 'Outlines of Army Proposals'.[68] Framed in consultation with the senior officers, this supported Wolseley's view that numerical increase was 'urgently, I may say imperatively necessary'.[69] He proposed adding ten battalions to the line; employing army reservists for 'little wars'; creating four battalions per infantry regiment, adding eighty men per infantry home army battalion, bringing each battalion up to 800; paying the infantry a clear 1s. as soon as they were of full age and efficient (as immature youths they would receive 9d.); ending the grocery stoppage for tea, sugar, milk, vegetables and the like, which cost an infantry soldier 3d. a day; and reducing their deferred pay on leaving the Colours. He also proposed allowing men to enlist in a regiment for three years, with the choice of then entering the Militia for a few years before passing into the Reserve or continuing with the Colours for a further nine years. The existing short service term was seven years with the Colours and five with the Reserve. In the Artillery he proposed longer service for the Garrison branch and increasing the Field branch by fifteen batteries.

Among the Auxiliary army he proposed bringing the Militia into closer connection with the line. The Militia would get more commissions; and officers in the line would be given inducements to serve in the Militia. If this was successful it would be extended to the Volunteers.[70]

On 9 December, while the cabinet considered his proposals, Lansdowne spoke in Edinburgh and set out the government's military policy. In an impassioned speech, while implying they had more to do, he explained what had been achieved: three new battalions, two new colonial battalions, more artillery, improved barracks, better defences and new training grounds on Salisbury Plain. Conscription had become a popular topic, he noted, and it might have to come, but he felt that 'the instincts of our countrymen are too strongly opposed to it'.[71]

The Queen was 'quite pleased' at the way Lansdowne 'laid the case before the country'.[72] *The Times* noted: 'Our correspondent "Reform" agrees with us in regarding Lord Lansdowne's speech as the most hopeful symptom that has yet appeared of a disposition in high quarters to look military facts in the face and shows that the Secretary of State for War is not yet dominated by the habit of mechanically repeating machine made opinions which is so painfully conspicuous in the letters of Sir Arthur Haliburton.'[73]

While the proposals were acceptable to the press, they met resistance in cabinet. Chamberlain, who disliked the linked battalions, was against adding ten new infantry battalions. He was in favour '(1) Of any increase in the artillery believing the Army should be especially strong in that arm. (2) Any expedients to improve the terms of the services and to secure a better class of recruits. (3) Of doing all necessary to make the Militia and Volunteers a really effective force. In my judgement Lansdowne's scheme does not do any of these things.'[74] He made no attempt to conceal his 'utter disbelief' in the policy which he described as 'an attempt to prop up a rickety and useless system'.[75] Lord James of Hereford, Walter Long, Aretas Akers-Douglas, Charles Ritchie and others expressed similar views.[76] Hamilton, who believed it impossible to set up any better system than what they had, felt Lansdowne's proposals would 'not altogether meet the difficulties'.[77] Hicks Beach would not defend them; Salisbury was 'frankly incredulous' and unwilling to speak up in debates.[78] Lansdowne believed the cabinet could demolish their critics who 'were clamouring for the abandonment of the present system', but 'if others find out that we are half hearted and they will find it out, the task is hopeless'.[79] Rather than raise unnecessary difficulties, he offered to resign. Salisbury refused the offer: 'I do not think you need anticipate any adverse vote on any essential portion. Some modification of figures may become necessary, but on them Governments have always to discuss and, if possible, to compromise.'[80] In the compromise, the

Treasury sanctioned six of Lansdowne's ten battalions and £115,000 less than he had requested for abolishing the grocery stoppage, a sum which Wolseley received with 'very great satisfaction'.[81]

By listening to his critics and adapting, Lansdowne conciliated many of their complaints. Dilke believed 'if honestly worked out and not spoiled by the War Office "Jacobins" the three year enlistment may perhaps lead to the right modifications of the system';[82] even Arnold-Forster recognised that he 'got a series of promises' from Lansdowne.[83] Although he was not sure they would all be accomplished, that there would be an attempt to carry them out was vouched for by the fact they were made by Lansdowne. However, he still wanted a promise to reform the War Office and criticised continuance of the linked battalions.[84] In a letter to Lansdowne the service parliamentarians accepted 'with satisfaction' his proposals while requesting greater attention to regimental *esprit de corps* and the 'reorganisation of all the land forces of the Empire with a view to their effective preparation for war'.[85]

Lansdowne's cabinet proposals also included decentralisation to improve efficiency and lessen bureaucracy, and he established a committee under Brodrick to report on this. Their report in March 1898 suggested that much of the business in the War Office, or with or between the districts, should be oral, general officers should have greater financial responsibility and there should be closer association between the military and civil departments. However, delegating financial responsibility was impossible 'unless the Treasury will consent to dispense with control over small matters of expenditure'.[86] Lansdowne 'in the main'[87] approved, although he believed they could simplify regulations even more 'if we had had leisure to take up such subjects'.[88] Arnold-Forster believed it did not go far enough and was 'a condemnation of the men who make it and the processes they have been working'.[89] The report raised few objections from service parliamentarians or the Liberal opposition. The military press remarked it had 'entirely missed its purpose' and the recommendations 'are for the most part so crude as to be unworkable'.[90]

Lansdowne moved quickly to implement his measures in late 1898. One obvious benefit he could demonstrate was bringing the Auxiliaries and Regular Army together in training and manoeuvres.[91] His 1897 Manoeuvres Bill balanced 'military considerations' and 'the interests of the public'[92] and he obtained funds to purchase 60 square miles of Salisbury Plain for use as a manoeuvring ground[93] and camp, and later permanent quarters.[94] He took a close interest in ensuring the land purchases caused minimal disturbance to farmers, but 'people will be disappointed if there are no manoeuvres in 1898 and I should like to have them on a grand scale. I have often wished that we could have combined Naval and Military manoeuvres – the landing of the Army corps in

Bantry Bay or something of that sort.'[95] In September manoeuvres were held in front of 80,000 spectators; 'the troops have come in for a good deal of praise and even *The Times* civil. But amongst the leaders of the others there has been flying about much envy, hatred, malice.'[96] Indeed, 'I have seen it said that these manoeuvres which cost the country something like £150,000 were a great waste of public money. I incline to the view ... that the manoeuvres would have been cheap at any price. It is at any rate, the first time in the history of this country that 50,000 men have taken the field in peace time.'[97]

Lansdowne saw great value in education for soldiers of all ranks, particularly for 'a private soldier as a means of fitting him for civil employment at the conclusion of his Army career'.[98] With Wolseley's help, military education was reorganised and the Staff College encouraged. Lansdowne also reorganised the nursing and medical branches. Inspired by Florence Nightingale, with whom he still corresponded, he amalgamated various nursing societies as support units in time of war. Aiming to popularise them, he amalgamated the Army Medical Staff and Medical Staff Corps and, with the Queen's consent, styled it the Royal Army Medical Corps.[99]

Lansdowne acted on Wolseley's suggestions for the education and medical departments, but not Wolseley's schemes for reinforcing South Africa. Wolseley threatened Lansdowne that 'sooner or later we shall have a violent explosion there. Are you prepared for it? Any student at the Staff College would say "No" to such a question', but 'There is no good reason that I know of why we should not be thoroughly prepared for it.'[100] He noted, 'As a soldier, I know what the Army wants. Lord L. does not and besides political exigencies influence him more than any Army wants even if he could appreciate what they are.'[101] Interestingly, in his evidence to the Royal Commission, Lansdowne stated that in the years between the Jameson Raid and 'the War' he never received from his military advisers any joint remonstrance for not strengthening the garrisons in South Africa.[102] Evidently, Wolseley criticised Lansdowne in private but not in public.

In fact, Lansdowne knew exactly what the Army wanted. With the Colonial Office he informed Hicks Beach that the troops sent out in 1897 were without transport and 'are now "immobile" therefore almost useless, either for offense or defence'.[103] Estimating transport would cost £60,000,[104] they should move as soon as possible and get the horses replaced or 'we might get into a serious mess there'.[105] When General William Goodenough, General Officer Commanding (GOC) in South Africa, fell ill, Lansdowne immediately replaced him with Sir William Butler, a member of Wolseley's 'ring', with instructions to report on the defence problem. Lansdowne foresaw the danger that in the event of further hostilities Britain would be outnumbered during the four to six weeks that would elapse before reinforcements could reach South Africa.[106]

Meanwhile, events in the Sudan raised the Army's profile. On 2 September 1898 the Khalifa and his 60,000 Dervishes were defeated at Omdurman, avenging the death of Gordon of Khartoum. Lansdowne found the news a great relief. He telegraphed Queen Victoria to suggest a GCB for Herbert Kitchener, Sirdar (Commander-in-Chief) of the Egyptian army.[107] In November, after the French withdrawal, he described the reconquest of the Sudan as the 'removal of a blot from our escutcheon and the tardy discharge of a national obligation' since General Gordon's death.[108] The war in the Sudan was a Foreign Office war, requiring little from the War Office beyond the dispatch of troops. That the War Office often played a minor role in managing overseas actions against foreign powers, played into the lack of thinking, resources and preparation given to such matters. However, during Lansdowne's term of office the once powerful Manchu, Ottoman and Persian empires were all in decay and the difficulty that this created for Britain was immense. Lansdowne could not avoid getting embroiled in overseas disputes.

In 1898, with threats to the Empire and an ill-equipped home army, Lansdowne saw the need to rearm soldiers with improved machine guns, breech-loading rifles and smaller-calibre ammunition.[109] Lansdowne was also responsible for arming coaling stations and fortresses. The War Office produced guns, carriages and ammunition at Woolwich Arsenal, explosives at Waltham Abbey and small arms at Enfield and Sparkbrook, but it also depended on munitions contractors. The Royal Ordnance Factories at Woolwich were in a 'muddle' when Lansdowne started at the War Office.[110] Blamed for 'delay, extravagance, and unreliability' they could not compete with the trade.[111] Friction and confusion were rife. Change was slow. Owing to financial considerations it was not until March 1898 that Lansdowne began to reorganise the factories and the Ordnance Department.[112] Frederick Donaldson, a civilian with a background in mechanical engineering, was appointed Deputy Director-General of the Ordnance Factories and the separate design branches were abolished.[113] The press criticised the exclusion of a military officer as 'not only a reflection but a direct injustice to the service'.[114] For James Edwards MP, the 'transference of the Ordnance Factories from the military to the civil side of the War Office is the gradual divorce of these factories from the Army'.[115] The death in December of William Anderson, the Director-General, gave Lansdowne an opportunity to mollify his critics. With Brodrick's advice, he decided to appoint a military man.[116] He also decided to reduce the Financial Secretary's responsibility for factories to that of finance alone. Previously the Director-General and his deputy were responsible to the Financial Secretary, and through him to the Secretary of State. Lansdowne thought this change would lighten the heavy workload of the Financial Secretary, but possibly he did not think highly of Powell Williams.

As part of Lansdowne's reorganisation, the Inspector-General of Ordnance became Director-General of Ordnance.[117] Edwin Markham, the Inspector-General, was 'weak'[118] and had not been a success,[119] and Lansdowne decided to replace him by Henry Brackenbury, who had been Military Member on the Viceroy's Council and was 'head and shoulders above all competitors'.[120] Brackenbury insisted that the Ordnance Factories be placed under his control. He told Lansdowne, 'Believe me there is no rest or peace for you outside putting the DGOF under the IGO.'[121]

Powell Williams, fearing it would discriminate against the trade, was strongly opposed to making the same officer responsible for manufacture and inspection. He also thought the factories should remain run by civilians, not military officers.[122] In cabinet, Hicks Beach and Chamberlain shared his views. The Chancellor opposed it for its implied sleight on civil control of military expenditure and Chamberlain was against weakening a colleague's responsibility. In defence of Powell Williams he remarked that Lansdowne's scheme was 'most mischievous' and Lansdowne was 'Brackenburyridden'.[123] Brodrick, who as a former Financial Secretary understood the system, was also against.[124] He believed that 'this change, if made, will content a very small number of military members of Parliament, who have worked up "The Times" – but it will be directly in face of experience, and of the decision of the cabinet in 1888, when the previous difficulties were fresh in mind'.[125] Devonshire, who had recommended such a change in the Hartington Commission report, could not see why, with 'good will and a desire to avoid difficulties, it should not succeed'.[126] Goschen also agreed. Salisbury shared this view but suggested the Defence Committee should investigate and decide.

Lansdowne defended the transfer: he was following the advice of four commissions[127] that had reviewed the question; financial control would remain with the Financial Secretary but the Director-General Ordnance Factories would draft proposals and calculations.[128] He disagreed that military control would discriminate against the trade. The committee – Devonshire, Lansdowne, Goschen and Hicks Beach – reported in favour of the proposal.[129] Brackenbury was officially appointed Director-General Ordnance in January 1899 and the following month Colonel Edmond Bainbridge became Chief Superintendent Ordnance Factories.

19

ORIGINS OF THE WAR
IN SOUTH AFRICA

IN EARLY 1896, William Waldorf Astor ended his six year tenancy of Lansdowne House. The Lansdownes returned to their London residence during the week, spending weekends at Bowood and one month each year visiting their Scottish properties, which were otherwise let out. The family continued to make annual visits to Ireland, where Lansdowne could genuinely relax. In 1898 William Rochfort was appointed head Irish agent to replace 'Towny' Trench. Apart from managing his estates, Lansdowne had many other duties. As a trustee of the National Gallery, in summer 1897 he negotiated for the nation the acquisition and housing of the Wallace collection at Hertford House.[1]

Bertie, his younger daughter, married Henry de la Poer Beresford, 6th Marquess of Waterford on 16 October 1897 at St George's, Hanover Square. He showed more interest in sport than politics, being a 'capital master of hounds, keen climber, fine polo player'[2] and ardent traveller. Within two years Bertie had two daughters. Evie and Victor Cavendish also had three children during this period. The Lansdownes loved their grandchildren. In 1895 Kerry, Lansdowne's elder son, joined the Grenadier Guards; in 1899 he was sent to South Africa. Lansdowne's other son, Charlie, received a commission in the Royals (Dragoons) and was with Roberts' staff in Ireland from 1898 until the Royals too went to South Africa.[3] Lansdowne's sister Emily and her husband Everard Digby and their three children continued to live at Buckshaw House, near Yeovil. Edmond Fitzmaurice, Lansdowne's brother, became Chairman of Wiltshire County Council in 1896 and Liberal MP for Cricklade in the 1898 by-election.

Lansdowne's health was largely good, apart from a foot operation in July 1897 and a fever in late 1898. Maud was a political hostess with grace and style. During the Diamond Jubilee celebrations, Lansdowne House hosted a number of parties, including one for Indian military officers.[4] On 25 June 1897 the Lansdownes entertained the Prince and Princess of Wales and foreign envoys. The Prince wrote, 'We dined at Lansdowne House at 8.30. A very large dinner, then went onto a ball at Grosvenor House, beautifully done.'[5] Lansdowne was made a patron and life member of the Army and Navy Veterans' Society and vice patron of the Royal United Services Institute.[6]

During 1899 relations with the South Africans worsened. On 8 June, three days after the collapse of the Bloemfontein Conference, Wolseley advised Lansdowne to mobilise 'at once on Salisbury Plain under the general who it is intended should command in South Africa in the event of war one of our three Army Corps as it might probably wake up the Transvaal to the fact that England was at last serious and by doing so prevent war altogether'. Lansdowne replied, 'there is now I think a general agreement that if there is to be a serious demonstration it should take a different shape. The proposal need not be further pursued.'[7] The 'different shape' that Lansdowne envisaged was conditioned by the need for public opinion to support a war in South Africa. As he later told the Royal Commission, 'I doubt extremely whether if we had gone, as I conceived prematurely, to Parliament in the month of June 1899, and asked for a large war expenditure, we should have got it'[8] – and, even if they had got it, it would have enabled their enemies to claim Britain provoked the war.[9]

In August, in consultation with Wolseley, he summoned Buller from Aldershot to inform him that if there was war in South Africa he would command. Buller hesitated, telling Lansdowne that he had never held independent command and had always considered himself as a better second in command in anything complex.[10] Eventually he accepted the offer. In mid-August, while the government maintained pressure on the Transvaal and brought public opinion along with them, Lansdowne produced a memorandum detailing the time it would take to mobilise and place an army in the field on the outbreak of war. He estimated it would take three or four months if nearly £1 million-worth of mules, carts and clothing was ordered immediately.[11] It was his view that 'I placed the Cabinet in full possession of the problem which lay before us. I gave them this "timetable" so that they might know what risk was incurred by the postponement of the expenditure, but I take my full share of the responsibility of the Cabinet for not having incurred that expenditure at the time.'[12] He accepted it was only political considerations that delayed those preparations being made.

Lansdowne's memorandum was a surprise to the cabinet. The implication of unpreparedness angered them. Salisbury told Chamberlain that he had never doubted the 'futility' of the War Office but he thought it 'uncivil' to criticise it just then. Recognising the 'scandal which will certainly be created by the conditions of our military preparedness', he held they should not spend any more money until it was certain that 'we are going to war'.[13] Chamberlain was alarmed by the timescale envisaged: the War Office 'are hopeless and it will be a mercy if they do not land us in a catastrophe'.[14] Goschen thought the four-month delay was preposterous.[15] He and Balfour urged Hicks Beach to sanction the money required, but no one else in the cabinet did. The Chancellor thought Britain 'may have to prepare for the worst',[16] but he was strongly opposed to further expenditure and no decision was taken.

After the cabinet meeting, Lansdowne went to Ireland while others went to Scotland for grouse or golf, believing war was improbable. During this break, Wolseley minuted Lansdowne, detailing Milner's anxiety about the need to send out 10,000 men.[17] Lansdowne informed his cabinet colleagues, but thought Wolseley had underrated the British force already in Natal.[18] His concern was that Milner, feeling the prolonged tension, might force war on the British;[19] they should avoid 'hurrying the pace and forcing on hostilities'.[20]

In early September, after the Transvaal government again rejected Britain's suzerainty of the Transvaal and any attempt for Kruger to meet Milner, Lansdowne realised war was imminent:[21] 'things would come to a head before we are many days or hours older and I shall be glad when our suspense is terminated'.[22] Whereas the soldiers previously found the politicians dilatory, they now complained they were moving too fast. On 5 September Buller was encouraged by Salisbury's private secretary, Schomberg 'Pom' McDonnell, whose views about Lansdowne matched his own, to go behind Lansdowne's back and give Salisbury a memorandum 'to startle the Cabinet'.[23] Buller believed that there must come a point when the military and diplomatic or political forces were brought into line. Before the diplomats presented an ultimatum, the military should be ready to enforce it.[24] Buller complained that he and his military colleagues at the War Office had no idea how matters were proceeding, had not been consulted and did not know how fast diplomacy was moving.

Wolseley echoed Buller's concerns, telling Lansdowne that the 'first intimation I have had that our negotiations with the Transvaal have reached an acute stage has come to me from Sir Redvers Buller. We have lost time. We have committed one of the gravest blunders in war, namely, we have given to our enemy the initiative. The government are acting without the complete knowledge of what the military can do while the military authorities on their side are equally without full knowledge of what the government expects them to do.'[25] While

1 Bowood House by B.P. Kennedy, 1851

2 Clan aged 18

3 Henry Thomas Petty-Fitzmaurice, 4th Marquess of Lansdowne, who died when Clan was 21

4 Emily Jane Mercer Elphinstone Petty-Fitzmaurice,
4th Marchioness of Lansdowne, aged 44

5 Lord Rosebery and Clan while at Oxford

6 (left to right): Charles, Comte de Flahaut, Georgiana de Flahaut, 4th Marchioness of Lansdowne and
Lady Emily Petty-Fitzmaurice (seated), Clan, Lady William Osborne, 4th Marquess of Lansdowne (seated),
Lord Edmond Petty-Fitzmaurice (standing) Margaret Mercer Elphinstone, Comtesse de Flahaut, 1865

7 Lansdowne and Maud Evelyn Petty-Fitzmaurice, 5th Marchioness of Lansdowne at Bowood, 1870

8 Lansdowne as Under-Secretary of State for War aged 27

9 Lady Evelyn Emily Mary Petty-Fitzmaurice (Evie), aged 4

10 Lord Charles George Francis Petty-Fitzmaurice (Charlie) aged 2½, Lord Henry William Edmund Petty-Fitzmaurice (Kerry) aged 4½

11 Envelope with Lansdowne's sketch on the occasion of his mother becoming 8th Baroness Nairne, 1874

12 Lansdowne, Kerry and Charlie, 1880

13 Maud Lansdowne aged 29

14 Evie and Lansdowne, 1880

15 Lady Maud, Beatrix Frances Petty-Fitzmaurice (Bertie), Victoria West (daughter to the British Ambassador to the US) at Rideau Hall, Ottawa, 1884

16 Lansdowne and Maud with their four children before their departure for Canada in October 1883. They are surrounded by some of Maud's family including the Duke and Duchess of Abercorn, The Marquess of Hamilton, Lord George Hamilton, Lord Ernest Hamilton, Lord Frederick Hamilton, Lord Claud Hamilton, Albertha, Marchioness of Blandford,

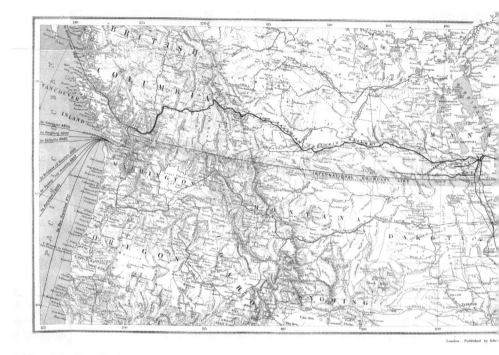

17 Map of the Canadian Pacific Railway by Edward Stanford

18 Lansdowne with Evie, friends and staff, Canada, 1885

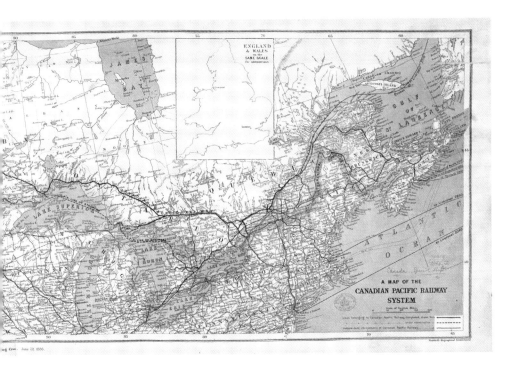

19 Rideau Hall, Ottawa, 1885

20 Bertie aged 8

21 Maud, Kerry and Charlie, Ottawa

22 Lansdowne and Charlie, Ottawa

23 Lansdowne in the uniform of the Lansdowne
    Toboggan Club, Ottawa

24 Maud having her hair cut by the butler (Hillier), New Derreen, 1886

25 Lansdowne and Maud with their children,
Meikleour, 1885

26 Cartoon presented to Lansdowne on his departure
from Canada, June 1888

27 Lansdowne and Maud with their children and staff on board P&O steamer *Sutlej*, enroute
to India, November 1888

28 Government House, Calcutta, 1890

29 Viceregal Lodge, Simla

30 Sitting room at Viceregal Lodge, Simla

31 Viceregal Hunt, Kuch Behar, 1890

32 Viceregal lunch party under a banyan tree, Barrackpore, 1890

33 Lansdowne and Maud with their staff at a picnic, Simla, 1891

34 Viceregal Party, Gwalior, 1891

AFGHANISTAN

BALUCHISTAN

KASHMIR

PUNJAB

SIND

RAJPUTANA

BAHAWALPUR

NORTH WEST PROVS. AND OUDH

CENTRAL INDIA

BERAR

CENTRAL PROVINCES

HAIDARABAD

MYSORE

MADRAS

ARABIAN SEA

Laccadive Islands

CEYLON

INDIAN

Herat • Kabul • Peshawar • Srinagar • Jammu • Lahore • Amritsar • Multan • Bahawalpur • Delhi • Moradabad • Bareilly • Kandahar • Khelat • Karachi • Haidarabad • Jodhpur • Ajmere • Jaipur • Agra • Gwalior • Ahmadabad • Baroda • Indore • Bhopal • Jabalpur • Nagpur • Amraoti • Surat • Bombay • Poona • Ratnagiri • Kolhapur • Goa • Haidarabad • Secunderabad • Bangalore • Mysore • Mangalore • Calicut • Cochin • Trichinopoly • Madura • Trivandrum • Madras • Pondicherri • Cuddalore • Salem • Trincomali • Colombo • Kandy • Galle • Dondra Head • Cape Comorin

Gulf of Cambay • Gulf of Cutch • Palk Strait • Gulf of Manar • Coromandel Coast • Malabar Coast

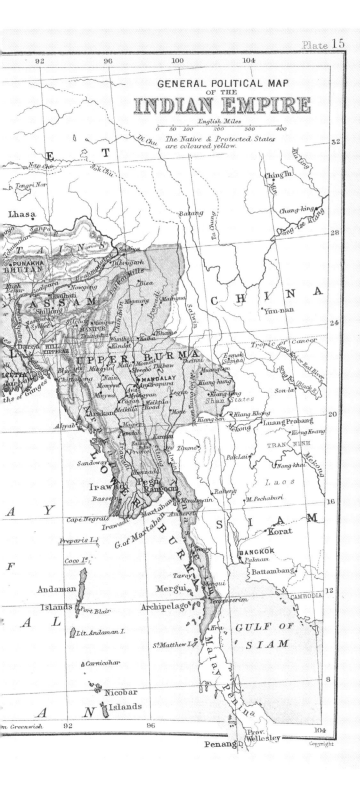

35 Constable's general political map of India, 1894

36 Lansdowne in Durbar with Maharaja Sir Pratap
Singh of Jammu and Kashmir, 1891

37 Statue of Lansdowne on the Maidan in Calcutta

38 Prince Albert, Duke of Clarence visits Calcutta, 1892

Wolseley and Buller were not *au fait* with the 'secrets of the Cabinet',[26] it is inaccurate to suggest that Lansdowne did not listen to or discuss matters with his military advisers. From his appointment in June, Buller was 'freely consulted' by Lansdowne and was given wide latitude while working at the War Office.[27]

The politicians at this stage had to deal with the situation in terms of what public opinion would stand. On 8 September the cabinet met to discuss South Africa. In light of War Office reports, Chamberlain suggested Indian forces should 'start for Natal as early as they can be moved'.[28] After the cabinet broke up, Lansdowne informed the Queen that he earnestly 'trusts that the government of the South African Republic will do nothing to precipitate hostilities. Should they do so after the arrival of these reinforcements there need be no apprehension for the safety of the Colony.'[29] To command the additional 10,000 troops and those already in Natal, Lansdowne, in consultation with Wolseley and Buller, appointed George White, the Quartermaster-General. Also on 8 September, Lansdowne had a stormy interview with Buller at the War Office.[30] He cautioned him for 'going behind his back' by writing to Salisbury and pressing for the dispatch of troops.[31] In evidence to the Royal Commission, Lansdowne stated Buller 'was perfectly aware of what was passing[;] if he was not aware it was his own fault, as he had ample opportunities of making himself aware'.[32]

Buller was still unhappy with the cabinet's decision and wanted many more troops sent to Natal. But Lansdowne did not see that the War Office could be expected to do more.[33] Furthermore, Wolseley had said he would stake his reputation that, after the reinforcements had arrived, everything south of the Biggarsberg hills would be safe. As the reinforcements left for Natal, Hamilton, the Secretary of State for India, reported to Curzon:

> The ease and rapidity with which the Indian Contingent has been told off and despatched contrast very favourably with the procrastination and want of decision of the War Office. Wolseley is quite played out; he has lost his memory, and his governing motive in arrangements for the Transvaal seems to be jealousy of the Indian establishment. Wood is half cracked and wholly deaf; White is to command in Natal, and Buller is hardly on speaking terms with the higher military authorities. The Department is a real danger to the nation, and until it is reorganised on the Admiralty system, civil and military being blended together, and working loyally together, we shall have no effective War Department. What disgusts me is the jealousy of the Indian Army, so constantly shewn ... Buller is, or rather was competent, but he lives too well, and from what I have seen of the War Office generally, I look with considerable apprehension upon the earlier

stages of any active campaign in South Africa ... Both Chamberlain and
Milner believe that, without war, no satisfactory settlement can be arrived
at. I am not certain that they are right; time is on our side, railroads are
being rapidly pushed on that will entirely circumvent the Transvaal, and
the influx of the British element must year by year increase.[34]

Was Hamilton being politely silent in not criticising Lansdowne, his
brother-in-law? He had been strongly critical of him during the Riel
affair while Lansdowne was serving as Governor-General in Canada.[35]

As the government continued to negotiate with Kruger, Lansdowne
sought cabinet authority to make immediate arrangements to collect, in
South Africa, the land transport and food supplies for an Army Corps.
This would take thirteen weeks, so it was 'really urgent'.[36] While his
proposal was discussed and agreed, Kruger's government were informed
that, unless they responded, they would receive an ultimatum. Meanwhile,
the War Office had further discussions on the line of advance in South
Africa. As in 1896, the Intelligence Department remained convinced
the Orange Free State would support the Transvaal[37] and preparations
should be based on 'the definite hypothesis of a hostile Free State'.[38]
Lansdowne informed the cabinet, noting that Buller would be able to
decide his own route to Pretoria across the Orange River.[39]

On 29 September the cabinet discussed the ultimatum to Kruger;
Chamberlain, Hicks Beach and Goschen were concerned as to how the
public would react, while Devonshire, Balfour and Lansdowne said little
except to approve the text. They agreed to continue preparations for
mobilising the Army Corps, call up the reserves and summon Parliament
for 17 October. Lansdowne, still hesitant, believed 'it may not be
desirable to call out the reserves a day sooner than is really necessary'
but soon enough for the War Office 'to equip them, perhaps to give them
a little course of musketry, to embark them, and to deliver them at their
destination by a date not later than that at which their land transport and
supplies will be ready for them in South Africa'.[40] He told Salisbury that,
if the latest date for the Queen to sign the proclamation was 7 October,
all the reserves would have joined by 21 October.[41]

At this point the Orange Free State declared an alliance with the
Transvaal and expelled British subjects; the Transvaal mobilised its
forces and adjourned the Volksraad. As the spotlight fell on the War
Office, there were signs that the principal individuals were pulling in the
same direction. On 3 October Lansdowne presented a memorandum
explaining that the War Office had decided to reach the Transvaal
via the Cape Colony and the Orange Free State. Wolseley and Buller
considered they should not reduce the strength of the Army Corps being
sent from Britain and that the force on its way from India should not

be reckoned as part of it. Lansdowne believed that the soldiers were right and that Britain would make a 'grievous mistake if, from motives of economy, we were to reduce the number of troops for which we are asked to provide'. 'We are going to fight an enemy more formidable than any whom we have encountered for many years past.'[42]

On 9 October the Transvaal government handed the British an ultimatum demanding immediate assurances by 5 p.m. on 11 October. Salisbury replied that 'the conditions demanded are such that Her Majesty's Government deem it impossible to discuss'.[43] Lansdowne congratulated Chamberlain: 'I don't think Kruger could have played your cards better than he has.'[44] Wolseley rejoiced 'beyond measure to think war must now come. Come it would most certainly sometime or other and now is best for us. Buller will, I am sure, end the war with complete success for England.'[45]

On the eve of war, four-fifths of the public rallied behind government policy; now the government needed to retain that support.[46] After the British victories at Omdurman and Fashoda, the public had no reason to suspect that a war against the Boers would be different. The opposition Liberal leaders were broadly supportive. Rosebery said, 'in the face of this attack, the nation will, I doubt not, close its ranks and relegate party controversy to a more convenient season'.[47] Campbell-Bannerman promised that his party would vote supplies and powers necessary for rapid and effective prosecution of a war rendered absolutely necessary by the Boer ultimatum and the invasion of British colonies.[48]

20

THE WAR IN
SOUTH AFRICA

HAVING SECURED SUPPORT for a war in South Africa, the government had to ensure that public approval and enthusiasm remained strong. That required a quick victory, and Lansdowne and his advisers had no doubt this was possible. George Wyndham, who had replaced Brodrick as Under-Secretary of State in October 1898, believed 'the Army is more efficient than at any time since Waterloo', a view shared by Lansdowne and Wolseley.[1] Such complacency was widespread; as one general said, 'we were all rather afraid the war might be over before we arrived in November'.[2] In the two weeks following the Royal Proclamation on 7 October, the reserves were mobilised and Lansdowne's adaptation of Cardwell was put through its first test in time of war. Doubting 'whether they will be as strong as we expected',[3] he was proved wrong by a 98 per cent return rate among reservists.[4] The need to send infantry to South Africa temporarily impaired normal training for home defence and overseas duties, so the War Office decided to mobilise some Militia infantry battalions.[5] Just as the successful call-up of the reserves silenced many critics of the War Office, so too did the partial embodiment of the Militia.

All this added enormously to military expenditure, and the cost of mobilisation to the end of 31 March 1900 was estimated at £11 million. Faced with the possibility of having to impose new taxes, Hicks Beach at first threatened to resign. However, when Parliament met on 17 October the House of Commons voted £10 million for the Army.

With funds secured, the whole of one Army Corps, except one cavalry regiment, roughly 41,000 soldiers, including Lansdowne's sons, began to embark.[6] The mobilisation was generally a success.[7] However, embarkations continued. Lansdowne observed that he was 'spending money at an appalling rate but I believe nothing to be more costly in the end than an unnecessary prolongation of war'.[8] To the War Office and the Admiralty, Buller's constant demands for more men during the next few months came as a surprise; some doubted that he even knew why he needed them. Between October 1899 and February 1900 Wolseley estimated 114,000 Regular troops and 28,800 Auxiliaries and colonials embarked for South Africa, the largest Army that had ever left Britain.[9] The mobilisation succeeded because of efficient cooperation with the Admiralty but also because of the Treasury's willingness to provide funds. After Hicks Beach's initial reluctance and then his belief that Lansdowne should limit himself to £9 million,[10] he raised no significant further objections.

Lansdowne's critics had few reasons for complaint. Campbell-Bannerman, who had some initial reservations about the system Lansdowne adopted, in particular the Army Board, admitted 'it has completely fulfilled the purpose for which it was created'.[11] Dilke criticised the cost of mobilisation and questioned the need for a home Army, but had not the 'slightest doubt' of the reserves answering the call, and embodying the Militia was the 'proper step'.[12] Service parliamentarians had no objections and Frederick Rasch commented that the 'War Office have disappointed the fondest hopes of their bitterest enemies.'[13]

In South Africa, the Army's performance was unimpressive. By the time Buller arrived on 30 October, White was trapped in Ladysmith, Cecil Rhodes and Colonel Robert Kekewich were surrounded at Kimberley, and Robert Baden-Powell was cut off at Mafeking. Buller regarded the situation as one of extreme gravity.[14] Lansdowne, who had known White since India, was glad Buller did not press for his dismissal and was confident White would hold out, although in England there was a great desire 'to get the knife into him'.[15] Buller reported 'we are still hanging on by our eyelids'.[16] Having previously agreed with the War Office to take the Orange Free State line of advance to Pretoria, he now decided to split his Army Corps into three: one army to relieve Kimberley, another to secure the Northern Cape, while he himself would proceed to Ladysmith. Lansdowne was 'not astonished' that Buller altered his plans, but he was concerned at Buller's choice of generals.

The defeat of all three armies within five days shocked the British authorities and the public. The Black Week, so called by H.H. Asquith, also shattered Britain's complacency about quick victory. When Buller told Lansdowne on 15 December that he was not strong enough to relieve Ladysmith and ought to let it go,[17] Lansdowne reacted unfavourably. Unable to ignore these grave misfortunes,[18] he warned Buller that the government would regard abandoning White's force and the consequent surrender of Ladysmith as a major national disaster.[19]

By the end of December there was a strong reaction of public disgust with the War Ministry's want of (military) foresight and much criticism of Lansdowne.[20] He and Balfour, who had joined him at the War Office the previous month, became bywords for weakness and Salisbury was described as a man of the past.[21] Most of the opposition maintained their broadly non-partisan attitude, but the civilian reformers held Lansdowne responsible for the defeats. Wilkinson accused him of personality flaws and of playing with national affairs.[22]

These personal attacks were nothing compared to those in some sections of the press. Unlike previous wars, 'the War' attracted a mass readership. Editors had expected prompt and decisive victory and dispatched numerous war correspondents, including Arthur Conan Doyle, Leo Amery and Winston Churchill. Much press reporting from the front was unreliable[23] and Lansdowne quickly made arrangements for strict censorship of telegrams from South Africa.[24] His unpopularity with editors made him an easy target for blame for the military blunders in South Africa. *The Spectator* suggested that 'a great nobleman is not the person to whom the country can look for a really thorough and merciless exposure of the causes of our present inefficiency'.[25] Black Week did not faze Queen Victoria: 'there is no one depressed in this house. We are not interested in the possibilities of defeat, they do not exist.'[26]

In the immediate aftermath of Black Week, Lansdowne made no public defence of the War Office or himself. It was Balfour who first denied War Office responsibility, in three speeches in early January 1900. Wolseley blamed Lansdowne for not listening to him,[27] and for thinking that he could do everything without Wolseley's help.[28] He resented having no part in 'the War' and 'that an older man than I has been allowed to command'.[29]

The setbacks of Black Week convinced Lansdowne that Buller should be replaced. His view was strengthened by the fact he could replace him with Roberts, who was willing to go to South Africa: 'my want of knowledge of the country would be made up by the many good men well acquainted with it whom I should have to assist me'.[30] In Roberts' opinion, Buller's mistakes made it clear that British strategy and tactics were both at fault, 'and that unless change is made at once our Army will be frittered away and we shall have to make ignominious peace'.[31] Lansdowne was persuaded that Roberts, assisted by Kitchener, should take command in South Africa. On 15 December he summoned Balfour from a dinner party to discuss the situation and spoke in favour of a Roberts–Kitchener combination. Balfour agreed that Buller should be replaced. Secrecy was essential as Kitchener was not popular with Wolseley and his 'ring'.[32] Although Salisbury was initially doubtful, the proposal to send Kitchener reconciled him. On the evening of

16 December the Cabinet Defence Committee confirmed that Buller must resign his command to Roberts.[33] Next day, Lansdowne met Roberts alone to discuss his appointment. Roberts, whose son died that very day while fighting in South Africa, accepted, stating that Kitchener's assistance was essential to him.[34]

Although the decision had already been taken, neither Queen Victoria nor Wolseley was aware of it.[35] When Wolseley heard, he was 'dumbfounded'. He told Lansdowne that Buller would rather resign than suffer such a humiliation and, even if Buller had made mistakes, he was a better man than Roberts. Queen Victoria intimated her astonishment through Arthur Bigge, her private secretary, a close friend of Buller's. 'Her Majesty was deeply aggrieved at the cabinet's behaviour. For not telling her of the decision to appoint Roberts, not seeking her advice, not consulting her before cabling Buller, and failing to consult Wolseley.'[36] Lansdowne's oversight occurred, it was later reported, because he contented himself with telling 'Bigge who was in London the whole story, and asking him to convey it to Her Majesty'.[37]

The Queen expected Roberts' former post of Commander-in-Chief in Ireland would go to her son, the Duke of Connaught. He himself wished to serve in South Africa, but was persuaded by the Queen, after she had consulted with Roberts and Lansdowne, to accept the position in Ireland. On 18 December Lansdowne telegraphed Buller to tell him of Roberts' 'appointment as Commander-in-Chief South Africa, his Chief of Staff being Lord Kitchener'.[38] Buller was as surprised as the Queen had been, remarking 'that it read like one to a girl who was being put in charge of a strict governess'.[39]

While Lansdowne's telegram upset Buller, so Roberts' appointment grated on Wolseley, who gradually lost interest in his work. After producing a memorandum on 29 December 1899 on the possibility of an invasion by France and measures to counter that,[40] and another on 30 January 1900 on what had been done in England, the Colonies and India to place a fighting Army in South Africa,[41] he took a noticeably less active role in the prosecution of the war.[42] The reasons for this may have been ill health and his anger that a 'charlatan'[43] and a 'cheat'[44] had obtained the South Africa command he had coveted; anger probably heightened by the adulation Roberts received as he turned the tide in South Africa. While Roberts' appointment distressed Wolseley, to some sections of the press it restored their faith in the government's seriousness to win 'the War': 'in sending out Roberts and Kitchener the government have done the best thing for restoring public confidence'.[45]

If they thought the team taking command of the Army in December 'remains all that we could wish it to be',[46] the deficiency in stores was certainly not. It triggered a further barrage of attacks against Lansdowne:

the 'military machine has never been kept in full working order' and 'war found us wanting in most essential preparations'.[47] Lansdowne accepted this criticism, purposely concealing nothing. In fact, he was prepared for it, since 'we have been struck by the inadequacy of our reserves of many kinds of stores'.[48] Brackenbury's report on the Ordnance Department, which Lansdowne had commissioned the previous January, found that the only items for which reserves were adequate were lances, revolvers, rifles and carbines. Brackenbury reported that this insufficiency was mainly because it was assumed that in the event of war output from the Ordnance Factories and trade would meet the demand. As a result, Britain was 'attempting to maintain the largest Empire the world has ever seen with armaments and reserves that would be insufficient for a third-class military power'.[49]

Both Lansdowne and Wolseley were surprised by the findings. Although Lansdowne certainly was aware before 'the War' that the Ordnance Department needed a thorough overhaul, which was why he 'brought in General Brackenbury with the Commander-in-Chief's entire concurrence',[50] he also believed 'great as our deficiencies were, the Army at that moment was probably better equipped than it had ever been before'.[51] Responding to the Royal Commission on questions of deficiency, he laid responsibility on Brackenbury's predecessor, General Markham.[52] By the time Brackenbury's report was completed, most of the existing reserves had been dispatched to South Africa and in many cases double that quantity had been sent. 'The War' had lasted just two months and was settling into a protracted state, forcing him to order equipment from all over the Empire and to borrow resources from the Navy.

In his recommendations on the department and its lack of reserves,[53] Brackenbury estimated that £11.5 million was the minimum required to make good the deficiencies. After some discussion by the Cabinet Defence Committee, Lansdowne appointed two departmental committees to examine Brackenbury's proposal, which Hicks Beach believed was wasteful, 'Owing to the rarity of important wars, the brief period for which guns, ammunition and stores remain "in fashion" before they are condemned as obsolete, and the cost of keeping such reserves in proper condition.'[54] Urged by his cabinet colleagues, he later reluctantly agreed to provide £10.5 million over three years from 1901. Lansdowne was disappointed, but after further conversations recognised that it was 'useless to press him to increase the amount'.[55] It is notable that, even though the deficiencies at the beginning of 'the War' were significant, Kitchener later reported that he had no reason to complain of delay by the War Office in complying with requisitions for ordnance: 'the stores and the equipment all came out, and we had at times one hundred and twenty days' supply on hand'.[56]

That Lansdowne accepted there had been a deficiency in reserves of stores did not appease his critics and only fed their view that he was unsuited to be Secretary of State. While it was easy for them to moralise on this subject, his critics could not agree on the lessons of the war. Although many clamoured for an inquiry, Lansdowne resisted: 'a long time passes while the inquiry is proceeding, and you are very fortunate indeed if you get advice on which you can act at once without further delay and without further investigation'.[57] He was also keen to avoid major reform with 'the War' in progress but, in consultation with the cabinet and the senior officers, he accepted the need for some emergency measures.

These measures dealt with two objects: firstly with additions to men and equipment and secondly as to strengthening Britain's defences.[58] Although Wolseley believed France might attack Britain, his opinion was not taken particularly seriously by the Admiralty, the cabinet or Lansdowne, and among the public it was of almost no concern – as Winston Churchill noted 'the fear of invasion seemed to influence our daily lives as little as the fear of death'[59] – though it could not be dismissed altogether and among the press it found followers.[60] Wolseley advised Lansdowne that a larger Army was required. Lansdowne agreed, but insisted that 'we must in the main rely upon materials already existing'.[61]

This idea was shared by other senior officers.[62] Giving greater prominence to the Auxiliary Army would increase its popularity,[63] Lansdowne thought, and weaken the arguments in favour of modified conscription. By tapping this resource he could raise 70,000 men.[64] Of the three forces comprising the Auxiliaries – Yeomanry, Volunteers and Militia – Lansdowne felt that Wolseley took 'too disparaging a view of the Militia's value'.[65] The patriotic fervour that took hold on the outbreak of 'the War' brought recruiting to new levels.[66] Lansdowne's emergency measures included a further twelve infantry battalions, more infantrymen enlisting for three years, thirty-six batteries of field artillery, seven of horse artillery and fifteen re-formed regiments of cavalry. Veteran soldiers re-enlisted for home defence as the Royal Reserve Battalion. All militiamen were made ready for action and thirty-six battalions saw service abroad; a reserve for the Militia was proposed and training opportunities were created for Militia officers. The office of Inspector-General of Auxiliary Forces and Recruiting was divided in two, and the new Inspector-General of the Auxiliary Forces had a subordinate to deal with the Militia. The Volunteers were given increased grants and encouraged to recruit up to full strength of 1,000 men per battalion and to recruit second battalions. They were given some Regular commissions to fill vacancies in the new infantry battalions and allowed to raise mounted companies. Legislation to provide buildings and rifle ranges was enacted and the ninety-eight batteries of Volunteer artillery were entirely rearmed, partly with a semi-mobile 4.7-inch gun. A Volunteer Bill empowered the government to accept, at any time, offers from Volunteers to serve in Britain. The Imperial Yeomanry was established and other Yeomanry received a month's training under canvas, an increased contingent allowance and a grant for travel.[67]

These measures did not go far enough for Wolseley. Upset by the cabinet's decision and sick of his position at the War Office,[68] he wrote: 'as the Cabinet refuse to adopt the measures by which alone I believe you could raise the troops I conceive to be essential for national safety, I feel compelled to resign my position as Commander-in-Chief'.[69] Lansdowne refused to accept his resignation. Lansdowne's measures also failed to convince the many critics of Army reform in Parliament and the press.[70] To Dilke they were an 'extravagant makeshift proposal',[71] and one of the service parliamentarians felt 'We have tried raising an Army by Voluntary enlistment and by making the Army popular, but we are now trying to raise an Army by invitation and imagination.'[72] *The Times* argued that the War Office 'has a rare opportunity' that has 'not yet been properly utilized'.[73]

21

FIGHTING THE WAR IN SOUTH AFRICA

WHILE LANSDOWNE WAS passing his emergency measures through Parliament, he was also ensuring the War Office's full support of Roberts' campaign. On arrival in South Africa, Roberts began a series of tactical reforms to address the weaknesses in the Army and bring 'the War' to an end.[1] Lansdowne did not believe in interfering with generals in the field[2] and made sure Roberts was given a free hand. He knew that if Roberts failed to recover the situation, the government's popularity would suffer. With minimal loss to civilian supremacy, Lansdowne loosened control, which satisfied the senior officers that they could prosecute 'the War' without hindrance. In bridging the gap between civilians and soldiers in London and at the front, Lansdowne also protected Roberts from interference and distractions as he advanced towards Pretoria, particularly from other generals impeding his plan of campaign. 'Please do not think about our Parliamentary difficulties or allow them to affect your plan', he informed Roberts in early 1900.[3] By maintaining this transparent and harmonious relationship,[4] Lansdowne ensured that Roberts had every chance to undertake a successful campaign.

While Roberts was preparing to advance to Pretoria, Buller was defeated at Spion Kop on 23–24 January 1900. The battle demonstrated the incompetent leadership of some generals and their failure to understand modern warfare. What began as a 'tea-time war' was now portrayed as an 'absent-minded war'[5] of military blunders.[6] The news coverage of Spion Kop nearly brought down the government. Lansdowne believed Buller's Army should be divided up and given to Roberts,[7] to whom he wrote, 'I confess I have no confidence in anything but the advance which you will be beginning a few days hence.'[8] Lansdowne also protested at Buller's demand for further reinforcements, advising

Salisbury that 'to weaken him [Roberts] in order to pour more troops into the Natal sieve would in my belief be sheer folly'.[9]

As the full implication of Buller's defeat became apparent, Chamberlain was not sure that the government would survive. When the situation was debated in the Lords, Lansdowne admitted that the government had possibly underrated 'not the numbers of armaments of the Boers but their value as fighting men'.[10] Denying that the government had been unprepared, he stated that his military advisers had claimed that, by sending out moderate reinforcements, they could secure the two colonies.[11] Interestingly, in evidence to the Royal Commission three years later he did admit that the government had been unprepared.[12]

Although the government survived, Lansdowne's publication of the Spion Kop dispatch in April caused further difficulties. Whilst it showed that the operation was muddled by generals who disagreed, Lansdowne believed publication was justified and the House of Commons would not have stood suppression of the facts.[13] It caused a 'howl'.[14] *The Times* said, 'It shows us the Secretary of State endeavouring to shift onto the Commander-in-Chief in the field responsibility that rightly belongs to the authorities at home.'[15] Salisbury was puzzled by Lansdowne's action. He thought the cabinet 'were all of one mind that it ought not to be published'.[16] With no official record of the cabinet having met, Lansdowne knew of no such decision. 'But our decisions are very often impalpable and perhaps I ought to have been able to construct one from materials afforded by Devonshire's yawns and casual interjections round the table,'[17] he commented sardonically to Balfour. Queen Victoria, who received copies of telegrams sent to and from South Africa, did not understand Lansdowne's action, and informed him that Roberts 'must not be interfered with by civilians at a distance who cannot judge the exact state of the case'.[18] Lansdowne concurred, while maintaining it was 'within the right of the Cabinet to endeavour to strengthen the hands of the general and to make him feel that the responsibility for severe measures if taken will not be his alone'.[18] Fearing that generals would lose the respect of their soldiers, she suggested that Lansdowne should resign, but Salisbury would not agree; the rest of the Liberal Unionists would follow Lansdowne and the government would collapse.

Many observers did not understand why this created such a sensation. Lansdowne's son, who was in South Africa, noted 'I suppose the fuss about Buller is really a political one, as he was Campbell-Bannerman & Rosebery's man for the W.O., and it is a fine chance for them to make political capital, without apparently being unpatriotic.'[20] The government escaped censure, although many of its supporters abstained. Making an example of Buller's incompetence was not Lansdowne's object, although 'Buller trusted too much to his subordinates and did not take measures to satisfy himself that his orders were carried out.'[21]

While Lansdowne's position in cabinet was not seriously affected, the press and public's opinion of him was further damaged and he was subjected to intense criticism and satire. To Rudyard Kipling, 'this here home government is about as slack-backed and muddleheaded as they can make 'em – specially the limp and luckless Lansdowne'.[22] Hector Munro, alias 'Saki', satirised Lansdowne in 'Alice in Pall Mall' as the White Knight. J.A. Spender, editor of the *Westminster Gazette*, who published the satirical short story, said it was quoted everywhere and set all of London laughing. He regarded it as symbolic of all War Secretaries who did not expect war.[23]

While Lansdowne was caricatured by the press and public, 'the War' with Roberts in command began with mostly successful British counter-offensives. On 11 February 1900 Roberts led his troops from the Modder River towards the Orange Free State in a great flanking march that ended in the capture of Bloemfontein.[24] On 15 February John French ended the siege of Kimberley, assisted by Roberts, who did the initial planning. The Boer line was finally broken between 21 and 27 February at the Battle of the Tugela Heights. The success of Buller's force at Pieters Hill, Railway Hill and Hart's Hill ended Boer resistance in Natal and they began to melt away. On 28 February Ladysmith was relieved, and so was Lansdowne:[25] 'the shadow of impending calamity, which has darkened our path for so long, is at last removed'.[26] Lansdowne went to Bowood for two days' rest, his first outing since November.[27]

As the generals in South Africa sensed a turn in their fortunes, so their petty jealousies began to materialise. They were of different backgrounds and temperaments and many were unsuited to their tasks. Lansdowne noted a lot of growling from 'the man in the street' and 'I might almost add the man in the Cabinet' over alleged failure to punish officers responsible for bad mistakes, but there were no calls in or out of Parliament for such action.[28] Roberts was less lenient and removed from command five generals, seven brigadiers and nine commanding officers for incompetence.[29]

With the surrender of Bloemfontein to Roberts on 13 March, some newspapers thought 'the first half of the Campaign is over'.[30] On 31 May General Pretyman, military governor at Bloemfontein, proclaimed annexation of the Orange Free State as the Orange River Colony. Roberts left Bloemfontein on 3 May 1900 and advanced towards Johannesburg, aiming to disconcert the enemy by going straight to their headquarters. Mafeking was relieved on 17 May and two weeks later Roberts captured Johannesburg. On 5 June Roberts entered Pretoria and, although there were two more battles, he declared 'the War' over. On 3 September he proclaimed annexation of the South Africa Republic. Britain now nominally controlled both republics, apart from the Northern Transvaal. Lansdowne felt that none of the cabinet, himself included, 'had an idea whether they were near or still far from the end'.[31]

While the situation stabilised, Lansdowne faced new challenges, including stories of medical negligence. Disease was a major problem and the death from typhoid of Prince Christian Victor, Queen Victoria's grandson, attracted public attention. *The Times* sent William Burdett-Coutts MP, and his report on the outbreak of the disease created a public sensation. Although it appeared to be an attack on the government, Lansdowne understood it was really aimed at the War Office. He questioned some of its contents, but realised there had clearly been great suffering because it was impossible to cope with the phenomenal outbreaks of disease that followed Roberts' advance. One criticism was the lack of nurses, a question that required Lansdowne's tact, particularly as the Army Nursing Service was associated with the Royal Family. When 'the War' began, this service had a lady superintendent, nineteen superintendent sisters and sixty-eight sisters, with no mechanism for expansion or bringing in reserves. The creation of Princess Christian's Army Nursing Reserve enabled the deployment of 1,400 trained nurses in South Africa up until May 1902. The difficulty in providing nurses during 'the War' was part of a larger problem with the Army Medical Department. In July, after charges of medical negligence were debated in the Commons, the government announced a commission of inquiry to report on the care and treatment of the sick and wounded during the war.[32] The findings revealed a lack of administrative and organisational ability among the principal medical officers, friction between civil surgeons and the Royal Army Medical Corps, and among the senior officers in the corps itself. Lansdowne's reputation did not suffer as it was widely accepted that he did more for the Royal Medical Army Corps than any previous Secretary of State.[33]

Over the summer the press and public began to probe the costs of the war. Hicks Beach urged the War Office to reduce expenditure. Lansdowne was unwilling until the situation in South Africa was clearer and it was safe to do so.[34] In the autumn, with costs still spiralling, Hicks Beach appealed to Salisbury and Chamberlain because Britain's finances were so bleak.[35] When he tried to impose a deadline for reducing the force, Lansdowne replied:

> In South Africa Robert's troops are all fully employed. The extent of the
> country which he is holding and the length of the railway which he has to
> protect are immense. To my mind it would be out of the question to take
> troops away from him at present. As to home troops I am not frightened
> by rumours of French preparations, but it is idle to deny that we are not

strong at home and the outlook abroad is not reassuring. I am indeed pressed by the soldiers to do more than we are actually doing. If we were to disembody now I think the commander in chief would be justified in protesting. No one is keener than I am for a drawing of our horns all over the world.[36]

Hicks Beach replied:

I could not ask you to take troops away from Roberts which he says it is necessary to retain. But, as I said, I am told that there is a very large force left behind in the Cape Colony and possibly also in Natal. As to home troops I do not see how Wolseley could in reason protest against the disembodiment of a force which he has just pronounced to be useless. I think you attach far too much importance to the soldiers' opinions on this matter which is a question of policy. I suspect that your soldiers want to make up abnormal armaments as long as possible in the hopes of making more of them permanent.[37]

While Lansdowne was considering this issue, Roberts wrote asking to rescind his command and return. Lansdowne thought he should become Commander-in-Chief of the British Army when Wolseley's term of office expired in December. Although this proposal 'really quite upset' Queen Victoria, for she had hoped her son, the Duke of Connaught, might take the post, she recognised Roberts' claim.[38] Lansdowne's son imagined it would be nice for his father to have Roberts at the War Office,[39] but Lansdowne himself had no such desire. By the end of August 1900 it was obvious that 'we shall be met next session by demands for fundamental changes both in the Army and the War Office. With regard to the Army it is admitted that the experience of the war has revealed many defects and that changes are inevitable. As for the War Office I am far from persuaded that there is such a case for a complete alteration of system.' Before new people 'laid rash hands on the organisation',[40] he hoped they would see what the staff thought of it and not refer questions of reform to a committee. Any such inquiry would be interminable and 'no department has been subject of so many enquiries as the War Office, no department is so much abused'.[41] If reform came from within, then should they not have a new Secretary of State as well as a new Commander-in-Chief? He wondered whether the public would be convinced that he, on whose advice the existing organisation was introduced, was free from leanings. 'Everything depends on the influence of individuals'[42] and, as the lessons of 'the War' emerged, he would not be the most suitable person to reform the office.[43]

Advising Lansdowne to avoid personal speculation, Salisbury did not accept his resignation. 'It is quite possible we may not be far from an election. We must all face it together. It would have the worst effect, if discussions about future resignations etc., were to be encouraged and get abroad just now. It would give the impression that we were falling to pieces.'[44] Lansdowne, although he had found the War Office the most thankless and 'irritating' post in government,[45] accepted his advice. According to Salisbury, 'Stanhope, Stanley and Gathorne-Hardy had all been criticised over War Office reform' and Lansdowne was only the latest victim.[46]

That Salisbury promoted him to the Foreign Office two months later showed his confidence in Lansdowne. On 21 October Salisbury told Akers-Douglas that he wanted to relinquish his double role[47] and would 'submit Lord Lansdowne's name for the Foreign Office'.[48] Queen Victoria insisted that Lansdowne hold office under the personal supervision of Salisbury, who on 26 October told Lansdowne that the Queen wished to know whether he would take the Foreign Office. Thus his role was settled in a most unexpected way.[49] He had expected relegation to an uneventful existence at Bowood or perhaps some easy-going post.[50] He replied to the Queen, in typically self-deprecatory terms, that he valued her offer the more because 'he does not disguise from himself that as Secretary of State for war he must often have seemed to you to fall short of Your Majesty's expectations'.[51] But he was 'glad to think that under the new distribution of offices he can look forward to the wise guidance of the Prime Minister'.[52] Ardagh thought the appointment well judged, 'at a time when it is most desirable to improve our relations with France. His French blood will stand him in good stead.'[53] Rosebery sent Lady Lansdowne his congratulations, 'even though they come from one who considered [his] army scheme inadequate!'[54] Maud wrote a little later:

> I was I must own very very much pleased when he was given the Foreign Office. He has been so much abused and so unfriendly criticised during the last year that at last I began to feel no one believed in him but me, so you can imagine when Lord Salisbury's letter came asking him to undertake what is the most responsible place next to the Prime Minister. I felt a most extraordinary sense of relief and delight to think that all the newspapers like the Daily Mail should get a slap in the face.[55]

Lansdowne was one of only three War Secretaries who spent more than five years in office. He believed that, of all departments, 'the War Office was par excellence the department of dilemmas'[56] but, despite imperfections in its constitution, the practice was better than the theory.[57] Having served under Cardwell, he understood its military system better than most, and respected its purpose and principles, but realised that it had its faults. The Empire had grown, special calls were made on the Army and the system was 'out of joint'.[58] Lansdowne's gradualism modified the system while preserving its basic structure, which had had the support of eight previous Secretaries of State, two Commanders-in-Chief and four Adjutant-Generals. Wolseley believed that the Army had already been reformed and needed only an increase in men, whereas Lansdowne adopted a more flexible view. By grafting many understated changes onto the existing system, he did more than either the military or civilian advisers were willing to do in rigidly defending the system. In implementing his changes he demonstrated the right political and managerial skills but also an awareness of and respect for public opinion.

Lansdowne's ability to manage the War Office was hindered by individual prejudices, rivalries and self-interests and its over-centralisation. There was no spirit of collaboration or appetite for reform. Overseas victories, which created national heroes and a sense of complacency, made his task more challenging. Most of his Army reforms were designed to be implemented over three or more years and should, he believed, be given a fair trial before further changes could be justified.[59] These measures were still new in October 1899, but with the war in South Africa they were put to the test and had a profound impact on how he managed 'it'. They allowed Britain to mobilise and dispatch the largest force to ever leave Britain's shores.

Historians have found Lansdowne wanting as Secretary of State, blaming him for the blunders of 'the War'. This fails to acknowledge that Lansdowne's decisions were not made in a vacuum, but in consultation and with the guidance of his military advisers and with the full approval of the cabinet. He accepted that they underrated the fighting value and endurance of the Boers,[60] and that not enough was done to prepare for war because of political considerations.[61] He believed the problem was one of personnel rather than the system.[62]

Contrary to the generals' view in 1899 that they had not been consulted, Lansdowne consulted the Army Board at every stage and once war was imminent 'it cannot be doubted that the generals knew perfectly well what they were going to South Africa for'.[63] Similarly, Lansdowne kept Roberts informed at every stage, giving him a free hand to successfully conclude 'the War'. Roberts said: 'Lansdowne has done everything which can be expected from a Secretary of State for War to push on the campaign.'[64] The precise delimitation of the civil and military spheres was (and is) always contended. By conceding some civilian authority as he did, Lansdowne met the wishes of the senior officers to administer 'the War' unimpeded, and yet without undermining the importance the cabinet placed on civilian supremacy. That the soldiers were frustrated is understandable. However, their failure to recognise political necessity, public opinion and the cost of their proposals made consensus impossible. In the longer term, Lansdowne's trust in military men and their judgement was damaged. By 1917, when he wrote the 'Peace Letter', he was clearly exasperated with the direction in which the generals were taking the First World War.

Lansdowne could not shake off political and bureaucratic constraints, but he was no mere prisoner of circumstances. Within the limitations imposed on him, he pushed through subtle reforms that prepared the way for Richard Haldane's later, wholesale restructuring of the Army. In this Lansdowne showed great political nous and practical sense. Hamilton considered Lansdowne the best War Minister since Cardwell.

22

THE FOREIGN OFFICE

LANSDOWNE ARRIVED AT the Foreign Office intent on forging closer relations with allies, particularly Germany. The Boer War had cost a fortune, Britain was financially crippled and Salisbury's foreign policy of engagement without commitment had become unsustainable. Nonetheless, Lansdowne wished to continue the prevailing orthodoxy that British foreign policy should be pragmatic, non-ideological, competent, patriotic, empire-driven and low-tax. Chamberlain disliked this adherence to the status quo, desiring an even more active foreign policy. Lansdowne avoided choosing between Chamberlain and Salisbury, but put his own stamp on foreign policy incorporating inclusion and transparency. What mattered to him most were stable international relations and Britain's leading role, maintaining the balance of power in Europe and Britain's interests beyond. His natural preoccupations were naval and imperial affairs. He also wished to recover his personal reputation in cabinet after his perceived failure as War Minister. With these objectives, Lansdowne set Britain on a new course that fundamentally altered British diplomacy.

Lansdowne insisted that ambassadors pursue international harmony with courteous exchanges. Within days of assuming office, he wrote to the ambassador in Berlin: 'I shall undertake the duties of my new office without, I hope, too many preconceived ideas, but I plead guilty to one – the idea that we should make every effort to maintain, and, if we can, to strengthen the good relations which at present exist between Britain and Germany.'[1] He wrote in similar language to the men in Washington and Paris, but Berlin mattered most.

Such openness would have been anathema to Salisbury, who by 1900 had served at the Foreign Office for over thirteen years and was associated with the policy of 'splendid isolation'. Salisbury favoured 'leaning to the Triple Alliance without belonging to it' because he saw no obvious advantage in signing a treaty: Russia and France were hostile; Germany would offer small compensation for the risk.[2] According to Count Paul von Hatzfeldt, the German ambassador in London, Salisbury was 'a man who in general cherishes no sympathies for any other nation, and in the transaction of business is moved by purely English considerations'.[3] It would take a lot to change the Prime Minister's mind on foreign relations.

By 1900 two factors had undermined the logic of isolationism: Britain was no longer the world's leading industrial power; and Germany and Russia threatened Britain's imperial and maritime interests. In 1870 Britain produced twice as much steel as Germany, its nearest competitor; in 1900 the United States and Germany were both ahead of Britain. Germany and France, vying for a new world role, were strengthening their navies and Russia threatened to control the north China ports from her naval base at Port Arthur.[4] Many younger diplomatists and cabinet ministers, notably Lansdowne, questioned the Empire's security. Shortly before retiring from the Foreign Office, Salisbury had been forced by the cabinet to open talks with Germany about China. The resulting agreement was politically profitable, creating distrust of Germany in St Petersburg and Paris. Lansdowne realised that British foreign policy was at a crossroads. In his new role he focused on the security issue, leaving Salisbury no choice but to accept further change.

To understand why Lansdowne was such a successful Foreign Minister, it is necessary to describe the context. Unlike the War Office, this department was one of action, talk and knowledge-sharing. This dynamic environment suited his temperament; he could focus on what mattered and bring out the best in himself and those around him. Unlike the sprawling War Office, where rivalry spoiled its smooth running, the Foreign Office was a smaller ministry where most recruits came from privileged backgrounds, and clerks, officials and diplomats tended to speak the same language. However, the younger generation saw the world through a different lens. Lansdowne wisely encouraged them to voice their opinions.

The Foreign Office in King Charles Street was a short carriage ride from Lansdowne House. At first, Lansdowne was distracted by 'an appalling number of threads to pick up', although he found it very interesting.[5] Salisbury appointed his son James Cranborne MP as Parliamentary Under-Secretary for Foreign Affairs. After five years working with Salisbury, Lansdowne accepted such nepotism without offence. Despite limited experience of foreign affairs, Cranborne was well qualified: an MP since 1885, punctual, un-argumentative and cultured. Lansdowne had known him for years, liked him and would have plumped for him anyway.[6] Parliamentary Under-Secretaries had restricted authority but they added weight to discussions.[7] They had to be aware of all the office was doing, supply information required by MPs, make statements in line with cabinet policy and defend that policy without offending foreign powers.[8] As Salisbury's eyes and ears, his role acquired added importance.

Day to day, the Foreign Office was run by the Permanent Under-Secretary, Thomas Sanderson, known as 'Lamps' because of his thick spectacles. He had been at the Foreign Office since 1859, in post since 1894, but was cautious in expressing opinions. Younger officials condemned his red-tapism and aversion to change. He admitted he was an 'official and narrow-minded'.[9] He oversaw the political and administrative departments, read dispatches and telegrams, might add comments, carried out the Foreign Secretary's instructions and dealt with British diplomats. Below Sanderson, the Assistant Under-Secretaries managed the overseas departments, commented on incoming dispatches, assembled information and papers, and drafted dispatches.[10] Officials did not all share similar ideologies and some were strongly for or against Germany and the other Great Powers. Lansdowne would have the final word.

There were six departments: Africa, African Protectorates, America, Eastern, Far Eastern and Western European. There were five administrative departments: Commercial and Sanitary, Consular, Financial (Chief Clerk's Office), Librarian and Keeper of the Papers, Treaties and Superintendents. To cope with the work, Lansdowne employed a private secretary and a précis writer. Eric Barrington, the private secretary, considered a snob by his colleagues, was responsible for organising appointments, staffing and discipline in the diplomatic and consular services, promotion and transfer of junior clerks and junior diplomats. During Lansdowne's five years the Office grew in size and each department had at least one senior clerk and up to six assistants and junior clerks. The Foreign Office was regarded as the most aristocratic of departments. Under Salisbury it had distanced itself from everyday life and the rest of Whitehall.[11] This gave ammunition to radicals, who argued that foreign policy was distorted by a cabal that welcomed diplomatic crises as justifying their existence, instead of pursuing peace and prosperity. Under Lansdowne, transparency – particularly with the Colonial, India and War Offices – became more normal and such criticism worthless.

The Foreign Office worked with the cabinet and British diplomats. A successful foreign policy depended on a close relationship between Foreign Secretary and Prime Minister, whose decision was final on important matters. Balfour, who succeeded his uncle as Prime Minister on 11 July 1902, wrote in 1923:

> you can't expect the Prime Minister not to interfere with Foreign Office business. It's only when you get a combination of two men who see absolutely eye to eye and work in perfect harmony that you can avoid it. Lansdowne and myself were one of the rare cases.[12]

Unless there was a crisis, the cabinet seldom interfered, though the Foreign Minister had to provide any information required. In 1900, although Lansdowne's reputation was at a low ebb, his position in the cabinet was strong, because he was one of those wishing to abandon Salisbury's policies. Chamberlain's wish to secure the Empire against possible threats, and Hamilton's and Balfour's for a strong India, put Lansdowne in a position to bargain with his colleagues.

For information and policy execution, the Office depended on diplomats. They summarised the opinions and moods of local press and politicians in daily telegrams to London. Decisions on foreign policy were usually taken in London and sent in official dispatches, supplemented by letters from the Foreign Secretary and Permanent Under-Secretary. Ambassadors rarely overstepped their instructions.[13] In dispatches they might be vague, but Lansdowne insisted on frankness about their sources and opinions in 'private' letters. Lansdowne found the letters and dispatches of Cecil Spring Rice, Chargé d'Affaires in Tehran, most interesting of all.[14] Spring Rice was a keen observer and his friends included the most influential public figures at the time. While he distrusted much about Germany and Russia, he was never malicious, always quite candid in setting down exactly what he thought.

Lansdowne would typically arrive at the Foreign Office at 11 a.m., read the telegrams, discuss them with the Permanent Under-Secretary and decide what line to take. He might need to see foreign ambassadors, generally in the afternoon, when he also dealt with the important dispatches, already scrutinised by the Supervising and Permanent Under-Secretaries. He would stay until 7 p.m. Any unfinished work would be sent to his house to be seen to between dinner and bed. Boxes with red labels were urgent, white labels were ordinary and green labels were intermediate. When cabinet and parliamentary business took him away from the Foreign Office, he had somehow to make up the time.[15] A Foreign Secretary needed to rapidly grasp important or decisive points in the papers submitted and appreciate the context and background. Conversations with foreign diplomats were an informal way of broaching complex questions, and he would keep a record of what he and they said.

Lansdowne's dealings with foreign representatives received little scrutiny by Parliament or the press. Foreign affairs involved negotiation and compromise with other states, ministers had less control over the outcome and issues seemed remote. Parliament had little influence on foreign policy, although radical Liberal MPs remonstrated on occasion. Constituents were more interested in domestic matters.[16] Peers were docile; there was bipartisan agreement on the main policies and on not embarrassing the government in debate.[17] Rosebery, the opposition Leader of that House, believed that if foreign policy were dictated by party, dictatorial empires such as Russia would have the advantage.

Although no longer Foreign Secretary, Salisbury was offered a room at the Foreign Office, if Lansdowne agreed. As a friend and colleague Lansdowne had no objection, and Salisbury got three rooms. Viscount Esher, the courtier and behind-the-scenes 'fixer', noted that 'Lansdowne is aware that ill-natured critics will say that Lord Salisbury remains there as Mayor of the Palace', but 'there is an advantage in the Prime Minister occupying rooms accessible from the principal offices without the necessity of running the gauntlet of prying reporters. We have made the Foreign Office to communicate with the Colonial, Home and India Offices.'[18] Until his retirement in July 1902, Salisbury exerted some influence, and his knowledge and advice were sought. Lansdowne kept him constantly informed and often awaited his approval before acting. Sometimes they corresponded three times a day on a subject.[19] Baron Eckardstein, First Secretary at the German Embassy, believed that Lansdowne managed Salisbury very cleverly, giving way on minor matters in order to carry important points.[20] Although Lansdowne never complained, by November 1901 Salisbury's domineering presence was hampering his ability to implement a new foreign policy. Brodrick, Secretary of State for War, felt 'Lansdowne is doing wonderfully well at the F.O. – always resourceful and only kept back by Lord S.'[21] Thereafter he found a way to assert himself and put his own stamp on foreign policy.

This new policy originated in the China Question. After the Sino-Japanese War of 1894–95 Britain could no longer rely on its navy to protect its global interests, and regional agreements proved unsuccessful. The decline of the Qing dynasty and the rise of aggressive powers on the borders of the British Empire, notably Russia, made fresh diplomacy urgent. As Lansdowne settled into office the Boxer troubles in China signified a threat in the Far East. In summer 1900 an uprising by the Boxer sect, devoted to the expulsion of all foreigners, spread across northern China. In Peking the Boxers besieged foreign legations and killed the German ambassador,[22] 135 missionaries, 53 children and many more converts.[23] The rebellion briefly united the European powers with the United States and Japan in sending an international force to relieve the Peking legations. Britain sent 3,000 troops, but the Germans took the lead since they planned to expand in China. Lansdowne came to accept that only agreement with Germany could prevent Russia from consolidating in Manchuria and, on 16 October, Salisbury made a limited agreement with Germany.[24] The German Foreign Minister and Chancellor, Bernhard von Bülow, concluded that Britain would do nothing about Russian influence in Manchuria. He was wrong, as after Russia's seizure of some British railway sidings in Tientsin, Lansdowne decided on a firm but unprovocative line. The Tseng-Alexeieff agreement in November 1900, permitting Russian troops in Manchuria, made this essential.

Equally alarmed were the Japanese. Baron Kato, the Foreign Minister, threatened that, if China yielded to Russia, then Japan would join other powers in partitioning the country. Count Tadasu Hayashi, ambassador in London, asked whether Britain would join Japan in demanding clarity from St Petersburg. Lansdowne asked Hayashi for more time, hoping that the crisis would facilitate rapprochement with Germany against Russia. This overlooked the question of the other Triple Alliance countries, Britain's relations with them being distant. Despite public Anglophobia, the German government made a move, encouraging Kaiser Wilhelm to visit his dying grandmother, Queen Victoria. Bülow advised the Kaiser that it would be a master-coup if this left the British with hopes of a firm relationship without binding or committing Germany.

The Kaiser took a leading part at the Queen's funeral on 2 February 1901. A few days before, on 25 January, he met Lansdowne at Osborne House, suggesting that Britain and France should pull together against Russian and American aggrandisement. At the end of January the Russians obtained a concession at Tientsin, which Lansdowne believed was territorial acquisition in violation of the Anglo-German China agreement.[25] He told Germany that the Powers should not recognise the concession, but Germany saw no threat to Chinese sovereignty. On 5 February the day the Kaiser returned home, Hayashi repeated his request for British help in warning the Chinese. Lansdowne agreed, then Germany agreed on 12 February and the USA also warned that the agreement should not be ratified. On 1 March the Chinese yielded, but asked the Powers to mediate between China and Russia.

Lansdowne expected to establish an Anglo-German-Japanese alliance that would secure British interests in the Far East. On 12 March he outlined a treaty with Germany that he believed would elicit a clear statement of German intentions. Salisbury dismissed it. Three days later Bülow ended doubts, announcing that the Anglo-German China agreement 'was in no sense concerned with Manchuria'. The three-way alliance on which Lansdowne had attempted to build his Far East policy was broken. The episode created ill feeling in London and Berlin, but contacts continued. On 18 March Eckardstein, First Secretary in London, suggested a general defensive alliance, directed only against France and Russia, and effective only when Britain or Germany was attacked by both those powers. Lansdowne doubted whether much would come of it as 'it would oblige us to adopt in all our foreign relations a policy which would no longer be British but Anglo-German'.[26] Lansdowne's interest was an arrangement for the Far East only.

Meanwhile, King Edward VII had ascended the throne. Lansdowne and the new King were not fond of each other. The King believed that Lansdowne was 'not a clever man you know, not clever at all'.[27] Ever since the Aylesford scandal in 1876, when Lansdowne believed the King was implicated in damaging the reputation of his sister-in-law Bertha Blandford, their relations had been uneasy. However, with Maud as Lady of the Bedchamber to Queen Alexandra, Lansdowne concealed his dislike. Even if the King could not interfere directly, he could make the Foreign Secretary's job easier or harder. Despite his political education, the King had little training in statecraft. Interested in foreign affairs, he overrated his political influence. However, he had an ability to evoke cordiality and popular sentiment. Lansdowne continued to send dispatch boxes to the sovereign.

The King's naivety damaged Lansdowne's further attempts at Anglo-German cooperation. Lansdowne was still hopeful of closer ties. On 5 August the King's favourite sister, Princess Victoria, Empress of Germany, died of cancer and he decided to visit Germany. Lansdowne prepared a memorandum on German relations for him, which mentioned many issues in dispute. The memorandum was meant for the King's eyes only; fortunately it was also discreet. When the King met the Kaiser on 23 August 1901 he handed the document to his nephew, who sent it to his own foreign office. No harm was done, but little good. With Lascelles, British ambassador in Berlin, present at Wilhelmshöhe Palace, the Kaiser told the King it was Britain's fault that Anglo-German talks had produced no tangible result and he earnestly desired a binding treaty. Lansdowne saw through such sentiment: 'as for a "complete understanding" between Germany and ourselves ... [it] cannot be fruitful of good results unless the conduct of the parties to it proves to the world that they are in loyal co-operation'.[28] He saw the chances of success were becoming fainter, though he did not rule it out. He told Lascelles the cabinet would discuss the question in the autumn.

Another possible solution to Britain's difficulties in the Far East, Lansdowne saw, was cooperation with Russia. But Lamsdorf, Russia's Foreign Minister, was unhelpful. Lansdowne thought it was a 'great pity that he will not play "*cartes sur tables*" with us'.[29] As to Russia's movements in Manchuria, 'We have already recognised its gravitation for railway purposes but we have a right to dissuade China from entering into surreptitious bargains. With a little "*bonne volonté*" and mutual confidence the whole affair ought to be capable of settlement.'[30] Charles Scott, ambassador in St Petersburg, believed the real danger was the weakness of the Tsar and the diverse opinions among his ministers, who had no strong leadership.[31] On 17 April 1901 Lamsdorf told Scott that Russia was friendly to Britain and 'with regard especially to China a thorough understanding which would enable them to render each other mutual assistance was not only practically possible, but even indicated by a true appreciation of their real interests'.[32] Lansdowne had sometimes to reprove Scott's blind faith in Lamsdorf's veracity.[33] On this occasion he advised Scott that Britain would not reject an offer, were one made.

On 1 February 1901, while Lansdowne awaited the Russians' next move, he submitted the names of peers to visit foreign courts to announce the accession of King Edward VII. Part of Lansdowne's success as Foreign Minister lay in his skill in using every opportunity to find out how the other Powers were thinking and then act. France was a case in point. Shortly before Lord Carrington set off, Lansdowne warned him that he might not receive a cordial welcome in Paris, where Boer sympathies ran high, but President Émile Loubet told Carrington that France was anxious for a good understanding with Britain, and Théophile Delcassé, the Foreign Minister, begged Carrington to tell the King that he would spare no effort to develop and maintain cordial relations. Clearly, if Britain wished for a friendly understanding with France, then this was possible. Such openness dispelled the view in British diplomatic circles that Delcassé was extremely uncommunicative, not to say secretive.[34]

In March Paul Cambon, French ambassador in London, proposed to exchange French fishing rights off Newfoundland for British territory in Gambia. He added *de son propre chef* that Britain should go along with the intended French plundering of Morocco and this would be part of the bargain – it was '*d'autant plus facile que tout cela ne nous appartient, ni aux uns ni aux autres!*' ('all the easier since the whole business is out of our hands, on both sides').[35] Cambon had an almost pathological suspicion of Britain in Morocco.[36] He also feared that Anglo-French conflict would only benefit Germany. Even if cross-channel relations had improved since 1898, and the Franco-Russian alliance had weakened, Lansdowne was unwilling to move so quickly. On 20 March he informed Cambon that 'he deprecated any attempt at a transaction on so vast a scale, and would rather avoid discussing it'.[37] His focus remained on the Far East and, since Germany remained uncooperative, a key objective was keeping on close terms with Russia.

The threat from Russia in Central Asia disturbed Lansdowne as much as in the Far East. Both powers saw Persia as central to their imperial economic and military interests. Russia wished to expand in Persia; Britain thought this would directly threaten India. The satellite territories of Turkey and Afghanistan were equally embroiled in the Great Game. According to Curzon, Viceroy of India, British prestige and influence in Persia had never sunk so low as it was in 1901. If Russia won the diplomatic duel and Britain did nothing, Salisbury warned, 'it would seem a lame and impotent conclusion'.[38] But Britain had no Central Asian foreign policy, except to recognise the Russian sphere of influence in the north and its own supremacy in the south. In September, partly because of the Shah's extravagance, Persia sought a new loan. Britain could assist but as Hamilton, Secretary of State for India, noted, Russia would certainly take Persia severely to task for evading their financial agreement: 'Lansdowne has inherited such a miserable hand in Persia, that it is difficult to suggest any lead which the Russians cannot overtrump.'[39] Curzon and the Government of India proposed to raise the loan for Persia. Lansdowne and Arthur Hardinge, Minister in Tehran, found this unacceptable because its terms were too onerous. Unable to finance British influence in Persia, Lansdowne turned to diplomacy.

In summer 1901, rumours reached Whitehall that Russia was seeking to extend its influence in Seistan, a strategically important state bordering India, under Persian control. Russia put financial pressure on its ruler, the Hashmat-ul-Mulk. Apparently the Shah was willing to pledge the revenues from Seistan as guarantee for a Russia loan. Lansdowne insisted the Foreign Office would not tolerate diversion of Seistan's revenues abroad or the intrusion of foreign authority there.[40] Hardinge was told to get a signed statement from the Shah to this end. Hardinge later explained to the Grand Vizier, Amir Mirza Ali Asghar Khan, Prime Minister of Iran, why Lansdowne insisted on this: 'the peculiar position in which the loan contracts had placed Persia toward Russia made it natural that we should demand special securities for our own interests in case these should be in danger of being mortgaged or sacrificed as the price of fresh Russian financial assistance'.[41]

While Persian finances remained unresolved, on 12 October Arthur Hardinge suggested that a friendly arrangement between Britain and Russia might give Persia the loan it sought; Britain could discuss terms with Russia as equals whereas Persia could not. This was supported by Francis Bertie, who ran the Asiatic and African departments in the Foreign Office. Lansdowne doubted that a joint loan would succeed, but he told the cabinet 'it may be of assistance to us hereafter to be able to appeal to the fact that we have made it, and the refusal of Russia would leave us with a comparatively free hand to make an arrangement of our own with the Persian Government'.[42]

On 29 October Lansdowne interviewed George de Staal, Russian ambassador to the United Kingdom, and proposed to deal directly with the Russian government on matters of mutual interest, emphasising Persia and China. It was merely an exchange of friendly words. Lamsdorf was said to favour the simultaneous advance of funds to Persia, but a Russian loan had nearly been concluded by Sergei Witte, the Russian Finance Minister, through the Russian Bank in Tehran. Charles Hardinge, First Secretary at St Petersburg, thought Witte would not care for Lansdowne's proposal;[43] in fact Witte would not listen to it.[44] The Russian loan was completed on 2 November. That month the India Office authorised the Indian government to offer a loan to Persia. Charles Hardinge suspected it was too late, lamenting that no British government 'has ever had a policy in Persia except that of drift'.[45] On 28 November Amir Mirza Ali Asghar Khan told Arthur Hardinge that Russia had vetoed a British loan. Persia was clearly subservient to Russia.

On 6 January 1902 Lansdowne sent Persia a dispatch outlining Britain's special interests. 'Having held back until the Persian government refused assistance from us under orders from Russia,' he told Curzon, 'there could be no doubt as to the propriety of speaking our mind.'[46] His attempt at an Anglo-Russian arrangement was over. 'I hope someday or other to bring out the fact that we offered the Russian Government to play *cartes sur table* with them about China and Persia, and that they refused.'[47] The dispatch was meant to warn Persia as much as Russia, that if she continued with expansion, war was likely. The dispatch marked a turning point. Despite further setbacks in 1901, Arthur Hardinge, Curzon and Lansdowne restored Britain's position at Tehran, and Russian supremacy was challenged. On 3 October the Amir of Afghanistan, Abdur Rahman, died, further weakening Britain's position in Central Asia. The succession of Habibullah, his son, brought into question the tenuous arrangements for defending India against Russia, which Lansdowne had considered when Viceroy. He told Curzon: 'and so the blow has fallen and the great crisis has arrived'.[48]

23

NEW IMPETUS AT THE FOREIGN OFFICE

FAILURE TO REACH agreement with Russia and Germany to resolve the Far East situation strengthened Lansdowne's case for an agreement with Japan. Until July 1901 Lansdowne had resisted Japan's efforts to obtain such a commitment, hoping Japan would support Britain anyway. Britain and Japan were not obvious partners, Japan being much less significant economically and politically. Lansdowne was concerned how the British cabinet and people would react.[1] Public opinion in Britain was convinced that Russian expansion in the Far East would take a long time to blossom; the Japanese were less sure. They worried about Russian expansion in Manchuria and were eager for Korean independence to strengthen their security.[2] Among the cabinet the idea met with approval from Hicks Beach, the Chancellor, who had concerns over naval spending, and from Selborne, First Lord of the Admiralty, who had recently been refused treasury funds to enlarge the navy and now feared for the safety of the Empire.

In September, after discussions between Hayashi and Claude MacDonald, ambassador in Tokyo, Lansdowne told Selborne that the Japanese were keen to move to a definite proposal.[3] On 10 October Hayashi produced a draft treaty. Lansdowne sent a copy to Salisbury, who raised none of his usual objections to all alliances.[4] He had previously recognised the value of an entente for the defence of the Chinese littoral. On 16 October Hayashi asked whether Lansdowne planned to include Germany. The reply was that it 'would be best to negotiate with you first and then later we can invite Germany to join in the negotiation and come into the alliances'.[5] On 5 November, in cabinet, Lansdowne put forward his case for a defensive alliance, operative if either party were attacked by two powers; Japan's interests in Korea would be safeguarded and neither party would make separate agreements with other powers regarding China or Korea.

Some cabinet colleagues thought the proposal inopportune. Balfour was anxious that, if the Japanese accepted, 'we may find ourselves fighting for our existence in every part of the globe against Russia and France, because France has joined forces with her ally over some obscure Russian-Japanese quarrel in Corea'.[6] Lansdowne dismissed this:

> the chances of the *'casus foederis'* arising are much fewer in the case of the Anglo Japanese agreement than they would be in that of an Anglo German agreement. The area of entanglement seems to me much more restricted under the former and, if this be true, the fact diminishes the difficulty of explaining to the Germans why we are prepared to face the one but not the other liability. The question we have to ask ourselves is whether we should allow Japan to be wiped out by France and Russia in the cases supposed. If the answer is 'no', may we not as well tell her so beforehand and get what we can out of the bargain.[7]

While the cabinet deliberated, Itō Hirobumi, Japan's elder statesman, visited London. Lavishly entertained by Salisbury and the King, who was 'much pleased with the proposed understanding' and hoped the Germans would not learn what was going on,[8] he decided Japan must complete the negotiations. At the end of December Hayashi informed Lansdowne that Japan would add to the treaty a statement that Japan had no aggressive motives in Korea and would qualify Britain's naval obligations by the words 'as far as possible'.[9] On New Year's Day 1902, Lansdowne advised accepting Hayashi's offer.[10] During discussions that day at Bowood, Itō assured Lansdowne that the Japanese were not double-dealing, as was suspected: 'I have no thought of a *double jeu*. We never contemplated an alliance with Russia as we do with Britain.'[11]

Lansdowne's positions in the cabinet and in the Unionist Party were still insecure. The overarching features of his proposal had the backing of Hicks Beach and Salisbury, but the devil was in the detail. Shortly after New Year, pressure from Salisbury and the cabinet forced Lansdowne to demand changes in Japan's refusal to limit her freedom of action in Korea. Both assenting to the changes on 30 January, Lansdowne and Hayashi signed the Anglo-Japanese Alliance treaty at Lansdowne House. It was limited to the 'Extreme East' and declared that the sole desire of the two governments was general peace in eastern Asia. There was a deliberate delay before publishing the treaty. The King believed the Germans should be informed twenty-four hours in advance of Parliament. Lansdowne agreed because, if they were notified informally, they could gauge the views of the Germans, who could not object later on.[12] On 13 February

Lansdowne outlined the terms to Parliament. Having described recent trends to alliances and arms races among the Powers, he entreated the Lords to look at this alliance strictly on its merits and not to be swayed by 'any musty formulas or old-fashioned superstitions as to the desirability of pursuing a policy of isolation for this country'.[13]

Parliament and even Liberal newspapers showed broad satisfaction, although some surmised Japan was now more likely to go to war against Russia. Sanderson thought the treaty would restrain Japan from war with Russia; Lansdowne thought this optimistic. The press saw the treaty as anti-Russian;[14] Lansdowne was determined to prevent war but, if there was one, Britain would not get involved. The alliance was a diplomatic defeat for the Russians, who immediately proposed a joint declaration by Russia, Germany and France, effectively accepting China's integrity while asserting a protectorate – a triple alliance against Britain and Japan. The Germans refused to consider it, but on 20 March 1902 the Franco-Russian declaration was published.[15]

With the shifts in geopolitics caused by uncertainty about China, Lansdowne recognised the practical worth of friendship with the USA, which became an important policy objective. Two major sources of friction were the Central American ship canal and the Alaskan-Canadian boundary. In February 1900 the Clayton–Bulwer Treaty (1850), which had given Britain and the US equal control of the projected canal, was renewed by the Hay–Pauncefote Treaty. In December 1900, as the treaty reached the Senate for ratification, Pauncefote informed London that it contained some amendments. Upset at this discourtesy, particularly as there was no hint of any negotiation, Lansdowne refused to approve them. Gentlemanly politics mattered to Lansdowne. He also believed that one particular amendment undermined the neutrality of the canal and was dangerously vague. In the summer, US Secretary of State John Hay and his advisers worked to conciliate all parties, and Lansdowne thought he could be more relaxed about American ideas of form, and on 18 November the treaty was signed. Britain gained little, but Lansdowne did persuade the US to pursue traditional diplomacy. Relinquishing outdated treaty rights without loss of respect satisfied him.

The Alaska Boundary dispute between the Russian and British empires began in 1821, and was inherited by the United States in 1867. The subject had been raised but never resolved during Lansdowne's time as Governor-General in Canada (1883–88). In late 1902, British naval intervention against Venezuela threatened the growing British-US rapprochement. That Germany and Italy were involved in the Venezuelan dispute complicated matters. Lansdowne was initially reluctant to join Germany in a peaceful blockade of Venezuelan ports, recognising US sensitivity about the Monroe Doctrine and Roosevelt's commitment to it.[16] Michael Herbert, the new ambassador in Washington, thought joint action with Germany would not be very palatable in the USA.[17] However, Cipriano Castro was a particularly troublesome despot and Lansdowne defused alarm by stating that Britain would not occupy Venezuelan soil. On 2 December he pressed for a declaration that Venezuela would accept the discrimination claims of foreigners and compensate them.[18]

Five days later, Britain and Germany declared a blockade and seized Venezuelan gunboats. Parliament and the press immediately criticised Lansdowne, condemning cooperation with Germany. Hamilton reported: 'Lansdowne for once was caught napping.'[19] The King was annoyed at being allied with Germany against an inferior country. Many Americans lamented Britain's choice of ally. Lansdowne was appalled at the anti-German feeling, telling Herbert that the Germans were cooperating fairly well.[20] Unperturbed, Lansdowne publicly restated his belief in the Monroe Doctrine; he told Balfour that Britain would not risk a diplomatic crisis with the US because of the German Navy. He thought it best to ask Roosevelt to arbitrate, and the cabinet approved. On 17 December Venezuela asked for arbitration, and Britain and Germany formally asked Roosevelt to arbitrate, but he declined, which Lansdowne regretted. On 13 February 1903 naval action ended and the blockade was lifted by the signing of the protocol.

After this, American animus made negotiations over the Alaska boundary more difficult. In October 1902 Britain and the US agreed to establish an impartial tribunal. In January six jurists were appointed.[21] Then, as US elections approached, Roosevelt adopted brash diplomacy. He needed Alaska to win the anti-British vote. Although Lansdowne disliked discourteous exchanges in international relations, he supported a settlement favourable to the American case, telling Balfour that Britain's representative, Alverstone, the Lord Chief Justice, would not willingly let the tribunal dissolve without this outcome.[22] On 20 October the final decision awarded the territory to the United States. Public opinion there was pleased, but Canadians believed that Britain cared more for US cordiality than for Canada, despite their patriotism during the Boer War. The Canadian members of the tribunal refused to sign the award. Lansdowne thought this undignified; it was better to resolve the Alaska dispute and have a clean slate with the US.[23] Since it strengthened Canadian security as well as relations with the US, Lansdowne was willing to give Canada less than it expected.

Although some at the Foreign Office thought it imprudent, Lansdowne defended Germany during the Venezuelan crisis because he valued rapprochement with Germany. Any tension would have jeopardised the Baghdad railway, which Lansdowne believed would strengthen the Ottoman Empire, politically and economically, and British commercial and economic links in the Near East against Russia. Internationalising the scheme would forestall Russian objections or retaliation. Germany and Russia had encouraged Turkey to strengthen her hold in the Gulf, a policy Lansdowne disapproved of. However, not wishing to range those powers against Britain, he allowed Turkey certain rights in the Gulf. In January 1902 the Ottomans granted the Anatolian Railway Company a new concession to lay track to the Gulf.

Lansdowne wanted to see British participation: 'It was clearly for our interest that the enterprise should be given an international character.'[24] French and German bankers discussed the project; the German government approached the Foreign Office. After consulting Salisbury, Lansdowne told Paul Metternich, the German ambassador, that Britain was not against the project but would expect an equal financial share for its goodwill.[25] Lansdowne had fought hard in cabinet and gained its support, although Curzon in India argued against, because 'the German emperor would sell us tomorrow for a wink from Russia's eye'.[26] However, suspicious of German designs, Russia abstained from the project. The line was clearly meant to connect Berlin with her East African colonies. After prolonged negotiations, involving European banking syndicates, the British government rejected the scheme because it gave insufficient security for international control or against one power getting preferential treatment. It became apparent by 1903 that the Germans were unwilling to share control of the project. Public opinion turned against it, convinced that politically the line threatened Britain's position in Egypt and India.

Balfour had all along supported Lansdowne in cabinet, so Lansdowne was dismayed when, in April, Balfour decided to pull out of the negotiations. Public opinion was one reason, but the principal cause was Joseph Chamberlain, who was sore at Lansdowne about Venezuela. He also had a motive, after being passed over in 1902 by the King in favour of Balfour replacing Salisbury as Prime Minister. Chamberlain saw a chance to draw attention to himself and his scheme of imperial preference, which was inconsistent with German cooperation. Lansdowne remonstrated with Balfour: 'but for Joe's bile the opposition would not be strong'.[27] Lansdowne still believed the Baghdad railway would be completed, but it divided him from Chamberlain in cabinet. In a speech he warned that Britain would regard a naval base or fortified port established in the Gulf by another power as a 'very grave menace to British interests' and would certainly resist it.[28]

The project was also perceived by some as harmful to British interests because of increasing tension in Turkey, Macedonia and the Far East created by Russian expansion. 'Macedonia' was the name European diplomats used for the Turkish provinces of Kosovo, Monastir and Salonika. After the Treaty of Berlin in 1878, Macedonia was given autonomy but, with no international control of implementation, the

Ottoman government failed to deliver. The cruel and cunning Ottoman Sultan, Adbul Hamid II, used *divide et impera* to play off the minorities of Macedonia, who included Bulgars, Serbs, Greeks, Turks, Vlachs, Jews and Armenians.[29] In 1902 the Christians of Macedonia revolted and the brutal response of Turkish soldiers reopened the Macedonian Question.

The task of reforming Macedonia was allotted to Austria-Hungary and Russia under the Vienna Scheme. The six-point plan included reorganisation of the gendarmerie to include Christians, an Inspector-General supplied by the Western powers, abolition of farm taxes and a general amnesty for political prisoners. The plan was revealed in early 1903, but Russia and Austria-Hungary showed no interest in enforcing it. This led to bloodshed and insurgency, leading to the Ilinden Uprising in August. The Foreign Office declared that Europe could not remain indifferent. On 4 September Lansdowne told Balfour that the Vienna Scheme had been a ghastly failure and British policy must change. Balfour proposed a conference of the powers; Lansdowne agreed,[30] but favoured caution, not snubbing Austria-Hungary or rushing to the front, but pushing for remedies and a wider scheme.[31] The new Lord Salisbury (formerly Cranborne) believed a conference would encourage rebellion, and force was the only remedy.[32] The King thought Britain should put her foot down and send a military attaché with the Turkish forces in Macedonia.[33] Lansdowne sent Francis Plunkett, ambassador in Vienna, a letter calling for an international gendarmerie, with Christians in Macedonia being given more officers and better access to administration and justice. On 30 September Emperor Franz Joseph I, Tsar Nicholas II and their Foreign Ministers met at Mürzsteg, south-west of Vienna, to discuss the initiatives proposed by the British and French.

In October Lansdowne received details of the Mürzsteg plan, incorporating some of his proposals. To prevent Britain and France taking the diplomatic initiative, Austria-Hungary and Russia insisted that Turkey introduce the Vienna Plan without delay.[34] Lansdowne thought the final scheme would not succeed, because it failed to put Europeans in control,[35] but he told Russia and Austria-Hungary that Britain would give the Sultan no hint of European disunity.[36] Had all the Powers not backed the scheme, Lansdowne might have been accused of doing nothing, giving way to the Russians or being too rigid in adherence to the Concert of Europe, but he had defused a situation in which British interests were slight and her risks great.[37] His cool-headedness paid off and he achieved a personal success.

During the next two months Lansdowne was 'occasionally seized by fits of wild impatience' at the inaction of Russia and Austria-Hungary.[38] As he later told Balfour, Austria-Hungary's attitude seemed inexplicable because it had no defined Near East policy, but only aspirations it could not achieve and would not share.[39] In November the Turks began a counter-offensive in Macedonia. This outraged Britons as much as the Bulgarian atrocities of 1876. The reforms had been ignored and only the gendarmerie had made progress; all concerned were disappointed.[40] Now that Britain had got her way, with friction, regarding military attachés, it was time to suggest some financial control in Macedonia; Lansdowne believed the corrupt practices of the 'oriental tax gatherer was the problem'.[41]

In 1904 Macedonia was divided into five sectors by the Powers; Drama was allotted to the British, who also ran the gendarmerie school at Salonika. Attempts to match district boundaries with racial distribution developed into internecine war.[42] The Powers put more pressure on Turkey, which had tried to thwart the foreign officers reorganising the gendarmerie. At the end of 1904 Balfour summarised the situation in a way Lansdowne would have agreed with,

> though there is but little hope of any suggestion of ours being accepted by the majority of the powers, it becomes a serious question whether for our own credit we should not formulate one. It is unfortunate that France should be so tied to Russia, or otherwise we might press for her assistance in a cause in connection with which neither of us has any selfish interest. Italy is friendly but suspicious of Austria: Austria is suspicious of Italy, and is hated by all the rival sects which are now tearing each other to pieces. Russia in her dealings with the Balkan Peninsula, as elsewhere, is moved much more by territorial aspirations than by philanthropy. Germany is anxious to make Turkey think her, her only friend, a prospect of which they are not hopeful.[43]

In May 1905 the Powers appointed international delegates to introduce financial reform. Lansdowne thought this a big step forward.[44] On 27 August the Porte (the government of the Ottoman Empire) was asked to instruct local authorities to recognise them, and the delegates were sent to Macedonia. Lansdowne's insistence on a financial commission to frame the Macedonian budget and oversee tax collection was the most beneficial reform of all.[45] Macedonia at this time demonstrated the self-interest of the Powers and their often-farcical foreign policy. Lansdowne's conciliatory approach bestowed on Britain an almost virtuous character.

The reason the Macedonian Question mattered to Lansdowne and why he did not let it escalate into a serious quarrel was that it impinged on Anglo-Russian relations in the Near East. After the failed attempt to assist Persia financially, Arthur Hardinge, ambassador in Tehran, pressed Lansdowne to invite the Shah to Britain, with the aim of securing for him an Order of the Garter and winning his friendship over Russia. It was assumed that the Russians would try to prevent his visit. They did not, but a clash between Lansdowne and the King nearly brought about the resignation of the cabinet.

The Shah expected to receive the Garter, as his father had previously. The King was adamant he could not because he was a non-Christian. Lansdowne advised the King to mark his reign with a new departure; the King refused. Arthur Hardinge, having arranged the visit, asked Lansdowne for a new posting; he believed he would be no use in Persia after this. Lansdowne – much respected by British diplomats for his willingness to listen to them and assert British interests firmly – refused. In August 1902 the Shah arrived in London with his ministers. Lansdowne danced attendance, combining some business with 'a good deal of doubtful pleasure', including a show at the Hippodrome. On learning that he was not getting the Garter, the Shah became depressed. Lansdowne feared the visit would be overshadowed by the rebuff. On 20 August he met the King on the Royal Yacht and gave him a memorandum explaining how the statutes could be amended. The King read it and, so Lansdowne understood, approved it. But three days later he informed Lansdowne that he was willing to consider any proposal to alter the statutes, but 'I never intended that these alterations should be rushed through in order to meet present difficulty, or that the Shah should know anything about it. I cannot have my hand forced.'[46] Lansdowne resented the implication he had exceeded his instructions. He told Balfour: 'the fact is the King wishes to change his mind again and would like to throw me over – that is a position which I could not possibly accept'.[47]

Lansdowne believed 'I have immolated myself' and the Foreign Office must explain to the press why the Shah had not received any decorations,[48] or there would be mischief-making in England, Russia and beyond. The King saw it as a personal matter and thought Lansdowne had treated him unfairly.[49] Lansdowne told Balfour: 'if the King remains obdurate there is so far as I can see only one way out for me, and that will be "out" in the most literal sense of the word'.[50] Two months after the Shah had left England and the cabinet had threatened to resign over the issue,[51] Balfour, who disliked the King as much as Lansdowne, explained how Lansdowne had acted under a misapprehension. Nonetheless, 'disavowal of the agent can hardly get rid of the obligation into which that agent has entered – As regards the country the refusal of the Garter would not merely deeply offend the Shah but would shake our credit in Persia. We have a very difficult game to play there. Russia has most of the cards, yet it may be disastrous for us to lose the rubber.'[52] The King, much depressed about it,[53] ordered a Garter mission to Tehran. The incident demonstrated that Lansdowne had begun to prove his worth, and that his colleagues and the Prime Minister were unwilling to lose him. It also showed how indispensable Lansdowne was to Balfour at this time.

24

FURTHER CHANGES IN DIRECTION

SHORTLY BEFORE THE Shah's visit, the war in South Africa ended and Salisbury resigned. Salisbury told Lansdowne: 'but for the war I should have done it sooner, for my strength does not enable me to do my work satisfactorily'.[1] Lansdowne was the first colleague to hear that Balfour had been asked by the King to take over. Lansdowne was intensely loyal and fond of Balfour; he enjoyed working with him, and told him that 'no one else could have taken Salisbury's place'.[2] In fact, Balfour never did properly fill his uncle's shoes.

Lansdowne's position was now quite secure. He had proved indispensable and he, Chamberlain and Devonshire were the most formidable members of the cabinet. All three were Liberal Unionists. Devonshire was an ally of Lansdowne's, also a Whig and an Irish landowner, and saw foreign policy through the same lens. Chamberlain was a radical imperialist. Lansdowne respected his ideology and political ability, until Chamberlain attempted to undermine the cabinet with tariff reform in 1903. But all that was in the future.

As Hamilton told Curzon,

the one man who has come on greatly during the last year is Lansdowne. He has a great natural aptitude for negotiation and diplomacy, he is much better off than he was a few years ago, from the death of his mother and an aunt, and Lansdowne House, having all the reception rooms on the ground floor, is very well adapted for entertainment. He, in fact, has been the main entertainer of the Party during the past year, and everything of that kind which he undertakes is thoroughly well done.[3]

To entertain in such style required an enormous staff of maids, valets, footmen, butlers, stewards, cooks, porters, coachmen, drivers and grooms. When not entertaining *en grand*, Lansdowne and Maud dined alone or with close friends or relatives. When there were important guests for dinner, the staff had 'to breech'; that is, wear a special evening uniform of red plush breeches, white stockings and pumps, white waistcoat and black coatee with flaps across the back. Male staff had four Henry Poole tailored outfits a year – two of day livery, one evening livery and one morning suit of striped trousers and morning coat. State livery – a special coat and waistcoat with the plush breeches – was worn only on special occasions. Staff also each had a box cloth carriage coat, a waterproof carriage coat, top hat and gloves, a motor coat and cap, and a black mackintosh for motor work.

Lansdowne was not concerned that Balfour might differ from him on foreign policy, but he realised Balfour's views would be different from Salisbury's. Balfour saw Central Asia as Britain's greatest problem and Russia as her worst enemy. He dismissed Lansdowne's view that a Russian entente was possible; but, like Lansdowne, he believed it was wise to ease the pressure between Britain and Russia by reaching agreement in Afghanistan and Persia.[4] Cabinet relations under Balfour did not strongly affect Lansdowne's policy. He pursued the same line as before, although with more chance to make his mark. Russian expansion remained the Foreign Office's biggest concern until after the Russo-Japanese War.

Early in 1903 rumours circulated that the Russians would declare a protectorate in Tibet. Curzon, Viceroy of India, pressed for a mission to go to Lhasa with a large military escort to negotiate a new agreement, including a resident British agent, and so pre-empt the Russians.[5] On 18 February Lansdowne pointed out to Alexander Benckendorff, the Russian ambassador, that Lhasa was 1,000 miles from Russia's border. As British India was much more interested than Russia in Tibet, any Russian activity there would suggest British influence was receding, and Britain would have to respond on a larger scale.[6] The cabinet unanimously advised Lansdowne to seek some *modus vivendi* to diminish the perpetual friction between the two powers in Central Asia.[7]

On 8 April Benckendorff told Lansdowne that Russia had no agreement with Tibet, did not contemplate one and had no intention of sending agents to Lhasa, but Russia could not ignore any British annexation or protectorate of Tibet, and would probably seek compensation elsewhere. Lansdowne responded that Tibet had a long frontier with British India, and trade and treaty obligations that Britain would enforce.[8] He wanted a satisfactory settlement from the Tibetans, with reparation for injuries. Curzon and Francis Younghusband, appointed to head the mission, believed that a British representative at

Lhasa would counter the Russian threat. Lansdowne doubted the wisdom of this but he believed that the mission, while it negotiated at Khamba Jong, demonstrated British moderation.[9] The stand-off between the Tibetans, Chinese and Younghusband continued until early October, when Lansdowne let the 'Indian fools' occupy the Chumbi Valley and advance to Gyantse, as they had been urging.[10]

On 12 November Benckendorff told Lansdowne that Russia saw the British invasion of Tibet as gravely disturbing.[11] Lansdowne was surprised, but he was astonished at Parliament's sensitivity, telling Curzon, 'You may kill as many black men as you please in Somaliland but when it comes to protecting our own frontier by advance to a place within 250 miles of it people shake with alarm.'[12] On 7 September Younghusband signed an agreement at the Potala Palace in Lhasa. Lansdowne was embarrassed by its terms, which were more punitive than the Russians had been told. After consulting Hamilton at the India Office, he decided that Ernest Satow, the British ambassador in Peking, should not press the Chinese government to sign anything since the convention might still be revised.[13]

Meanwhile, Russian rivalry with Japan had escalated. In April 1903, Russia agreed to evacuate the second zone of Manchuria, but on terms that gave them complete control. If war came in the Far East, Britain was not keen to support Japan whose army was thought to be inferior to Russia's.[14] With a war between their allies seemingly possible, Britain and France moved to settle their own disputes. On 11 March Lansdowne advised Edmund Monson, British ambassador, in Paris that the King was cruising in the Mediterranean and on his return wished to meet President Loubet.[15] On 13 March Loubet welcomed a visit from the King; it would do even more good than London imagined.[16] The King arrived on 1 May to a reserved reception, but Paris gradually thawed. At the Hôtel de Ville and the Élyseé Palace the King spoke of rapprochement, and the visit was seen as successful. But even before the King arrived, a return visit had been arranged for 6 July.

On 7 July, at Cambon's prompting, Lansdowne and Delcassé met at Lansdowne House. As Lansdowne noted, 'a good understanding with France would not improbably be the precursor of a better understanding with Russia, and I need not insist upon the improvement which would result in our international position, which, in view of our present relations with Germany, as well as Russia, I cannot regard with satisfaction'.[17] This would reduce military and naval expenditure. Lansdowne saw few disagreements between them that could not be settled. The whole question hinged on Britain and France accommodating each other in Egypt and Morocco. Evelyn Cromer, Consul-General of Egypt, advised Lansdowne to take advantage of the situation.

Britain's main interest was control of the trade route via Suez to the Red Sea, and on to India, but Britain had never had a free hand in Egypt. On 10 September 1902, Lansdowne explained the Egypt–Morocco barter to the cabinet: it was worth some sacrifice to get a comprehensive settlement and minimise future trouble. Legally, all the Great Powers had to consent to reforms in Egypt, and there were concerns about Germany. Lansdowne believed, as did Cambon,

> that we shall have to reckon with Germany. Metternich has made several inquiries as to what we were about and the newspapers have made so many disclosures of late that they probably know the whole story, even if they did not know it before. It would not surprise me if they were to ask for Rabat. I do not know what our Admiralty would say to this, but the French have always assumed that we were to keep other Powers out of Morocco, and the Spaniards cannot bear Germany, and impute to her the most sinister designs.[18]

The negotiations met obstacles but by New Year 1904 terms were all but agreed, except for territorial compensation. At the eleventh hour, France demanded a valuable tract on the right bank of the Niger, part of the *spolia opima* of Chamberlain's campaign against the French in 1898. Lansdowne thought this, and their demands in Newfoundland, unreasonable; Balfour said it would be an international misfortune if negotiations failed. Finally, on 8 April an usher in the Foreign Office announced Cambon at Lansdowne's door. On a table lay the result of their efforts. Surrounded by staff, they signed the Anglo-French Entente-Cordiate.[19] It granted freedom of action to Britain in Egypt and to France in Morocco, if France allowed for Spain's interests there. Britain agreed to French control of the upper Gambia, defined the Nigerian frontier in France's favour and conceded the Los Islands (off French Guinea); France abandoned certain fishing rights off Newfoundland. British and French spheres of influence in Siam were delineated, and rivalry between their colonists in the New Hebrides was ended. *The Times* thought that

> the whole significance of the Agreement will be missed if it is jealously scrutinized as a mere barter of concessions from one country to the other. Its importance and its worth are really of a deeper kind. It is a landmark in the policy of the two nations, because it represents for the first time a serious attempt to see their worldwide relations steadily and to see them whole. It cannot, we think, be called anything but a satisfactory settlement of the material points at issue. But transcending its significance in this respect is the value it must possess and the weight

it must carry as a substantial pledge of the essential unity of our interests and desires. That value, as a great factor in the peace of nations, we believe it will retain.[20]

The agreement was broadly welcomed. The King wrote:

it has created a very good impression all over the civilized world! Though many countries may not like it as there are some (which shall be nameless) still I feel convinced that for the sake of peace it is one of the greatest diplomatic successes that we have had for a long time![21]

Concluding the agreement denied Lansdowne his holiday, but he was pleased. On 11 April he told Maud, 'I have been touched at the pleasure which my little French success has given you – you are I believe the pit and gallery to which I am playing most of the time.'[22]

One dissenter was Rosebery, former Foreign Secretary, friend of Lansdowne's and Liberal leader in the Lords. He believed the agreement would mean war with Germany in the end. Publicly he said, 'this unhappy agreement is much more likely to promote than to prevent unfriendliness'.[23] Lamsdorf expressed Russia's satisfaction; Germany kept silent, sure that Britain and France would quarrel eventually. On 23 March Delcassé gave assurances that France would still allow trade in Morocco. Germany, having insisted that trade was their only interest, had to be satisfied.[24] Spain had commercial interests there and was very suspicious. Lansdowne strove to reassure them that their interests had been respected,[25] but Spain appealed to Germany for support. Bülow thought the Spanish were acting as British agents and suggested to Lansdowne that they arrange joint backing for Spain against France.[26] He believed talks between Spain and France would come to nothing or split Britain and France. He was disappointed. On 3 October Spain signed the Franco-Spanish agreement, receiving a strip of northern Morocco as a neutral area.

Implementing the Anglo-French treaty required the consent of Russia, Germany, Italy and Austria-Hungary to the Egyptian Khedivial Decree.[27] Lansdowne expected Germany to blackmail Britain,[27] but he hoped to isolate Germany by offering the other powers diplomatic concessions.[28] On 10 May Benckendorff informed Lansdowne that Lamsdorf and the Russian government would not oppose the Khedivial Decree if Britain gave assurances on Tibet.[29] Lansdowne pressed Italy and Austria-Hungary. The Italians agreed on 22 May, in exchange for a concession on Abyssinia. Four days later, Austria-Hungary assented. Germany wanted a general settlement embracing Samoa, South Africa and trade with British colonies. Britain refused and Germany hinted it might turn to Russia; at the end of May Lansdowne concluded they must hold Germany at arm's length.

As part of his diplomacy, Lansdowne made full use of his family connections and residences. Lansdowne House was the venue for many dinners and dances, notably those during visits by the Shah of Persia in July 1902, President Loubet in July 1903 and King Alfonso of Spain in June 1904. After a dinner at Lansdowne House on 9 August 1902 (Coronation Day), Maud insisted on going out, despite her son Charlie trying to deter her. In the crowded streets, she, Edward 'Blackie' Hope, Lansdowne's best friend, and Almeric FitzRoy became separated from the other dinner guests. Maud behaved with pluck and good humour; they extricated her and got her to the park, where she sat down exhausted.[30]

In these years, Lansdowne always made time for his wife and growing family, while managing his estates. Each year they spent three months (summer, winter and spring) at Derreen, where, on 31 July 1903, King Edward and Queen Alexandra paid them a visit during a tour of Ireland. Children of the local school presented the Queen with a bouquet. Down at the pier, she was initiated into the mysteries of prawn fishing.[31] Under the Wyndham Land (Purchase) Act of 1903, Lansdowne sold off parts of his other Irish estates to tenants. In England and Scotland, agents helped him manage the estates. Financial difficulties forced him to sell off parcels of the Bowood estate.

Lansdowne's daughters Evie and Bertie gave birth to five children and, on 16 February 1904, Kerry, Lansdowne's elder son, married Elsie Hope, daughter of 'Blackie' and Consie Hope. She was eighteen, thirteen years younger than Kerry. The Lansdownes were pleased by the marriage, and Lansdowne gave the couple part of the estate at Sheen Falls in County Kerry. In 1901 Lansdowne's other son, Charlie, joined the staff of Lord Roberts, Commander-in-Chief until 1904; in 1905 Charlie rejoined his regiment at Lucknow in India. Lansdowne's brother, Edmond Fitzmaurice, was MP for Cricklade during Lansdowne's years at the Foreign Office. In 1905 his biography of Earl Granville, Lansdowne's political mentor, was published. When the Liberals came to power in December, he was offered the post of Foreign Secretary if Sir Edward Grey refused it, which he did not. Edmond instead became Under-Secretary of State for Foreign Affairs. At the 1906 general election he did not stand for Cricklade and was ennobled as 1st Baron Fitzmaurice of Leigh in Wiltshire. The presence of brothers on different sides in Parliament was not generally newsworthy, although the fact that Edmond represented foreign affairs in the Lords had its own piquancy. The men resembled one another in many respects, but Edmond was a staunch Liberal and a more zealous free-trader on tariff reform than his brother.

Lansdowne's role as Foreign Secretary involved not only geostrategic decisions but also the policing of corrupt states. Congo was one. The Berlin Conference (1884–85) recognised many European claims in Africa, including a personal possession of King Leopold II of the Belgians, called the Congo Free State (CFS). On 12 May 1894 the British government leased parts of the Upper Nile Valley to King Leopold as sovereign of the CFS. Two months later, without consulting Britain, Leopold granted a concession to the Société Générale Africaine, which transferred it in turn. With absolute control of people, produce and minerals entirely in Leopold's hands, Lansdowne was concerned that under the 1894 'lease' HMG had no precaution against an abuse of authority. By 1903 it was impossible to keep secret the sinister activities and appalling cruelties of the CFS from which Leopold was making a fortune. Rubber sales, 80 per cent of Congo's exports, had increased fifteen times in eight years.[32] Britain had to define its attitude.

In a Commons debate on 20 July 1903 it was alleged that the Congo administration cared less for the welfare and government of the natives and more for revenue collection pursued by methods tantamount to slavery. The armed forces of the state were said to be recruited from the most savage tribes, who terrorised even their own officers. On 4 June Lansdowne ordered Roger Casement, British consul in the Congo, to go into the interior and investigate. While awaiting his report, Lansdowne wrote on 8 August to Britain's envoys in the countries that had signed the Treaty of Berlin to say he was aware of very serious allegations of ill-treatment of natives and he proposed a conference on trading rights in the Congo basin because, in his opinion, 'the prevailing system was inconsistent with Article I of the Berlin Act, providing for freedom of trade there by all nations'.[33] Leopold's principal Congo secretary dismissed the allegations. None of the powers responded except Turkey.

Published on 11 December 1903, Casement's report created a sensation.[34] He said that, as part of commercial exploitation, unspeakable atrocities were constantly and systematically perpetrated upon the natives with the knowledge of Congo officials. In February 1904, Lansdowne forwarded the report to Edmund Phipps, ambassador at Brussels, and to all signatories of the Berlin Treaty with a request to reply to his dispatch of August. In April the Congo Reform Association was set up in London, with Edmund Morel as secretary. This was, in effect, the world's first human rights organisation. In May, Charles Dilke, a radical Liberal MP, led the opposition attack, urging stronger action than writing dispatches. Edward Grey said the Congo State must answer to the Belgian Parliament. He also called for a conference to revise the Berlin Treaty of 1885. Lansdowne's brother, Edmond Fitzmaurice, pleaded for consular courts and even hinted that a warship might be sent to occupy Boma.

The Congo government objected that Casement's report was based on only a brief visit, to which Lansdowne replied that Leopold should appoint a commission of inquiry for himself. After deliberation, the Congo government agreed,[35] but asked for a copy of Casement's report so that they could interview the same witnesses. Lansdowne agreed, subject to their coming to no harm. On 31 July the Congo government appointed a special commission, which arrived in October 1904 and left in February. Lansdowne insisted that its moral authority would be destroyed if it held no public sittings. The Congo agreed, even allowing the British consul to attend closed sittings. Its report in October 1905 contained scathing criticism; it caused a sensation in Belgium and vindicated most of Casement's report. In 1906 Lansdowne, no longer Foreign Secretary, described the Congolese system as 'bondage under the most barbarous and inhuman conditions and maintained for mercenary motives of the most selfish character'. Grey, then Foreign Secretary, and Fitzmaurice, Under-Secretary, agreed completely with Lansdowne.[36]

During his time as Foreign Secretary, Lansdowne rarely found himself at loggerheads with the opposition Liberals over foreign policy. Domestic policy was another matter, Ireland particularly. In 1903 the Irish political situation had improved with the Wyndham Land (Purchase) Act, whereby sale was made attractive to both landowners and tenants by the British government paying the difference between the asking price and the tenant's offer. The economic situation improved, although political friction remained between Home Rulers and Unionists. Lord Dunraven, a discontented Unionist, took matters into his own hands. He had become disappointed by the Irish Parliamentary Party, notably in O'Brien's resignation and the vehement campaigning of the Nationalists. In August 1904 he created the Irish Reform Association, which met in Dublin and adopted a tentative programme of devolution for Ireland. To develop their preliminary report into a definite scheme, Dunraven sought help from the Irish government. The Chief Secretary for Ireland, George Wyndham, was ill, so it was Sir Antony MacDonnell, Under-Secretary for Ireland (who had been an Indian administrator during Lansdowne's viceroyalty), to whom Dunraven spoke. Lansdowne admired MacDonnell and had secured his appointment as Under-Secretary, stating he was fearless and just, and would not truckle with the Nationalists.[37] But many Unionists, particularly in Ulster, suspected him of Home Rule leanings. Although he was initially reluctant to help, he agreed to meet Dunraven on his yacht the following month. He agreed to draft the Reform Association's first policy declaration and the financial and legislative details for their second statement. To avoid any misunderstanding, he informed Wyndham on 10 September. He received no answer.

On 20 September 1904, MacDonnell spent a night at Derreen and showed Lansdowne a typescript substantially identical to the second manifesto. Lansdowne did not read it very carefully, attaching little importance to it because he understood Dunraven and his friends were responsible for the proposals and that MacDonnell had provided only redaction. He did ask if Wyndham knew what he was about, and MacDonnell answered that he did. This second report was published on 26 September. *The Times* called it an 'insidious project' and alluded to the involvement of Dublin Castle and MacDonnell. Unionists attacked it because it seemed like an advance towards Home Rule and Nationalists criticised the fact that it did not envisage an Irish Parliament. Wyndham, who did not recall MacDonnell's letter of 10 September, was alarmed. He immediately wrote to *The Times*, denying knowledge of the report, denying that anyone had sought his views on the matter and stating that the Unionist government was opposed to new legislative bodies in the United Kingdom. On Wyndham's advice, MacDonnell broke off contact with the Reform Association, but he was violently abused.

On 17 February 1905, the Lords debated the contacts between Dunraven and MacDonnell. During the debate, which Almeric FitzRoy said was more heated than any other he could remember, Lansdowne spoke lucidly and openly, deflecting the brunt of the Liberal Party's attack. He argued that MacDonnell's position was quite exceptional and that he had acted with the full knowledge and approval of Lord Dudley, Lord Lieutenant of Ireland. When Lansdowne sat down, Ashbourne, Lord Chancellor of Ireland, whispered in his ear, 'My boy, I have never heard so much fat put on the fire in a few minutes!' Lansdowne's speech did not satisfy his critics. Unionists in Ulster and elsewhere strongly suspected there had been a government plot to bring in some form of Home Rule without their consent; some of the Liberal press believed that, if they vindicated Wyndham's actions, the latter might recover his reputation in Ulster by making MacDonnell a scapegoat.

The government majority was cut to fifty, including just six Irish Unionists. On 6 March 1905, Balfour announced Wyndham's resignation. Lansdowne was upset and did not approve,[38] but the controversy had destroyed Wyndham's value to the Irish Office. *The Times* and the opposition, scenting that the Unionists had become enfeebled, probed further in late September and October, attacking Lansdowne and Balfour. On 12 October, at the Liberal Unionist Council in Nottingham, Lansdowne put paid to the MacDonnell mystery. He stated that Balfour never promoted Home Rule proposals, and neither Balfour nor his cabinet knew that Dudley and MacDonnell were mixed up in devolution. Lansdowne thought his audience was convinced, but *The Times* was not. Irritated by this, Lansdowne told Balfour that George

Buckle, the editor, was irreconcilable.[39]

Balfour thought Lansdowne's speech was excellent and Wyndham was grateful for it, although he doubted it would satisfy the Ulster party, 'but then nothing ever will'.[40] Joseph Chamberlain, then under attack from *The Times*, told his wife, 'It's just like Lansdowne, it's manly and it's straightforward and it ought to put an end to the controversy.'[41] However, in a letter to Lansdowne, MacDonnell questioned the truth of his statements. Lansdowne was disappointed by his former colleague. He did not believe he had misrepresented him but offered to discuss the matter should he visit London. He later made a note that MacDonnell called at Lansdowne House in October or November. The matter was dropped and never revived.

25

THE TRANSFORMATION OF
THE FOREIGN OFFICE

DUNRAVEN'S DEVOLUTION SCHEME caused minor political discomfiture for Lansdowne and Balfour in comparison to Joseph Chamberlain's drive for colonial preference and tariff reform. In May 1903, Chamberlain publicly rejected free trade and set about dividing the cabinet over the issue. With no clear lead from Balfour, the situation worsened. By the end of September Chamberlain had resigned to organise a national campaign for tariff reform, unaware that Devonshire and three hard-line free-traders – including Hamilton, Lansdowne's brother-in-law – had also left the government. Lansdowne deplored the whole situation. He was so fond of Devonshire that he could not help taking it to heart, and later said his retirement was a colossal mistake.[1] But, 'having failed egregiously with the uncle, I have tried to prevail with the nephew [Victor Cavendish]. He would like to stay with us, and I think his qualms can be overcome.'[2] In this, Lansdowne was successful. Maud deeply regretted her brother's decision.[3]

In the reconstructed cabinet, Lansdowne stayed at the Foreign Office and succeeded Devonshire as Unionist Leader of the House of Lords and Deputy Leader of the Unionist Party. Leadership of the Lords gave him much anxiety: he felt he knew nothing about English politics or subjects such as licensing, education or local government; and he was much affected by the radical newspapers' delight in arguing that his War Office failures disqualified him from the post. Maud asked Cavendish and Balfour to persuade him.[4] Lansdowne accepted and, on 13 October, became Leader of the Lords, like his grandfather fifty-seven years earlier. He was particularly useful as a foil to discontented Irish peers, although the job added enormously to his workload at the Foreign Office. By this time he had more than proved his worth in cabinet and had recovered his reputation as a minister.

Chamberlain now created further political turmoil in attempting to convert the country to tariff reform. Without Devonshire's support, he took control of the Liberal Unionist Association (LUA), intending to rebuild it and use it as an instrument of fiscal policy. In July 1904 he persuaded Lansdowne to become Vice President. Lansdowne accepted in order to act as a brake on Chamberlain – a part Balfour had intended for Devonshire.[5] On 14 July, at the Albert Hall, Lansdowne and his Liberal Unionist colleagues stood on a platform beneath a banner proclaiming 'Learn to Think Imperially'. The LUA declared that only imperial union and preference could save the Unionist Party. As a member of the Cobden Club,[6] Lansdowne was regarded as a free-trader; however, on this occasion he praised Chamberlain's ideal of fiscal preference, while leaving a good deal of ambiguity about the taxation of food.[7] As the Unionist Party wobbled, so Lansdowne's position in cabinet grew firmer. Brodrick noted that

> Lansdowne has been terribly overwhelmed with business lately, with the continual *pourparlers* both with Russia and Japan, with the negotiations with France, and the leadership of the House of Lords, and the deputy leadership of the party thrown in. He takes the chair for us in cabinet and does it exceedingly well. I really believe, if so great a national misfortune were to happen as anything which incapacitated the Prime Minister, that Lansdowne would be the only man who could replace him. And that is the more remarkable as it is little more than three years since that his administration of the War Office had most unjustly become a by-word.[8]

Having gained the respect of cabinet, Lansdowne initiated restructuring of the Foreign Office without concern that his colleagues would raise objections. Simultaneous with his efforts to smooth Britain's relations with the Great Powers, in 1903 he began overhauling his staff and administration, increasing the authority of senior officials, encouraging junior clerks to develop specialist knowledge and devolving much of the work. His first task was to get the right people in the right posts, after which he established a committee to report on departmental efficiency. From these findings he introduced a general registry for the archiving and retrieval of correspondence as well as a special cipher room.

In December 1904, Lansdowne proposed introducing a special examination for entry to the Foreign Office; this required a sound liberal education, a leaning towards the literary rather than the scientific, and certain personal qualifications and aptitudes that no examination could reveal. The object of the exam was to show what a candidate might become, not what he was at that moment. Lansdowne attached much weight to composition: as he commented in a memorandum, honours graduates had shown they could express their ideas in their own language, but it was hardly possible to overrate the value of a clear, orderly style.[9]

During Lansdowne's time at the FO, commerce became far more prominent in negotiations. In late 1902 some Liberal newspapers alleged apathy at the Foreign Office in promoting British trade, but by November 1905 the commerce department was dealing with 10,000 cases a year. Lansdowne thought the explanation was obvious: civilised nations were now less inclined to extend their territory, and looked to extend their markets instead. Tariffs were manipulated in such a way that 'most favoured nation' could mean something very different in reality; in future, Lansdowne believed, Britain should seek agreements that specially provided for her interests. The Entente Cordiale of 1904 was his first success in this.

Relations between Russia and Japan were strained to breaking point, and in December 1903 war seemed imminent. Lansdowne mentioned unofficially to Cambon, the French ambassador, that such a war might involve Britain and, if so, France's treaty obligations might make it difficult for her to keep out. Cambon was aware that the Anglo-Japanese agreement required Britain to intervene only if Japan was assailed by two other powers, and advised Lansdowne to pour as much cold water as possible upon the embers.[10] Long before this, the cabinet had decided that financially Britain could not afford to go to war in the Far East. Austen Chamberlain, the new Chancellor, and son of Joseph, told Lansdowne that the cost of a large-scale war would be ruinous.[11] Moreover, the cabinet assumed that if it came to war, Japan would be defeated, so they were determined to avoid negotiations that would oblige them to assist the Japanese. Lansdowne thought prevention a better option and argued they should strive to achieve that. He believed the British people would not support a Russian invasion of Japan. He proposed appealing to France and the United States for mediation, believing that if Russia were accommodating in Manchuria, he could urge Japan to accept the best bargain they could obtain over Korea.[12]

Balfour disagreed. He had less faith in the Japanese and was less interested in the Far East. A war between them would end in Russian victory, but 'an invasion of Japan by Russia on any important scale is I believe impossible. A war therefore would not "smash" Japan in the sense of wiping it out.'[13] On 29 December Hayashi met with Lansdowne under instructions to show that Japan was not the aggressor in the dispute. Lansdowne listened and informed him that, in a Russo-Japanese war alone, he should not rely on the terms of the Anglo-Japanese Alliance. He also refused Hayashi's request for a guaranteed £20 million war loan, and in this he was supported by both Balfour and Austen Chamberlain who disapproved for economic and political reasons. Chamberlain believed the markets needed a chance to digest the large bond issues from the Transvaal war.[14] Hayashi was bitterly upset and Anglo-Japanese relations became strained.

On 6 February 1904, Japanese destroyers under Admiral Tōgō torpedoed three Russian battleships anchored at Port Arthur (Lüshen Port, China), clearing the way for troop landings in Korea. As London prepared for a Russian victory, Balfour told Lansdowne that Japan's defeat would mean Russia going to war with China. On 21 October, in crossing the North Sea, Admiral Rozhestvensky's Russian fleet found itself surrounded by Hull fishing boats at Dogger Bank. Nervous Russians, without provocation or enquiry, fired torpedoes, sinking one vessel and killing two fishermen. While the majority of the cabinet were ready to declare war on Russia, Lansdowne was strongly against. He instructed Charles Hardinge, ambassador in St Petersburg, to inform Lamsdorf of what had occurred and, since the action had seemed deliberate, the widespread indignation it provoked in Britain. Among the political parties to speak most critically were the Labour Party, whose leaders were usually opponents of militarism, but were particularly bellicose because the victims were working men.[15] Lansdowne believed that, if the admiral had been negligent, 'it will be the duty of H.M.G. [His Majesty's Government] to require ample apology, complete and prompt reparation, as well as security against recurrence of such intolerable incidents'.[16]

Lamsdorf, who was horrified, offered the assurance sought. The Tsar wrote:

> The English are very angry and near boiling point. They are even said to be getting their fleet ready for action. Yesterday I sent a telegram to Uncle Bertie [King Edward VII], expressing my regret, but I did not apologize. I do not think the English will have the cheek to go further than to indulge in threats.[17]

The King did not think the Tsar's regret was sufficient: 'The Russian admiral must be punished for his conduct and we have a _right_ to demand it.'[18] Lansdowne believed Russia would not accept such humiliation.[19] Opinion at the Foreign Office was that any inquiry should be carried out by the British. Hardinge told Bertie, British ambassador in Paris, that he presumed Britain did not want war because it would be a general calamity; the area of operations might extend indefinitely and only Germany would benefit.[20] Russia agreed to pay compensation, and the two countries referred other aspects to a commission of inquiry at The Hague.[21] The affair pushed Russia closer to a German alliance. Driven by the Kaiser, the Germans pressed Russia to join a continental league against Britain. Nothing came of this because neither Britain nor Russia was as eager for war as the French and Germans had assumed. It was the end of an epoch in which Anglo-Russian conflict seemed the most likely threat to international relations. After November 1904, the conflict was indefinitely postponed.

Contrary to London's expectation Russian attacks proved indecisive and in January 1905 Japan took control of Port Arthur. Britain had steered clear of the war in the Far East, but now Lansdowne saw an opportunity to profit from its eventual outcome to improve Britain's imperial position and renew the Anglo-Japanese Alliance on better terms. As Claude MacDonald, the ambassador in Tokyo, put it:

> The moment when we can be of the greatest use to them, the moment when they will definitely decide whether they will go with us in the Far East of the future or come to an arrangement with the Russians, will be during the peace negotiations. If we stick to them and prevent other nations interfering, I think we shall continue to have a say in matters Eastern.[22]

On 12 February 1905, at a dinner in London celebrating three years of the alliance, Komura, the Foreign Minister, and Katsura Tarō, the Prime Minister, announced their wish to extend the agreement in duration and scope.[23] On 24 March Hayashi confirmed that this was the general feeling in Japan. Lansdowne instructed Mortimer Durand, Britain's ambassador in Washington, to inform President Roosevelt.[24] The Japanese needed to safeguard their new position, especially in Korea, and deter Russia from considering revenge.[25] They wanted to make the alliance 'more solid'.[26] Britain had less need to renew the alliance, but Lansdowne believed Japan

> could insist on maintaining her paramount interest in Corea and on the retention of Port Arthur. We should be ready to act with the United States in opposing attempts by neutral powers to force Japan to abandon either of these interests.[27]

On 31 May Lansdowne circulated a draft treaty to some cabinet ministers and military experts, who accepted it with far smaller demands than in 1902, showing how far Lansdowne had come since then. Four days later, the Japanese fleet crushingly defeated the Russians at Tsushima.

On 12 August 1905, Lansdowne and Hayashi signed the Second Anglo-Japanese Alliance at Lansdowne House. This was a new alliance, not just a renewal of 1902. The terms were different, as was the emphasis, which was offensive in tone. One article provided that any attack on the territory or interests covered in the treaty of either signatory would at once bring in the other signatory to wage war alongside its ally. The alliance now included India and accepted Japan's 'paramount political, military, and economic interests' in Korea, whose independence was not recognised. The alliance was to last for ten years.[28] As peace talks between Russia and Japan were about to start, with the likelihood of changes to their territorial rights, it was decided not to publicise the new treaty yet. However, news leaked out at the end of August and the details were confirmed on 27 September. Lansdowne informed France at the beginning of September and, as a favour from one foreign minister to another, asked Cambon to reassure the Russians. Lansdowne was still eager to negotiate with Russia:

> We are extremely anxious that the Russian government shall not regard the new alliance as an unfriendly act towards itself. I go further and say that in my opinion our compact with Japan in no way excludes the idea of a friendly understanding with Russia covering the future developments of our policy in those regions where the interests of the two powers are in contact.[29]

Lamsdorf, speaking privately, remarked that the treaty had a very bad effect in Russia and left an unpleasant impression on the Tsar.[30] Witte, the Finance Minister, denounced it.[31]

On 5 September the Treaty of Portsmouth formally ended the war in the Far East. Russia's weakened state was both a benefit and a risk to British diplomacy. The Franco-Russian alliance had acted as a break on Germany in Europe. Without a strong Russia to contain her in the East, Germany was free to assert herself in the West. Lansdowne was, however, less concerned by Germany than his colleagues and the British press. He remarked, 'I have perhaps become so much used to the querulous tone of the German government that it produces less effect on me than it does upon our colleague. I am at any rate more inclined to meet it with ridicule than with violent indignation.'[32] Lansdowne's optimism was short-lived.

On 12 March 1905, Bülow, the German Chancellor, announced that Germany urgently needed to assert its rights in Morocco. Worse, at the end of March the Kaiser visited Tangier, proclaiming he would protect Moroccan independence and would not recognise agreements made without his consent, in effect challenging the Anglo-French Entente Cordiale.[33] On 9 April Lansdowne told Lascelles, British ambassador in Berlin, 'we can hardly regard this ebullition as an isolated incident. There could be no doubt that the Kaiser was much annoyed by the Anglo-French agreement and probably even more so by our refusal to vamp up some agreement of the same kind with Germany over the Egyptian question. We shall, I have little doubt, find that the Kaiser avails himself of every opportunity to put spokes in our wheels.'[34] Delcassé, the French Foreign Minister, came under attack from his pro-German Chamber of Deputies and Prime Minister for his firm line against Germany. Lansdowne was inwardly annoyed and appalled that the Germans could discredit the entente.

On 1 May Edward VII arrived in Paris on an informal visit. In support of Delcassé's views, he assured the French government that Germany would not dare make war but, if it did, France could rely on British support. Lansdowne was assured that the entente was in excellent shape. At the end of May he wrote to Cambon, inviting him to discuss how they might deal with the various complications at hand. As if to emphasise the gravity of the situation, he concluded that he was not quite sure whether he had made it clear to Cambon that

> there should be a full and confidential discussion between the two governments, not so much in consequence of some act of unprovoked aggression on the part of another power, as in anticipation of any complications to be apprehended during the somewhat anxious period through which we are at present passing.[35]

Unsupported by the French government, Delcassé's further attempts at strengthening the entente failed and he was forced to resign. He warned the Chamber of Deputies that Germany would now be more insolent and exacting than ever. That day, the Kaiser ennobled Bülow as a prince. On 12 June Lansdowne remarked to Bertie, the ambassador in Paris:

> Delcassé's resignation has, as you may well suppose, produced a very painful impression here. What people say is that if one of our Ministers had had a dead set made at him by a foreign Power, the country and the Government would not only have stood by him, but probably have supported him more vigorously than ever, whereas France has apparently thrown Delcassé overboard in a panic. Of course the result is that the entente is quoted at a much lower price than it was a fortnight ago.[36]

While Lansdowne's faith in the entente was shaken by the French government's inability to deal effectively with German bullying, he was equally perturbed by King Edward's bullying of the Kaiser. Lansdowne found the King's animosity to his nephew as annoying as Germanophobia in general. In August he reported to Balfour that the King had 'the Emperor on his brain' and his constant abuse of his nephew was doing 'a great deal of harm'.[37]

Lansdowne wished to temper the King's impatience with the Kaiser because German intrigue was rife. In August Lansdowne heard from Charles Hardinge, ambassador in St Petersburg, that the Kaiser and Tsar Nicholas of Russia had met the previous month in the Björkö Sound in the Gulf of Bothnia, where they signed a secret mutual defence accord. Witte and Lamsdorf were not present nor consulted; they both insisted the treaty should never take effect unless approved by the French. Lamsdorf believed the treaty was all in Germany's favour and might embroil Russia in Anglo-German rivalry.[38] In fact it subsequently strengthened the Entente Cordiale by convincing the timid French government that German diplomacy was set on breaking the Franco-Russian alliance. The intended continental league was soon also thwarted by the new Anglo-Japanese Treaty, the Treaty of Portsmouth between Japan and Russia, the proposed Franco-German conference on Morocco, and loans to Russia by the French, who had no intention of joining the league and antagonising Britain. Russia dared not threaten France. France had no desire to break with Britain, and Germany was further isolated.

Lansdowne's foreign policy was not as Eurocentric as his successor Edward Grey's was, but he recognised the importance of the entente. During 1905 the service departments enquired about a potential war between Germany and France, and Lansdowne was informed that Germany would violate Belgium's neutrality. He considered that, in a European war, the powers would almost certainly form groups and the theatre of war would extend around the world.[39] It was later suggested by Cambon that Lansdowne wished for an alliance with the French but he had no intention to go so far.

However, in the final months of 1905, military and naval talks began about Franco-British cooperation in a war against Germany. Recollections of those close to the matter at that time do not mention any official discussions before the new government took office in December 1905. In an interview between Lansdowne and Harold Temperley, the diplomatic historian, in July 1926, Lansdowne revealed his view that the entente was the same at the end of his period of office as at the beginning, except that military and naval experts on both sides got together and talked about possible schemes of cooperation, 'as was their business, and talked indiscreetly as they always will do!' Temperley concluded that Lansdowne meant by this that he as Foreign Secretary had not authorised any such discussions, and there is no evidence that he did.[40] On 20 December 1905, Cambon informed King Edward that neither country had discussed their military plans. It is evident that Lansdowne was eager to maintain the entente but unwilling to develop it into a core element of his foreign policy in the form of a military alliance.

By autumn 1905, Balfour and his colleagues accepted they would soon lose office. The government had become weakened by Chamberlain's fiscal demands and growing discontent among the electorate. Lansdowne discussed the matter with Balfour and saw that the arguments in favour of immediate resignation were very strong: 'We could in no conceivable circumstances have retained office for more than a few weeks.'[41] Before the Liberals could strike the first blow, Balfour forced the opposition into office. On 4 December the government resigned and Lansdowne left the Foreign Office. He was delighted to have fewer official engagements and he expected to have more private ones.[42] In the election of January 1906 seven of Lansdowne's cabinet colleagues lost their seats, including Balfour himself. The new House of Commons contained 400 Liberals, 157 Unionists, 83 Irish Nationalists and 30 Labour members. It was the greatest victory ever for the Liberals,[43] a party Lansdowne had once supported.

As Foreign Secretary, Lansdowne altered British foreign policy for ever. Not wishing to enlarge the British Empire and aware that its power was declining, he recognised that international friendships based on mutual interests were the best safeguard of imperial security. The special relationship with the US, the Japanese alliance and the entente exemplify this. Inheriting an imperial strategy concentrated on curbing Russian expansion in the Near and Far East, Lansdowne had no preconceived foreign policy. He worked with events and allowed himself to be directed by the force of developments. A remarkable aspect of his first three years in office was the rapidity with which he was prepared to change policy and defend German outrages. He was profoundly frustrated that he could not put Anglo-German relations on a better footing. Unlike the majority of his departmental colleagues he was not anti-Germany. Even after the Kaiser's intrigues and attempts to weaken the entente in 1905, Lansdowne remained on cordial terms with him. Lansdowne was never regarded by the Germans as an enemy. This says as much about Lansdowne's personality as it does his policy, which was inclusive.

Another important break with his predecessor, Salisbury, were Lansdowne's reforms in the Foreign Office. Few in Whitehall saw the need and value of commercial reports and representation as clearly as Lansdowne did by 1905.[44] While most departments still thought largely in terms of power, prestige and strategy,[45] the Foreign Office under Lansdowne became more active in encouraging trade. At the War Office he had come to appreciate that international decisions depended on knowledge-sharing in Whitehall, so he ensured that the War, Admiralty, Colonial and India Offices were informed of Foreign Office matters. He and his department, with Balfour's support, began to take more notice of the opinions of the Committee of Imperial Defence[46] and reports from the Intelligence department.[47] Britain's relations with foreign allies became more transparent and the Foreign Office became far less insulated under Lansdowne.

Shortly before leaving the Foreign Office Lansdowne was a guest of the Junior Constitutional Club at a congratulatory dinner given in his honour on the occasion of the conclusion of the Anglo-Japanese Treaty. Addressing the 375 guests Lansdowne remarked:

> I think most of us in this country have been brought up to the idea that upon the whole it was better for us to avoid any alliances of whatever kind. There has been a prejudice against alliances. They have been spoken of as 'entangling alliances,' and our people are supposed not to like such entanglements. But I own that in my humble opinion the time for holding these opinions seems to me to have passed by. We have only to look at what is passing in other parts of the world. Other nations are grouping themselves together. Other nations are also arming themselves to the teeth, and in these days the shock of war comes with much greater suddenness and rapidity than it came in the days of our forefathers. I venture to say to you that in these times no nation which intends to take its part in the affairs of the civilized world can venture to stand entirely alone… I wish to raise my voice against the assumption that because there has been an approximation between Great Britain and two great and friendly Powers [France and Japan] there must necessarily be an estrangement between ourselves and any other Power or Powers. The suggestion seems to me to proceed upon the altogether untenable theory that the stock of international good will and international good manners is so limited that if a certain amount of it has been served out there is none left for any of those who may afterwards apply for it.[48]

Many years later Lansdowne spoke of his period at the Foreign Office as 'incomparably most interesting'.[49] By temperament, education, training and natural aptitude, he was well suited to the role. He inspired confidence among foreign representatives and his colleagues in the department and diplomatic service. The cabinet even believed he was worth resigning for. On leaving office he received the Royal Victorian Chain, the highest decoration of the Royal Victorian Order, conferred on those who had served the monarch with distinction. His successor, Edward Grey, broadly speaking followed Lansdowne's policy, albeit that he concentrated largely on Europe. Subsequent events in foreign affairs were largely the result of adopting a military rather than diplomatic strategy to guarantee security. Lansdowne had more faith in diplomacy, as did Cambon, who later said of the entente: '*Puisse cette entente subsister, car sans elle, je ne vois en Europe que trouble et confusion.*'[50]

26

LIVING WITH
THE LIBERALS

LANSDOWNE WAS NOT surprised by the Liberals' landslide victory in January 1906, but he was deeply concerned for his own 'shattered party', especially its leadership. Despite Balfour losing his seat at Manchester East, Lansdowne was optimistic he would stand again. In the meantime, keeping the party intact was essential and he believed that Chamberlain should lead, even though 'wry faces will be pulled, and malcontents will be worse content than ever'.[1] The new Prime Minister Henry Campbell-Bannerman and the Liberals had a majority only in the Commons, so the House of Lords, where Lansdowne was Unionist Leader, would determine the fate of legislation. It was critical that the Unionists should 'not make a tactical blunder at the outset'.[2] Balfour thought the same, except he was more determined to thwart the Liberals' political agenda than was Lansdowne.

While Lansdowne was concerned by the social reforming ambitions of the new government, he was satisfied that Edward Grey, the new Foreign Secretary, favoured continuity in foreign affairs and that Richard Haldane, the new Secretary of State for War, would continue the military policy of his predecessors. It was Balfour's view that the Unionists, whether in office or not, should control the destinies of the Empire. To achieve this, the House of Lords became 'Mr. Balfour's poodle', as Lloyd George put it.[3] Such an abuse of power was destructive to the Unionists and, in 1911, to the House of Lords itself, but Lansdowne failed to see this at the time. He became a willing accomplice to Balfour. When Lansdowne agreed in 1903 to succeed Devonshire as Unionist Leader of the Lords, he undoubtedly had no idea that he would find himself in the middle of the bitterest constitutional struggle of his generation.

To understand why Lansdowne accepted Balfour's strategy, we must look beyond simple motives of class and electoral advantage. Since the 1870s parliamentary reform had made the House of Commons increasingly strong while weakening the power of the Lords. Salisbury believed that the Lords' duty was not to act as a pale shadow of the Commons but to represent the permanent feelings of the nation and uphold them. While Prime Minister in 1885, 1886–92 and 1895–1902, he argued that, since the views of the Commons and the will of the people were not always in accord, the House of Lords had a duty to reject contentious bills and refer them back to the electorate. Lansdowne himself did not strictly adopt Salisbury's referendal theory, but he and Balfour – in defiance of accepted parliamentary government – continued to invoke this theory to justify the Lords' legislative veto.

Before the new session of Parliament, the Unionists focused their attention on the party leadership and the direction it should take. Although Balfour won his seat in the City and returned to lead the Unionists, the party was deeply divided between Balfourites, Chamberlainites and Unionist Free Fooders,[4] whose peers Devonshire hoped might form a swing group in the Lords. One sign of the impending crisis was where party members chose to dine at the various eve-of-session dinners. Concealed behind these choices was the reality that the House of Commons was about to collide with the House of Lords. Preparing for the inevitable, Lansdowne wrote to Devonshire that

the political situation had been so profoundly altered by the result of the elections that you may attach less weight than you did to the reasons which formerly led you to think that we had better dine apart. I am as much impressed as you are by the apprehension of a collision between the two houses. Whether the best way of mitigating the risk is to establish within the H. of L. such a 'buffer' party as you apparently contemplate, I am by no means sure.[5]

Devonshire and many others, however, had no wish to put their differences to one side for the sake of party unity.[6] Lansdowne could not prevent further ructions. As he told Balfour:

we shall have to consider very carefully the line to be taken in both Houses and if Joe [Chamberlain] is to understudy you, I am by no means confident that his line will be that which I should approve. If Joe insists on pushing his views, the schism will become deeper, and the Unionist party will degenerate into two feeble and mutually suspicious groups. It is not necessary that we should recant our opinions as to retaliation or colonial preference, but the country has pronounced decisively against them, and we must accept the verdict. With a majority of over 200 against us, we are – for the moment, at all events – relieved of the necessity of bringing forward a constructive policy of our own. I particularly dislike the idea of tarring the H. of Lords with the brush of Protection.[7]

Attempting to save Unionist Party unity on terms that were not disastrous to it and their reputations, Lansdowne warned Balfour that it was up to him to make a move towards Chamberlain and 'to explain how it has come to pass that while, a few weeks ago, you resigned on account of the differences within the party, these differences have now been composed'.[8] He advised Balfour to avoid making any alliance with Chamberlain based upon acceptance of tariff reform and severing relations with Unionists who refused to accept the full Chamberlain programme. He believed any such alliance would fail within six months.[9]

On 7 February Chamberlain demanded a meeting with Balfour, hoping to persuade Balfour to accept his policy and remain leader. The alternative was a fight to decide policy, with the leadership being decided later.[10] Lansdowne offered Lansdowne House for the event, even though 'I shall be sorry that it should hereafter be associated with the memory of a discreditable and useless episode'.[11] The conference was attended by over six hundred Unionist politicians, and the 'Valentine letters'[12] (later published) were widely seen as Balfour's surrender to Chamberlain. The meeting demonstrated that the Unionists were still deeply divided, but an agreement had been made and the opposition party prepared itself for the challenge ahead. Although Lansdowne urged that 'the fiscal question does not occupy the whole area of our political life',[13] he was more concerned by the impending clash between the Liberal majority in the Commons and the Unionist majority in the Lords.

In 1906 the Lords' ability to delay, examine, scrutinise, revise and, if necessary, throw out bills passed by the Commons gave it considerable influence. The House of Lords was a key element in the British constitution, so much so that changes to it would trigger constitutional issues including the role of Parliament and Whitehall and the future of the monarchy. Among the general public and the press, the Lords was seen to perform an invaluable service, one that justified its place in the constitution. As mentioned, Salisbury believed that one function of the Lords was to refer important legislation to the electorate whenever it could be argued that the government, relying on the House of Commons, had no mandate for its measures. By such reasoning the Lords should look to the nation or electorate for direction and guidance.[14] However, the Lords was also seen as a bastion of privilege, inherited wealth, high society and finance.[15] This reality was easy for the new Liberals and the emerging Labour Party to exploit.

Although most peers belonged to one of main parties and took a party whip, they were not constrained by party discipline. The Leader and the Chief Whip of the Unionist Party were dominant, but they had few means to persuade reluctant peers. Most were hereditary peers; only a third were life peers or bishops, and they were not subject to expulsion or removal. Unionist peers occasionally rebelled, but rarely in the cause of Unionist democracy. Debate in the Lords differed markedly from that of the Commons. As Henry Lucy, the political journalist noted, 'in the Lords only the big men speak, and when they have had their say all is over'.[16]

Business between the two Leaders of the House and the whips was arranged ad hoc.[17] Unlike the Commons where Members conducted much of their business in the Commons lobby, the peers rarely gossiped and their lobby had 'a deserted, almost ghostly look, intensified by the upright rails and hooks placed for hats and coats'.[18] The workload of peers was not usually demanding, with fewer votes taken than the Commons. In fact, many peers rarely visited or took little interest in proceedings. However, the demand upon Lansdowne as Leader of the Opposition was great. Until 1906 the Lords commonly sat from 4.30 p.m. on Monday, Tuesday, Thursday and Friday; from 1906 onwards it was Monday to Thursday.[19] The House was, in general, poorly attended. At dinner time, especially, it would be quite empty. A slovenly grandeur characterised its members, who often arrived dressed as if they had come directly from their country estates. The calibre of debate, however, was generally high with peers speaking on subjects where they had special knowledge or experience. Communication between backbenchers and Leaders was weak, and Unionist peers met only periodically.

Lansdowne was responsible for all opposition business in the House. It was his duty to express the collective views of his party on formal occasions and to give procedural advice when requested. His long career in Parliament made him perfectly suited for the task. He had no preconceived idea of how to manage the House, except to avoid bringing the two Houses into conflict.[20] Having earned the respect of his colleagues in government, Lansdowne accepted his new role with confidence. His opposite number in 1906 was Lord Ripon, previously Viceroy of India and then Lord Privy Seal. Like Lansdowne, Ripon was from a long line of Whigs. One of the older members, he had served in government with Lansdowne's grandfather. Lansdowne respected Ripon as an example of sound and dignified parliamentary methods. The Unionist peers were managed by William Waldegrave, the Chief Whip, and his deputy. There was not much for the deputy to do, but the Chief Whip was Lansdowne's principal agent. Like his Liberal counterpart, he managed the 'whipping in' of peers for the divisions that took place each session, as well as acting as Lansdowne's eyes and ears in and out of the House, namely at the Carlton Club. Lansdowne did not get on well with Waldegrave, whom he considered incompetent and slow, as well as taking hardly any interest in coordinating action with his Unionist counterpart in the Commons. The Lords Chamber, completed in 1847, was a sumptuously decorated room measuring only 45 by 80 ft. The fittings and furnishings were designed by Augustus Pugin in the gothic style. From the stained-glass windows depicting the monarchs of England and Scotland, to the solid brass gates at the entrance of the Chamber, each weighing some three-quarters of a ton, to the ornate gold-gilded Royal Throne, the Chamber was the most lavishly embellished in Parliament. Members entered through an antechamber, 39 by 33 ft, where they could informally discuss matters during sittings or collect messages from the doorkeepers, who controlled access to the Chamber. This was the arena in which the fiercest constitutional struggle of Lansdowne's career was fought.

As they prepared for the new session of Parliament, Lansdowne suggested to Balfour: 'It is essential that the two wings of the army [Unionist Party] should work together, and that neither House should take up a line of its own without carefully considering the effects which the adoption of such a line might have upon the other House.'[21] Since there was no existing machinery to do this, he proposed a committee of four or five members from each House, to meet at least once a week to exchange ideas and plan strategy. It might also appoint subcommittees ad hoc, on which any prominent members of the opposition might serve.[22]

Balfour replied that Lansdowne's idea should be carried out in some form. In effect, they would hold a shadow cabinet once a week, for

> there has certainly never been a period in our history in which the House of Lords will be called upon to play a part at once so important, so delicate, and so difficult. I conjecture that the Government's methods of carrying on their legislative work will be this: They will bring in Bills in a much more extreme form than the moderate members of their Cabinet probably approve: the moderate members will trust to the House of Lords cutting out or modifying the most outrageous provisions: the Left Wing of the Cabinet, on the other hand, while looking forward to the same result, will be consoled for the anticipated mutilation of their measures by the reflection that they will be gradually accumulating a case against the Upper House, and that they will be able to appeal at the next election for a mandate to modify its construction.
>
> This scheme is an ingenious one, and it will be our business to defeat it, as far as we can. I do not think the House of Lords will be able to escape the duty of making serious modifications in important Government measures, but, if this be done with caution and tact, I do not believe they

will do themselves any harm. On the contrary, as the rejection of the Home Rule Bill undoubtedly strengthened their position, I think it quite possible that your House may come out of the ordeal strengthened rather than weakened by the inevitable difficulties of the next few years. It is of course, impossible to foresee how each particular case is to be dealt with, but I incline to advise that we should fight all points of importance very stiffly in the Commons, and should make the House of Lords the theatre of compromise. It is evident that *you* can never fight for a position which *we* have surrendered; while, on the other hand, the fact that we have strenuously fought for the position and been severely beaten may afford adequate ground for your making a graceful concession to the Representative Chamber.[23]

Although Balfour's analysis was perceptive, he hedged around Lansdowne's request for formal machinery and coordination of tactics. What did take place was conducted by letter or at ad hoc meetings between himself and Lansdowne. The inner circle remained very embryonic, met only sporadically and was quite casual.

The ensuing conflict, which resulted in the Parliament Bill of 1911, began over education. The bill, which would have amended the Unionist Education Act of 1902 and ended public support of religious schools, met violent opposition, as much for excessive disturbance of the existing system as for theological considerations. It has been suggested that the government could have claimed an electoral 'mandate' for the bill in that it had the support of many Nonconformists, who had been raising objections to the Act ever since it was introduced. After the measure passed the Commons in July, it went to the Lords. Lansdowne objected to the bill on its own merits as well as the tactics employed to pass it. He was acutely sensitive to the grievance felt by teachers of religious instruction and that of parents whose children they taught.[24] After the bill passed its second reading in the Lords, Lansdowne informed peers that they 'did not part with one jot or tittle of our right to deal with it at some future day'.[25] This was the first public indication that he was willing to use the power of the House to suppress Liberal legislation.

On 24 October the Bill went to the committee stage in the Lords and was fundamentally altered by the Unionists. On 21 November Crewe (Lord President of the Council) and Ripon told Lansdowne that the situation was extremely grave: if the Lords persisted with its amendments, they were certain the Commons would refuse to discuss them. If so, Lansdowne told them, the Bill would be lost; the House of Lords could not be expected to submit to such an affront. Whatever they thought of the amendments, they had all been supported by weighty arguments and many had been framed to meet expectations raised by the government. It was inconceivable to Lansdowne that ministers would allow one House of Parliament to deal so offensively with proposals made by the other. On 6 December the Lords passed the amendments; four days later, the Commons began discussing them.

On 12 December the Commons voted 416 to 107 to reject the Lords amendments *en bloc*. Irish MPs voted with the government. Crewe and Asquith, Chancellor of the Exchequer, pressed the Unionists for compromise. Lansdowne, who liked Asquith, wondered why. After thirty-eight years in politics Lansdowne knew when individuals had reached their limits and would not budge; it was clear to him that neither Balfour nor the other Unionists in the House of Commons wanted a compromise. Had he believed that they were acting irresponsibly, he would have suggested alternatives, but he was convinced the bill was unworkable and let things be.[26] On the 18th, at Crewe's invitation, Lansdowne, Balfour and Cawdor (the former First Lord of the Admiralty) met Crewe, Asquith, Augustine Birrell (President of the Board of Education) and, at the King's suggestion, Randall Davidson (Archbishop of Canterbury) for an informal conference at Crewe's townhouse in Curzon Street. Adjourning in the afternoon, the conference resumed in the evening but there was no agreement over the question of teachers, without which, to Lansdowne, it was useless to discuss other questions.

The hardening of party lines after 1900 and the Liberals' strength in 1906 had made a successful meeting of party leaders impossible.[27] Even this informal conference failed; the forces of moderation could not stem rising party sentiment, and its failure fuelled the bitter struggle that both parties were inciting. On 19 December, in the Lords, Lansdowne contrasted the Crewe House conference favourably with past conferences, but debate on the bill reached deadlock. Lansdowne moved and the Lords voted by 132 to 52 that 'this House do insist upon its amendments to which the Commons have disagreed'.[28] Next day, the government decided not to proceed further. Campbell-Bannerman said:

> It is plainly intolerable that a Second Chamber should, while one party in the State is in power, be its willing servant, and when that party has received an unmistakeable and emphatic condemnation by the country, the House of Lords should be able to neutralize, thwart, and distort the policy which the electors have approved.[29]

Had the government raised the question of their electoral 'mandate' earlier, it would have been seen as utterly unconstitutional for the Lords to block the government bill. Presumably the Unionists did not expect the Liberals to adopt this tactic. Knowing that those who objected to the support of Anglican teaching from public funds had nearly all voted Liberal in the last election and would continue to vote Liberal, the Unionists calculated that there were no Unionist votes to be lost by wrecking the bill.[30]

Lansdowne's language and behaviour over the Education Bill were out of character. A year earlier, in government, he believed the political outlook for Britain and the Empire was secure. Now he was less certain. A year earlier, as Leader of the Lords, Lansdowne had had full autonomy to direct his fellow peers. There is evidence to suggest that after 1906 this was no longer the case and that Balfour had instructed his front bench to put pressure on Lansdowne. To suggest that Lansdowne was nothing more than Balfour's agent would be unfair, but evidently he had in some sense signed up to Balfour's plan. British domestic affairs were not of much interest to him; but they were to Balfour, who had made the politics of the everyday and the party his cause. During 1906, Lansdowne and Balfour were selective, letting through bills for which the government had a mandate or that directly benefited the working classes.

The Trade Disputes Bill, which had its second reading in the Lords on 4 December, was a classic case of Unionist manipulation. The bill protected unions against being sued for damages incurred during a strike; it had the support of the Labour Party, partial support from the Liberals (but no electoral mandate) and ambivalence from Unionists, who got many trade unionists' votes. In Lansdowne's view it was very unjust, even dangerous, but on second reading he advised his colleagues against rejection or amendment. He believed that most labourers saw the bill as their right and, since it was an affair of the labouring classes, they were bound to have their way in a democracy. All the Lords could do was point out the injustice and probable evil consequences of it.[31] He warned the party that this was a period when conflict and controversy might be inevitable and they should 'move with great caution and join issue only on favourable ground, which this was not. Even if their Lordships won, the victory would be fruitless.'[32] This tactic had two results: it deprived the government of a chance to build its case against the Lords and it gave organised labour a privilege that was repugnant to the lawyers in the Liberal cabinet.[33]

27

UNIONIST BLOCKING

BY 1909, STILL in good health, Lansdowne was a grandfather to twelve children. He and Maud made regular visits to Derreen where he gardened, hunted and fished, and sailed a small yacht he kept in Killmackillogue harbour. After a spell of dry weather in August 1908, the well that supplied the house held only a few inches of water and the rivers still less, so salmon and sea trout were at the mercy of poisoners. A bucket of spurge tea tipped into the river by an innocent child was enough to destroy the fishing. Although Lansdowne's own pools escaped, the practice was widespread in Munster.[1]

With his financial burdens increasing, Lansdowne sold more of his Irish land. Meikleour in Perthshire was let to the Duke and Duchess of Bedford, but he was proud of Bowood, liked it to be appreciated and regularly filled it with friends and family.[2] On 20 July 1907, King Edward, Queen Alexandra and Princess Victoria visited and stayed the night. On 11 November 1907, as Lady of the Bedchamber in Waiting, Maud was in attendance at the railway station at Windsor to welcome the German Emperor and Empress. Four days later, Lansdowne and Maud attended the state banquet in their honour. Lansdowne still thought well of the Emperor, although many people were now against Germany. Lansdowne's parliamentary commitments led him to decline invitations for the positions of Chancellors of Oxford University and of Bristol University. He did, however, accept an honorary Doctorate of Law from the University of Leeds.

Kerry, Lansdowne's elder son, did not win a seat in the 1906 election but was elected to serve on the London County Council for West Marylebone (1907–10). He and his wife Elsie lived in Mansfield Street, London, and Sheen Falls, Ireland. Evie, Lansdowne's elder daughter, and her husband Victor lived at 37 Park Lane, London, and Holker Hall, Cumbria, until on 24 March 1908, when the 8th Duke of Devonshire died and Victor inherited Chatsworth, Hardwick Hall, Bolton Abbey, Compton Place, Devonshire House in London and Lismore Castle in Ireland. Evie became very interested in the collections Victor had inherited, and in preserving and restoring them.[3] Hugh Tristram de la Poer Beresford, born 1 October 1908, was Bertie's and Henry Waterford's sixth and final child.

In September 1906 Lansdowne heard that Charlie, his younger son, stationed in India, was taken with Violet Mary Elliot-Murray-Kynynmound, third and youngest daughter of Lord Minto. Lansdowne approved. In August 1908, Charlie proposed to Violet. She thought that he had 'gone off his head' and told her father that it would not happen for a long time.[4] Next month she accepted. Lady Minto was comforted to have such 'golden' in-laws whom they had 'known since Canadian days'.[5] Lansdowne, who adored Violet, was thrilled. The couple married in Calcutta in January 1909. Lansdowne could not attend because a statute forbade a former Viceroy from entering India. Maud went, with her brother Frederick Hamilton.[6] In 1909 Charlie became an equerry to the Prince of Wales, who in May 1910 succeeded to the throne as George V. Charlie's career as equerry pleased Lansdowne immensely.

On 12 February 1907, Parliament opened, with the King's Speech arousing little reaction. In the debate on the address in reply to the King's Speech, Lansdowne allowed himself more freedom than usual; Almeric FitzRoy thought it was the best speech in either House and that Lansdowne's attitude to the government programme was unexceptionable.[7] Questioning the government's proposal to revise the working of the Parliamentary system and Constitution, because of the 'unfortunate differences between the two Houses', he urged the Peers to do so upon broader grounds than that and to not discount House of Lords reform.[8] It was Lord Newton, a progressive Unionist and later Lansdowne's biographer, who made the first move. Lansdowne was not enthusiastic about Lords reform, but he was not hostile in principle and certainly did not want to block discussion of Newton's bill, which proposed a stricter and more meritorious membership.[9] However, he felt strongly that Unionists should not move in haste. On 7 May, after Newton introduced the second reading, Lansdowne put up Cawdor, a breezy and business-like peer,[10] to delay the bill by referring it to a select committee. Aware that the Liberals wanted nothing to do with this bill and would be highly critical if the Chairman was a Unionist, Lansdowne asked Rosebery, the former Liberal Prime Minister, to chair it.[11] The Rosebery Committee proposals of 1908 were defective in certain details and their impact was minimal. The report failed to address relations with the Commons or representation of the parts of the United Kingdom and the colonies. It left open the issue of the Lords' veto and was not even discussed in that House.[12]

Campbell-Bannerman, the Prime Minister, thought the Liberals would be foolish to review membership of the Lords before revising its powers. Ignoring the reform debate, he proposed a suspensory veto, whereby if a government bill did not pass in the Lords after it had passed twice more through the Commons, it could become law regardless.[13] Backed by a strong socialist feeling in the country, on 24 June 1907 Campbell-Bannerman put his scheme before Parliament. He promised to limit the Lords' veto so that 'within the limits of a single Parliament the final decision of the Commons should prevail'.[14] Naturally this roused the Unionists. Lansdowne wondered at the eccentricities of the Prime Minister and his colleagues.[15] Balfour questioned how the Prime Minister could attempt a fundamental and vital alteration in the constitution when he had no claim to be carrying out the will of the people;[16] Lansdowne would surely have agreed. Balfour could not find support in the Commons, and Campbell-Bannerman's motion was passed by 432 votes to 147, but in the end the government failed to act on it. The Liberals realised that, unless coupled with truly popular reforms that were resisted by the peers, an attack on the Lords' powers would fail.[17]

Lansdowne ended 1907 campaigning in Sheffield, Glasgow and Dalkeith, arguing that public opinion was against weakening the House of Lords, that tariff reform was needed to supply new revenue to meet new demands,[18] and that the government had attacked the Lords to divert attention from their failure to maintain law and order in Ireland.[19] Britain faced recession and the Liberals after two years in power had little to brag about. However, warfare continued in the Unionist Party, where tariff reformers and free fooders were still fighting, even though tariff reform was now party policy. Asked to support candidates from Cromer's group of Cobdenite free-traders, Lansdowne pointed out that constituencies had freedom to select their own candidates – if they wanted tariff reformers, there was nothing Central Office could do.[20] He hoped goodwill would bring about unity. This, the only significant formal attempt to reconcile free-traders with the rest of the Unionist Party, was doomed from the start.[21]

While the parties continued to brawl, Campbell-Bannerman suffered a series of heart attacks. On 1 April 1908 the dying Prime Minister dictated a letter addressed to the King, asking to resign. Asquith was summoned to Biarritz to kiss hands with the King, who was on holiday there. Campbell-Bannerman died at Downing Street on 22 April. In the new cabinet, Ripon retired as Liberal Leader of the Lords. Lansdowne was sorry to see him go:

We have the big battalions in our House, you have them behind you in the Commons, and if you are good enough to commend the manner in which our forces have been handled, we may be permitted to recall the fact that your superior strength elsewhere never led you to deal with us otherwise than fairly and considerately.[22]

This very gentlemanly view of party politics helps to explain why intra- and inter-party warfare was so challenging to Lansdowne, and not a top priority. Ripon's successor was Lord Crewe, also Colonial Secretary, who was tall, good looking and charming, a radical Liberal, loyal to his party and a poor public speaker. Like Lansdowne, he was a Whig, although his Whiggery was more temperamental than ideological.[23]

The key members of Asquith's cabinet included Lloyd George as Chancellor of the Exchequer and Winston Churchill as President of the Board of Trade. In September Edmond Fitzmaurice, who had been ennobled in 1906, succeeded Lord Wolverhampton as Chancellor of the Duchy of Lancaster. Lansdowne was delighted for his brother, who he believed had long deserved cabinet rank, and commented that 'the government could not have a more efficient "maid of all work" to use Dufferin's phrase'.[24] He did not mind sitting opposite his brother in the House of Lords and over the following years dealt with Edmond's often critical questioning with tact and patience. Asquith, a Liberal imperialist and husband of the socialite and author Margot Tennant, moved in the same society as Lansdowne. They were on good terms and the Asquith children often visited Bowood. However, with Asquith as Prime Minister, this friendship was severely tested.

The principal new measures were the Licensing and the Old Age Pensions Bills. The Liberals had no mandate for these bills, which were purposely introduced to focus conflict with the Unionists. The Licensing Bill fixed a ratio of public houses to population in each licensing area; most voters thought it futile, oppressive and insincere, so the Unionists fought it. The Old Age Pensions Bill aimed to reduce poverty among the elderly by providing non-contributory pensions from the age of seventy; it was first read in the Commons on 28 May 1908.

On 3 July Lansdowne held talks at Lansdowne House to establish his colleagues' views on the Pensions Bill. Some of them voted to reject it outright. Lansdowne believed it would undermine the Poor Law system and would cost the nation as much as a full-scale war, but he was against rejection. In the Lords second reading debate on 20 July Lansdowne set out his case for accepting the measure:

[T]his Bill, though not strictly speaking a money Bill, is essentially a Bill of a financial complexion [and] has been supported by colossal majorities in the House of Commons.... [W]ere they to reject it he had no doubt the Opposition would seize with avidity the opportunity of representing the Lords as having attempted to rob the aged and deserving people of this country.[25]

He also told the Lords that should they reject the bill they would be accused, not without reason, as having interfered with the House of Commons privilege, which established almost undisputed control over the finances of the country.[26] It is notable that a year later, in debating the Budget, Lansdowne had changed this view on interfering with money bills. Many peers accepted under protest and the Old Age Pensions Bill passed the House by 123 to 16, receiving the royal assent on 1 August. The result might be seen as testament to Lansdowne's indomitable ability to lead the House. However, it was not so, and many peers – especially Irish peers, who viewed Lansdowne as a traitor after he encouraged them to pass the Evicted Tenants Bill of 1907 – were in revolt.[27]

One result of the Old Age Pensions Bill was to strengthen resistance to the Licensing Bill. On 24 November Lansdowne assembled a party meeting at Lansdowne House to discuss it. He was in favour of dealing with the bill in a way that could not be misunderstood. This was not a Finance Bill, and he was for outright rejection. At the meeting were 'backwoodsmen' who had never spoken in the Lords; some had never been there. Willoughby de Broke joked that some had mistaken Lansdowne House for the House of Lords, and thought the bill was being decided then and there. The meeting agreed to reject the bill and 'adjourned for a good lunch at the Carlton Club'.[28]

Almeric FitzRoy was left sensing that 'therein the timidity of property, which is the prevailing characteristic of the House of Lords, expressed itself, as I think, disastrously for the future of that assembly. When sectional fears come to be manipulated for party ends, the claims of the House to the impartiality of a revising Chamber must necessarily be abandoned.'[29] On 27 November peers rejected the bill by 272 votes to 96. FitzRoy noted:

> all the information I gather from authoritative sources goes to show that Lord Lansdowne capitulated to the thinly veiled threat of a Tory revolt. Thus it came about that a reasoned amendment was adopted, charging the Bishops, who may still in some feeble degree be held to represent the conscience of the community, with supporting a measure that violated every principle of equity. Lord Lansdowne's standing difficulty as the Whig leader of Tory Peers, coupled with his scrupulous regard for the obligations of any position he accepts, could not make head against the vehemence of a large section of his supporters.[30]

To suggest, as FitzRoy does, that Lansdowne was railroaded by his own party in the Lords would be a mistake. Lansdowne did not capitulate. His amendment for the rejection was based on his view that the bill as it stood was intolerably unjust: while the government had promised to deal fairly with the brewing trade the compensation offered to them was not nearly adequate.[31]

After the 24 November meeting, Lansdowne wrote to Jack Sandars, Balfour's private secretary, thanking him for his assistance and ammunition in the debate. It was not the first time that Lansdowne had taken counsel from Sandars, often regarded as Balfour's other self. Undoubtedly Lansdowne and Balfour were singing from the same hymn sheet. However, there was angry criticism that the fate of the bill was decided by these two men, who denied the House of Lords the right to consider the details of the bill. A sarcastic piece in the *Sunday Chronicle* called Lansdowne the 'Great Dictator':

> See Lord Lansdowne sitting in the centre of the long red bench to the left of the Woolsack – a dark, pale man, with subdued energy in every fibre of his frame. His restraint of manner and his restraint of language strike you at once. He never goes straight to the point. He edges off, makes circles round it, and, instead of denouncing, quietly questions. He toys with his pince-nez, keeps his voice to a conversational tone, and having said his say, sits down. He is a sombre-clad man. His lips are straight and his chin strong. The brow, high-domed is thoughtful. But the eyes – so bright, so keen, so penetrating, dominate the countenance. He walks quickly: he sits with folded arms, and concentrates his attention. There is a thin atmosphere of mystery about him – the man who keeps himself to himself, and never speaks except when it is necessary. Such is the Dictator in the House of Lords.[32]

This article was among Lansdowne's personal papers, perhaps to remind himself how he was perceived. He must have sensed that he was becoming what he most abhorred, a figure of notoriety. Lansdowne was still in charge of the Lords, but he was losing control of it.

28

THE PEOPLE'S BUDGET

LANSDOWNE DID NOT look forward to the New Year of 1909. The government had lost support in the country, it had realised the futility of putting contentious measures of social or political reform through the House of Lords and it needed new revenue to pay for pensions and naval expansion. Clearly their next move would be a controversial budget. Parliament opened on 16 February. The Prince of Wales noted that he and and his wife May drove in state to the House of Lords and stayed for the debate: 'Lansdowne made an excellent speech, but Crewe was bad and hesitated.'[1]

While awaiting the Budget, Lansdowne dealt with the Indian Councils Bill, which amended his own Act of 1892 and would appoint Satyendra Prasanno Sinha as law member to the Viceroy's Supreme Council. Fearing that the government was yielding to Indian extremists by rushing the GOI into constitutional changes, Lansdowne protested that such an appointment went far beyond party politics.[2] He was convinced that no single Indian could claim to represent all India's creeds and castes on the Supreme Council. 'To my mind that "is the last thing to be touched".'[3] Minto, the Viceroy, agreed it would be 'quite impossible' to find anyone who could, but that should not debar anyone.[4] He told Lansdowne it was 'not a question of racial representation, but whether a first-rate man should be disqualified because of his race'. He explained that new conditions governed India.[5] The bill received the royal assent.

The 'People's Budget', introduced on 29 April, was a hammer blow. To Lansdowne and his Whig values, it was a monument to reckless finance, based upon principles that were the fallacies of socialism. To Lloyd George, an instinctive Chancellor of the Exchequer and a muddle-headed land reformer with a personal aversion towards Unionist landlords, it was war. In hindsight, the Budget was fairly unexciting; it was the taxation that was controversial. Needing £16 million more revenue to pay for old age pensions and eight dreadnoughts, Lloyd George taxed the rich. The land tax raised less money than it cost to collect and was repealed in 1920,[6] but he also raised income tax from 1s. to 1s. 2d. in the pound for unearned incomes over £2,000, with a super tax of 6d. in the pound levied on incomes over £5,000 (payable on the amount by which incomes exceeded £3,000), and increased death duties from 8 per cent to 15 per cent for all estates over £1 million. A daughter of the Duke of Rutland recalled that 'We all thought papa would die. He looked too ashen to recover.'[7] Laying the basis of democratic taxation in Britain by breaking with the principle that taxation was simply for revenue, the Budget was an attack on landowners and the rich as a class, most of whom supported the Unionist Party.[8]

It took six months, seventy days of debate and 554 divisions to get the measure through the Commons. Outraged, many Unionists united during the summer to delay the Budget. Balfour and Lansdowne played little part in this campaign. During June, as agitation in the country grew, neither leader spoke in public.[9] Their failure to give a firm lead during this period damaged the anti-Budget protest. On 16 July, after six weeks' public silence on the matter, Lansdowne stated rather ambiguously:

> I do not think you will find that when the time comes, the House of Lords is at all likely to proclaim that it has no responsibility for the Bill and that because it is mixed up with the financial affairs of the nation, we are obliged to swallow it whole and without wincing.[10]

Until 9 August, when Lloyd George announced concessions on land duties, the Unionist leaders had not committed themselves publicly. Thereafter, as the summer weather suddenly cooled, they revealed their policy. Balfour believed outright rejection was the only possible course. Lansdowne did not, since 'there are lions in every path',[11] and urged caution. Initially he favoured a proposal by James Garvin, pro-Unionist editor of *The Observer*, to throw out the land clauses by amendment, with some other portions of the bill kept as a counterpoise. He saw this as a case of 'tacking' – that is, getting a highly political measure passed by tacking it onto a Finance Bill – and believed that the Lords could answer the 'class selfishness' argument their opponents would use.[12]

However, Lansdowne accepted that rejection might become inevitable, in which case many peers might leave the Unionist Party, and it could lead to financial chaos if the government deliberately allowed a crisis, saddling the Lords with responsibility. Among those to warn Lansdowne, the ever cautious Hicks Beach (Lord St Aldwyn), thought rejection 'the worst gamble I have ever known in politics'.[13] Even though in two centuries the Lords had never rejected a Finance Bill, constitutionally they were entitled to reject one but not amend it. Of this Lansdowne had been assured by the Unionist jurist Albert Dicey. Therefore, Lansdowne believed that this was not a case for elaborate arguments on constitutional precedents; Unionist action should be determined on broad grounds of policy.[14]

Over the summer Lansdowne was kept busy with tiresome bills sent from the Commons, ranging from Irish land to town planning. He took no holiday and became quite weary. Lloyd George and his Liberal colleagues spent the summer goading the peers into rejecting the Budget, thus triggering an immediate general election. Rabble-rousing speeches, such as Lloyd George's at Limehouse, set an uneasy tone. The King, who was essential to the Liberals if the Lords were to be outwitted, was upset by such tactics and put pressure on Asquith to remonstrate with his Chancellor. A week after Limehouse, Unionists were depressed by the High Peak by-election, won by the Liberals with 5,609 votes to their 5,272. Lansdowne was equally distressed by Lloyd George's taunts, comparing him to 'a swooping robber gull, particularly voracious and unscrupulous, which steals fish from other gulls'.[15]

It was clear that Lloyd George's attacks on the rich had support among the electorate and, if the Budget were rejected, the Liberals would win the general election. However, Lansdowne did not believe that Limehouse or High Peak justified changing course or that Lloyd George's arrogance had done more than dismay Unionists. Balfour thought otherwise. He believed that Lloyd George had transformed the debate, and the bill must be stopped. Over the following weeks he and Jack Sandars, by disquisitions on government tactics, gently prodded Lansdowne into accepting total rejection. While Lansdowne listened, he also gathered opinions from free-traders, who wished the Budget to pass, and tariff reformers, who wanted it rejected because it threatened to destroy part of their case for protection.

At this stage, Lansdowne might have stopped Balfour in his tracks by threatening to resign. That he did not was because his position as Leader of the Unionist peers was not strong enough. Balfour could have used one of his front bench contacts in the Lords to overshadow Lansdowne in debate, essentially silencing him. Maintaining that the Lords could not pronounce until they knew the bill's fate in the Commons, Lansdowne did his best to avoid pushing the Lords in any direction. He was not purposely stalling but building his case. As he told Curzon in early September, it was extraordinarily difficult: he thought that if they confessed they had become impotent in this crisis, the House of Lords would lose its standing, and entirely discourage moderates who looked to them for support.[16] But impotent is exactly what they had become, driven by the clamour of the unthinking section of the Unionist Party.

Balfour's decision to reject the Budget, made in early October, was arguably one of the most disastrous political decisions of the past one hundred and fifty years. Lansdowne must share the blame, for he was jointly responsible with Balfour. Lansdowne's argument for rejection is best explained in a letter he wrote to Lord Balfour of Burleigh. Contradicting his former argument for making amendments, he had decided that if the Lords dealt only with land and licensing, 'they would be accused of deserting their fellow-sufferers and thinking of their own skins'. Moreover, they would get 'into controversies upon the technical right of the Lords to amend Money Bills and the right of the Commons to "tack" extraneous matter on to the Finance Bill'. The real issue would be obscured. Left with no option but to reject or accept, Lansdowne favoured rejection because the finance bill was

a new departure of the most dangerous kind, to which the House of Lords has no right to assent until it is sure that H.M.G. [His Majesty's Government] have the support of the country. We must, I think, assume that, if there is a general election, we may be beaten at the polls; but to my mind the consequences of acquiescing in a measure which we know to be iniquitous, and have denounced as such, would be more deplorable than the consequences of defeat.

I am assured on what I believe to be good authority, that even if we let the Budget go through, Government will appeal to the country early in the year. This seems likely, for the popularity of the Budget will not increase as time goes on, and H.M.G. would appeal with all the trumps in their hand after what would be regarded as an ignominious capitulation on the part of the Opposition. To my mind, in such an event, the position of the H. of L. would have been gravely and permanently impaired. We could never in future, however outrageous the financial policy of a Radical Government might be, claim the right to stand in its way. I think it, then, quite conceivable that we shall be defeated, but I take it as certain that the Radical majority would be greatly decreased. This would be to some extent a justification of our conduct, and we should be far stronger if we were no longer a mere handful in the House of Commons. If the majority either way is to be a small one, it would, I think, be better for us to be in a large minority than in a small majority.

Your fear is that such a defeat would involve the virtual destruction of the H. of L. as a second Chamber. I am much less afraid than you are of this result. The Radicals will no doubt do their best to confuse the issue and to make out that a verdict in favour of the Finance Bill carries with it a *carte blanche* to deal with the H. of L. But the destruction or reform of the House of Lords is not to be accomplished in a few weeks or months; and when the heat and fury of the general election has spent itself, the country will,

I believe, be quite able to discriminate between the two issues and I do not believe the country desires a Single Chamber system. By the time the H. of L. issue is ripe for treatment, the popularity of the Budget will, unless I am mistaken, have greatly diminished. We shall not, in my opinion, get through the present crisis without two general elections.[17]

Lansdowne's analysis of the situation created by rejection reveals not only his determination to preserve the credibility of the House of Lords as a revising chamber, but his belief in Salisbury's referendal theory. Although Balfour had mentioned that, in the event of a second general election, the Liberals would have to depend on the Irish Nationalists, and that Home Rule would re-surface and help the Unionist Party to win that second election, it is notable that Lansdowne does not hint at this. Lansdowne spoke of defending the Lords. Balfour spoke otherwise, but they wished to make common cause. Shortly after Lansdowne made his case for rejection, Lloyd George with deadly eloquence made it clear that the House of Lords would never be the same again.[18] On 4 November the Budget finally passed the Commons, and cabinet discussion for the first time assumed that the Lords would reject the Budget. Beatrice Webb, a founder of the Fabian Society, wrote that the political world was convulsed with excitement: if the Lords rejected the Budget, they were gambling with all they held dear.[19]

On 16 November Lansdowne gave notice of the historic amendment that would destroy the Finance Bill. When the bill came up for second reading he moved 'That this House is not justified in giving its consent to the Bill until it has been submitted to the judgment of the country.'[20] FitzRoy, whose grandfather had been a Whig Prime Minister, found Lansdowne nervous and ill at ease, with some misgivings about the course he was taking. He inferred that it had been forced on Lansdowne by the clamour of the Unionist press and the fears of the tariff reformers: 'Whig scruples have been ruthlessly sacrificed to Tory passion and the petulance of wire-pulling demagogy.'[21] Margot Asquith thought the Lords were mad, but prayed they would help the Liberals to a good majority in the election that would follow: 'There will be hot fighting for four weeks and not much holiday.'[22] For most government bills the Leader of the House would speak first, but, on 22 November, Lord Crewe, having moved the second reading, refused to speak further, disgusted at the Unionist tactics. So Lansdowne, suffering from a head cold, spoke instead, warning the House that they had no right to assent to the Budget until the electorate had indicated its approval. After five days of debate, the Lords voted on 30 November.

On that grey November afternoon, the house met as usual at 4 p.m., but long before that every entrance to the Chamber was besieged and the galleries were soon full. The Peeresses' Gallery filled by 1 p.m., and Maud Lansdowne was there. Suffering from hoarseness, Lansdowne opened the debate by proposing his amendment. Unusually, the sitting was not suspended for dinner at 8 p.m. and it was 11.30 p.m. before Crewe uttered his last words of protest and Earl Loreburn, the Lord Chancellor, put the question that the Finance Bill be read a second time. There was a murmur of contents and a roar of discontents before the peers proceeded to the division lobbies. When they reassembled in the Chamber shortly before midnight, Loreburn announced that the peers had rejected the Budget by 350 votes to 75.

Lansdowne's argument that this was punitive social legislation masquerading as a Budget did not satisfy his critics. Two days later the Commons voted by 349 to 134 that the Lords' rejection was 'a breach of the constitution and a usurpation of the rights of the Commons'.[23] Asquith accused the Lords of rejecting the Budget 'not because they love the people, but because they hate the Budget'.[24] Asquith's dramatic charge was telling and immediately found support in his party. But it sidestepped the fact that the Commons (and many senior Liberals) had admitted previously that the Lords had a right to reject a Finance Bill, though not to initiate or amend one, so Asquith's invective was rather cheap. Nonetheless, Lansdowne's decision created a situation unparalleled in the history of Parliament. Hubris had overtaken strength. He knew the high risk he was running but, once committed, showed no sign of wavering. If anything, he became more resolute, remarking a few days later that the Lords were fortified against any attack, quoting a Zulu proverb, 'He who charges into battle may be killed. He who runs away from the battle will be killed.'[25]

The immediate reaction among Unionists was supportive, giving Lansdowne's position as Leader a short-term boost. Newspapers were divided equally: Liberal papers were instructed by their editors to mourn the decision and the abuse of privilege, while the Unionist press took the opposite view. In Lansdowne's mind, there was no question that the Lords had overstepped their privileges; he had simply done what he believed was right in the circumstances. That he saw such a dire situation so positively was echoed in a letter to the editor of *The Times*, arguing that the 'weaknesses of the House of Lords are the real sources of its strength, and of its hold upon the nation'.[26] Far more than the House of Commons, with its Labour and Irish supporters, the Lords represented the fundamental conservatism of the English people, their wariness and love of tradition. However that might have been, times were changing and for Lansdowne to fail to appreciate the political reality and significance of the Liberal election victory of 1906 and reject the budget was in my opinion a mistake. By forcing further political deadlock, his action left Parliament facing a far greater political revolution.

29

THE 1910
GENERAL ELECTIONS

ON 3 DECEMBER 1909, Lansdowne spoke in Plymouth to a crowd of 7,000. He made no apologies for rejecting the Budget: the House of Commons was notoriously out of touch with the British people and the House of Lords was fighting for popular liberties.[1] Asquith responded to the Lords the same day, securing an immediate dissolution. The eight-week campaign began erratically but gathered momentum after Christmas. On 15 January 1910 polling began and, unlike present-day voting, continued over several days, finishing on 10 February.[2] Circumstances did not help the Unionists. Trade had recovered that summer, the economic depression had lifted and the party was still divided. The Liberals made their campaign on the Lords' veto and its power to destroy Liberal legislation, not simply the Budget. Realising the future of the Lords was threatened, Lansdowne campaigned principally on Lords reform, in speeches at Plymouth, Liverpool and Salisbury. He admitted that the House was imperfect and too large but, as he told Balfour:

I am convinced that we should make a great mistake if we were to pledge ourselves to changes which would, in effect, give us a second elective chamber. This would, in the truest sense of the word, be a revolution, for which no necessity can be shown.

He envisaged reforms based on the Rosebery Committee proposals on the selection of peers, but 'with an open mind as to changes of a more courageous description'.[3] How 'courageous'?

I should always believe in the preponderating power of the House of Commons, and it is my belief that if you were to set up a House of Lords fortified by some process of election, or otherwise placed in a position analogous to that of the House of Commons, you would inevitably find that the House of Lords would claim what it does not claim now, which is co-ordinate power with the popular House.

This has always been the argument against House of Lords reform and continues to be so today.

Lansdowne believed that merely possessing a peerage should not confer the right to legislate, so, if the government wished to change the membership of the House, he would negotiate. He still believed they could avoid the issue of the Lords' powers to resist the will of the Commons. Balfour shared his view. Lansdowne also believed that any reform of the House of Lords should 'be the work not of one political party but of both political parties working together'.[4] But Lansdowne's faith in government support could not have been more mistaken. The Liberals wanted simply to destroy the Lords' veto.

Both parties might have been expected to outline their proposals on the House of Lords; neither did so. Liberals disagreed on the detail and Unionists were reluctant to formulate policy during an election. After the final polls were taken on 10 February the result was: Unionists 273, Liberals 275, Irish Nationalists 71, Independent Nationalists 3, All for Ireland 8 and Labour 40. With a government coalition majority of 124, and more influence exercised by the Irish and Labour, under Arthur Henderson, the election made a veto limitation likelier. Lansdowne saw the result as a vote against the Lords and all landlords, but he noticed that where Unionists won they did so because of tariff reform. The Unionists would have to address this question. However, Lansdowne's immediate[5] concern was what line the party should now take about the Lords.[6]

On 21 February the new Parliament opened. Aside from the Budget, for which the election gave a conclusive mandate, the government programme included bills on education, licensing, plural voting, disestablishment of the Church of Wales and Home Rule for Ireland. During the debate on the address, Lansdowne kept the House in a state of tension while he exposed, 'in incisive and often scathing sentences, the weakness of the Government's position'.[7] Although his performance was praised by Unionists, his lack of urgency for reform of the Lords brought criticism, especially from Rosebery.

Lansdowne had accepted that the general election was a mandate for the Budget and that it had to pass,[8] and so his principal duty, and Balfour's, was to safeguard the British constitution against efforts to place powers of legislation entirely in the hands of one Chamber.[9] The government's position was less clear: they were divided on whether to focus on Lords reform or veto legislation. However, five weeks later, wishing to give a strong direction to his cabinet, Asquith announced proposals to abolish the Lords' financial veto and limit their legislative veto. He hoped that tackling these powers first would lead to more radical reform later.

On 21 March three resolutions were tabled in the Commons:[10] to bar the House of Lords from interfering with a money bill, to allow the Commons to pass any bill after three successive sessions whatever the Lords decided, and to reduce the life of Parliament from seven to five years. On 5 April the government resolutions, then under discussion in committee, were passed under the guillotine.[11] Nine days later, Asquith stated that veto resolutions would be immediately introduced into both Houses of Parliament; if the Lords rejected them, the government would ask the King to agree to a large creation of Liberal peers. The coalition having reintroduced the Budget, it passed the Commons and was let through the Lords without a division in a few hours. On 29 April it received the royal assent.

Two months earlier Lansdowne had been inundated with suggestions for Lords reform from Unionist supporters, many of whom had met violent antipathy to the hereditary principle during the electoral campaign, particularly in Scotland and the north of England. Unless the principle was abandoned or pushed into the background, they believed the Unionists would lose further seats in future. Lansdowne dismissed such impressions, given when the political temperature was so high. He feared that excessive concessions might fail to win new supporters while alienating existing ones, who would not understand why, after such an election result, the party should precipitately abandon its positions.[12] On 3 March Rosebery joined Lansdowne, Balfour and other senior Unionists at Lansdowne House to discuss the future of the Lords. Opinions differed widely and no definite scheme emerged. Lansdowne was less inclined than Rosebery and some others for radical reform. Lansdowne's opinion at that time carried great weight, especially because he was conservative in this matter and anxious to carry the mass of the Lords with him.[13]

On 14 March, with the House in a curious mood, Rosebery introduced three resolutions to set out the principles of reform. Three days later, Lansdowne concluded the debate, stating that the Lords should preserve its historic continuity and should not change its name, renounce the hereditary principle or reduce the number of hereditary peers. Against election by county councils or anyone else, he thought that a number of new members might be allowed to take seats as life peers, nominated by the government for a substantial term. Many found his speech disappointing. Rosebery was especially disheartened, telling Lansdowne, 'if you cannot go beyond the limits that you appeared to lay down last night, the House of Lords plan will be stillborn'.[14] Lansdowne agreed to differ, but said he would try to meet him as far as he could.[15]

Rosebery's resolutions were passed on 22 March, but events soon made them irrelevant. On 29 March Asquith moved his veto resolutions, intending that they become a bill to limit the Lords' powers. This eliminated any ideas that Lansdowne had entertained of negotiating Lords reform with the government. On 14 April Asquith threatened that if the Parliament Bill was rejected, another election would follow, with the government sure that the judgement of the people would be carried into law. On 21 April Lansdowne convened another meeting to discuss what the Lords should do. Austen Chamberlain noted a rather rambling discussion, but it appeared that the House of Lords had better '*brusquer le dénouement*'[16] rather than delay it.[17]

Before Parliament reconvened, the political atmosphere was changed by the death of King Edward VII on 6 May. His successor, George V, lacked political experience, although as heir apparent he had studied more state papers than had his father. With experience as a naval officer and a country gentleman, he was quite conventional and patriotic. It seemed clear to Lansdowne that, in deference to the new King, a political truce would follow. While the constitutional crisis was put on hold, Asquith informed the King that he wished to reach an understanding with the Unionists so as to avoid a second election. This idea took the form of an inter-party constitutional conference. Lansdowne's position at this time was led by party considerations. He believed that moderate Unionists would be glad to avoid a crisis, or at least postpone it, and that another general election would be an outrage. As matters stood, the party was not in a position to amend the Veto Bill.[18]

On 16 June the constitutional conference began, with Asquith, Lloyd George, Crewe and Birrell for the government, and Balfour, Lansdowne, Austen Chamberlain and Cawdor for the opposition. Meeting in Asquith's rooms in the Commons, they discussed relations between the two Houses over finance, procedures in case of persistent differences and reconstruction of the Lords. Some progress was made on finance and constitutional questions before the summer recess. This exasperated those keen to continue the inter-party war. Edward Carson, the Irish Unionist, voiced the feeling of many: 'it is impossible to fight whilst the generals are in friendly conference'.[19] Crewe offered his country house, Crewe Hall, to continue talks during the summer. Lansdowne thought this a thoroughly bad idea; the public would not understand: 'It would be at once said that the whole affair was a picnic, and that business of such importance ought not to be transacted in an environment of such a kind.'[20] Critics would say they had been 'softened' by champagne and country house luxury,[21] and his concerns were accepted by his colleagues. Crewe thought the Constitutional issue was so far from ordinary political controversy that the usual restrictions did not apply.[22]

After the conference resumed on 11 October, the participants discussed the treatment of constitutional bills and Irish Home Rule. Insurmountable difficulties arose when they tried to agree the size of Lords representation at joint sittings and the definition of constitutional legislation. Lansdowne, who dominated the Unionist side, was never eager to enhance the agreement; he remained cautious and guarded throughout. Lloyd George even referred to him as an ineffectual echo of Balfour. Lansdowne's negative attitude certainly reflected his lack of interest in tariff reform and his strong views about Ireland and the Union, but his principal fear was that the government was forcing them to pay too high a price. On 4 November both sides admitted that negotiations had broken down.

The cabinet decided on immediate dissolution when Parliament returned on 15 November, but Asquith could not say anything until negotiations with the King were completed. While seeking the King's permission for a dissolution, Asquith also asked for a guarantee that, in the event of a Liberal victory and the peers not surrendering, the King would use his prerogative to create enough peers to enable the Parliament Bill to be passed. The King reluctantly agreed, believing that he had no alternative to giving the guarantee. In fact, there was an alternative. Lord Knollys, the King's private secretary, who was a Liberal, failed to mention that he knew that if the King refused Asquith's request and the government resigned, and Balfour was asked to form a government, he would do so.

While the House of Commons waited for more information, the Lords were in no mood to wait upon the government. Unaware of the full extent of discussions between the King and the Prime Minister, Lansdowne, with an air of 'aloofness and hawk-like suavity', moved to invite the government to submit without delay the Parliament Bill for consideration and decision.[23] Rosebery's resolutions were debated and disposed of with no opposition. Crewe accepted the motion with some bitterness, subject to the Unionists promising not to amend the bill. Lansdowne believed this would make the debate unreal. The following day the King agreed to the creation of peers, subject to it remaining a secret between him, Asquith and Crewe, and the Lords having an opportunity of debating the Parliament Bill before Parliament was dissolved for a second time.

On 23 November, quite unaware of the new power in the hands of the government, but aware of the forthcoming election, Lansdowne introduced some resolutions along the lines discussed at the constitutional conference, aiming to settle differences between the two Houses. These involved a reconstituted and reduced House of Lords, settlement of bills in cases of deadlock of one year or less by joint committee of both Houses and, in cases of greater gravity, where it had not been submitted for the judgement of the people, decision by referendum. The Lords were also prepared to forgo their constitutional right to reject or amend money bills provided that provision was made against 'tacking' and that a joint committee of both Houses with the Speaker of the House of Commons as chairman, exercising only a casting vote, would decide whether a bill was purely financial or not.[24] The resolutions challenged merely the preamble of the Parliament Bill, not its substance or the relations between the two Houses. In reality they would have been difficult to implement. Joint sittings were a novel device, and defining the importance of bills by such a subjective test was considered difficult. Lansdowne had drafted his proposals with support from Balfour, who thought some of his ideas 'ingenious' and better than his own,[25] and Curzon. The resolutions were carried without a division, but government peers refused to support them. The debate was notable for the enthusiasm shown by some traditionalists for drastic reform. Although most of the proposals had been supported by Unionists in the constitutional conference, they were not welcomed by other Unionists.

Lansdowne's focus now moved to the election. He was not too confident about it but 'the prospect is much better than it was. If the Radical Government comes back with a materially reduced majority, their position will be far from strong, and we shall I hope, be able to put up a pretty good fight, and perhaps secure very substantial changes in the Government scheme.'[26] The Unionists knew they would not win by defending the House of Lords alone. They decided to oppose Home Rule rather than support tariff reform. On 29 November, the day after Parliament dissolved, without having consulted anyone in his shadow cabinet except Lansdowne, Balfour pledged in a speech at the Albert Hall to submit tariff reform to a referendum if the Unionists came to power. The pledge was conditional on the Liberals doing the same with Home Rule. Lansdowne strongly supported this as Unionist Party policy, believing that the tactical advantages were unquestionable.[27] The pledge satisfied the free-traders by ending the fiscal quarrel but upset the Chamberlainites and other tariff reformers who believed it was a betrayal, sacrificing protectionist policies in favour of resistance to the emasculation of the House of Lords.

On 3 December polling began for the last general election to be held over several days; the results were announced on 19th. Any expectations of a dynamic campaign were overshadowed by an atmosphere of exhaustion. Concerned that the Parliament Bill was a challenge to democracy and a threat to the unity of the Empire, the Unionists largely campaigned on the issues of the referendum and the Irish Union. The

Liberals chose to attack on the peers versus people theme. The Liberals won 272 seats, Labour 42, Irish Parliamentary and Independents 84 and the Conservative and Liberal Unionists 271. The total poll was down by over a million. Control of the political situation fell to the Nationalists and Labour, and both parties were determined to see the Parliament Bill passed. Lansdowne admitted his share of responsibility for Balfour's pledge, telling Austen Chamberlain, one of the senior Unionist tariff reformers:

> That the pledge might have embarrassing consequences I was fully aware, but the ordinary voter would have been quite unable to appraise this argument at its proper value, and if we were right in supposing that the announcement would help us achieve success, or to avoid defeat or disaster the risk was, it seemed to me, worth running. The results of the election are disappointing, but I refuse altogether to believe that they will lead to the passing of the Parliament Bill in anything like its present shape.[28]

The fact that the Liberal government had been returned by the country as strong as they went in placed the King in a very difficult position. Balfour noted that 'an unscrupulous ministry could do any amount of damage if the King has not the alternative of calling into existence a Ministry which can secure an adequate parliamentary support in the existing House of Commons, or can hope to obtain that support by an appeal to the country'.[29] He also realised there was no alternative ministry. Lansdowne saw it differently:

> I cannot conceive that the Unionist party will have anything to gain by taking office. A third general election within a period of less than 10 months is to my mind unthinkable and without a third general election we remain helpless. My hope, I will say my expectation is that the conditions will not remain unaltered and that the situation will develop when Parliament gets to close quarters with the Parliament Bill and the country begins to realise the monstrosity of that measure and the superior advantages of the unionist counter scheme. I am without information as to the advice which has been given or may be given to H.M. [His Majesty] by his ministers or as to the reception which that advice is likely to meet. But I earnestly trust that both advisers and advised will perceive that it would be altogether wrong and unconstitutional to demand or to give pledges upon a purely hypothetical basis. The crisis has not yet arisen. There will surely be time enough to decide how it shall be dealt with when it has.[30]

Not knowing that the King had already guaranteed the creation of peers, Lansdowne was sleepwalking into further difficulty.

30

THE KING

DURING CHRISTMAS WEEK 1910, John Revelstoke, senior partner at Barings Bank, family friend of the Lansdownes and close friend of the King, informed Lansdowne that pressure was being put on the King to agree – and Revelstoke believed he could not refuse – to create peers should the Lords not pass the Parliament Bill. Lansdowne told Balfour it was really hard on the King and dangerous to the Commonwealth that he should be left with no help from him or Balfour.

On 27 January 1911, at Windsor Castle, the King noted a little talk with Lansdowne, who also noted it in his diary:[1]

> H.M. told me that the P.M. and Lord Crewe had both told him that when Parliament met, finance would, in the first place, have to be dealt with; then the Parliament Bill in the House of Commons, where it would be taken before Easter. H.M.G. expected to pass the Bill through both Houses before the Coronation. Other business of importance would probably be carried over until the autumn.
>
> H.M. went on to say that the two Ministers referred to had assured him that proposals for the amendment of the Parliament Bill would be fully considered in both Houses, and any arguments advanced by the Opposition carefully examined with a view to a 'compromise'.[2]

Lansdowne thought their language sounded reasonable, although it contrasted with what Crewe had said previously, and that the situation might change greatly as the discussion proceeded. On the subject of the King being forced to create peers to overcome the resistance of the House of Lords, Lansdowne told the King that such a step might become inevitable, but it had been universally condemned as violently straining the constitution. 'It was a step which I felt sure H.M. would be reluctant to take, and his Ministers not less reluctant to advise; and I thought it not unfair to say that, up to a certain point, we should be justified in bearing this fact in mind when considering whether it was desirable to offer resistance to the Government proposals.'[3] As the King dwelt on the improbability of Balfour being able to form a ministry and go to the country if the Parliament Bill were rejected, Lansdowne agreed, but he urged the King to be cautious; it would be 'most unwise for any of those concerned, either in government, the Opposition, or, the King himself to commit themselves finally to any particular line of action, or allow it to become known that they had done'.[4] But of course the King had already committed himself to creating peers.

On 5 February the Lansdownes launched the political session with a dinner party for their Unionist colleagues, in the sumptuous surroundings of Lansdowne House. After the meal there was a reception for over a thousand people, including Unionist MPs, candidates and party workers, notables of all political parties, the ambassadors of Austria-Hungary, Russia, Italy, France, Spain and Japan, the US chargé d'affaires, the ministers of China, Belgium, Greece, Sweden, Switzerland, Mexico and Brazil, and the councillor of the German Embassy.[5] One might wonder, given Lansdowne's precarious finances, how he could afford it. He had to sell assets: in March Rembrandt's *Mill* was sold for £100,000 to Joseph Widener, an American collector, and in May the Kinneff estate in Scotland was sold.

Parliament was opened on 6 February by the King, and the Parliament Bill, unchanged, was taken after the address. Moira Lyttelton, daughter of the 10th Duke of Leeds and great-niece of Maud Lansdowne, in an interview in 1972, recalled this as a tremendously bitter time – her parents thought they would be ruined and nothing would be the same again. She drew an analogy with the Suez Crisis of 1956 when Lady Eden felt the Suez Canal was flowing through her drawing room, dividing her friends and acquaintances. Maud might have felt the same. At Bowood in 1911 Maud asked Moira whether she would like to ask two young men to bring up the numbers for a party. When Moira suggested Arthur Asquith, the Prime Minister's son, Maud said he probably would not be welcome there, so he was not asked. Such feuds occurred between political families that the social fabric was unhinged.[6]

The Parliament Bill was read a first time in the Commons on 21 February. It passed by 351 to 227. That same day, Lansdowne gave notice of a bill to amend the constitution of the House of Lords. He did so against his better judgement, on the advice of party string-pullers and Curzon, who insisted that Lords reform would act as a delaying tactic. Lansdowne was obviously uncomfortable with his decision because he later told Sandars he was not sanguine about the results of their reform bill.[7] He thought it would be a death blow to the existing and conventional House of Lords. Lansdowne's announcement brought a mass of divergent correspondence and by mid-March he had to tell Balfour that their people were hopelessly divided on reform.[8] Aged sixty-five, Lansdowne was now less energetic and his health less strong. During March and April, suffering from throat trouble and a violent cough, he made little progress on his bill. As he followed the Commons debates on the Parliament Bill, he realised that the government intended to ride roughshod over the Unionists and would do the same in the Lords.[9]

After ascertaining Balfour's views, Lansdowne introduced the Reconstitution Bill on 8 May. Lansdowne's House was to be restricted to 350 members, with no hereditary peers except royal princes, who would be summoned if they were not Lords of Parliament as defined by the bill. Of the 350, 100 were to be elected by the hereditary peers themselves, 120 representing districts were to be indirectly chosen by electoral colleges, 100 members were to be chosen by the government of the day, and 30 royal princes, bishops and law lords were to retain their seats, some for life and others for 12 years. Lansdowne argued that there would be no large reduction in the number of members of the House; no member of it would be there by purely hereditary right; and continuity of tradition would be maintained by the election carried out by hereditary peers.[10]

Lansdowne's speech fell very flat. Still unwell, he looked pallid and wasted;[11] some colleagues thought he seemed too apologetic and would have had a better reception if he had been bolder.[12] Margot Asquith noted that his reform scheme was received in icy silence; she wished she had been there. She thought things were going well for the government.[13] Lansdowne told Roberts the 'occasion <u>was</u> a rather trying one' and he was scarcely fit.[14] Many peers thought it a tactical mistake to confess any imperfection in the Lords; Unionist diehards like Willoughby de Broke saw no need for any reform; many 'backwoodsmen', aware they would be made victims, demanded angrily why they should be sacrificed for the convenience of Lansdowne. The Reconstitution Bill was read a second time on 22 May, passed without division and was never heard of again.[15] Lansdowne's leadership suffered further.

With Lords reform out of the way, on 23–24 May the Parliament Bill had its second reading in the Lords and passed without a division. The debate made little impression and the bill went to committee. Lansdowne warned that it would be heavily amended. The polemicist Wilfrid Scawen Blunt thought the Lords had committed suicide, without a division and without glory: 'Never was a position so frittered away.'[16]

Although Lansdowne's health improved in June, further misfortune struck in August when his eye was punctured, colliding with a beetle while cycling one evening at Derreen. He wrote a poem about it that included the lines:

'A beetle is as good,' says he, 'and better, than a Lord,
And of us two, if one goes down, 'tis the Marquis should be floored.'[17]

On 18 May 1910, before the funeral of King Edward VII, Kaiser Wilhelm II and Kaiserin Augusta visited Windsor to lay wreaths on the tombs of Queen Victoria and King Edward. That evening, they and their daughter, Victoria Louise of Prussia, were guests of honour at a banquet at Lansdowne House. Among other Germans in attendance were the ambassador and various statesmen, admirals and generals. The large dining room was decorated with pink carnations, the grand hall and stairway with white and pink flowers. After dinner, various distinguished persons were invited to meet Their Imperial Majesties and listen to a German band.[18] On 20 May the German Embassy reported to the Chancellor, Theobald von Bethmann-Hollweg, on the visit. Lansdowne was said to be reserved and silent, 'a man who may be efficient in his way and a good diplomatist, but he runs between blinkers, has no broad views'.[19] Such a view quite overlooked Lansdowne's ability to see ahead.

On 22 June 1911, George V was crowned King of the United Kingdom and the British Dominions, and Emperor of India, at a brilliant and solemn ceremony at Westminster Abbey. The Lansdownes were one of the few aristocratic couples who drove to the service in their state coach. Maud wore a dress embroidered with 'the beehive beset with bees, diversely volant' of the Lansdowne crest, among heavily embroidered leaves. Crowned by the King's side was his wife, who, at his suggestion, took the name 'Mary', although she was christened Victoria and informally known as 'May'. During the service Lansdowne carried the Royal Standard. Next day the Lansdownes were at Devonshire House with Victor and Evie to watch the Royal Progress.

On 28 June the Parliament Bill began its committee stage in the Lords. In the days that followed the bill was mutilated by amendments similar to those rejected in the Commons. On 4 July, Lansdowne introduced a referendum amendment which was carried on a division on 5 July by 253 to 40.[20] This amendment and others made by the Lords left Asquith noting that the bill had been transformed as if no general election had been held.[21] At the time, Lansdowne was accused of failing to give the Unionists a firm lead. In fact, he feared a revolt within his party and was determined to proceed on constitutional lines in a conciliatory manner. He was struggling less with the government than with the more extreme

Unionists. This group, known as 'the diehards', resisted any surrender of power by the Lords; they thought emasculating the Lords was as foolish as swamping it with Liberal peers. Led by Willoughby de Broke, who had little parliamentary experience but much charisma, and some of the Cecils, who had enormous parliamentary experience and knew Lansdowne well, the diehards believed the Unionist leaders of both houses had become ineffectual compromisers and should be replaced by true Tories.[22]

On 18 July Lansdowne noted a conversation with Balfour and Lloyd George, in which Lloyd George told them bluntly that he had the King's guarantee over the creation of peers, that Asquith would make an announcement to that effect in the Commons on 24 July, and the government would not send the bill back to the Lords until the peers had been created. Lloyd George also said that he would communicate the King's interview to Lansdowne officially if this was less distasteful to peers than an announcement in the Commons. Finally, if the Lords persisted with amendments, he would regard the bill as lost and they must take the consequences.[23] In his recollection of the meeting, Lloyd George, who had a strong personal dislike of Lansdowne, recalled that Lansdowne,

> the fussy little shop-walker, looked utterly smashed, so miserable and so broken I was really sorry for him. Up to that moment he had never believed that we had got the guarantees. That explains all their insane action during the last few months.[24]

Lansdowne, who was far too discreet to reveal his views of the deal made between the King and the Prime Minister, was very shocked:

> we had all of us anticipated that our amendments would be sent back to us with the usual statements of the House of Commons objections, and that we should thus be given an opportunity of reconsidering the situation. It was, as far as I was aware, an unheard of thing to throw out our amendments en bloc and tell us at the same time, that, unless we undertook, while the Bill was still in the hands of the House of Commons, to accept it in its House of Commons' shape, peers would be created in sufficient numbers to overwhelm our resistance.[25]

Such politics would have been unheard of a decade earlier. Lansdowne's world was facing extinction.

31

THE FINAL STAGES OF THE PARLIAMENT BILL

AS THE LINES were drawn between Unionists and Liberals, so too were lines drawn between Unionists. Willoughby de Broke sent to Lansdowne House on 11 June 1911 a resolution signed by seventeen peers, with twenty-four more in support, to accept any amendments to secure the Lords' powers, 'notwithstanding the possible creation of peers or the dissolution of Parliament'.[1] On 12 July thirty-one diehard peers met at Lord Halsbury's house. He informed Lansdowne they were determined to follow through the 11 June resolution. Willoughby de Broke believed they were strengthening Lansdowne's hand; in fact, this put him in a position of great embarrassment.[2]

On 20 July Morley, temporarily replacing Crewe as Leader of the Lords, moved the third reading of the Parliament Bill. It was passed and returned to the Commons with the Lords amendments on which the diehards insisted. Lansdowne showed little sign of retreat but he was less insistent than the diehards, stating that to throw overboard any part of the changes that the Unionists had deliberately introduced into the bill would be, to say the least, a very unusual parliamentary manoeuvre and that they would not be prepared to recede from some of their amendments as long as they were 'free agents'. Dealing with the facts before him Lansdowne informed the peers he would pursue the controversy upon constitutional lines.[3] Asquith's reaction was swift. As agreed on 18 July and thought less provocative to the peers, he wrote to Lansdowne and Balfour, stating that he would ask the House of Commons to disagree with the Lords amendments; should necessity arise, he would ask the King to exercise his prerogative so as to pass the bill in much the same shape as it left the Commons, and the King had signified his willingness to act on that advice.[4]

On 21 July, in sweltering heat, some 170 peers met at Lansdowne House to be informed of Asquith's reaction. The party was deeply divided on how to proceed: some wished to resist, entailing the creation of peers; others, including Balfour and Lansdowne, felt they should accept the inevitable and let the bill pass. During the meeting it was disclosed that both Unionist whips in the Lords, Waldegrave and Victor Churchill, had joined the diehards. That they were not immediately replaced was taken to indicate Lansdowne's weakening position. From accounts of those present at this meeting, it is clear that Lansdowne displayed feebleness. Throughout his career he listened to all sides of an argument before taking a decision. In the heated atmosphere that afternoon, an immediate and definite lead was needed to channel the passions of those present. This he was unable to give. Two days later, he wrote to Norfolk:

> further resistance becomes useless and worse when once it is established beyond question that they have secured the King's full support and that the Bill must become law in its House of Commons shape. I told you that I should not be sorry to see a certain number of token peers created, so as to afford an absolute demonstration that we were not free agents, but I do not think the supporters of His Majesty's Government will permit them to take this course, the disadvantages of which are, from their point of view, obvious. There is another consideration which weighs with me. A dissolution is not within our reach, but I am also convinced that our party do not desire one and probably would not face one, and the knowledge that this is so has greatly strengthened the view which I have expressed above.[5]

Over the following weeks Lansdowne suffered for his indecision at the meeting. His followers – the non-diehards – were in the majority, but the revolt against Lansdowne gathered pace. Forming a committee under Halsbury, the diehards realised that Lansdowne was following policy, not principles, whereas they would rather die in the ditch than let the bill pass. Meanwhile Curzon, a non-diehard, established the Hedgers. This splinter group, which supported Lansdowne, believed that a House of Lords with a two-year veto would be better than allowing its virtual destruction, followed by Irish Home Rule, Welsh disestablishment and other radical measures. As Curzon later noted:

> I threw myself energetically into the fray and organised the forces which ultimately enabled Lord Lansdowne to prevail. Every day for a fortnight a committee met in my house Lord Lansdowne constantly attended. He intimated that his attitude, which was held by the diehards to have been

mainly responsible for the end result, brought him a <u>great deal</u> of personal vituperation. 'But I was unable to see that there were two sides to the matter and how foolish the policy of the diehards would have been was sufficiently demonstrated in the ensuing two years'.[6]

On 24 July Lansdowne met the King, who was agitated, but seemed anxious not to create more peers than necessary and said that was the view of ministers.[7] The Prime Minister had told him he would be satisfied with a majority of one for the bill. His description of his ministers' plans matched that given by Lloyd George. When the King asked Lansdowne whether that was the usual course, he replied that it certainly was not and described what he believed to be the proper procedure when the two Houses differed. The King asked whether a course less offensive to peers would make any difference; Lansdowne said it would have made a great difference at first, but it would be difficult for ministers to make any change now and, after Mr Asquith's announcement, it would probably not produce much effect. His Majesty said the Prime Minister had suggested a conference between the leaders, after adjournment of the debate due to begin that day.[8] The King's anxiety was so great that he decided not to attend Goodwood Races.

As the Unionist party split further, Balfour withdrew. According to Albert Dicey, the Unionist jurist, 'with all his clearness in debate he does not seem to see the immense effect of a few plain words of authority spoken at once'.[9] Concerned by this, Curzon and Lansdowne persuaded Balfour to write a letter replying to a Unionist peer supposedly seeking advice. The imaginary peer was Newton, later Lansdowne's biographer. In the letter, published on 25 July, Balfour said he had never thought he should intervene in the affairs of a House to which he did not belong; nor had he joined in the vigorous propaganda of some of its members:

> But this is not because I have any doubts as to the advice which I ought to give to those who seek it. On the contrary, my views are clear. I think the majority in the House of Lords should support its leader; I agree with the advice Lord Lansdowne has given to his friends; with Lord Lansdowne I stand; with Lord Lansdowne I am ready, if need be, to fall.

Balfour warned the diehards that

> the crime of the government is that by a gross misuse of the prerogative they have made the second chamber powerless, and fighting in any effective sense impossible. Fighting means, or ought to mean, something real. It means damaging the enemy, hampering his operations. I fail to see how the course proposed by those who refuse to follow Lord Lansdowne is to attain

any of these objects. It would in my opinion be a misfortune if the present crisis left the House of Lords weaker than the Parliament Bill by itself will make it; but it would be an irreparable tragedy if it left us a divided party.[10]

Balfour's letter inflamed the diehards further. They held a dinner to celebrate the stand taken by Halsbury and others, while maintaining that it was not a demonstration against Balfour or Lansdowne, or even a criticism of them. However, the root of their complaint was clearly the Unionist Party's need for new leaders.

Two days earlier, at Curzon's suggestion, Lansdowne had written to ask the views of every Unionist peer not already pledged. Unable to win but unwilling to perish, Lansdowne reiterated that the best course was submission. Their insistence on his amendments would swamp the House of Lords with peers and paralyse its future action without impeding the passage of the Parliament Bill. From the replies, Lansdowne understood that should Halsbury collect seventy-five or more followers the bill would be lost. Lansdowne therefore needed to know how many Unionist peers would if necessary vote for the government. As Leader of the Lords, he could not undertake this sensitive task himself, so, to avoid provoking indignation, private enquiries were made. In a private letter to Balfour he explained why, if the Halsburyites took their own line, a few Unionist peers might take a different line of their own and go further than he and Balfour were willing to:

> they will not be numerous, for most of those who have said they were prepared to vote with the government plainly indicated that they would go into the Government lobby with me only if I went there.[11]

Balfour wished Lansdowne to publicly state his disapproval of any of his followers actively voting for the bill, and drafted a letter to serve his purpose. Lansdowne was reluctant to intervene directly. However, on 1 August it appeared in the press, as a letter from Lansdowne to Camperdown:

> You published in *The Times* of the 28th instant an important letter in which you announced that you were prepared, when the Parliament Bill came back to the House of Lords, to vote with the Government if by doing so you could help to avoid a creation of peers. During the last few days I have been repeatedly asked whether I was in favour of the course which you are yourself prepared to take, and whether I was in any way responsible for your suggestion. I am anxious that there should be no room for doubt as to the course which I have recommended to those who are good enough to support me in the House of Lords. My advice has been in favour of

abstention from voting, and, in order to make my position clear, I may add that in no circumstances should I consider myself justified in voting with the government when the Bill returns to our House.[12]

The letter in fact provoked resentment among some of the timid peers, who supported Lansdowne. Margot Asquith told Curzon that

no one made such a mistake as Lansdowne by writing his letter. Henry [Asquith] said to me from the first 'how I wish it could all be hurried up' – Lansdowne you will see will start with courage and be completely knocked off by a few threats from the others. I shall be very sad to see Arthur [Balfour] and Lansdowne beaten on the post.[13]

John St Loe Strachey, the Editor of the Spectator, was very unhappy about Lansdowne's letter and wrote to the *Daily Mail*:

What is the true inwardness of the movement which has Lord Halsbury for its figure-head. As you say, it is nothing less than a plot against Mr Balfour. The situation was bad enough and serious enough when the danger before us was that to the great evils of the Parliament Bill were to be added the evils of the destruction of the House of Lords and the ruin of the peerage. Now we have in addition the risk of the deposition of Lord Lansdowne and Mr Balfour, and such deposition, I am convinced, must mean at this juncture the ruin of the unionist party.[14]

Perhaps it was not, as Dicey thought, that Balfour did not see the value of 'a few plain words', but rather his difficulty in making them plain enough, because *The Times* and the *Daily Mail*, newspapers owned by Lord Northcliffe, published articles inferring from the letter that Lansdowne did not really wish to dissuade his friends from voting for the government.[15]

On 9 and 10 August 1911 the Lords assembled for the final debate on the Parliament Bill. The temperature in Parliament was over 100 °F (37.8 °C). Viscount Simon noted of the first day's debate that 'what added immensely to the sense of excitement was that no one knew how the division would go'.[16] Peers abandoned their usual formality, even indulging in personal altercations. In place of Crewe, who was still unwell, Morley opened for the government by moving consideration of the Commons' disagreements with the Lords' amendments. Lansdowne set the tone for the Unionists by dismissing the government concessions, but most of his argument was directed at his own rebels. He ended by referring to a long constitutional struggle ahead and the undesirability of divided counsels among Unionists.[17] Almeric FitzRoy wrote that

Lord Lansdowne, who always shines in a position of extreme difficulty, acquitted himself of the task he had to perform with the greatest tact, polish, dignity and address, and but for the fact that he appealed to a section of the House impenetrable to reason and proof to the dictates of prudence, his allocution could not have failed of success.[18]

Twenty minutes after midnight, Midleton, formerly St John Brodrick, moved adjournment. On 10 August Balfour left for Austria, stopping over in Paris;[19] Asquith was recovering from laryngitis. Meanwhile, in the Lords that afternoon, Midleton opened the debate on behalf of those supporting Lansdowne. Morley spoke next:

> if the Bill should be defeated tonight His Majesty would assent – I say this on my full responsibility as the spokesman of the Government – to a creation of Peers sufficient in number to guard against any possible combination of the different Parties in Opposition by which the Parliament Bill might again be exposed a second time to defeat.[20]

Violet Asquith noted: 'one of the most thrilling evenings of my life. I was in the House of Lords from 4 onwards.'[21] On leaving the House that night, Lady Halsbury refused to shake hands with Lansdowne when she and her husband met him. The government majority included twenty-nine Unionist peers who voted with them. The diehards took 114 votes, including two bishops.

Arthur Bigge, the Unionist private secretary to George V, returned to Buckingham Palace and reported the night's events to the King, who noted in his diary, 'so the Halsburyites were thank God beaten. It is indeed a great relief to me – I am spared any further humiliation by a creation of peers'.[22] Wilfrid Scawen Blunt noted, 'the Lords have voted their own death by a majority of 17. They have played their game with inconceivable stupidity, making miscalculation after miscalculation.'[23]

The diehards were bitterly disappointed: infuriated at the weakness of Unionist leadership, infuriated at fellow Unionists who had voted for the bill and despondent at their defeat.[24] Wyndham told his wife:

> Of course we can never meet George Curzon or St John Brodrick [Midleton] again, nor can we ever consent to act with Lansdowne or Balfour if they summon Curzon to their counsels. I will *never* bow the knee to the Harmsworth Press. I will *never* meet Curzon at a council convened by Balfour.[25]

On 12 August Lansdowne told Roberts, who had voted with the diehards, that nothing distressed me more than to find myself at this crisis differing from so many of my oldest friends and the extreme violence of some of them was to my mind unpardonable. But all that will, I hope, blow over unless some of the malcontents are so foolish as to set up a 'vendetta' and persecute or excommunicate their opponents. That would lead to a permanent estrangement and to the ruin of the party.[26]

On 19 August Wicklow told Lansdowne that he thought the government would probably not have had the courage to carry out their threat: they had succeeded in a great game of bluff.[27] Lansdowne thought otherwise: had the government lost the bill they would have created a large number of peers. If Asquith had tried to evade his party's pledges, their Irish and Labour supporters would have turned him out of office within three months.[28]

Despite the drama for those involved, the public showed little interest, preoccupied with the Agadir Crisis, the threat of war with Germany, and a number of strikes, including dockers, firemen, seamen and possibly railwaymen.[29] The Parliament Act became law in autumn 1911 and with it the last bastion of landed power was successfully emasculated and the power of the Lords was irrevocably weakened. The Liberals could press on with their radical programme, notably the National Insurance Act. Lord Newton wrote:

> looking back, after an interval of eighteen years, it is difficult to resist the melancholy conclusion that the humiliating defeat of the Unionist party over the Parliament Bill was due more to the tactical error of rejecting the Budget of 1909 than to any other cause.[30]

On 22 August Lansdowne wrote to his daughter Evie, from Derreen, that he was picking up slowly, 'but as Carlyle said "all H–ll is rumbling in my innards, & I am as weak as a kitten"'.[31] Maud was aware that her husband would get a lot of abuse, but

> it doesn't really matter if he has done right & there can be no doubt that his policy for the country is sound though to the young and ardent unionist it may seem cowardly.[32]

She was proud of his speech on 9 August during the final debate on the Parliament Bill, which she attended. She told Evie: 'if the end of all this is his resignation of the leadership, I shall not be sorry'.[33]

Maud's remark about leadership was at the centre of the dispute, not only at individual but at party level. Lansdowne was from an older generation that favoured caution and the status quo. The younger generation saw things differently. After he defiantly rejected the Budget, Lansdowne pursued his usual diplomatic approach of inviting wide expressions of opinion, well aware that his room for manoeuvre was restricted. Unfortunately, his enemies were inflexible. With party tempers so frayed, it would have made little difference whatever course he took. The diehards were simply dissatisfied with the leadership and direction of the Unionist Party. They wanted change and new leaders.

32

NEW DIRECTION

IMMEDIATELY AFTER THE Parliament Bill passed the Lords, the diehards regrouped and campaigned to depose Balfour and Lansdowne:

> it is utter nonsense to pretend that we or any Conservatives or Unionists can ever support Balfour and Lansdowne and their followers. They have by their miserable folly and dishonesty done their best to wreck the party.[1]

Lansdowne thought their pronouncements 'rather ridiculous and inconsistent with the professions of those who assured us that this was merely a passing difference and that the solidity of the Party was to remain unimpaired'.[2] Maud reckoned the diehards would not rest until they were rid of both leaders. She told Evie: 'I can't help feeling it would be better for them both to retire now, before they are asked to do so, but I don't think Clan agrees with me.'[3]

The pressure put on Balfour was immense and he informed Lansdowne privately a few days before announcing his resignation as party leader on 8 November 1911. This saddened Lansdowne, especially that it was so soon after the events of August; the public would think Balfour had been driven from office by an unscrupulous cabal at a time when Britain was threatened at home and abroad. He informed Balfour: 'people will say that, even at the cost of grave personal inconvenience, your first duty is to remain at the head of your party', adding 'if you are no longer to lead us, I do not see how I can usefully stay where I am'.[4] Yet, despite Balfour's departure, Lansdowne decided to stay on as opposition Leader of the Lords. This might seem very odd, especially for an old-style politician whose interests in politics were bound up in Balfour's leadership, but he was persuaded by Sandars that his departure would cause a political crisis and remove the whole basis of personal argument on which Balfour rested his case.[5] Moreover, Lansdowne, even after eight years, had more to do in the Lords. The government would soon legislate on Irish Home Rule and socialism would continue to threaten the second Chamber. Resisting such forces mattered to Lansdowne.

Within five days of Balfour's resignation, 232 Unionist MPs met at the Carlton Club and elected Andrew Bonar Law as their Leader in the Commons. Born in Canada, the son of an Ulster Presbyterian minister. Having made a fortune in industry, he became an MP in 1900. He was regarded as rather dull by comparison to Balfour. He was a new type of leader, having never attended public (private) school or university. His business experience convinced him of the benefit of tariff reform and his upbringing made him value the Union between Britain and Ireland. On 12 November Lansdowne wrote to him:

> I wish you a successful leadership, and I feel no doubt that it will be successful. We ought to keep in pretty close touch with one another – it is very important that the unionist front benches should from time to time take stock of the political situation.[6]

Lansdowne believed that Bonar Law was probably for the best,[7] but he found it 'rather horrid to begin working with a new man' at the age of sixty-six.[8] However, he treated Bonar Law with unfailing courtesy. He displayed on occasion a hint of superiority, but this owed more to the fact that Lansdowne was older and was more senior in the party hierarchy. Lansdowne did not conceal that he missed Balfour dreadfully; as his wife remarked, 'I never took in just how devoted they are to each other.'[9]

Although the Parliament Act reduced the Unionist advantage in the Lords and enabled the Liberals to press on with their legislative programme, it did not bring about the destruction of the House of Lords. Furthermore, the Act's preamble envisaged sweeping Lords reform in the future but this was not pursued and the House remained unreformed until years later. After the heated debates of the summer, the Lords fell into a depressed state, with poorly attended, uninspiring debates during the autumn. Lansdowne did his best to invigorate the House with the support of Curzon, whom he saw as his natural successor.

On 25 September 1911, two months before the change of party leader, Lansdowne wrote to Curzon setting out his view of the situation. He was inclined to replace the party whips, who had joined the diehards the previous July. Arthur Steel-Maitland, party chairman, suggested Willoughby de Broke; Lansdowne thought he would be excellent, but 'his conviction as a poacher was too recent to make it possible for us to equip

him with the keeper's velveteens just yet'.[10] Lansdowne's nephew Victor
Devonshire replaced Waldegrave, and Victor Churchill was retained.
Forming an opposition cabinet proved a problem for Lansdowne and
Bonar Law because the rules were unclear. During the next six months
this caused them perpetual trouble. To omit people caused offence; to
invite them would lead to intangible claims for office when the party
came to power. As a result, they convened the shadow cabinet only when
important or contentious issues or authoritative party pronouncements
made it imperative.[11]

As further Liberal legislation reached the House of Lords, Lansdowne
showed little hostility to it. On 11 December, as Parliament was prorogued
for the year, Lansdowne advised his colleagues on the National Insurance
Bill. Although he questioned the scheme's cost and cautioned that no
social legislation of its magnitude had ever been attempted without a
previous inquiry, he advised the Lords to accept it. On 16 December the
bill was given the royal assent. That month King George V and Queen
Mary visited Delhi and announced that it would become the capital
of India, along with the reorganisation of the province of Bengal. On
his return the King summoned Lansdowne for his advice on the Delhi
announcement. Although Lansdowne had reservations about the cost
of the project he took a non-partisan line with the King, advising him
that any criticism in Britain would be directed more at the government's
methods, which were to keep the matter shrouded in secrecy, than at the
changes that were being contemplated.[12]

After new year, Lansdowne and Bonar Law set about uniting their
party. On 12 February 1912 it was remodelled as the National Unionist
Association of Conservative and Liberal-Unionist Organizations. On
18 April, at Lansdowne House, the Liberal Unionist peers and MPs
unanimously approved this merger.[13] It was ratified on 9 May. A few
months before this, on 14 February, Parliament was opened by the King
and Queen on a dull and cloudy day. Lansdowne believed the legislative
programme was preposterous, with obvious omissions, but his principal
concern was for the Unionists. To the free-traders in his party, tariff
reform and food taxes had caused the election defeat, distracted the
party from the fight against Home Rule and damaged party support.[14]
To the Chamberlainites, tariff reform was essential, while food taxes
offered new revenue and gave preference to imperial produce. Shifting
the Unionist Party away from these issues and focusing on the Irish
question and Home Rule was Lansdowne's challenge.

On 29 February the first shadow cabinet since Balfour's retirement
met at Lansdowne House to discuss food taxes and the referendum
pledge. Bonar Law left the initiative to Lansdowne, who suggested that,
for the moment, the party should leave food taxes as part of their tariff

reform policy, but they were no longer bound by Balfour's 1910 pledge to put tariff reform to a referendum. Those present decided to follow his lead, but keep their discussion secret.[15] By 10 October journalists were pressing Lansdowne for a statement on the pledge. He told Bonar Law,

> I think you agree with me in believing that an explicit statement upon this point is inevitable, and in my opinion we shall gain rather than lose by it. There is a kind of impression abroad that we are trying to shirk the question.[16]

Lansdowne insisted on being able to announce their policy before Bonar Law or anyone else because

> I was consulted by Balfour when the pledge was given, and I repeated it in all the speeches which I delivered at the time of the election.[17]

Lansdowne suggested repealing the pledge at the November 1912 party conference, Bonar Law agreed.

While tariff reform was divisive, Ireland offered the best chance to unite the party and win an election. Abolition of the Lords' veto paved the way for the Government of Ireland Bill. Even before the final battle in August 1911, the Liberals had been planning for Home Rule and its effects on the United Kingdom. Lansdowne was uneasy about Home Rule, but he did not believe the anti-Home Rule cry would catch on as it had in 1886 and 1893. When Curzon raised the matter in September 1911, Lansdowne told him

> People have got much more used to the idea than they were, and there is an intense desire to relieve the Westminster Parliament of some of the work which it now does so badly. Quite apart from this, the old anti-Home Rule movement derived a great part of its strength from the abhorrence created by crimes and outrages which are fortunately of rare occurrence today.

As an alternative policy he mentioned that

> the best antidote to Home Rule was the completion of the land purchase policy embodied in George Wyndham's Act.[18] Its financial collapse has been an unmitigated misfortune, but we must endeavour to keep it going, and this is, I think, possible. I have no doubt whatever that the demand for Home Rule has become infinitely less active in those areas where Purchase has prevailed. You will I daresay have noticed that many of the members of the Government connect their Home Rule policy with a scheme of Home Rule all round.[19] I have myself always been ready

to treat respectfully proposals for a further devolution of public business to local bodies, but that is very thin ice, and as you may remember I got into hot water for allowing Antony MacDonnell to talk to me about his Devolution scheme. Up to the present time I have heard of no policy which we could, and Redmond [Irish Parliamentary Party leader] would, look at for a moment. Upon the whole, I do not think we shall make much of a fight against Home Rule unless its financial bases prove to be vulnerable. This is, I think, almost sure to be the case, but we cannot make the most of this argument until the Government Bill has been produced. As to your question, if the Home Rule Bill were to survive the two or three years' struggle in both Houses of Parliament, and if the majority of the electors declared themselves in favour of it? I do not see how we could resist further or encourage Ulster to do so.[20]

In December 1911, Home Rule matters escalated in and out of Westminster and Lansdowne was absorbed with separatism:

We must dismiss the idea of a separate Parliament for Ulster. Ulster will not accept such a Parliament upon any terms. Let us continue the Balfour policy in Ireland. No administration can possibly be worse for the material well-being of Ireland than a partisan Administration controlled entirely by one great Irish faction. We stand for the Union and the Constitution, for the Union which we mean to preserve, for the Constitution which we hope to re-establish.[21]

On 11 April 1912, two months after the opening of Parliament, Asquith introduced his Home Rule Bill. It resembled the Bill of 1893, which the House of Lords had rejected, providing for an independent bicameral Irish Parliament, but reduced the number of Irish representatives able to sit at Westminster to forty-two. The Irish Parliament would consist of an upper house of forty senators and a House of Commons with 164 members. Ministers from the two Houses would form an Irish executive, headed by the Lord Lieutenant. It would have no control over army and navy matters, foreign relations or trade. A ban was proposed on legislation discriminating for or against any religion. The Parliament could levy new taxes (but not customs duties) that did not conflict with existing legislation; a joint board would decide on 'conflict'.[22]

Unionists in England and Ireland were generally opposed to Home Rule, but views differed. Some saw it as a purely domestic affair; others, like Lansdowne, saw it as part of an imperial issue where minorities mattered.[23] Ulster attracted many British advocates, but southern Unionists, fewer in number, and their British supporters were divided between those resigned to Home Rule and willing to watch Ulster make the best terms possible and those strongly against it and willing to condemn desertion by Ulster. While Lansdowne kept a low profile, he believed as strongly as Bonar Law about defending Ulster, though 'I should probably have used language rather less suggestive of readiness to carry a rifle in her defence'.[24] Unionist meetings culminated on 28 September with Ulster Day. Edward Carson, leader of the Irish Unionist Party, and about half a million people signed Ulster's Solemn League and Covenant, in protest against the Home Rule Bill. Lansdowne sent a message of sympathy.

During the summer of 1912, Lansdowne tackled the land question and regeneration of rural Britain, which Lloyd George had made his own. With a general election due in 1915, Lloyd George's land campaign was both an attempt to strengthen the Liberal's position against the Unionists and to maintain Liberal support against the threat of socialism: he saw tackling landownership and agriculture as a way of winning rural votes. Unlike the Liberals, the Unionists did not have a formulated land policy, although they favoured small-ownership as a means of fortifying private property and as a barrier to socialism. Even if their party was still the preserve of the landowning class, neither Lansdowne nor Bonar Law could afford to appear as mere instruments of this faction. However, appearing to ignore their interests would inflame them and jeopardise votes on other matters including Ireland. In June Lloyd George announced his campaign: courts to fix fair rents, security of tenure for farmers and tribunals to set minimum agricultural wages.

On 25 July Lansdowne took up the matter. As a Whig landowner, defender of private property and manager of his estates, he was better informed than most about land. He acknowledged that across Britain estates were in decline and more small owners were needed and would generally be a good thing for the country. Indeed 'the old tendency to accumulate land has been replaced by the tendency to disperse it' under pressure from taxation and burdens on property. He cited a real estate company that in four months had sold land worth £1.25 million. His speech to the Rural League was not just a response to Lloyd George but a reminder that land had been an issue for his party and class for many years. He sketched a bold policy of state support for smallholders, alongside rural cooperatives, as in Denmark, and aid in building cottages where they were badly needed and scarce because landowners and local authorities could not afford to build them. State intervention was needed to promote rural housing, agricultural education and rural banks, with loans to sitting tenants dispossessed by their land being sold. Schemes would begin prudently and experimentally.[25]

No form of tenure would give the cultivator the same security, interest, responsibility and self-respect as ownership. No tenant in a precarious and fluctuating business like agriculture wanted the kind of state intervention that then existed in Whitehall, 'presided over by a Minister with ideas, who may be here today and gone tomorrow'. Lansdowne realised that the only real argument against publicly assisted purchase was financial, but no better use could be made of public credit than settling independent, hard-working cultivators on English soil. Lansdowne saw this as a better future for land policy than the Radicals' dream of 'setting the land free' and 'restoring the people to the land' by piling rates and taxes on it until landowners had to sell; 'rural people would easily see how totally that ignored their needs'.[26]

While Lansdowne endeavoured to unite those interested in agriculture – owners, farmers and labourers – he also strove to unite the Unionists. Although the political situation was less favourable to the government that at the beginning of 1912, the deterioration of their prestige was less marked than expected for a government in its seventh year of office. On 14 November Lansdowne attempted to score political points over the Liberals and settle tensions about tariff reform. He told the National Unionist party conference that the Liberals were asking people to believe that the Irish Home Rule Bill was a first step towards some great scheme of decentralization for the country and of federation for the British Empire.

> It is not by these insincere proposals that you will bring the Dominions closer to the Empire. We Unionists desire to draw them nearer to us but we are convinced that the soundest foundation for such a closer union of the Empire is to be found in the establishment of closer commercial relations between the different parts of the Empire and that is why we have given Tariff Reform a foremost place in our policy.[27]

The Unionists had promised a referendum on tariffs if the Liberals put Home Rule to a referendum, but the Liberals had not done so. Therefore, the Unionists were free to deal with tariffs in any way they chose.[28]

The speech was well received. Bonar Law added 'I concur in every word which has fallen from Lord Lansdowne', bringing further applause. But some free fooders were dissatisfied. In December a campaign was started for a renewal of the pledge. Lansdowne had to consider whether abandoning food taxes would unite the party any better than retention. Privately, he believed they were done with food taxes. As uncertainty developed, both leaders considered stepping down, but that would have plunged the party into even greater confusion. In January 1913 the deadlock ended when Carson met Bonar Law and Lansdowne and discussed compromise. The outcome was a signed memorial from 231 of the 280 Unionist MPs, affirming the party's commitment to tariff reform and imperial preference, and both leaders' willingness to postpone food taxes until after another election.

Lansdowne accepted the modification, as there seemed to be no change of principle. As Maud noted, 'neither Clan or Bonar Law will resign, but it is rather humiliating to have to eat your own words and naturally the radical papers will crow over it, but there it is, I suppose it has to be done. Clan is very quiet over it all.'[29] Lansdowne told Edmond Fitzmaurice, his brother, 'it has not been a pleasant episode and I should not have been displeased if it had ended in my retirement into private life – but it has revealed the strength of Bonar Law's position, due partly to his own merits, which are incontestable, and partly to the impossibility of discovering another leader in his place'.[30] It left Lansdowne very sad. He told Evie that a politician's sixty-ninth year ought to bring him the prospect of peace. The decision spelt a deepening of the crisis of Conservatism and set the Unionist Party on a new political course, associated with extreme measures.

To supporters and opponents, Lansdowne and Bonar Law were the only possible leaders to deal with Home Rule. In October 1912 Parliament had reassembled and Asquith pressed ahead with his Home Rule Bill. He moved the guillotine resolution, allowing twenty-seven days in committee, seven for the report stage and two for third reading. Many important provisions and amendments were passed without any discussion. On 13 December, when Lansdowne and other senior Unionists met to consider how the Lords should deal with the bill, a large majority favoured simple rejection at second reading. Lansdowne thought this wise.[31] On 1 January 1913 Carson and two other MPs moved an amendment excluding the nine Ulster counties. To make the threat of resistance more credible, he argued that without the use of force Ulster Protestants would never submit to Home Rule,[32] but he also wanted to separate Ulster from the rest of Ireland. Carson's amendment was rejected. The Commons passed the bill with a majority of 110.

The bill then went to the Lords where, after a four-day debate of exceptionally high quality, Lansdowne wound up for the opposition. He said the debate had shown the bill to be ill-considered, unworkable and bound to fail. Home Rule had not been prominent in the government programme until an election showed they needed the Irish vote, but this was not a matter for Ireland alone. Ulster believed the bill was fatal to her best interests, had no confidence in the safeguards and resented bitterly that it should be forced through under the Parliament Act. 'She also refuses to believe that you are going to coerce her into submission to a yoke which is hateful to her.'[33]

On 30 January 1913 the Lords rejected the bill by 326 to 69. It had passed its second reading in the Commons on 9 May 1912; since, under the Parliament Act, two years had to elapse between this date and the Commons passing the bill again, it could not be sent back to the Lords until 9 May 1914.[34] However, meanwhile, on the day the Lords rejected the bill, a Home Ruler won a by-election at Londonderry, giving them a 17-to-16 edge in Ulster.[35] To most Unionists the future of Home Rule had come down to the exclusion of part of Ulster.

33

HOME RULE PROGRESSES

ON 10 MARCH 1913 Parliament reconvened and the Home Rule Bill made progress. No amendments were allowed, so there was no committee or report stage, and the Commons passed the bill on third reading after three days. On 9 July, after taking widespread advice from colleagues and advisers, Lansdowne gave notice that at second reading in the Lords he would move 'that this House declines to proceed with the consideration of the Bill until it has been submitted to the judgment of the country'.[1] His amendment was so phrased to challenge the principle of the Parliament Act while serving for the Lords' second rejection of the bill on 15 July. This was an extraordinarily risky decision – one might question whether he had learned nothing from 1909 – and brought the crisis to a head. As in 1909, Lansdowne doubted that the government would oblige the Unionists, but unlike in 1909 he was confident that the Unionists would beat them if there were an appeal to the country.[2]

Crewe, Leader of the Lords, dismissed the idea of an election, sneering that Ulster would not care a snap of her fingers for the views of Wiltshire peasants or Glamorganshire miners. Lansdowne urged that an election would be priceless to the government, for 'if they won they would know that they had not misread the opinion of the country'.[3] He concluded, 'if the country wants this bill, we are ready to let them have it'.[4] The King agreed with the Unionist position. He believed the government was 'drifting' and making his position as constitutional monarch more and more difficult.[5] On 24 July he learned that an arrangement might be made for Ulster to 'contract out' of Home Rule for ten years, with the right to join in if approved by referendum.

Having spoken with Asquith and other senior government officials, the King summoned Lansdowne to Balmoral to understand the opposition's view. On 6 September they had a long conversation. The King was anxious about the political situation, and did not disagree with the Unionists' tactics. Lansdowne minuted their conversation in a memorandum:

> He [the King] reminded me that in the general election of 1906 the issue had been, not without success, represented as between the Houses of Lords and the people. He was afraid that if we were to resist his ministers now the issue would be represented as between the people and the sovereign. He had dwelt with such earnestness on the difficulty of the position in which he would find himself if he were to be called upon next year either to refuse his assent to a Bill which had run its full course under the Parliament Act, or to sanction a measure which would be resisted to the bitter end by Ulster, and would probably occasion bloodshed and necessitate the employment of his troops for the purpose of coercing the recalcitrants. The Prime Minister had told him that as a Constitutional sovereign it would be impossible for him to disregard the advice of his Ministers, and that, whatever happened, His Majesty's position would be 'unassailable' so long as he followed that advice.

Lansdowne said he would be sorry were it deliberately admitted that the King must automatically assent to anything his ministers chose to present to him. The question seemed to Lansdowne to depend on the circumstances. As he later noted, 'What were the circumstances of the case? It was doubtful whether any mandate for Home Rule had been given by the electors; they certainly had given no mandate for the Bill now before Parliament. On the other hand, it was now doubtful that the passing of the Bill would mean civil war in Ireland.'[6]

As to Asquith's observations on the referendum, Lansdowne admitted that there was some force in his argument that they could not compel the electors to consider Home Rule and nothing else. Nevertheless, if the government looked likely to agree to a referendum, he felt sure that the Unionist leaders would treat the verdict of the people as affecting the Home Rule Bill only. As for settlement by consent, Lansdowne said:

> I thought His Majesty was right in giving little encouragement to the idea of a formal conference. I did not think such conferences were of much use without a certain amount of previous agreement, but the two parties were wide as to the poles asunder upon Home Rule on the lines of the present bill. I should deprecate the idea of a conference upon the basis of Home Rule with the exclusion of Ulster. His Majesty had mentioned the Carson amendment, and I said that this amendment had been moved only upon the assumption that, so far as the House of Commons was concerned, the

Home Rule Bill was likely to become law; but it certainly did not indicate a readiness on our part to accept Home Rule, and I should deprecate the idea of going into conference with an admission that Home Rule had become inevitable. I said that I was not much alarmed by the anticipation that the failure of the Home Rule bill would be followed by disturbances in other parts of Ireland. There might be ebullitions but I did not think the feeling for Home Rule in the South and West of Ireland approached in intensity the feeling against Home Rule in the four counties.[7]

Lansdowne left Balmoral to join Maud at Meikleour, where on 12 September they entertained Bonar Law, who was on his way north to meet the King. Meikleour was at this time very well equipped for sport, with plenty of shooting and fishing. However, apart from a bowling green in the village, there was little to do for guests who preferred not to hunt animals and for his staff when off duty. Lansdowne addressed this by building a nine-hole golf course in the park. According to one of his household staff, he did this because he found that the staff smelt strongly of beer after spending their afternoons at the bowling green.[8] In summer 1912 Bonar Law had been one of the first guests to play on the new course. As a keen golfer, he enjoyed the round, but Lansdowne chose to walk.[9]

On 11 September *The Times* published a letter by Loreburn, former Liberal Lord Chancellor and chairman of the 1911 cabinet committee on Home Rule, appealing for an inter-party conference and pleading that ministers would not under any circumstances use military force against rioters.[10] Loreburn was sympathetic to Home Rule All Round, the idea being to devolve wide areas of government to Parliaments in Ireland, Scotland and Wales, limiting governments' dependence on the Irish Parliamentary Party.[11] Lansdowne, aware that the King was working towards settlement by consent, believed the letter would strengthen his attitude,[12] but the idea seemed nebulous and had caught on only because everyone was looking for some way out of their difficulties.[13]

At Balmoral, Bonar Law was more emphatic with the King than Lansdowne had been about the effect if the government attempted to use troops in Belfast before they were backed by the moral force of public opinion.[14] Lansdowne thought the practical difficulty of giving Ireland 'a sort of Home Rule' while north-east Ulster remained an integral part of the United Kingdom would be even greater than Bonar Law supposed. After reading the latter's Balmoral report, Lansdowne told him:

I doubt whether it would be possible to obtain for it the requisite measure of approval from the unionists of the south and west of Ireland, while on the other hand the kind of local government which would be given to the rest of Ireland would fall far short of Nationalist ideals and be contemptuously refused by the Irish leaders.[15]

Lansdowne was against the exclusion of Ulster, pure and simple. On 2 October he told Bonar Law he would be very sorry if Unionists offered this as a solution, though 'we may have to fall back upon it, but only when we are in our last ditch and we are not there yet'.[16] While Bonar Law adopted a course of less resistance, Lansdowne set out his views:

(1) Our demand is for a general election, and we should concentrate upon this as much as possible.

(2) It is not our business to make overtures for conferences or anything else.

(3) We ought not to go into conference if there is to be a preliminary bargain under which we should be compelled to accept the Bill, subject to special treatment for Ulster.

(4) We ought not to refuse an 'open' conference if one is offered to us. I should myself prefer to use the word 'discussion' rather than 'conference'. For the purpose of such a conference the Government need not be compelled, as a preliminary, to withdraw their Bill, nor need we be compelled to accept it, with or without conditions.

(5) We admit that some form of extended local government should be given to Ireland, but it might be on a provincial and not a national basis, and it must leave room for the recognition of Ulster and be of such a kind as to be capable of incorporation in, or at all events not inconsistent with, a general measure for the relief of the Imperial Parliament.[17]

Speaking on 25 October, Asquith dismissed the possibility of a conference and proposed to the Unionist leaders 'an interchange of views and suggestions, free, frank, and without prejudice' – but he set two conditions: nothing must be done to interfere with the setting up in Dublin of a subordinate Irish legislature with an executive responsible to it, and that nothing must be done to erect a permanent and insuperable bar in the way of Irish unity.[18] Lansdowne thought it was brazen effrontery of Asquith to assert that his conditions contained no loophole or ambiguity. He was glad, however, that the Prime Minister had brushed aside the idea of a conference. He felt strongly on this: if one had been proposed, 'I think I should have asked to be excused from taking part in its deliberations'.[19] He felt that

the proper solution of this question is a reference to the electors of this country. Failing that, we are ready to consider special terms for Ulster, accompanied by such changes in the Bill as the special treatment of Ulster may render necessary. If both these things are refused, then we shall give

Ulster, in and out of Parliament, all the encouragement we can in the resistance she makes. We shall hold His Majesty's Ministers responsible for any disasters which may result from their conduct. We shall regard the settlement thus imposed on us as lacking in authority, and we shall hold ourselves free to reopen it should the opportunity arise.[20]

While Lansdowne and Bonar Law worked towards uniting the Unionist Party and pressing the government to let the electorate decide upon Home Rule, the situation was taking its toll. On 8 December Bonar Law wrote to Lansdowne: 'I think we are a curious pair of leaders, for it is evident that you are not enjoying it, and at this moment I would give a good deal to be out of it, too.'[21] For both men the Irish problem was becoming an overarching concern and their tempers were beginning to fray.[22] At the same time, Asquith was in a panic about it and was probing the Unionist leaders to establish the limits of their flexibility and the bottom line for a deal.

Neither Lansdowne nor Bonar Law were in any mood to give up the fight, but Asquith met Bonar Law on three occasions to convert him to a proposal of Edward Grey, the Foreign Secretary, for 'Home Rule within Home Rule' and United Kingdom-wide devolution. Lansdowne did not believe this was a solution to the issue; Asquith 'has no doubt been told that it is absolutely necessary for him to make a move of some kind, but I do not suppose that he sees his way out'.[23] Asquith held further meetings with the Unionists, and sent Carson some ideas that were apparently not a serious offer but a means of drawing the opposition into defining their terms. His paper, a variant on 'Home Rule within Home Rule', seemed to Lansdowne a patchwork that would probably please no one.[24]

By 30 November 76,757 men had joined the Ulster Volunteer Force and large imports of rifles were reported. In Dublin, a counter-force, the National Volunteers, was organised on 25 November. By the year end, exclusion of Ulster was generally accepted in principle, but most people assumed that, in a referendum or general election, Home Rule would be rejected.[25] Lansdowne looked ahead to 1914 with foreboding:

> The only prophecy upon which we can safely venture is that no one is likely to have a good time.[26]

34

RISING MILITANCY

JUST AS MILITANCY emerged during the Home Rule Crisis in 1913, so the land question also provoked increasing militancy among agricultural labourers over the issues of housing, working conditions and low wages. On 21 June 1913, Lansdowne outlined Unionist land policy to the West Derbyshire Unionists (constituents of his son Kerry), with a plea for the revival of agriculture. He wished to see state aid to increase the number of owner-occupiers and deal with inadequate village housing. He touched on cooperation, rural education and agricultural credit. Maud noted that it was 'a good deal above the heads of the audience and they were bored to death with it though they tried hard to be very nice, but heaps of them trespassed out, long before the end of the speech'.[1]

The world was changing rapidly and gentleman politicians were no longer revered or even listened to. The public wanted new promises, and Lloyd George exploited the mood. He said Lansdowne's proposals meant an open mind for the labourer and an open mouth for the landlord, given a large bonus. He ignored Lansdowne's assurance that his policy would put no burden on the state.[2] Despite demands from senior Unionists, Bonar Law refused to lead on the land question. A further split in the party seemed likely. That summer a powerful movement emerged among younger Unionists aiming to disarm Lloyd George, who was then vulnerable, by restoring the combination of Conservatism with social reform. With the momentum from Lansdowne's land debate, some of them drafted an agricultural manifesto, proposing a voluntary movement among landowners to encourage wage increases by lowering rents. Although their schemes differed, Lansdowne offered them his support.

At the end of September Lansdowne's land policy was again attacked on the grounds that the state would incur enormous liabilities without adequate security. Steel-Maitland, Unionist chairman, wrote to *The Times* defending Lansdowne, showing the liability to be small and well secured, and urging a party conference on land. Lansdowne told Bonar Law, 'I am dismayed at the idea of introducing fresh complication into a question which is sufficiently complicated already.'[3] However, the conciliation movement gained fresh impetus when William Joynson-Hicks, an influential backbencher, joined them. Under pressure from the radicals in their party, the Unionist leaders were compelled to take further steps.[4] In October 1913 Lloyd George launched his land campaign and over the following months he spoke enthusiastically on the issue. But this was largely a sham fight as some of the other Unionist policymakers, notably Milner, were no less radical than Lloyd George in their approach to the land question.[5] Lansdowne avoided directly being drawn into a fight, deploring Lloyd George's unscrupulous bombast.[6] The land campaign diverted attention from the Irish issue, but had been little discussed by the cabinet and had never fully caught on.

Suffrage militancy also increased in 1913. Lansdowne and Maud were opposed to female suffrage, although neither voiced their opinion publicly. Like many political hostesses, Maud was active behind the scenes in promoting her own career and her husband's. Lansdowne was content to avoid the suffrage issue. In August 1913 Robert Cecil, a supporter of the Conservative and Unionist Women's Franchise Association, approached Lansdowne to find out if he would receive a small deputation of suffragettes, including the suffragist Millicent Fawcett. The suffragettes knew that Lansdowne did not support their movement, but it was growing and statesmen of all parties would have to reckon with it – and they thought the Unionists might soon be in power.[7] Lansdowne did not think that the interview would serve any useful purpose and he was not prepared to make any statement about what the Unionist Party might do.[8] In 1914 the House of Lords rejected a bill for the enfranchisement of women; among those who voted against was Lansdowne. Suffragettes picketed Lansdowne House. Not wishing to confront them, he sent them a letter in reply to their demands.

With such developments taking shape, on 5 February 1914, Lansdowne and Bonar Law met party officials at Lansdowne House to review policy in Parliament.[9] The Irish Crisis dominated people's thoughts, and they decided to continue with their demand for an election on Home Rule, even considering laying hands on the Army Annual Act to prevent the use of troops to coerce Ulster. Lansdowne himself was against such action and it was eventually dropped. On 11 February, during the opening sessions of Parliament, Lansdowne, chose to focus on Ulster, stating that 'the conversations [between Bonar Law and Asquith] of which we have heard so much have failed; that is a matter of notoriety … What

Ulster wants is to be left out altogether ... If the complete exclusion of Ulster were to be offered to us ... accompanied by new precautions for safeguarding the interests of those Unionists who do not happen to be within the excluded area, then I should be prepared to consider [it].'[10] The atmosphere in the Lords differed markedly from that in 1911. Lord Plymouth, who sat on the opposition front bench, did not foresee a repeat of the disunity in 1911, but 'I do think my duty is to see what line of action Lansdowne recommends before I commit myself to any course which may not be in accordance with his views'.[11] Most other peers had absolute confidence in Lansdowne and Bonar Law, believing that neither would agree to a compromise.[12]

On 9 March the Home Rule Bill began its third round. Asquith announced an Amending Bill for the concession to Ulster on the basis of county option and six year exclusion.[13] Bonar Law did not reject this but declared on 19 March:

> if he chooses to put his new suggestions into his Home Rule Bill, and if he submits these suggestions to the country by a Referendum and the country decides in favour of them, then I have the authority of Lord Lansdowne to say now that, as far as his influence in the House of Lords goes, that body will offer no impediment to carrying out completely the decision of the will of the people of this country.[14]

Asquith's response was overshadowed by the Curragh incident in Ireland. Given the choice of marching against the Ulster Volunteer Force or dismissal, fifty-seven cavalry officers and General Hubert Gough, their commander, at the Curragh Camp, the main base for the British Army in Ireland, chose to leave the Army. The situation put Asquith in a dilemma: if an example was made of the officers, there would be further resignations; if they let them off and promised not to coerce Ulster, their position would be damaged. The government refused to accept the resignations. Gough refused to move without a guarantee, in writing, that the Army would not be used against Ulster. On 22 March Jack Seely, Secretary of State for War, and Sir John French, Chief of the Imperial General Staff, gave four Curragh officers a written undertaking that the government would not use the Army in Ireland or elsewhere to maintain order so as to crush political opposition to the policy or principles of the Home Rule Bill. French also approved a note, written by Gough, assuring his officers that their soldiers would not be pressed to enforce the present Home Rule Bill on Ulster.[15]

The shadow cabinet, meeting at Lansdowne House on 21 and 23 March, decided to back the cavalry officers. On Monday 23rd, Lansdowne spoke in the Lords on the Army and Ulster because few of us can recall any occasion upon which there has been greater public anxiety, I would almost say acute distress, in the mind of the public than that which has arisen in connexion with these incidents. I should like to suggest that by sending great bodies of troops into Ulster at this juncture they are doing exactly what is most calculated to provoke the kind of collision which they are so anxious to avoid. We [the Unionists] may, I think take credit to ourselves for having been true prophets in regard to this matter. We have told you – ever since you set out on this disastrous policy – that it would lead you to civil war. Civil war is coming nearer to us with every day that passes. We have also told you that, should we ever find ourselves engaged in conflict or with the prospect of a conflict close at hand, you would be putting an intolerable strain on the discipline of the Army. It has become apparent within the last few hours that that strain is getting perilously near to the breaking point. If only half of what we hear is true, it seems clear that unless you are able completely to reassure the Army you will find you have struck a blow shattering to its discipline and disastrous to its efficiency.[16]

The government, unable to explain the blunders and feebly attempting to play down the incident, inflamed suspicion. In the following days, the Unionists could have further discredited the government, but did not take full advantage. On 25 March Asquith announced Seely's resignation and cancelled the (now public) offer made to Gough. On 30 March, much to the surprise of the opposition, Asquith announced he would become War Minister himself. Many Liberal peers and MPs now recognised an even greater need for compromise, which appealed equally to Lansdowne and other senior Unionists, anxious for the future. Lord Brassey told Lansdowne that he believed it was 'a plot of Churchill's and Lloyd George's to force the pace so as to be able to raise the Army cry at an election, when it came'.[17]

During April 1914, knowing the Home Rule Bill would pass the Commons a third and final time on 25 May, there were attempts to rekindle the idea of Home Rule All Round. On 1 May Lansdowne addressed the Primrose League. He was reported as saying that the opposition would consider overtures from the government, but their objection to Home Rule remained unalterable. By the exclusion of Ulster they meant exclusion for as long as she desired it and Parliament willed it. Unionists would not give anyone a blank cheque, but they would examine any federal scheme with an honourable place for Ulster if consistent with other UK interests.[18]

If we entertain proposals based upon the exclusion of Ulster, do not let it be thrown in our teeth that we are converts to Home Rule.[19]

However, the federalist schemes failed to bring about compromise.

On 5 May Bonar Law told the shadow cabinet that he and Carson had been invited to meet Asquith, who, he expected, would demand that the Unionists accept any agreed compromise and pledge that, if returned to power, they would give it a fair trial and not amend it. He thought this was fair and that it would be impossible to repeal the bill once passed. Despite the potential for civil war in Ulster and bloodshed in Dublin, Asquith maintained his strategy, planning to see the Home Rule Bill through under the Parliament Act, then deal with Ulster by an Amending Bill. Lansdowne was very anxious not to be committed to accepting the bill as a condition of excluding Ulster. During May and June he and his colleagues prepared for the Amending Bill. Unlike in 1911, many diehards, including Willoughby de Broke, offered Lansdowne their 'unflinching and active support' in their opposition to a Parliament in Dublin, but warned him that they would not agree to the exclusion of Ulster.[20] Milner urged Unionist peers to defeat the Amending Bill and block anything that might help the government. Lansdowne and other senior Unionists were so impressed by his arguments that he was asked to join the shadow cabinet.[21] He subsequently established a procedure committee to consider party tactics.[22]

On 25 May, with only the Royal assent between the Home Rule Bill and the statute books, a group of southern Unionists, chaired by Midleton, wrote to the *Irish Times* to say that setting up a Dublin Parliament was dangerous to the Empire and oppressive to Unionists in the three southern provinces, that if the Home Rule Bill was amended so as to avert civil war they desired an immediate general election on the principle of Home Rule, and that further delay by the government would simply increase unrest.[22] Forcing Asquith and the Liberals to a choice between dissolution and potential civil war was acceptable to many Unionists. Lansdowne worried, however, that 'if Asquith makes a really tempting offer there will be a serious cleavage and Asquith is probably aware of this'.[23] Moreover he was alarmed at Midleton and others canvassing like diehards, asking people to promise to reject proposals that were not yet known, and told him:

we all desire a general election, but it is surely worthwhile, before we talk of 'insisting' upon one, to ask ourselves (1) whether we can insist effectually and (2) whether we are setting to work the right way to win the general election when we have got it.[25]

On 31 May the King suggested that the Lords should pass the Amending Bill on second reading; it was everyone's duty to do their utmost to prevent civil war.[26] He told Devonshire he had reason to believe the opposition could get their own terms – namely, exclusion of the whole province of Ulster with no time limit – and that there would be an early general election. He seemed to think a settlement of the whole question by consent was possible and was most anxious it should happen.[27]

When the Lords reassembled after Whitsuntide, Crewe announced that the Amending Bill would be introduced in the House of Lords on 23 June. Lansdowne responded this gave them little time to consider the Amending Bill and they would not be rushed. They desired to know the government's whole Home Rule policy in ample time, but Crewe provided no satisfactory answer. The press believed the government had not made up their minds.[28] On 23 June Crewe introduced the Amending Bill, by which any Ulster county could opt out of Home Rule for six years – the formula the Unionists had rejected on 9 March. Lansdowne declared: 'My own impulses lead me to desire to see the Irish nation one and undivided and to see that one and undivided nation remain under the "British Flag".' However, if Home Rule was forced on them in its present form, he accepted that the separation of all or part of Ulster might be the only alternative to civil war; but with that solution, the time limit must be abandoned and Ulster left free to come in when she was willing.[29]

The murder of Archduke Franz Ferdinand on 28 June, in Sarajevo, disrupted the debate and Asquith was pressed for a rapid settlement to the Irish Question.[30] Lansdowne saw more clearly than his colleagues the impending calamity taking shape in Europe. The tragedy shocked him. He wrote to Count Albert Mensdorff, the Austro-Hungarian ambassador: 'It is appalling. I need not assure you of our sympathy. We are perhaps more touched than others because as you know, His Imperial Highness was good enough to honour us with his friendship. We have never forgotten the visit which he paid to us when we were in India, and on occasions when in subsequent years, he came to this country, he was always more than kind to us all.'[31]

As the Irish Crisis continued, the Lords debated the second reading of the Amending Bill on 1 July and the third reading on 14 July. Lansdowne supported the second reading to gain time, though

it really is a 'freak' Bill, a Bill worthy of a place in a museum of constitutional curiosities. It is, to begin with, a Bill to amend another measure which is not yet upon the Statute Book. A Bill intended to amend a Bill which according to the government cannot be bettered; and we say what an extraordinary thing it is that a Bill which cannot be bettered is going to be resisted by the most important Province of Ireland at the point of the bayonet.[32]

However, he advised the House against voting down the measure since it was evident that 'there is a great Irish problem to be solved, that it requires investigation, that it requires to be dealt with courage and with sympathy, and that we cannot fall back upon a mere policy of negation and destructive criticism'.[33] The Unionist peers altered the bill to nine-county exclusion rather than county by county, and permanent partition of the island, not just for six years.[34] The result was further impasse, which bought Asquith some time. Then the King announced that he wished to call a multi-party conference to push matters forward, and the Unionists, who like Asquith recognised that delay might avert dangerous consequences, agreed. Lansdowne, who was not immediately informed, accepted that no other reply was possible.

From 21 to 24 July Asquith, Lloyd George, Lansdowne, Bonar Law, John Redmond (Irish Parliamentary Party leader), John Dillon (Irish Nationalist), James Craig (Irish Unionist) and Carson, with James Lowther, the Unionist Speaker of the House of Commons, as chairman, met at Buckingham Palace. King George gave a short speech calling for generous compromise and then left the room to allow the politicians to get on with their work. The conference failed, and it is generally assumed that this was only to be expected. Asquith noted that Lansdowne and Bonar Law gave no help towards a settlement.[35] The Amending Bill was postponed. Before it could be reintroduced, the Irish Crisis was overtaken by the Great War.[36]

35

THE OUTBREAK OF
THE FIRST WORLD WAR

As EUROPE PREPARED for war, the British government wavered
between those in favour and those against entering the war, with no
clear lead from Asquith and a divided cabinet. Shortly before Austria-
Hungary declared war on Serbia on 28 July 1914, Lansdowne realised
that the complications in Europe had altered the situation in Ulster and
Asquith's ability to reach agreement. As a former Foreign Secretary with
a wide understanding of European statesmen and statecraft, Lansdowne
was well positioned to act. During the final days of July he pressed the
government for information on the situation and rallied his colleagues.

On Friday 31 July, with many rumours of war flying around,
Lansdowne surprisingly chose to leave London. But it was the Bank
Holiday weekend and he had invited a large house party to Bowood,
including the German and Russian ambassadors. A tea was also
planned in the park to celebrate the birth of Lansdowne's grandson.
Devonshire, Lansdowne's son-in-law, stayed in London and promised
to inform Lansdowne of any developments. The position for Edward
Grey, the Foreign Secretary, and the whole government was critical, but
most serious for Lansdowne was a report going around Europe that the
Unionist Party would oppose any action by Britain.[1]

On Saturday 1 August France ordered mobilisation of her
armed forces. Germany did likewise, declaring war on Russia almost
immediately. Lansdowne was convinced that if Britain hung back it
would mean indelible disgrace and lasting danger. Hearing the news
late that afternoon, Lansdowne drove to Lansdowne House, in a hurry,
according to his driver.[2] That evening senior Unionists, including General
Henry Wilson, met at Lansdowne House to discuss the government's
inaction and an offer of full Unionist support. Next day, Lansdowne

meant to breakfast late but, after very little sleep, was woken by an urgent message from Austen Chamberlain, who arrived at 9.20 a.m. and urged Lansdowne to go to Downing Street to see the Prime Minister before cabinet at 11 a.m. At 10 a.m. Lansdowne and Chamberlain met Bonar Law, who was reluctant to press matters. But, after discussing the situation with them, Bonar Law wrote to Asquith:

> Lord Lansdowne and I feel it our duty to inform you that in our opinion, as well as that of all the colleagues whom we have been able to consult, any hesitation in now supporting France and Russia would be fatal to the honour and to the future security of the United Kingdom, and we offer His Majesty's Government the assurance of the united support of the Opposition in all measures required by England's intervention in the war.[3]

The letter was sent to Downing Street immediately by Lansdowne's car, arriving before the cabinet meeting. It strengthened the 'war party' and the cabinet edged towards action. Although the Unionists were prepared for a possible cabinet break-up and the formation of a coalition government, Lansdowne was strongly against it. As he told Maud, 'Things may end in a split, and our being approached, but a change of govt. would be deplorable at such a moment.'[4] Supporting the government rather than seeking office was the primary motive of the Unionist leaders. The following morning, Lansdowne and Bonar Law met Asquith and re-affirmed their support, laying great stress on Belgian neutrality and supporting the entente with France.[5] The Prime Minister was tired, and anxious to get rid of them. Shortly after Germany declared war on France, Grey explained to a silent House of Commons the narrowing range of options. Lansdowne, who was present, thought it was a magnificent performance.[6]

On 4 August the Germans crossed the Meuse river, Britain demanded that Belgian neutrality be respected, and the Unionists learned that British mobilisation was incomplete, delaying the Expeditionary Force. Lansdowne discussed the matter with his colleagues and they agreed to write to Haldane, the Lord Chancellor, for the immediate dispatch of 100,000 men. Lansdowne was anxious to write again to Asquith but it was too late to reach the cabinet meeting that afternoon, at which five ministers resigned. Later that day Lansdowne met Haldane, who explained that

> the cabinet had carefully considered the question of sending out the Expeditionary Force, and still had in mind the possibility of despatching it. They had, however, come to the conclusion that it would have been unwise to take this step at the very outset, for several reasons. (1) The

despatch of so large a portion of the Home Forces before the completion of mobilization would have dangerously weakened this country and would have rendered it impossible to send the fleet far from our own shores. If the country had been denuded of the fleet, Germany might have been tempted to attempt a coup. (2) If we had sent 150,000 men to the German frontier, the German army might have made a prodigious effort to surround and annihilate our force. (3) The neutrality of Italy enabled France to make use on the German frontier of a large number of troops who would have been otherwise employed in watching the Italian army.[7]

After discussion, the Unionists suspended criticism of the government and offered support of measures to avoid financial panic and continue industrial production, even if there was no obvious market for goods.[8] Lansdowne became a daily visitor in the Commons press gallery. One reporter noted:

one of the most surprising things about the sittings of the Lords is the celerity with which business can be disposed of in a period of emergency, and another is the absence of anything like excitement. The Assembly is perfectly calm and attended by a smaller number of peers than in ordinary party warfare. The reason of this is that as the Commons begin business an hour and a half sooner than the Upper Chamber, noble Lords have the opportunity of learning in advance any important statement which the Government has to make in connection with the war.[9]

On 6 August, as the Germans attacked France through Belgium, Lansdowne stated in the Lords:

our diplomacy seems to have been throughout absolutely sincere. I wish I could say the same of the diplomacy to which it has been opposed. We may at any rate say this, that we embark in this tremendous contest with no sinister ambition, no selfish motives, with a clear conscience, and with clean hands, and I believe we have the public opinion of this country behind us.[10]

On 12 August the British Expeditionary Force began operations. A few days earlier, Asquith had announced that the government still intended to see the Home Rule Bill on the statute book that session. Lansdowne was prepared to challenge this proceeding, since ninety MPs (seventy Unionists and twenty Liberals) had joined the Colours, with more to follow.[11] Lansdowne advised Crewe that controversial business should be set aside and after the truce was over, each side should stand where it stood before. Crewe saw great difficulty in giving effect to this principle. Lansdowne recognised this, telling Crewe, that Unionists would be ready to agree an arrangement, if necessary by legislation, to secure the Liberals against losing any advantage they had under the Parliament Act on the Welsh Church or Home Rule Bills:

> I could not see that a postponement in these conditions need involve any injustice to the Nationalist party. The government were pledged to the view that the Home Rule bill ought not to pass into law without the simultaneous passage of an amending bill. They had found it impossible to solve the difficulty of framing such a bill. The negotiations had dragged on since the month of March, and the collapse of the Buckingham Palace Conference had shown that the problem was almost insoluble. The attitude of Ulster was threatening, and the situation was by no means favourable to the Home Rule cause. But apart from this it seemed to me that the attempt to get the Home Rule Bill on to the statute book was a mere piece of tactics which ought not to be resorted to at such a moment as this.
>
> We had some discussion as to the possibility of a settlement by consent based upon the exclusion of a part of Ulster. I again reminded Lord Crewe of the breakdown of the conference. It seemed to me almost inconceivable that after all that had happened, anyone should be able to hit upon a scheme which would be accepted, not only without discussion, but without very acrimonious discussion. A discussion which I felt sure all of us would be most reluctant to take a part in in present circumstances.
>
> With regard to the Welsh Church Bill, Lord Crewe admitted that there were strong reasons against proceeding with disendowment at the present time. He was evidently in favour of an arrangement under which the bill would not come into operation for some time, but he desired to bring this Bill also on to the statute Book. I repeated my objection to the policy of pressing on legislation of this kind when the international situation was so grave. I added that an amply sufficient reason for postponing further consideration of the Bill was to be found in the fact that it has been referred to a select committee of the House of Lords with the approval of HM Government. The committee had not yet reported, and obviously there had been no time for the public to consider the important evidence which it had collected. Lord Crewe repeated that HM Government had to reckon with the great body of their supporters, who would probably not be content with anything short of obtaining the Royal Assent for both bills without further delay.[12]

On 7 September the cabinet, goaded by the Irish Nationalists, voted to continue with Home Rule, obtain the royal assent and then suspend its operation for the duration of the war. The Welsh Church Bill would receive similar treatment. Lansdowne was upset that the government had taken advantage of the fact that Parliament was not in the mood to think about domestic politics.[13] On 14 September he introduced the Controversial Legislation (Suspension during War) Bill, which equitably postponed the two controversial measures. Asquith remarked,

> it is of course, innocent though it looks, a most provocative measure, for it would leave the whole work of this Parliament at the mercy of the next House of Commons, who must be elected in the autumn of next year, and if it had the minutest Tory majority would by a single vote deal a death blow at Home Rule, Welsh Dist. and the rest.[14]

The Lords passed Lansdowne's bill on 16 September; the Commons rejected it. On 17 September the Speaker of the Commons certified that the Home Rule and Welsh disestablishment bills complied in all respects with the Parliament Act, and the royal assent to those measures, the suspensory bill and several emergency bills 'would be signified before the prorogation'.[15] On 18 September, at the end of this momentous session, the King's Speech was read amid an impressive silence, followed by a quite unexpected display of loyalty and patriotism.[16]

On 21 September 1914, Lansdowne spoke at a non-party gathering in Nottingham, called by the mayor to stimulate recruiting. He summarised the events that led to the war and showed how deeply Britain's honour was pledged. The *Westminster Gazette* said,

> it has been suggested that the time has come when the war might be treated as a drawn game, 'not quite, I think,' said Lord Lansdowne. True that Belgium has been ravished and her cathedrals and churches destroyed, but 'the smashing blow at the allies has not yet been delivered, and we are holding our own well.' The time has not yet come for declaring the innings closed. 'The game is a game worth winning, and under Providence we mean to win it. Our cause is a just cause, and it is a cause not only of England but of civilization and humanity.'[17]

In the early days of the war Lansdowne advised Unionist peers against criticising the government's methods of prosecuting the war.[18] As both of his sons enlisted with their former regiments and were sent abroad, he was filled with patriotism. In late October Lansdowne was laid up by severe cystitis. While recovering from an operation, he was told of Charlie's death in action west of Ypres on 30 October. He and Maud were heartbroken. Balfour wrote to say, 'You and I are getting old, and I, at least, have no desire for a long life, but the bitterness of seeing our juniors taken from us in the full vigour of manhood never seems to diminish. Yet we may at least be proud.'[19]

Lansdowne was due to attend Parliament on 5 November and address the Dolphin Society on the 13th, but had to cancel both. Balfour took his place at the banquet and Curzon spoke in the debate.[20] The Prince of Wales, visiting the front in November, took a photograph of Charlie's grave and Queen Mary sent Lansdowne a copy of it.[21] During Lansdowne's convalescence, Curzon led the opposition peers and briefed him; 'the House of Lords is strange without Lord Lansdowne, and everyone hopes that he will be able to return to his place before this short session is closed'.[22] The Prime Minister, using Sir Maurice 'Mongie' Bonham Carter, Asquith's private secretary, as messenger, sent Lansdowne copies of Sir John French's telegrams.[23]

Towards the end of 1914 Lansdowne and his colleagues were dismayed at the stalemate on the Western Front. They believed that the war was being mismanaged. As the party that 'knew' about war, they were frustrated not to have more direct input and that by January 1915 their influence had been reduced by the loss of 139 Unionist MPs who had volunteered, as opposed to only 41 Liberals. Unionist criticism was especially directed against Churchill, who in late October had deserted his office and visited the front. Lansdowne thought it was outrageous 'to play the kind of pranks[24] which Churchill has been playing to the general bewilderment of everybody at the front'.[25] He advised Asquith, notably on dispatching extra men, but he was given no information about the availability of soldiers, arms, ammunition or equipment.[26]

Seeing the need for action by the Unionists, Lansdowne decided to initiate a debate in the Lords when they met on 5 January 1915. As he was still unwell, he authorised Curzon to raise certain questions of policy:[27]

It would clearly be desirable that Kitchener [the Secretary of State for War] should give us another statement as to the progress to the war. If he makes one, the occasion would, I should think, be appropriate for a discussion on the recruiting question. I do not suppose Kitchener will tell us what his plan is, but I think we might well insist upon an assurance from him that the point has not escaped attention, and that a careful enquiry is already in progress as to the conditions and limitations under which some form of compulsion might be resorted to in the event of a sufficient number of recruits not being forthcoming.[28]

Reading newspaper coverage of the debate, Lansdowne thought the government's performance was lamentable and did not inspire confidence. It seemed that the government were not interested in opposition ideas, and the Unionists must reconsider their tactics.[29] Curzon noted that

Kitchener told us absolutely nothing. He simply plays with us and the public, delivers a few generalities about the war which any schoolboy who had read the morning papers could compile in 10 minutes. As to what the government are after about recruiting who can tell? Kitchener literally discourages it by his frosty remarks.[30]

Asquith's attitude was expressed to his close friend Venetia Stanley:

one cannot help smiling when men like Lansdowne and St John [Midleton] and Curzon who led us into the Boer War with no preparations at all cavil and carp and criticize.[31]

When Parliament reassembled on 2 February, Lansdowne was there. The *Daily Sketch* noted that

his appearance has not altered for a long time – the same shade of grey in whiskers and moustache, the same neat black bow tie, the same precise frock coat, and the same black spats. And there is the same touch of hauteur and the same punctilious correctness in his Parliamentary demeanour.[32]

During the debate Lansdowne sought

from His Majesty's Government some indication of the kind of conditions under which our business in this House is likely to be conducted during the present session. We have no desire on this side of the House to break the truce or to revive Party hostilities. We want to know how we stand with regard to the terms of the truce, and what measure of responsibility we who are parties to the truce can be held to have assumed. We must add that we cannot altogether abandon our right of criticism. Then we desire to add this, that any assistance which we are able to give to the Government – and we are glad to give it – any abstention on our part from criticism of the Government, any confidence which we receive at the hands of the Government, must not be interpreted either in or outside Parliament as implying that we have accepted any responsibility either for the ordinary business of the country or for the measures which are being taken to prosecute naval and military operations against the enemy.[33]

In the following months the Unionists accepted legislation on Welsh disestablishment but not on the drink trade; Lloyd George thought that excessive drinking by workers was damaging productivity and proposed the state purchase of the trade. Lansdowne disagreed; insobriety reduced efficiency and slowed production, but so did other factors, notably high wages (no incentive to work harder), large profits said to be earned by manufacturers (workers demanding their share) and long hours (making workers stale and indifferent). It would be disastrous to set up a government monopoly on drinking that then failed for lack of public support or because it could not be enforced. By mid-April, with mounting opposition from Unionists and many of his cabinet, Lloyd George dropped the idea.

As the Unionist leaders continued to take a stand on the prosecution of the war, Asquith invited them to attend the War Council on 10 March. Churchill thought he had invited 'a lot of ignorant people to meddle in our business'.[34] Lansdowne accepted, although he and Bonar Law felt they were in an invidious position. Five days later they declined to attend further meetings, fearing it would weaken their position in the party and thus their support of the government.[35] Asquith arranged for them to receive all papers prepared for the War Council, whose secretary noted 'how astonishing is the influence of party politics'.[36]

Where the Unionists could challenge the Liberals was over Army recruitment. On 13 May Haldane, Lord Chancellor and former War Secretary, announced that a bill to amend the Army Act was 'an approach to the principle of applying compulsion'. Lansdowne was glad to see the government grappling with this grave problem. At Lansdowne House the next day, senior Unionists agreed to focus not on munitions or strategy, but conscription. This was controversial because it went to the core of what the war was for and how it should be fought. Aiming to force the hand of the cabinet while offering their full support, they would give it non-party legitimacy.[37] However, Admiral Fisher's departure from the Admiralty overshadowed their plans and Lansdowne's draft letter to Asquith was not sent.

Discussions at Lansdowne House turned to Fisher's resignation and the conduct of the war. Lansdowne believed that managing the war under the existing party system was unsustainable. He detested the idea of coalition and was concerned about his health and increasing deafness, but 'we have to do the best we can'.[38] Bonar Law thought the same. Coalition would enable Asquith to extend the party truce and avoid a general election.[39] On 18 May a shadow cabinet discussed coalition, and the idea found favour. That night Asquith and Bonar Law jointly declared to an astonished House of Commons their decision to form a coalition government with twenty-two members: twelve Liberals, one Labourite, one non-party member and eight Unionists.

While Lansdowne was assured of a place, among those who urged him to accept was Margot Asquith, wife of the Prime Minister. She got Devonshire to wire Lansdowne to say that 'he <u>must</u> join'[40] and would be 'very useful in foreign affairs with Grey so upset'.[41] She thought that Lansdowne was '<u>straight</u> which I find unique almost'.[42] On 26

May Lansdowne and Bonar Law spoke at the Carlton Club about the invitation to join a coalition. Lansdowne explained that

> in our view that was an offer with which it was right for us to comply. We felt sure that if we had declined it the country would have judged us hardly. I suppose that every gentleman here has at the back of his mind a dislike to Coalition governments. In ordinary circumstances, I fully admit that the dislike is reasonable and ought to prevail, but we are not in ordinary circumstances to-day.[43]

That same day he was appointed Minister without Portfolio, the first since his grandfather in 1856. Newspapers reported that he would share the Foreign Office with Grey, whose health and sight were failing. Fortunately, Grey was devoted to him and delighted at his appointment.[44] Early in June Grey was instructed to rest. Crewe took charge at the Foreign Office, with Lansdowne to assist him. Aged seventy, he was the oldest member of the new cabinet, which also included Balfour and Curzon. Although there had been previous coalitions, never before had all the chief political leaders of the different parties been included. The national emergency made it more urgent.

Lansdowne found it easy to work alongside Asquith, who as a Liberal Imperialist shared similar ideas. Bonar Law was less comfortable and found Asquith regularly exalted Curzon over him. Curzon became more ambitious, believing that, as they were in coalition, the post of opposition leader had, *de facto*, lapsed. Asquith was their head, and the rest, including Bonar Law and Lansdowne, were on equal terms. Although Lansdowne still had influence and was regarded as 'useful'[45] to the cabinet, he did not have the same energy as its younger members. His contribution to the war effort was far-reaching, but he knew his limitations. The two main issues facing the new cabinet on 27 May were the Dardanelles and conscription; underlying both was the question of Asquith's leadership.[46] On 29 May Asquith appointed a cabinet committee on the Dardanelles, though it also oversaw other campaigns; it replaced the pre-coalition War Council. Among its members were Lansdowne, Bonar Law and Balfour. While a member of this committee, Lansdowne gave full support to the Dardanelles campaign. In November Asquith announced a new War Committee on which Lansdowne, as a former War Secretary, was offered a place, but not Bonar Law. Lansdowne was unsure about accepting and wrote to Asquith on 9 November:

> My views:
> (1) You suggest a committee of 6. I am convinced that a smaller body would do better work, and command more confidence. I cannot believe

that the Chancellor of the Exchequer [Lloyd George] ought to be a full member of the committee. If he and I were left out you could remain with 3 or plus Kitchener [War Minister] 4.

(2) I am painfully conscious that I could not be of much service to the committee although I might not impede its deliberations by superfluous talking. I had made up my mind for private reasons not to join the government when it was formed and did so only because I thought my abstention might have created a wrong impression. I have for some months been in rather indifferent health and dread the coming winter.

(3) (I have not seen Bonar Law since Saturday, and do not know what he will do, but) I anticipate that he will resign. If he does, could you not give the Colonial Office to George Curzon and summon him occasionally to the War Committee? Of course he would prefer full membership and if you adhere to the larger number you may be disposed to admit him.[47]

On 11 November Asquith noted that 'dear old Lansdowne refused to serve', so he 'was obliged to take on B. Law'.[48] Whether Lansdowne was justified in refusing his place on the committee is debatable. It sat for six weeks and then collapsed due to infighting between its members and their heavy workloads, including their departments of state, international conferences, cabinet work and parliamentary duties.[49] In correspondence with Churchill, who had resigned from his post as First Lord of the Admiralty and returned to his regiment in France, Lansdowne remarked that if he had had a regiment to rejoin he would have done likewise. He noted that by the time Churchill returned to politics, he would find Lansdowne 'if still in any sense alive – beyond all doubt politically extinct'.[50] While Lansdowne reflected on his future he continued his commitment to the war effort. During November 1915, along with Curzon, Selborne and Crewe, Lansdowne precipitated a political crisis over Asquith's decision to abandon the Dardanelles. But losing the support of the senior military advisors, including Kitchener, they were forced to concede their fight.

Asquith had said early in the war that he did not foresee conscription, but as the numbers volunteering declined he had to revise his position. In May 1915, 135,000 men enlisted; in September 71,000. Without drastic action, Britain could not maintain seventy divisions in the field, as Kitchener wished.[51] No issue divided the coalition government as much as conscription. In general, Unionists supported it and Liberals opposed it; but some Liberals who defended individual rights were willing to accept compulsion as a necessary sacrifice to safeguard fundamental liberties. On 29 June, as the government formulated their ideas, Walter Long, President of the Local Government Board and pro-conscription, introduced a bill on National Registration as a litmus test for conscription. The bill would enable the authorities to determine who should serve at home and who should be accepted into the Army. Asquith sought Lansdowne's views. Lansdowne saw the 'value of an inventory' with volunteers, but thought the government should 'make it quite clear that in our view registration is valuable, both on account of the information which a register would furnish, and because we may have to use compulsion if the voluntary system fails to give us all we require'.[52] The bill became law on 15 July. Lansdowne was impatient for conscription. As with Long, he thought that Asquith carried 'the policy of "wait and see" to a most dangerous extent'.[53] Asquith's delay was an attempt to defuse the situation and buy time; his concern was how to convince the country that compulsion was necessary. In early August he appointed Crewe to chair a war policy cabinet committee to gather information about compulsion from ministers.

On 15 August (Registration Day), males and females between the ages of fifteen and sixty-five, across Britain, had to tell canvassers their name, occupation, current employment and skills useful to war work. Some 29 million forms were issued across England, Scotland and Wales. The information was sent to the Local Government Board and copied onto new forms: white for females, blue for males of non-military age or fitness, and pink for fit males aged eighteen to forty-one; men in essential occupations were marked with black stars. According to the War Office, based on the statistics collected there were 5,039,181 names on pink forms, with 1,462,136 starred, which, allowing for medical rejects, left about 1,788,500 men available for possible recruitment.[54] These figures reinforced the argument that the country's manpower needed organising in a better way, and balancing the needs of industry with those of the military required a solution along authoritarian lines.

Six weeks before the War Office arrived at its numbers, Asquith instructed Lansdowne to chair a committee on the National Register to find out the extent of availability for recruiting. Lansdowne's report was based on registered men of military age between nineteen and forty-one living in England and Wales, and the numbers differed little from the War Office. In fact, Kitchener used Lansdowne's figures in compiling his own, adjusted to include eighteen-year-olds and men living in Scotland. At the end of September Lansdowne reported that there were about 1,283,673 men available for recruitment in England and Wales. Adding 10 per cent for returns not yet received, he estimated the total at 1,412,040.[55]

While Lansdowne was producing his report, Crewe's war policy cabinet committee met twelve times in August before producing three sets of reports with suggestions for and against conscription. Asquith was in a fix because to force conscription would have split the coalition and undermined his leadership. To keep the conscriptionists and Lansdowne

39 Tenants and staff reception to the Lansdowne's return from India, Bowood, 1894

40 Lansdowne skating on the lake at Bowood, 1895

41 Lansdowne as Secretary of State for War, aged 53

42 Shooting party at Sandringham, 7 November 1901. Standing L–R, Lord Farquhar, Lord Crichton, Lady
Suffied, Sir Francis Knollys, Princess Victoria, Marquess of Ormonde, Prince Charles of Denmark, Count
von Plessen, Sir Stanley Clarke, King Edward VII, Colonel Arthur Davidson, The German Emperor, Earl
of Clarendon, Count Metternich, Prince of Wales, Queen Alexandra, General Sir Dighton Probyn, Miss
Knollys, Sir Frank Lascelles, Sir Donald Mackenzie Wallace, Lord Churchill. Seated L–R. Lady Constance
Butler, Princess Charles of Denmark, Countess of Dudley, Marchioness of Ormonde, Marchioness of
Londonderry, Marchioness of Lansdowne, Marquess of Londonderry, Marquess of Lansdowne, R Sassoon

43 The opening of King Edward's First Parliament, 14 February 1901. Lansdowne's
brougham passing with Irish Guards lining Whitehall

ALICE AND THE WHITE KNIGHT.
(*With apologies to Sir John Tenniel.*)

44 Alice and the White Knight Cartoon by Sir Francis Carruthers Gould. Lansdowne's promotion from the War Office to the Foreign Office was ridiculed in some sections of the press. Hector Munro, alias, 'Saki' lampooned him in his 'Alice in Pall Mall' satire as the White Knight who fell off one horse, the War Office, on to another, the Foreign Office

PEEROTS ON TOUR.
Chorus (*with conscious pride*). " Yes, we sat upon the Budget on the flo-o-or,
A thing we had nev-ah done befo-o-ore."
(Lords Lansdowne, Halsbury, Londonderry, and Curzon.)

45 Shortly after the Peers rejected the People's Budget on 30 November 1909, Asquith called a General Election for January 1910. It was virtually a referendum on the budget and the peers. Lansdowne, along with former members of Balfour's ministry and the former Viceroy of India were under the spotlight

STANDING FOR HIS TRADE PHOTOGRAPH (CHRISTMAS AND NEW YEAR SEASON, 1908-9).
(Lord L-nsd-wne.)

46 Between 1906-1909 with the Liberal's in power 158 bills were sent up by the House of Commons to the House of Lords which received the royal assent, and of these 65 were amended by the peers. Ten bills were rejected or wrecked

PARDONABLE CURIOSITY.

Lord Crewe. "THIS, I THINK, IS THE INSTRUMENT YOU WERE ENQUIRING ABOUT?"
Lord Lansdowne (*on his way to trial*). "THANKS. I THOUGHT I'D JUST LIKE TO GLANCE AT IT."

47 The second 1910 General Election, which lasted from 2 to 19 December, focused squarely on
constitutional reform to curb the power of the House of Lords

48 The visit of King Edward and Queen Alexandra to Bowood, 20 July 1907

49 Lansdowne House, London, 1911

50 Lansdowne aged 68

51 Lansdowne with his grandson George Mercer
Nairne (later 8th Marquess of Lansdowne) at
Bowood, 1916

52 Lansdowne fishing at Glanmore River, County Kerry, 1914

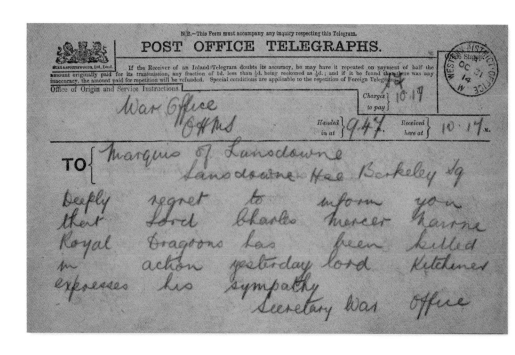

N.B.—This Form must accompany any inquiry respecting this Telegram.

POST OFFICE TELEGRAPHS.

If the Receiver of an Inland Telegram doubts its accuracy, he may have it repeated on payment of half the amount originally paid for its transmission, any fraction of 1d. less than ½d. being reckoned as ½d.; and if it be found that there was any inaccuracy, the amount paid for repetition will be refunded. Special conditions are applicable to the repetition of Foreign Telegrams.

Office of Origin and Service Instructions.

War Office

OHMS

Charges to pay 10·17

Handed in at 9·47

Received here at 10·17

TO { Marquis of Lansdowne
Lansdowne Hse Berkeley Sq

Deeply regret to inform you that Lord Charles Mercer Nairne Royal Dragoons has been killed in action yesterday lord Kitchener expresses his sympathy Secretary War Office

53 Telegram from the War Office notifying Lansdowne of the death of his son Charlie on 30 October 1914

54 Aerial view of Bowood, 1917

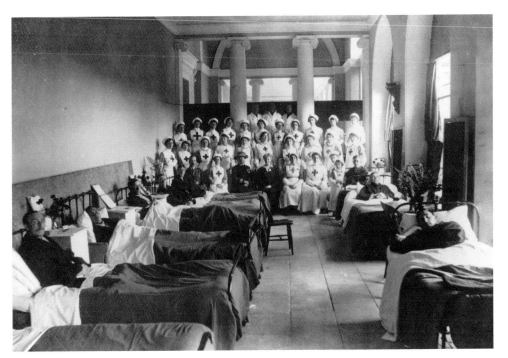

55 Maud with nurses and soldiers, Bowood Hospital, 1918

56 Lansdowne inspecting cattle in the Terrace Field, Bowood, 1921

57 Drawing room at
Bowood, 1914

58 Bowood from the
terrace, 1914

59 The Library at
Bowood, 1914

60 The sculpture gallery
at Lansdowne House,
London, 1919

61 Lansdowne judging the Lauragh Village School Sports Day, County Kerry, 1914

62 Lansdowne inspecting a fallen tree in the garden of Derreen, County Kerry

63 Derreen House, 1921

64 Derreen House after it was destroyed by the Irish Republican Army in 1922

65 The Second Asquith ministry, a wartime coalition government was formed on 25 May 1915. From Left to Right. Arthur Henderson, Austen Chamberlain, Thomas McKinnon Wood, Winston Churchill, Andrew Bonar Law, The Earl Kitchener, Herbert Henry Asquith, The Marquess of Crewe, David Lloyd George, Lewis Harcourt, Reginald McKenna, The Lord Buckmaster, Sir Edward Grey, Sir John Simon, Walter Runciman, Augustine Birrell, Walter Long, The Earl of Selborne, Sir Edward Carson, The Earl Curzon of Kedleston, Arthur Balfour and Lansdowne (seated in the foreground)

67 Lansdowne and Lord Hugh Cecil at Windsor, 1922

66 Rembrandt van Rijn's *The Mill* sold by
Lansdowne to settle debts for the record price
of £100,000 to Joseph Widener in March 1911

68 Queen Mary with the Lansdownes at
Bowood, 1922

69 Lansdowne aged 80 with his family. Back Row L–R Lord John Charles de la Poer Beresford, Lady Anne Cavendish, Margaret Mercer Nairne, Unidentified, Countess of Kerry, Viscount Calne and Calstone, Earl of Kerry, Lord Edmond Fitzmaurice, Lady Katharine Petty-Fitzmaurice, Lord Ernest Hamilton, Lord William de la Poer Beresford. Seated L–R. Lady Maud Cavendish, Lady Everard Digby, 9th Duchess of Devonshire, Marquess of Lansdowne, Marchioness of Lansdowne, 9th Duke of Devonshire, Lady Osborne Beauclerk, Lord Osborne Beauclerk, Front Row L–R George Mercer Nairne, Lord Edward Petty-Fitzmaurice, Lord Charles Hope Petty-Fitzmaurice

70 Lansdowne's funeral, Bowood, 8 June 1927. Surrounded by estate workers, Lansdowne's coffin is carried on a farm cart led by two white Shire horses

at bay a little longer, he appointed Edward Stanley, 17th Earl of Derby, a committed conscriptionist, soldier and Unionist, as Director-General of Recruiting at the War Office, to undertake a final canvass under the voluntary system. Derby requested all males aged eighteen to forty-one, not in a starred occupation, to make a public declaration. Each man's pink card from the National Register was copied onto a blue card and sent to his local parliamentary recruiting committee. Each man was asked either to enlist directly or to 'attest' his willingness to serve when called, in a kind of compulsory voluntarism. Each man's details were put on a white card, used to assign him to a married or unmarried age group. There were forty-six groups.[56]

Shortly before the Derby Scheme began, Kitchener announced a scheme of his own for a revived militia ballot under which men eligible for recruiting would be conscripted by lot.[57] It was similar to the Militia Ballot Act introduced by Lansdowne when he was War Secretary in 1899. Kitchener threatened to resign if it was not accepted, and C.P. Scott, editor of the *Manchester Guardian*, wrote that 'Lloyd George, Churchill, Curzon, Carson, Bonar Law, Long and Lansdowne were determined to press for adoption of the plan in place of the Derby scheme'.[58] Scott thought they might resign over the matter; if so, that was not because they believed in Kitchener's idea but because any form of compulsion hinted at by so popular a figure as the War Secretary was better than the existing system of voluntarism. Although the situation was swiftly defused by Asquith, the conscriptionists soon looked to the Derby Scheme for their growing body of evidence in favour of compulsion. The survey was conducted in November and December 1915. Lansdowne described it as a 'hurricane recruiting campaign'.[59] It obtained 318,553 medically-fit single men but some two million did not attest at all. This left the government short and a clear case for conscription could now be made.

In light of this, on 5 January 1916 Asquith introduced the National Service Bill in the Commons. The Lords treated the first reading of the bill – now the Military Service No. 2 Bill – as a mere formality, and on 25 January Lansdowne moved the second reading, which was passed without a division after four hours' debate. In defence of leaving Ireland out of the bill, Lansdowne stated there would have been no chance of agreement if they had brought in Ireland. Great Britain, on the whole, had been vehemently pro-Derby; he did not think there had been any pro-Derby feeling in Ireland.[60] To include Ireland, and then strike it out in deference to objections, would be bad tactics.[61] The first conscription law of modern times received the royal assent on 27 January.[62]

Many Unionists, including Lansdowne, were dissatisfied by the limited scope of the plan and were adamant that general military conscription was necessary. Attacked by the Unionist War Committee, established in January 1916, the Unionists in cabinet could no longer prop up the coalition government with schemes of limited conscription. As Asquith came under further attack, the coalition cabinet reassembled the Military Finance Committee to consider the manpower question. Lansdowne, Asquith, Austen Chamberlain and Reginald McKenna were selected as members. Within two weeks the committee reported that limited compulsion could not remedy the manpower shortage. The report was as significant for its unintended consequences as for what it did do. It brought the matter to a head and compelled Lloyd George to take a leading role. The cabinet was divided. As Frances Stevenson, Lloyd George's secretary and mistress, recorded, 'If Asquith will not accept compulsion whole-heartedly, then they will resign, & D. [David Lloyd George] with them. The doubtful point is whether the Unionists, or which of the Unionists will resign.'[63]

Lansdowne was party to the negotiations between Bonar Law and Asquith as the two pre-war leaders fought for position. Asquith eventually conceded that it was better to accept an unpleasant outcome on his own terms than have something worse forced upon him by his opponents. On 2 May he introduced the Military Service Bill, which applied the existing Act to all men aged eighteen to forty-one regardless of marital status and extended, for the duration of the war, the service of time-expired men. It received the royal assent on 25 May. The outcome weakened Asquith's position; soon new disputes arose about how conscription could be made to work.[64]

36

THE FALL OF THE ASQUITH COALITION

ALTHOUGH THE GOVERNMENT was aware of growing tension in Ireland, it failed to recognise the gravity until it was too late. The Easter Rising on 24 April 1916 was a surprise to Lansdowne, who thought 'the Dublin business is pretty mischievous' and 'it may take some trouble and loss of life to restore order completely'.[1] Two days later Lansdowne was put on the spot, being the only government minister present in the Lords. Uncharacteristically, he was not fully informed; he acknowledged that the government had been warned but 'there was nothing like a specific warning that this particular trouble was to be expected'.[2] The mismanagement of the affair and the execution of the rebels angered the public and converted many to the rebel cause. While some Unionists complacently believed it had put paid to Home Rule, it did the opposite.[3]

In the weeks that followed and with Asquith's support, Lloyd George began negotiations with the Irish. Lansdowne and the other Unionists in the cabinet approved, assuming that Home Rule would not come into operation during the war. In mid-June Lloyd George published a summary of his plan. Home Rule would come into effect immediately in twenty-six counties; the six north-eastern counties would remain within the United Kingdom. MPs from the twenty-six counties would be able to sit in a new Parliament in Dublin and also in Westminster. A cabinet minister would oversee the six-county territory. The authorising act was to remain in force for twelve months after the war; if Parliament had not by then 'made further and permanent provision for the Government of Ireland', the act would be extended by Order in Council 'for as long as might be necessary'.[4]

Although the scheme found favour with Irish Unionists and Nationalists, public opinion in Britain believed that Ireland should not distract attention from the war. At Westminster most senior Unionists, including Bonar Law, accepted Lloyd George's plan, but Lansdowne, along with William Selborne and Walter Long, did not. They were motivated by principle but also by complex personal issues; Lansdowne put his objections in a memorandum:

> The proposals seem to me profoundly alarming. Even if the Minister of Munitions [Lloyd George] succeeds in patching up a truce, I doubt whether it will be a lasting one; but to my mind the idea of a truce on such conditions will be deeply resented by many of those who now support the Coalition government. The recent disturbances have no doubt, as the Prime Minister points out, generated a widespread desire for a settlement, but they have certainly not softened asperities or disarmed suspicion. In many quarters it would be contended, that on the contrary, the outbreak, which no one will attribute merely to the desire of the people of Ireland for local self-government, has revealed the existence of subterranean forces which will continue to be formidable, no matter what the system of government may be. The settlement which we all desire must be contingent on the discovery of a modus which will be acceptable (a) to Ulster, (b) to the Home Rule party, and (c) to the people of this country. I should like to add, particularly if we are to proceed upon the basis of exclusion, that the settlement should contain (d) some features intended to reassure, so far as possible, the loyal minority outside the excluded area.
>
> Is the scheme propounded by the Minister of Munitions likely to fulfil these conditions? I fear not.
>
> In the forefront of it stands the old, and I think much discredited, plan of proceeding by exclusion. I have always myself thought that any measure of Home Rule which presented to the world as a new Irish 'nation' an Ireland from which Ulster or any part of it was excluded would be a deplorable and humiliating confession of failure, and if Home Rule is to come I should prefer a measure embracing the whole of Ireland, with safeguards for the minority wherever found. It should moreover not be forgotten that any scheme of exclusion, whether of the whole province or of certain portions of it, will require extensive alterations in the Act, and particularly the reconsideration of its financial provisions. Is this then the moment for imposing upon the country, in the guise of an interim arrangement, a bold and startling scheme which at once concedes in principle all that the most extreme Nationalists have been demanding, viz. the disappearance of Castle government and the establishment of an Irish Parliament with an Irish Executive responsible to it? The triumph of lawlessness and disloyalty would be complete. We may delude ourselves by urging that the arrangement is merely provisional, but the capitulation will be palpable, and its significance will not be diminished by the exclusion of Ulster or a part of that province.[5]

Lansdowne proposed an interim arrangement:

(a) The Lord Lieutenancy should be abolished.
(b) The promise of a royal residence and occasional visits from the sovereign.
(c) The appointment of a Secretary of State for Ireland to be assisted by,
(d) An Irish council, probably a Committee of the Irish Privy Council. Such a committee might deal with the question of disarmament, the Civil Service, and the appointment of magistrates.
(e) These steps might be accompanied by the promise of an enquiry into the whole question of Devolution.[6]

On 1 June Parliament was adjourned and three days later Lansdowne left for a short break at Derreen. He told Margot Asquith, 'I am rather ashamed of myself for being here, but I have not been going strong lately, and my doctor prescribed change of air, and found his patient more docile than usual. I am not even making believe to study the Irish question.'[7] If Lansdowne was docile, he was also concealing an aching heart that his favourite daughter-in-law, his dead son Charlie's widow Violet, was about to marry John Astor, son of William Waldorf Astor.

When Parliament returned on 20 June, it was clear that the Irish issue would cause deep divisions in the coalition. In cabinet next morning, four Unionist ministers, including Lansdowne,[8] stated that they could not accept the scheme. Asquith was unmoved and remarked that, if they parted, they did so without any ill feeling or any intention to mislead.[9] The next day eighty Unionist MPs met and demanded 'insurance of sufficient protection for southern Unionists; guarantees that Home Rule would not endanger the war effort; and the permanent exclusion of the designated counties'.[10] On 23 June Selborne told Long, 'there can be no possible justification of the Prime Minister's conduct to us. p.s. The cause is darkness not dishonesty but the result is the same.'[11] The cabinet met twice on 24 June. Lansdowne and Long continued to speak out against the settlement. Lansdowne expected the cabinet to break up. Among his Unionist colleagues, Bonar Law, who backed Redmond, Leader of the Irish Parliamentary party and Carson, Leader of the Irish Unionist party, and Balfour, who thought it was a unique opportunity to satisfy the Ulster Unionists, both spoke in favour of agreement. Except for the *Morning Post*, which was a voice for southern Unionists, the Unionist press supported an immediate settlement. As the crisis heightened, Asquith appointed a subcommittee to devise further safeguards to maintain effective and undisputed imperial control of all naval and military conditions in Ireland.[12] Lansdowne was very unhappy with the situation and detested the idea of leaving the government, but could not see how he could remain and defend an indefensible policy; meanwhile, he informed Crewe that he would take no final steps 'until after Tuesday's cabinet [27 June]'.[13]

Selborne, unwilling to wait any longer, resigned from the cabinet on Monday 26 June. That day, Lansdowne told Long, 'I am glad you did not let them announce your resignation. Selborne might just as well have held his hand.'[14] Had Long resigned with Selborne, it would have brought the party 'close to a smash', which Lansdowne was determined to avoid.[15] Two days later, Long told Selborne that he only stayed on because Lansdowne asked him.[16] On 1 July Lansdowne told his brother Edmond, 'we might have known better than to entrust Lloyd G. with these negotiations, but we had the best possible reasons for supposing that there was no question of granting a National Parliament before the end of the war'.[17] Lansdowne chose not to resign because he was satisfied by the subcommittee's amended terms. Asquith, sensing agreement was in sight, announced these safeguards on 5 July to his cabinet, which was still divided.

Balfour, Bonar Law and Carson endorsed the scheme. They did so again on 7 July at a Unionist Party meeting attended by 160 MPs and Lansdowne. This upset Midleton as no Unionist peers were invited; it appeared that Bonar Law was determined to consult only his own followers. During five hours of discussion, Bonar Law regretted the circumstances that made the scheme necessary, but thought Home Rule was now inevitable. He told the southern Unionists that their position would 'not be made worse by a settlement now than a settlement at any future time', adding that he understood Lloyd George had plenary powers. Lansdowne argued strongly that he did not. Despite Bonar Law's assurances, there was such support for the views of Lansdowne and Long that the meeting adjourned without a vote or resolution.[18] However, William Hewins, a Unionist politician and economist, believed the Unionists would not split.[19]

By now the cabinet had agreed to draft a bill, outlined by Asquith on 10 July. He said little of the security arrangements, important to Unionists, although he affirmed that the reunification of Ireland 'can never be brought about without the free will and assent of the excluded area'. Doubts remained.[20] Lloyd George said the settlement was provisional. The following day, Lansdowne resumed his attack. In the debate about the Easter Rising and Lord Charles Hardinge's Commission of Inquiry into its causes, he alluded to the Amending Bill then being drafted, stating that it would be 'permanent and enduring' and adding that for the remainder of the war, Britain would govern Ireland by a modified version of the Defence of the Realm Act, which the Parliament in Dublin would not be able to challenge.[21]

The Irish leaders were furious, believing Lansdowne made the speech to wreck the settlement. No one assumed that he would be allowed to discredit the proposal while he remained in cabinet. Asquith had great difficulty persuading them not to ask point-blank whether it represented government policy. In a press statement, Redmond condemned Lansdowne's comments as 'a gross insult to Ireland' and amounting to a 'declaration of war on the Irish people'.[22] His remarks elicited from Lansdowne a letter published in *The Times* on 14 July:

> In making my statement as to the character of the amending bill, I did not intend to go and I do not consider that I did go, beyond the declaration made by the Prime Minister in the House of Commons on the 10th instant – that the union of the six counties with the rest of Ireland 'could only be brought about with, and can never be brought about without, the free will and assent of the excluded area.'
>
> My statements with regard to the government of Ireland during the interval which must elapse between the present moment and the passing of the amending bill represented what I believed to be the views of the government and were made after consultation with the Prime Minister and others of my colleagues.[23]

Lansdowne believed that the sudden production of the draft bill was meant to rush him and his colleagues, and the bill's language, especially about the six counties, did not reassure him. On 19 July he and Long persuaded the cabinet to underline the permanence of exclusion and reduce Irish representation at Westminster – making it clear that the nature of partition settlement was enduring. At this, Redmond threatened to oppose the bill at every stage. This was exactly the result Lansdowne wished for. He told Selborne 'the "Irish settlement" broke down under its own weight, and we are well out of it'.[24]

On 27 July the government bowed to the opposition of southern Unionists and the Irish party and abandoned the scheme. Dublin Castle government was restored. On 30 July H.E. Duke became Chief Secretary of Ireland and Lord Wimborne returned as Lord Lieutenant. The crisis sharpened the differences between Unionists on questions of patriotism and principle. Bonar Law and Balfour believed these could be reconciled over Ulster, but Lansdowne did not: safeguarding the minorities in the west and the south was their duty, and the principle of the Union remained paramount.

Lansdowne devoted much of summer 1916 to Irish affairs, but also spoke in the House on other pressing war-related matters. The war was not going well, Jutland caused disappointment and Kitchener's death on 5 June was a shock.[25] Lansdowne told Margot Asquith:

most of us knew his faults but during the intimacy of the last twelve months I had certainly discovered a side to his character of which I was unaware and it attracted me very much. Maud has had a tender spot for him in her heart ever since she went to India for our Charlie's wedding when Kitchener was kind beyond words to her as well as to him and little 'Vi' [Violet Mercer Nairne, Charlie's wife] of whom K. was very fond. I was sure his death would shock you and Asquith deeply. It has saddened me more than I can say. I expect the P.M. will have to appoint Lloyd George. I say so on the assumption, which may be unwarranted, that the munitions department is now working at full speed, and that the machinery of production has been completely set up. Failing him, George Curzon is worth considering, he is resourceful and courageous and has infinite powers of work, but I fancy the House of Commons will want the new minister to be one of them. I don't think Derby would do, though I should like to see him in the government.[26]

On 6 June Asquith appointed Lloyd George as War Minister. Next day the Somme offensive began, the greatest disaster in British army history, with 60,000 casualties on 3 July alone, one third of them killed, ten times the German losses. When it ended, on 19 November, the front had advanced 7 miles at a cost of 620,000 men killed, wounded, missing or captured. Public confidence was eroded further by Zeppelin raids on England, which cities had no defence against. German resistance was clearly stronger than expected. Lord Northcliffe became convinced Asquith had to go, and his newspapers, including *The Times* and the *Daily Mail*, began attacking the Prime Minister.

The failure of the 1916 campaign sharpened debate more than ever. In early 1916, Loreburn had begun corresponding with Lansdowne on the disaster of the prolonged war and the view from Germany. Lansdowne was unconvinced. Referring to comments by Grey, he wrote:

I do not think it can fairly be argued that the war has been prolonged in order that Russia may reap certain advantages at Constantinople. I should put it this way: that the war is being carried on in order that the Germans may be beaten. Not till Germany is prepared to make certain concessions which we would agree are reasonable and indispensable could it be said that the war is being prolonged in order to secure special advantages for any one of the allies. So far as we are aware, Germany is not by any means yet prepared to meet even the minimum requirements upon which every one of us would insist.[27]

Until the end of October 1916, Lansdowne publicly maintained the government policy of a fight to the finish. But privately, after Verdun and the Somme, his faith in military success had dwindled. The death of Raymond Asquith, whom he knew well, was a reminder how the death of a son means one's life can never be the same again.

During 1916 a number of civilian leaders became sceptical of military victory. The German Chancellor, Theobald von Bethmann-Hollweg, had never believed in it. His doubts were mirrored by István von Burián, Austria-Hungary's Foreign Minister. Joseph Caillaux, former Prime Minister of France, noted growing support for peace. M. de Fleuriau, at the French Embassy in London, admitted that influential people were asking whether in twelve months hence France would get better terms from Germany than today.[28] In July Sergey Sazonov, the Russian Foreign Minister, urged concessions to the Poles, but Tsarina Alexandra's Germanophile faction had him dismissed after he proposed autonomy for Poland. His replacement, Boris Stürmer, a favourite of the Tsarina, wanted a separate peace with Germany. The generals – everywhere except Russia – had shifted the opposite way. Paul von Hindenburg and Erich Ludendorff, who took over the Western Front in summer 1916, both sought decisive victory. Robert Nivelle, who replaced Joseph 'Papa' Joffre on 13 December as supreme commander of the French and British armies, believed he had the secret of defeating the Germans.[29] Much the same happened in Britain. Those who had earlier promoted conscription now began to side with Lloyd George, aiming at outright victory. Many Unionists, including Bonar Law and Curzon, did the same. Lansdowne did not. Having originally supported militarising the country, he now thought it futile to expect to win by continuing as they were. Britain was at a crossroads and the choice was a 'knock-out blow' or a negotiated peace.

Lansdowne concluded this after reviewing intelligence reports of moderate opinion in Germany and discussing with Loreburn the British government's inadequate approach to the war. The intelligence showed a conflict between German annexationists and moderates; the latter had made peace overtures[30] on 23 June 1916.[31] With encouragement from entente moderates, a belief grew that a coordinated challenge to the annexationists would succeed. As politicians and soldiers across Britain and the Continent began firmly questioning the direction of the war, Asquith was forced to listen. At the end of October Asquith decided to ask the War Committee on what terms peace might be concluded. Lansdowne seized the opportunity. On 13 November 1916, he circulated a memorandum suggesting that the War Committee consider a somewhat different problem: what were the prospects of being able to 'dictate' the kind of terms that all Britons would like to impose on their enemies. It was a precursor to his 'Peace Letter' a year later:

We are agreed as to the goal, but we do not know how far we have really travelled towards it, or how much nearer to it we are likely to find ourselves even if the war be prolonged for, say, another year. What will that year have cost us? How much better will our position be at the end of it? Shall we even then be strong enough to 'dictate' terms?[32]

Questioning the ability of the Army to achieve victory, and the effect of prolonging the war, Lansdowne highlighted the number of casualties, the depletion of resources and the financial burdens.

All this it is no doubt our duty to bear, but only if it can be shown that the sacrifice will have its reward. If it is made in vain, if the additional year, or two years, or three years, finds us still unable to dictate terms, the war with its nameless horrors will have been needlessly prolonged, and the responsibility of those who needlessly prolong such a war is not less than that of those who needlessly provoked it.[33]

Unless his concerns could be shown to be groundless, Britain should not discourage any movement, no matter where it originated from, favouring an exchange of views about a settlement. Concluding with a goad to Lloyd George's call for a 'fight to the finish – to a knock-out', he indicated that such an approach ought surely 'to depend on our naval, military and economic advisers' views and upon the result of the careful stock-taking, domestic and international of each of the allies'.[34]

Rising to Lansdowne's bait, Lloyd George immediately instructed William Robertson, Chief of the Imperial General Staff, to inform the government whether his generals believed they could give the enemy a 'knock-out blow'. Robertson was contemptuous of Unionists and Liberals alike, and thought Lansdowne was 'a good man grown old and weak'.[35] Believing civilian heads of department should stay in their offices and obey orders, he summarised the war situation and its prospects in ten paragraphs. He cuttingly concluded,

as for ourselves, there are amongst us, as in all communities, a certain number of cranks, cowards and philosophers some of whom are afraid of their own skins being hurt, whilst others are capable of proving to those sufficiently weak-minded to listen to them that stand to gain more by losing the war than by winning it.[36] We need to have courage in London as have our leaders in the North Sea and in France. The whole art of making war may be summed up in three words – courage, action, and determination. In peace time half-and-half measures may not be very harmful. In war time they are deadly. We must make up our minds either to fight or make peace. The most pernicious and paralyzing thing that could happen would be to try and make war while in our hearts we are afraid to take punishment. My answer to the question is that I am 'satisfied that the "knock-out blow" can and will be delivered' if only we take the necessary measures to give us success, and take them in time. We shall win if we deserve to win.[37]

Lansdowne replied that Robertson's note was surely not a very helpful contribution to the investigation that the cabinet had authorised on 13 November 1916:

The question which was then raised cannot be disposed of by confident assertions as to the temper of the army which no one ever doubted, by moving exhortations to steadfastness, and still less by vehement denunciations of those who, not less patriotic or ready to submit to sacrifice than their neighbours, nevertheless desire a more searching examination of the problem than it has yet received. Sir William Robertson evidently understood me to suggest that we should seek an opportunity of bringing about an inconclusive peace. I made no such suggestion. I have read my note over carefully, and I search in vain for any passage which could be read as indicating that I desired to flinch from the efforts which we are making, or that I was reluctant to submit to the sacrifices which a prolongation of the war must bring with it. Sir William misunderstood my meaning. I hope I misunderstand his when I ask him not to include me (as I fear he does) among the 'cranks, cowards, and philosophers,' who think that 'we stand to gain more by losing the war than by winning it.' I hope he will forgive me for adding that those who ask questions which the Cabinet think worthy of a respectful answer will not consider that they are answered when they are told that such questions are an 'insult' to the fighting services.[38]

Lansdowne's witty retort to Robertson earned him a private word of praise from Asquith and silenced Grey, but his suggestion was rejected by the cabinet. Bonar Law was appalled by the memorandum. The cabinet discussed it on 22 November, and Bonar Law sensed an undercurrent of sympathy for Lansdowne's views. Frances Stevenson, Lloyd George's secretary, noted after speaking to Lloyd George about the meeting, 'It was agreed that there should be time given for the consideration of the Document & the matter brought up again. It looks as though if Lansdowne is outvoted he will have to resign. You cannot have a man in a War Cabinet who thinks we ought to make peace.'[39]

The shared disgust at what Lloyd George, Bonar Law and Carson considered Lansdowne's 'defeatism' ultimately drove them into a close triumvirate against the elder statesman. Nor did the memorandum persuade Austen Chamberlain that peace by negotiation was necessary or possible at that stage, but it strengthened his conviction that Britain's conduct of the war should be radically revised.[40] In the weeks that followed, Asquith's grip on power slipped and Lansdowne saw that the fate of the coalition hung in the balance. He reported to Evie a rumour that the malcontents meant to break up the government over votes for soldiers or Admiralty administration and that Lloyd George was deep in the conspiracy, ready to displace Asquith. Lansdowne spoke up for Asquith, 'who with all his faults, seems to me the best available leader'.[41]

On Thursday 30 November Bonar Law told Lansdowne and some other Unionist colleagues that he, Carson and Lloyd George had discussed Asquith's future and the War Council. He met a cool response. Next day Lansdowne wrote to him:

> the meeting in your room yesterday left 'a nasty taste in my mouth'. I did not like your plan, and I am by no means convinced that the alternative is all that can be desired.
>
> You will I have no doubt have another talk with [Lloyd] George, and we shall I assume hear the result. I know you will not mind my making two observations.
>
> 1. I hope you will not commit <u>yourself</u> irrevocably to George until you have given us another opportunity of considering the situation. I underline the word 'yourself', because it would be beyond measure painful to me to think that at such a moment you could entertain the idea of dissociating yourself from the other Unionist members of the Cabinet.
>
> 2. I think we all of us owe it to Asquith to avoid any action which might be regarded by him as a concerted attempt to oust him from his position as leader.[42]

Lansdowne was against his Unionist colleagues becoming allied with Lloyd George and the 'knock-out' party, particularly as he planned to call a secret session in the House of Lords to debate his memorandum. Bonar Law replied that evening: 'I recommended both Asquith and [Lloyd] George to have it out with each other and I consider therefore that for the moment the matter is out of my hands.'[43] But it was not out of his hands; Bonar Law was up to his neck in intrigue.

On Sunday 3 December *Reynold's News* printed a story that Lloyd George would resign if his proposals were not accepted and would then appeal to the country. Carson was in cahoots with him, and Bonar Law would probably resign too. Bonar Law called a meeting at his house for those Unionists who were in London. Lansdowne and Balfour were absent, Lansdowne at Bowood with Grey and the Salisbury family as his weekend guests. Possibly he hoped to convince Grey of his Lords idea and the benefits of negotiated peace. Attending Bonar Law's meeting were Curzon, Chamberlain, Long and Robert Cecil, Salisbury's brother. Bonar Law told them that Asquith had rejected Lloyd George's latest memorandum on reconstructing the War Council. They agreed on a resolution to Asquith:

> We share the view expressed to you by Mr Bonar Law some time ago that the Government cannot continue as it is.
>
> It is evident that a change must be made and in our opinion the publicity given to the intention of Mr Lloyd George to make reconstruction from within is no longer possible. We therefore urge the Prime Minister to tender the resignation of the Government. If he feels unable to take that step we authorise Mr Bonar Law to tender our resignations.[44]

Their stated object was stable government by combining the forces behind Lloyd George and Asquith, but they did not believe that a government under a Unionist Prime Minister would have any success. Curzon reported the meeting to Lansdowne:

> we know that with him [Asquith] as chairman, either of the Cabinet or War Committee, it is absolutely impossible to win the War, and it will be for himself and Lloyd George to determine whether he goes out altogether or becomes Lord Chancellor or Chancellor of the Exchequer in a new Government, a nominal premiership being a pro tem compromise which, in our view, could have no endurance.[45]

Asquith was alarmed by the threat of resignation. He sent for Lloyd George who, they had settled, was to be chairman of the new War Committee, although Asquith would have supreme and effective control of war policy. At Bonar Law's suggestion, a press statement was issued at 11.45 p.m on Sunday 3 December, saying that the Prime Minister would advise the King to agree to reconstruction of the government. Accounts differ as to the events on 4 December, however: according to Lord Crawford, at 1 p.m. Lansdowne, Chamberlain, Cecil, Curzon, Crawford and Long met at the India Office to discuss the situation. It is probable that Asquith saw Bonar Law in the early afternoon and Lansdowne at 5 p.m. After his meeting with the Prime Minister, Lansdowne went to the Colonial Office and met with the senior Unionists. He told them that he thought Asquith would come to terms with Lloyd George.[46] On Tuesday the political crisis became acute when Asquith, encouraged by some of his colleagues, denounced the agreement. Lloyd George sent his resignation to the Prime Minister. At 7 p.m. after further discussions with Unionist and Liberal colleagues, Asquith offered his resignation to the King.

Lansdowne was not pleased at the way the business was handled and thought Asquith was badly treated. That same day, Tuesday 5 December, he decided to stand down. Maud told Evie:

B Law is absolutely led by the nose by Lloyd George. It is very terrible that all this should happen in the middle of the war. I trust that Clan will not re-enter any government, it is too much for him now, and his blood pressure the last two days has been very high. He and Asquith seem so very fond of each other, & I think he had been a great comfort to A. who naturally cannot but admire his wonderful high mindedness & great courage in speaking out his mind & his loyalty.[47]

At 3 p.m. on Wednesday 6 December the King summoned Asquith, Bonar Law, Arthur Henderson, Lloyd George and Balfour to discuss the question of a National Government. Asquith was resolute he would not serve under anyone else and that the Prime Minister should preside over the new War Council. Bonar Law and Lloyd George insisted that the chairman should be Lloyd George. The talks lasted 90 minutes.[48] Lansdowne reported to Maud that

there was a great conclave at B. Palace, and I believe B/L [Bonar Law] is still wrestling with his difficulties – we shall know more tomorrow. It is amusing to find that in their difficulties they turn to A.J.B [Balfour] to help them out![49]

At 7 p.m. Bonar Law and Lloyd George returned to Buckingham Palace. Bonar Law met the King first and explained that he must give up his attempt to form a government. The King then saw Lloyd George, whose government was prepared, with a majority of Unionists.

Next day, Lansdowne told Maud, who was at Bowood, that

I had almost made up my mind to take refuge in flight, but things do not seem to be settling quite satisfactorily and I had probably better stay where I am.

I gather that the large majority of the Liberal members of the late cabinet will not serve under Ll.G [Lloyd George] – If that be so the Unionists will be reluctant to join a Georgian ministry, and there may be difficulties as to policy as well as personnel. The whole business is deplorable and a sad exhibition of national impotence.[50]

Lansdowne's faith in his Unionist colleagues was misguided; Lloyd George had formed close ties with Bonar Law, Curzon and Austen Chamberlain. Later that day Lloyd George met some leading Unionists to discuss appointments. Lansdowne was not invited. Lloyd George, who disliked his political ideology, had no intention of appointing him. At 7.30 p.m. he told King George V he would be able to form a ministry. He kissed hands as Prime Minister.

On 11 December 1916, the ministers of the late government gave up their seals to the King at Buckingham Palace. Maud told Evie:

> Well! Clan is at last free & I am more relieved than words can say, but he is <u>very</u> low, & like a fish out of water; since he was 23, he has been in public life, & it was <u>his</u> life, now he feels it is over for ever. On Tuesday [12 December] he sat below the Government front bench in the H. of Lords, the 1st time for 48 years; he has always been on the front-opposition, or government bench. However, I hope he will soon settle down.[51]

Lansdowne thought, 'The collapse of H.M. Government was catastrophic, and will puzzle the historians who have to account for it. Changes were, I am convinced, inevitable, but I certainly did not expect this particular dénouement. We shall someday, no doubt, go back to party lines, but it will never be quite the same again.'[52]

He told his brother Edmond:

> I had made up my mind not to enter any new combination, I shall be 72 next month & of late I have been feeling my years more and more. It would be idle to expect that I should be able to remain in office for any length of time, and the furrow which we have got to plough is going to be a very long one.
>
> But if I had had any doubts, or been shaken in my resolve by friends who wished me to stay, the new arrangements would have rendered me more fixed than ever in my resolve; the position of a Cabinet minister without a department has its drawbacks – a minister without a department to run or a cabinet to sit in would find himself in an intolerable position. The new company has an abundance of 'stars', and is apparently going to receive a liberal measure of support – I shall do what I can in a humble way to help it.[53]

One other outcome of the government restructure was that it ended Lansdowne's idea of a secret session in the Lords to discuss his memorandum and a negotiated peace. All his former colleagues who joined the front bench were now firmly in support of the 'knock-out blow'. As Parliament settled back to work, Lansdowne noted 'there was a rather amusing *chassez croisez*[54] in the H. of L. Crewe established himself in the centre of the front opposition bench – Haldane moved across to join him. Halsbury came back to the government side – several back bench peers crossed the floor in order not to sit behind Haldane. I established myself below the gangway which seems to me, for the moment at any rate, my proper place. But I should not wonder if there was to be a fresh grouping in consequence of these changes.'[55] On 19 December, along with Crewe, Curzon, the new Leader of the Lords, paid tribute to Lansdowne and his thirteen years as Leader.

SECTION 3

WAR AND PEACE

37

OUT OF OFFICE

ON 14 JANUARY 1917, Lansdowne celebrated his seventy-second birthday, depressed at being 'out of work'. He looked less worn, but his family worried that he had not enough to do, since walking, motoring, tree-cutting, picture-hanging and even china-shifting were all for various reasons barred. Even worse, he had surrendered his long-serving private secretary, a civil servant. Maud thought he should stay in London, where he could see people more easily and go to the House of Lords, but he would soon tire of the Lords with nothing very definite to do.[1]

With the onset of war, attempts to reform the Lords had been abandoned. However, the success of the Speaker's Conference on Electoral Reform, which ended on 23 March, raised new hopes for the Unionists.[2] Following a suggestion by Walter Long, Bonar Law and Curzon set about arranging the conference to report on reform. They urged Lansdowne to take the chair. Maud was keen for him to accept; he might forget his troubles and his concern about his prostate gland. Lansdowne worried 'quite terribly about the war' and no longer 'heard the private news that those in office hear which is often consoling and counter balances the other bad things'.[3] Lansdowne had no wish to be chairman, writing to Austen Chamberlain:

> I refused partly because I am getting rapidly deafer and can't hear what is said, perhaps muttered, round the table and partly because my health is not all that can be desired and I ought in common prudence to avoid new commitments. My tormentors have, however, returned to the charge, and use an argument which has practical strength viz. that they cannot find anyone else – I should be able to meet it more effectually if I could suggest a good name.[4]

The chair was taken by Lord Bryce; Lansdowne was among the twenty-seven commissioners. After forty-eight sittings, it reported to the Commons on 24 April 1918. As *The Times* said, Lords reform was 'of real moment to the Empire, but it is in no sense an urgent war measure'.[5] Few MPs even read the report, and its recommendations did not become part of the British constitution because in a more democratic age the second Chamber was no longer a major issue.

Lansdowne was also a witness at the Dardanelles Inquiry.[6] It reported on 12 February 1917, placing responsibility on the War Council, Churchill, Fisher and Kitchener. Lansdowne wished publication could have been avoided, commenting that 'Winston seems to me to come better out of it than Asquith & Kitchener, altho' Winston's methods were extraordinary.'[7] He also spoke in debates on the Mesopotamia Report,[8] which concluded that the transport and medical shortcomings showed that the military system of India was radically unsound.[9] Lansdowne condemned Lord Kitchener's system of centralisation and one-man power, which he, with experience as viceroy, had strongly deprecated at the time. He also agreed with Chamberlain that the government muddled the report and that

> if a little more promptitude and courage had been shown in dealing with those responsible the final muddle might have been avoided and I am afraid that such blunders are characteristic of the present system and our cabinets were too numerous, too discursive, and too weakly handled, but it seems to me that cabinets are wanted, and that they afford invaluable opportunities for timely criticism and suggestion as to difficult questions of policy, having little connection with the war, but nevertheless quite unimportant enough to concern the reputation and stability of the whole government or a particular Department![10]

As public hostility to Germans and Germany escalated in Britain during 1917, suspicion was thrown upon the Royal Family. On 19 June King George V changed the surname of his own family from the distinctly Germanic Saxe-Coburg-Gotha to Windsor. He also appointed a committee of the Privy Council, which included Lansdowne, to take evidence and report the names of 'enemy' British peers or princes. Among those implicated were the Duke of Albany (also the Duke of Saxe-Coburg-Gotha, a reigning prince of a German state), the Duke of Cumberland (exiled Crown Prince of Hanover living in Austria) and Prince Albert of Schleswig-Holstein (an officer in the German army), all descendants of Queen Victoria. While Lansdowne was willing to reckon with public opinion, he questioned whether one 'can punish or humiliate the holders of these decorations by publicly depriving them of their honours'.[11]

The Lansdownes played their part in the war effort, and most of the staff at Lansdowne House and Bowood joined the services. Lansdowne House became the headquarters of the Officers' Families Fund,[12] set up in 1899 by Maud and Louisa Wolseley, wife of Lansdowne's former colleague. With Queen Mary as Patron, the fund had raised over £310,000 by 1916 and apportioned £210,000 in nearly 10,000 cases. The fund also helped in other ways: it found paid employment for the wives, widows and daughters of officers, and its clothing department filled a house in Hertford Street. Owing to rationing the Lansdownes stopped giving official dinners until, in April 1917, finding that no Unionist reception had been arranged on the eve of the new Parliament, Maud held an evening reception at Lansdowne House, preceded by dinner for party members.[13] They avoided bomb damage from Zeppelin raids, although Lansdowne noted on 4 October 1917 that part of a shrapnel shell 'fell 10 yards from the dining room window & the porter had collected numerous other interesting souvenirs – one sees boys and girls picking them up in Berkeley St. as if they were children collecting shells at the sea side'.[14]

As part of what was called 'women's work in time of war', Maud helped the British Red Cross Society (BRCS). She had, in fact, long been involved with the organisation. Lansdowne became chairman of the BRCS Council on 12 May 1915, and in June he addressed a public meeting at the Mansion House and raised £87,000 for the Lord Mayor's Appeal. In September he launched an appeal to the Dominion states and Colonies for 'Our Day' on behalf of the BRCS and the Order of St John of Jerusalem. When Charles Hardinge, Viceroy of India and Lansdowne's former colleague, advised him against appealing in India he replied, pragmatically, 'we have to be sturdy beggars, and must be prepared for an occasional refusal'.[15] On 8 December 1915, announcing that Our Day had raised £797,458, he thanked the Dominions for their 'incalculable service' in money and men, but even more for the moral strength they had given to Britain's cause.[16] In 1918 the Our Day appeals raised £3.8 million.

Lansdowne was asked to become head of the Wiltshire Territorial Association. In May 1915, two groups of yeomanry – 520 of the North Somerset and 1,980 from the Wiltshire, Dorset and Hampshire – camped at Bowood. On 29 May Lansdowne, in khaki uniform, opened one of twenty-five YMCA tents set up to provide recreation and refreshment. He said of his home, 'never had he been prouder of it than at that moment'. Asked whether he was alarmed at handing over the place to soldiers, he remarked, 'even if there was a little bit of cutting and disfigurement, this was not the time for such considerations to prevail'.[17] The camp lasted until the end of September.

At the end of September 1914, Maud turned the stables at Bowood into a hospital, fully equipped with twenty beds. On Christmas Eve, patients and nurses sang carols outside the dining room while the Lansdownes were at dinner, only to be interrupted by three patients who returned from the nearby village of Calne very drunk.[18] The following August Freddy Hamilton, Lansdowne's nephew, was staying at Bowood and kept the nurses and patients in convulsions of laughter, which Lansdowne thought was not good for the patients.[19] His daughter-in-law Violet Astor came to help and the hospital took some casualties from Loos and the Somme. In March 1917 the principal matron and two sisters left, and voluntary nurses took over. Maud made herself commandant so that if the new nurses had anything they were not happy about, they would have a right to talk to her about it.[20]

Because of shortages, the hospital committee took steps to secure coal and coke before each winter. Although the impression persisted that the rich had plenty of comforts, this was not so. When Maud visited the hospital, she ate with the staff and was counted for the daily rations. Otherwise she would not have got her ration of bread, sugar, butter or milk.[21] She told her daughter in Canada:

> The food question is becoming most difficult. Without potatoes or very much bread, one feels very empty – I really am sorry for the servants, I am trying barley bread which is good and saves wheat flakes, but it is most indigestible. Alice gave us bacon for breakfast yesterday, Lansdowne & I have not had it for over two months, & we felt quite greedy about it; I am sure it is very good for us all having to do without a good lot that we have been accustomed to. It certainly makes one appreciate any little extra.[22]

In December 1917 there were great numbers of wounded. Maud received an urgent appeal for more beds at Bowood and made room accordingly, bringing the total to sixty, but that was full capacity.[23] That Christmas, as usual, Maud was kept busy with hospital entertainments.

While Lansdowne understood the menace of the German submarine campaign, supported national food security and advised his tenants to break up inferior grassland if it could be used more profitably for national purposes, he disliked gesture politics in time of war, especially the Corn Production Bill.[24] On 27 April 1917, Lloyd George confirmed the new agricultural policy of increased self-sufficiency, proposing to take another 3 million acres of grassland as 'fresh land' for the 1918 harvest: 'It is obviously an injustice to the community that a man should sit on land capable of producing food and either, selfishly or indolently, refuse to do anything. So the government must have the right to enforce cultivation in those cases.'[25] This suggestion was not, however, directly mentioned in the Corn Production Bill. What concerned Lansdowne was not only the indiscriminate ploughing of pasture and its effect on milk production, but the assumption that a farmer who demurred must be selfish or lazy, whereas he might be convinced that ploughing that land would be a fatal blunder agriculturally. He cautioned the government: 'you may want to have a sword. Do not draw it unless you are obliged, and do not rattle it about too much in the scabbard. These men are people whom you can lead, but they are not very easy people to drive.'[26] Lansdowne's opposition to the Corn Production Bill and the ploughing of land failed to find support. The bill became law on 21 August 1917; a month earlier, as recommended by his local agricultural committee, Lansdowne was 'trying to find 40 acres to plough in the park. A very doubtful experiment.'[27]

During the war the Lansdownes made few visits to Derreen and Meikleour. The latter, sadly associated with Charlie, his dead son, 'spells the great disappointment of my life'.[28] For their war efforts, Maud was among eighteen people appointed to the new Order of the Companions of Honour, and Lansdowne became Chancellor of the Order of St Michael and St George.[29]

38

MOVES TOWARDS PEACE

WHILE LANSDOWNE DID his utmost to support the war effort, he still worried that the government's 'knock-out blow' was unrealistic. His memorandum of 13 November 1916 had given Bonar Law and Lloyd George the impression that older politicians were weakening in their will to win. There were many, including Austen Chamberlain, who believed Britain's approach required radical changes.[1] Overseas, many statesmen believed that new methods of conducting the war were needed. In March 1917, ahead of the Imperial War Conference, Jan Smuts of South Africa and Robert Borden of Canada, stressed that Dominion prime ministers wanted a clearer statement of war aims.[2] In April Charles I, the Emperor of Austria and King of Hungary indicated his willingness to discuss a separate peace; Ottokar Czernin, his Foreign Minister, wanted to compel Germany into making peace by threatening to desert her. On 22 January Woodrow Wilson, President of the United States, appealed for an end to conflict in Europe on the basis of 'peace without victory'; two months later the United States declared war on Germany – albeit as an associated power, not an ally. Following the February Revolution and the Tsar's abdication, Lansdowne was not surprised to see instability continue in Russia as the provisional government was challenged by the Bolsheviks. He told Evie: 'I am glad Bowood is not in Russia – but you may live to see trouble in this country if things go less well than people want.'[3] Whatever Lansdowne believed, for the first eleven months of 1917 he kept silent in public about a negotiated peace.

The objectives of Lloyd George's government were the same as its predecessor, but to sustain them it needed popular support for the war. The 'knock-out' policy assured them of this. They distrusted

German-led peace initiatives as intended to create tension between Britain and the United States. In June the War Cabinet took new steps against pacifist propaganda. In the following months a regulation was introduced requiring any leaflet, pamphlet or circular relating to the war or negotiation of peace to carry the name and address of author and printer, with a notice that it had been submitted before publication to the Press Bureau and been passed. This regulation was simply announced to the Commons on 15 November. The *Morning Post* was the only newspaper that welcomed it. The *Westminster Gazette* warned that it would rebound on the government.

While the War Cabinet was determined and successful in cracking down on pacifist propaganda, their attempts to formulate war aims had largely failed, there was disagreement about what was theoretically desirable and there was little conviction that it could all be achieved, even if the war lasted long enough. In June the request of Maurice Hankey, secretary to the War Committee, for authority to begin secretarial arrangements for the eventual peace conference was rejected for fear that this 'might create a peace atmosphere or give the impression that the government were making preparations for a peace conference'.[4] The Vatican's attempt on 1 August to broker a peace came to nothing as Richard von Kühlmann, Germany's Foreign Minister, remained resolute that Germany's political system demanded German hegemony over the Continent, including security of Alsace-Lorraine. Germany's stance would not have mattered anyway since Lloyd George considered such a compromise inconceivable. Any hope of peace between Germany and the Allies seemed unlikely during summer 1917.

On 8 November Lenin declared that the Russian provisional government had been deposed and the Bolsheviks had taken power. Next day the Italians suffered a major defeat at Caporetto. While there was now no question of Britain abandoning the Allies, there was concern that the Allies might abandon Britain. On 16 November Georges Clemenceau, '*Le Tigre*', became the 85th Prime Minister of France, declaring his intention to make 'a war to the end'. Much of the British press welcomed his appointment. Four days later, Field Marshal Haig launched the Battle of Cambrai. On the first day the British advanced $4\frac{1}{2}$ miles; the Germans reinforced their position; Haig halted the advance. Disappointment in Britain was strong.

As the direction of the war drifted further from victory and Lansdowne's patience with military solutions faded, so the issue of the more general and longer-term outcomes of war came to concern him. He decided to act on his conviction in what became one of the most courageous moments of a long career built on independence and integrity in politics. As was his habit, established in his early twenties when he inherited his estates, he first sought advice and then proceeded cautiously. In mid-November 1917 he turned to his oldest colleague, Balfour, then Foreign Secretary. After a conversation with Balfour at Horse Guards Parade, he sent him a nine-page memorandum.[5] He also produced a list of questions he would like to ask in Parliament:

Whether in order to meet the misleading statements which are constantly made as to the objects with which the country is waging war, H.M.G. are prepared to state –

(1) that they do not seek to bring about the destruction or dismemberment of either of the Central Powers;

(2) that they do not desire to impose upon those Powers any form of government other than that of their own choice;

(3) that they do not desire to destroy or paralyse those Powers as trading communities, but that they are determined to secure for this country, from sources upon which it can depend, an adequate supply of the essential commodities;

(4) that they are prepared to examine, in concert with other nations, the great group of international problems, some of recent origin, connected with the question of 'freedom of the sea';

(5) that they will insist upon the adhesion of our enemies to an international arrangement under which ample opportunities would be afforded for the settlement of international disputes by peaceful means, and of such a nature as to make it hereafter impossible for any Power to provoke a sudden war until an attempt has been made to bring about a peaceful solution;

(6) that our general aims in regard to territorial questions have been stated in broad outline, that we recognise that no complete settlement of these questions can be reached without full discussion, but that such a discussion has been rendered impossible by the refusal of the Central Powers to put forward a corresponding statement of the aims which they have in view.[6]

That same week he also explained his position to Colonel Edward House, Woodrow Wilson's chief adviser on European politics, who happened to be in London. House, who knew Lansdowne socially, noted that

I found Lansdowne of a peculiarly pacific turn of mind. He condemned the folly and madness of some of the British leaders. He thought it was time for the British to realize that in the settlement they need not expect to get what he termed 'twenty shillings to the pound.' He believes that definite war aims should be set out – aims that are moderate and that will appeal to moderate minds of all countries. He specifically set forth five or six things he thought necessary to be done and, strangely enough, Conservative that he is, we scarcely disagree at all. [He advocated] a more liberal sea policy, bordering on the plan for the freedom of the seas, which indeed he was good enough to say he had obtained from me during my last visit here. He thought it would be necessary to give Germany an assurance as to our future economic policy which would not in any way restrict German trade. He was moderate in all his ideas.[7]

Having read Lansdowne's proposals, Balfour replied sympathetically, but cautiously and tactfully, to each of Lansdowne's points:

I do not know that this is a very suitable time for discussing peace matters. I rather think not. But I send you the following observations, for what they are worth, on the various statements which you propose to elicit from His Majesty's Government by Question in the House of Lords or by some other method.

(1) I certainly do not desire the destruction or dismemberment of Germany, if by 'Germany' is meant that part of Central Europe which properly belongs to the German people. I do not think, therefore, that the transference of Alsace-Lorraine to France, or the re-creation of so much of the historic Poland as is really Polish, constitutes dismemberment. But the Germans think differently, and this introduces the inevitable ambiguity into the proposed answer to your first question.

(2) A similar ambiguity attaches to the proposed answer to your second question. I certainly do not, for example, desire to compel Germany to adopt full-blown Parliamentary institutions; but I do not want to see a form of Government established in say, (German) Poland to which Germany would strongly object. These observations, which are true of Germany, may surely be applied, 'mutatis mutandis,' to Austria also.

(3) I quite agree that we do not wish to destroy Austria and Germany as 'trading communities'; but nothing ought to be said which hampers the attack on German commerce as a war measure, or (if it should prove necessary) the threat of post-war action in case Germany shows herself to be utterly unreasonable.

(4) As regards sea-power, it has to be observed: (a) that the phrase 'freedom of the sea' is extremely vague and is differently interpreted by different Powers; (b) that the abuse of sea-power should not be distinguished, either in logic or in law, from the abuse of land-power; and (c) that it is a subject which concerns neutrals as much, or almost as much, as belligerents, and cannot therefore be decided at any Conference where belligerents alone are represented.

(5) This last criticism applies also to this, but of course we are all in favour of it.

(6) I am in general agreement with this, though perhaps I might be inclined to make some changes in the wording.[8]

Lansdowne later wrote of his dealings with Balfour cited above – the memorandum, his draft questions of 16 November 1917 and Balfour's reply of 22 November – that

> I had for some time been anxious to give prominence to my five points. I had more than once pressed on Balfour the desirability of doing this. I had left with him a memo which we had discussed. I urged the necessity of finding some means of focussing on the matter in a few concise sentences. I sent him my draft questions as a proposal for giving effect to this. His dated 22 November was adverse; he dwelt on inevitable ambiguity of answers, and difficulty of an official explanation.
>
> Our interview took place on the eve of his departure after the Primrose service on Monday [26 November].[9] I agreed to abandon action in Parliament, and admitted that it might be undesirable to press the Government. I therefore proposed to put my view before the public in the form of a letter. He did not dissuade me. I said that I was anxious not to publish anything misleading or which might seem unfair to the F.O. [Foreign Office], and that I would gladly have shown him my draft, but that was impossible as he was to leave at 8.30 that evening [for the Paris Conference]. Did he object to my showing the draft to Hardinge [Charles Hardinge, Permanent Under-Secretary of the Foreign Office], in order that he might tell me if the letter contained any inaccuracies? He assented, adding 'Hardinge knows my thoughts.' I showed my letter to Hardinge [on 27 November]. He made one or two suggestions not touching questions of principle. He observed that it was 'statesmanlike' and would 'do good.'[10]

On 28 November Lansdowne saw Geoffrey Dawson, editor of *The Times*, who refused to publish the letter and warned Lansdowne to do nothing until the Paris Conference was over. That evening Lansdowne met Harry Burnham, proprietor of the *Daily Telegraph*, in the House of Lords, told him the history of the letter and asked him to publish it. He immediately agreed to do so, remarking that it was a good letter and he would give it prominence.[11] Lansdowne's letter was published on 29 November under the title 'Co-ordination of Allies' war aims'. Later known as the 'Peace Letter', it is cited here in full:

> Sir, - We are now in the fourth year of the most dreadful war the world has ever known; a war in which, as Sir W. Robertson has lately informed us, 'the killed alone can be counted by the million, while the total number of

men engaged amounts to nearly 24 millions.' Ministers continue to tell us that they scan the horizon in vain for the prospect of a lasting peace. And without a lasting peace we all feel that the task we have set ourselves will remain unaccomplished.

But those who look forward with horror to the prolongation of the war, who believe that its wanton prolongation would be a crime, differing only in degree from that of the criminals who provoked it, may be excused if they too scan the horizon anxiously in the hope of discovering there indications that the outlook may not after all be so hopeless as is supposed.

The obstacles are indeed formidable enough. We are constantly reminded of one of them. It is pointed out with force that while we have not hesitated to put forward a general description of our war aims, the enemy have, though repeatedly challenged, refused to formulate theirs, and have limited themselves to vague and apparently insincere professions of readiness to negotiate with us.

The force of the argument cannot be gainsaid, but it is directed mainly to show that we are still far from agreement as to the territorial questions which must come up for settlement in connection with the terms of peace. These are, however, by no means the only questions which will arise, and it is worth-while to consider whether there are not others, also of first-rate importance, with regard to which the prospects of agreement are less remote.

Let me examine one or two of these. What are we fighting for? To beat the Germans? Certainly. But that is not an end in itself. We want to inflict signal defeat upon the Central Powers, not out of mere vindictiveness, but in the hope of saving the world from a recurrence of the calamity which has befallen this generation.

What, then, is it we want when the war is over? I know of no better formula than that more than once made use of, with universal approval, by Mr. Asquith in the speeches which he has from time to time delivered. He has repeatedly told his hearers that we are waging war in order to obtain reparation and security. Both are essential, but of the two security is perhaps the more indispensable. In the way of reparation much can no doubt be accomplished, but the utmost effort to make good all the ravages of this war must fall short of completeness, and will fail to undo the grievous wrong which has been done to humanity. It may, however, be possible to make some amends for the inevitable incompleteness of the reparation if the security afforded is, humanly speaking, complete. To end the war honourably would be a great achievement; to prevent the same curse falling upon our children would be a greater achievement still.

This is our avowed aim, and the magnitude of the issue cannot be exaggerated. For, just as this war has been more dreadful than any war in history, so we may be sure would the next war be more dreadful than this.

The prostitution of science for purposes of pure destruction is not likely to stop short. Most of us, however, believe that it should be possible to secure posterity against the repetition of such an outrage as that of 1914. If the powers will, under a solemn pact, bind themselves to submit future disputes to arbitration, if they will undertake to outlaw, politically and economically, any one of their number which refuses to enter into such a pact, or to use their joint military and naval forces for the purpose of coercing a power which breaks away from the rest, they will, indeed, have travelled far along the road which leads to security.

We are, at any rate, right to put security in the front line of our peace demands, and it is not unsatisfactory to note that in principle there seems to be complete unanimity upon this point.

In his speech at the banquet of the League to Enforce Peace, on May 28, 1916, President Wilson spoke strongly in favour of 'A universal association of nations to prevent any war from being begun either contrary to treaty covenants or without warning and full submission of the cause to the opinion of the world.'

Later in the same year the German Chancellor, at the sitting of the Main Committee of the Reichstag, used the following language:

When, as after the termination of the war, the world will fully realise its horrible devastation of blood and treasure, then through all mankind will go the cry for peaceful agreements and understandings which will prevent, so far as is humanly possible, the return of such an immense catastrophe. This cry will be so strong and so justified that it must lead to a result. Germany will honourably co-operate in investigating every attempt to find a practical solution and collaborate towards its possible realisation.

The Papal Note communicated to the Powers in August last places in the front rank:

The establishment of arbitration on lines to be concerted and with the sanction to be settled against any State that refuses either to submit international disputes to arbitration or to accept its awards.

This suggestion was immediately welcomed by the Austrian Government, which declared that it was conscious of the importance for the promotion of peace of the method proposed by His Holiness, viz., 'to submit international disputes to compulsory arbitration,' and that it was prepared to enter into negotiations regarding this proposal. Similar language was used by Count Czernin, the Austro-Hungarian Foreign Minister, in his declaration on foreign policy made at Budapest in October, when he mentioned as one of the 'fundamental bases' of peace that of 'obligatory international arbitration.'

In his despatch covering the Allied Note of January 10, 1917, Mr Balfour mentions as one of the three conditions essential to a durable peace the condition that:

Behind international law and behind all treaty arrangements for preventing or limiting hostilities some form of international sanction might be devised which would give pause to the hardiest aggressor.

Such sanction would probably take the form of coercion applied in one of two modes. The 'aggressor' would be disciplined either by the pressure of naval or military strength, or by the denial of commercial access and facilities.

The proceedings of the Paris Conference show that we should not shrink from such a denial, if we were compelled to use the weapon for purposes of self-defence. But while a commercial 'boycott' would be justifiable as a war measure, and while the threat of a 'boycott' in case Germany should show herself utterly unreasonable, would be a legitimate threat, no reasonable man would, surely, desire to destroy the trade of the Central Powers, if they will, so to speak, enter into recognisances to keep the peace, and do not force us into a conflict by a hostile combination. Commercial war is less ghastly in its immediate results than the war of armed forces, but it would certainly be deplorable after three or four years of sanguinary conflict in the field, a conflict which has destroyed a great part of the wealth of the world, and permanently crippled its resources, if the Powers were to embark upon commercial hostilities certain to retard the economic recovery of all the nations involved.

That we shall have to secure ourselves against the fiscal hostility of others, that we shall have to prevent the recurrence of the conditions under which, when the war broke out, we found ourselves short of essential commodities, because we had allowed certain industries, and certain sources of supply, to pass entirely under the control of our enemies, no one will doubt, subject, however, to this reservation, that it will surely be for our interest that the stream of trade should, so far as our own fiscal interests permit, be allowed to flow strong and uninterrupted in its natural channels.

There remains the question of territorial claims. The most authoritative statement of these is to be found in the Allies' Note of January 10, 1917. This statement must obviously be regarded as a broad outline of the desiderata of the Allies, but is anyone prepared to argue that the sketch is incomplete, or that it may not become necessary to re-examine it?

Mr. Asquith, speaking at Liverpool in October last, used the following language: 'No one pretends that it would be right or opportune for either side to formulate an ultimatum, detailed, exhaustive, precise, with clauses and sub-clauses, which is to be accepted *verbatim et literatim*, chapter and verse, as the indispensable preliminary and condition of peace.'

'There are many things,' he added, 'in a world-wide conflict such as this, which must of necessity be left over for discussion and negotiation, for accommodation and adjustment, at a later stage.'

It is surely most important that this wise counsel should be kept in mind.

Some of our original desiderata have probably become unattainable. Others would probably now be given a less prominent place than when they were first put forward. Others again, notably the reparation due to Belgium, remain, and must always remain, in the front rank, but when it comes to wholesale re-arrangement of the map of South Eastern Europe we may well ask for a suspension of judgement and for the elucidation which a frank exchange of views between the Allied Powers can alone afford.

For all these questions concern our Allies as well as ourselves, and if we are to have an Allied Council for the purpose of adapting our strategy in the field to the ever shifting developments of the war it is fair to assume that, in the matter of peace terms also, the Allies will make it their business to examine, and if necessary to revise, the territorial requirements.

Let me end by explaining why I attach so much importance to these considerations. We are not going to lose this war, but its prolongation will spell ruin to the civilised world, and an infinite addition to the load of human suffering which already weighs upon it. Security will be invaluable to a world that has the vitality to profit by it, but what will be the value of the blessings of peace to nations so exhausted that they can scarcely stretch out a hand with which to grasp them?

In my belief, if the war is to be brought to a close in time to avert a world-wide catastrophe it will be brought to a close because on both sides the peoples of the countries involved realise that it has already lasted too long.

There can be no question that this feeling prevails extensively in Germany, Austria and Turkey. We know beyond doubt that the economic pressure in those countries far exceeds any to which we are subject here. Ministers inform us in their speeches of 'constant efforts' on the part of the Central Powers 'to initiate peace talk.' (Sir E. Geddes at the Mansion House, November 9.)

If the peace talk is not more articulate, and has not been so precise as to enable His Majesty's Government to treat it seriously, the explanation is probably to be found in the fact, first, that German despotism does not tolerate independent expressions of opinion, and second, that the German Government has contrived, probably with success, to misrepresent the aims of the Allies, which were supposed to include the destruction of Germany, the imposition upon her of a form of government decided by her enemies, her destruction as a great commercial community, and her exclusion from the free use of the seas.

An immense stimulus would probably be given to the peace party in Germany if it were understood:

(1) That we do not desire the annihilation of Germany as a Great Power;

(2) That we do not seek to impose upon her people any form of government other than that of their own choice;

(3) That, except as a legitimate war measure, we have no desire to deny to

Germany her place among the great commercial communities of the world;

(4) That we are prepared, when the war is over, to examine in concert with other Powers the group of international problems, some of them of recent origin, which are connected with the question of 'the freedom of the seas';

(5) That we are prepared to enter into an international pact under which ample opportunities would be afforded for the settlement of international disputes by peaceful means.

I am under the impression that authority could be found for most of these propositions in Ministerial speeches. Since the above lines were written, (1), (2) and (3) have been dealt with by our own Foreign Minister at the public meeting held in honour of M. Venizelos at the Mansion House. The question of 'the freedom of the seas' was amongst those raised at the outset by our American Allies. The formula is an ambiguous one, capable of many inconsistent interpretations, and I doubt whether it will be seriously contended that there is no room for profitable discussion.

That an attempt should be made to bring about the kind of pact suggested in (5) is, I believe, common ground to all belligerents, and probably to all the neutral Powers.

If it be once established that there are no insurmountable difficulties in the way of agreement upon these points, the political horizon might perhaps be scanned with better hope by those who pray, but can at this moment hardly venture to expect, that the new year may bring us a lasting and honourable peace.[12]

The letter produced a sensation. To the general public, even to Lansdowne's friends and family, it was a 'bolt from the blue'.[13] *The Times* said the letter 'reflects no responsible phase of British opinion and in all the Allied countries will be read with universal regret and reprobation'.[14] The *Daily Mail* announced, 'if Lord Lansdowne raises the white flag he is alone in his surrender'.[15] The *Daily Express* reported, 'the letter will serve no useful purpose' and such a peace by negotiation could only mean gigantic preparations for further wars.[16] The *Morning Post* commented, 'it is appalling to think that a mind so constituted and open to such illusions should have so long led the Unionist Party, and had so much to say in the direction of Imperial policy. Little wonder if Unionists have lost all their bearings with such a hand at the helm.'[17]

The letter was published in the *New York Times* and reported in other leading US newspapers. Cecil Spring Rice, ambassador in Washington, noted that 'the general attitude of the numerous editorials which have appeared on the subject has been one of disapproval'.[18] Louis Tracy, a British journalist on the staff desk in New York, told Northcliffe that 'Lansdowne's letter created the worst possible effect here. It was most bitterly resented by all loyal Americans.'[19] Some Americans took a different view. Harry Garfield, a presidential adviser, wrote to President Wilson that the letter 'seems to me to run with your purpose and I can well believe brings you both encouragement and relief'.[20] The French press vilified the letter, the Dutch commented with unconcealed satisfaction and where German papers published the letter it was considered the 'beginning of England getting reasonable'.[21]

With the letter's publication, the futility of war re-emerged as a political issue, but Lansdowne himself also became a political issue. Liberal and Unionist leaders had to defend themselves to their own parties. On the morning the letter appeared, Lloyd George was in Paris for the first meeting of the Inter-Allied Conference at Versailles. He told Lord Islington, then Under-Secretary of State for India, that Lansdowne's letter very nearly broke up the Paris Conference. Nobody among the Allied representatives would believe that such a document, coming from so cautious and experienced a man, could have been published without the tacit consent of his old colleagues. Lloyd George said that, had he been at the Conference by himself, it would have defeated him; but four or five colleagues spent the whole day visiting people and giving assurances.[22]

On 30 November Colonel House told Lloyd George that he was wrong to oppose Lansdowne's ideas and making a mistake in not insisting at Versailles on a resolution on a statement of the Allies' war aims. However, next day, as the delegates failed to agree, House announced that the USA could not be party to any of the draft declarations under discussion. Lloyd George, sensing the mood in Paris and the opportunity to extricate himself, announced that he had been prepared to support a public statement that the Allies would discuss revised war aims with a 'decent' Russian government, but he would no longer do so, as it would look like an endorsement of Lansdowne's point of view.[23] The Allies agreed that no joint declaration on war aims for Russia was possible. House told President Wilson that the failure to formulate agreed war aims was all the fault of the entente.[24]

The British government immediately issued a significantly inaccurate statement about Lansdowne's intervention:

> Lord Lansdowne in his letter spoke only for himself. Before writing it he did not consult nor, indeed, has he been in communication with any member of the Government, His Majesty's Ministers reading it with as much surprise as did everybody else.
>
> The views expressed in the letter do not in any way represent the views of His Majesty's Government, nor do they indicate in the slightest degree that there is any change or modification in the war policy of this country.[25]

On 4 December Balfour issued a memorandum and betrayed his friend of over fifty-six years, leaving him to suffer alone at the hands of his detractors:

> I understand that during my absence in Paris a statement has been made about my supposed connection with Lord Lansdowne's now famous letter which gives an entirely false impression of what really occurred. I have not yet had an opportunity of reading the letter in question, but from all I hear it must have gone outside the subject discussed in the following correspondence.[26]

Evie later declared that

> I don't believe Arthur B. ever did face the question of publication. He so seldom faced anything, and would be inclined to agree with father as to the substance of the memorandum to save himself trouble.[27]

Balfour never corrected his story. It says much of Lansdowne's character that after the war not only did he and Balfour remain close colleagues,[28] but to his dying day Lansdowne refused to contradict, publicly or privately, the claim that he had acted alone. It was typical of his complete loyalty and patriotism that he would not embarrass his colleagues or the wartime government.

Bonar Law also dissociated himself from Lansdowne's 'Peace Letter'. While wishing privately to remain a friend of Lansdowne, he publicly repudiated him, believing that, unless he did so, the government's whole attitude might become suspect at home and abroad.[29] On 30 November, at the Unionist national conference, he declared,

> I disagreed absolutely not only with the arguments, but with the whole tone of his letter. I think it is nothing less than a national misfortune that it should have been published, now of all times.[30]

As Lansdowne put it, he was 'officially excommunicated' and, although he and Bonar Law remained on friendly terms for the rest of their lives, their political paths drew apart. Rudyard Kipling, musing on why the *Daily Telegraph* published it when *The Times* did not, told Stanley Baldwin,

> I fancy it appeared there because the proprietor is a Hebrew and was suffering from cold feet. It is a semitic complaint. But the origin of his letter must be much more interesting. I am, as you know, a low minded soul and I expect the poor old bird (who is ga-ga) was worked upon as a 'patriot and a statesman' by someone – female for choice – in the Liberal interest.[31]

This speculation that Margot Asquith might have influenced Lansdowne's decision to write the letter is ridiculous. Overnight, Lansdowne became one of the most reviled men in England. He was not surprised by the reaction, but he noted that 'the newspaper attacks are past all belief'.[32] While his letter made the concept of patriotism more convincing to the Unionist party and its constituents, it drove the two sections of the Liberal party further apart. Although the 1918 General Election was still over twelve months away, Lansdowne's letter assisted Lloyd George's supporters in preparing their campaign strategy as a fight between pro-war and anti-war parties. This is all the more remarkable considering Lloyd George's objection to the Boer War in 1899. On 30 November, when Jack Sandars, Balfour's private secretary, passed him on Bond Street, Lansdowne remarked, 'I don't suppose you will speak to me!'[33]

To understand the origins of the letter one must appreciate that it was the result of lengthy meditation on the war and its course, as well as experience. Lansdowne was not a pacifist or defeatist as his detractors claimed; he had been War Minister and, as Foreign Secretary, he had helped to establish the framework within which continental war became possible. This is not to suggest that he was responsible for the causes of the conflict, but he understood the decision-making that led to war. He had lost his youngest son, and watched powerlessly as friends and colleagues lost their children too. He saw the mounting cost of the war in financial and human terms and believed it unsustainable.

To read Lansdowne's letter simply in the context of the war is to miss its true message, which was about positioning: Britain's place in the world, but also the way the country was ordered. While expressing a direction in which foreign policy could move, Lansdowne's letter was also intended to give rise to certain movements within domestic politics.[34] His objective was not reactionary, although he realised that the suffering inflicted by the war might end in widespread revolution. Such disorder, the obliteration of a generation and fear of an uncertain future impressed Lansdowne deeply with the need to speak out. He saw clearly that pursuing a negotiated peace would mean working with political forces that would eventually overpower the class and way of life in which he had been brought up. That price seemed worth paying with so much at stake. Just as Lansdowne never felt any need to defend his motives, he never elaborated on the meaning of the letter beyond stating 'it speaks for itself'. It did that, but essentially it spoke for his values – values nurtured over a lifetime, values that he believed were worth salvaging from the pre-war world. That these values did not appeal or seem relevant to a younger generation added to the sensation it stirred up. He was quite unrepentant about it, remarking that it did 'good both at home and abroad; but if I had had more of the wisdom of the serpent, I should have added a good deal of padding as to my abhorrence of anything which could be called a German Peace'.[35]

Lansdowne's letter did resonate strongly, however, among individuals who believed in a compromise peace. On 3 December Loreburn wrote to the *Pall Mall Gazette* that

> Lord Lansdowne's letter is an exceedingly able and far-seeing document. The letter has been called a surrender. As a matter of fact, it contains no hint at this. On the contrary, Lord Lansdowne expresses his wish to beat the Germans.[36]

Edward Grey, the former Foreign Secretary, thought 'the outcry against it absurd – it was a wise discussion of possibilities in an uncertain situation'.[37]

Among others who were sympathetic to Lansdowne's ideas were Asquith, Esher, Haldane, Sanderson, Robert Cecil and the Archbishop of Canterbury. Not many people endorsed Lansdowne's proposals in public, except for pacifists and known anti-war figures. Ramsay MacDonald, for the Labour Party, welcomed the letter. He hoped it would open up a new approach to European problems, which Britain had to face, and promote a new spirit. Arthur Henderson thought the letter timely and hopeful; he suggested that public figures with similar views should band together and exert 'benevolent pressure on public opinion'.[38]

By 10 December Lansdowne had recovered from the initial outburst against him. In one of the few documents where he expressed his views, he told his daughter Evie:

> I have for some time felt that it was somebody's duty to put this view of the case before the public. My friends in the Government were strongly opposed to a debate in the House of Lords, which would have served my purpose, and they were probably right, as they would have been closely interrogated and forced to say something or maintain an undignified silence. I have been snowed under with letters from all manner of folk – a few hostile, but mostly in complete sympathy with me. The prevailing note is: you have had the courage to say what we have been thinking for ever so long.[39]

After the Allies had failed to agree on a joint statement of war aims in Paris, President Wilson broached the subject. On 4 December, without discussing it with Colonel House, he addressed the US Congress, calling for peace when German power was broken. He began by declaring that

America's object was to win the war and they would not be diverted until then. He would regard the war as won only when the German people told them 'through properly accredited representatives' that they were 'ready to agree to a settlement based upon justice and reparations of the wrongs their rulers had done'. He envisaged a peace settlement that guaranteed 'full, impartial justice' for enemies as well as friends: 'No one is threatening the existence or the independence or the peaceful enterprise of the German Empire.'[40] Wilson's address contained many parallels with Lansdowne's letter. Parallels which Lansdowne pointed out in an interview with the *New York Times* on 5 December. Among those close to Lloyd George and willing to support Lansdowne's case was Robert Cecil. He tried to persuade the Prime Minister that he had misunderstood Lansdowne's letter, which was not a desire for peace on any terms:

> I venture to think that a great mistake has been made, particularly in the press, in the treatment of Lord Lansdowne and his letter. Lansdowne is not a traitor, nor is he senile, still less is he corrupt, and to suggest these things about him merely tends to throw doubt on the strength of the cause of his opponents. If you compare closely the substantive demands made by Lansdowne and Wilson, my impression is that you will find comparatively little to choose between them.[41]

Lloyd George did not agree, citing Wilson's unswerving devotion to a victorious war as a fundamental difference. However, on 14 December, making his first public speech since Lansdowne's letter had been published, he seized on Lansdowne's recent comments in support of Wilson's policy and attempted to undermine him. Speaking at Gray's Inn he brushed it aside, declaring flippantly,

> Recently a highly respected nobleman startled the nation by a letter which gave rise to very considerable apprehension. I now understand that [he] had not intended in the least to convey the meaning which his words might reasonably bear. That all the time he was in complete agreement with President Wilson and only meant to say exactly the same thing as the American President said in his recent great speech to Congress. I might be forgiven for saying that if Lord Lansdowne simply meant to say exactly the same thing as President Wilson it was a great misfortune that he did not carry out that intention. However, it is satisfactory to know that Lord Lansdowne was misunderstood both by his friends and his critics and that the whole weight of his authority and influence may be reckoned on the side of the enforcement of what I call the Wilson policy.
> I shall therefore pass on from this letter to the view which it was supposed to advocate, but did not, to the opinions which are held and

expressed by a number of people in this country. It is true they are in a minority, but they are a very active minority. The Lansdowne letter brought them out into the open. They thought that at last they had discovered a leader with a view to forcing this country into a premature and vanquished peace. The danger is not the extreme pacifist. I am not afraid of him. But I warn the nation to watch the man who thinks that there is a halfway house between victory and defeat, who thinks that you can end the war now by setting up a League of Nations with conditions as to arbitration. That is the right policy after victory. Without victory it would be a farce.[42]

Lloyd George never mentioned Lansdowne's letter directly in his memoirs but he was alarmed at the momentum it gathered. Wishing to stall matters he restated victory would continue to be an essential condition of government policy.

On 14 December Maud wrote to Evie:

Ever since Clan's letter to the D.T. [The *Daily Telegraph*] on the 29th of November we have lived in a whirl of the most scurrilous abuse & hundreds of letters of the most grateful thanks (some of them quite beautiful) to Clan for his courage in speaking, & giving his views on a subject which was bound in many quarters to be received with execration. I have always been proud of him, but I don't think I ever really realized <u>what</u> a <u>big</u> man he was till now. It is difficult to describe the abuse & the names he has been called particularly in London. Clan remains quite calm through it all, & says 'they may call me a coward & traitor, I don't mind in the least, I should have been a coward & a traitor to my country, if I had held my tongue feeling as strongly as I did, that we were giving no thought to the future or what our proposals in the want of overtures for peace would be, only going on blindly slaughtering Germans, and having the best of our country either maimed or slaughtered & not really advancing a bit.'

My men in the hospital here [Bowood] tell me that every Tommy at the front will be grateful to Clan, & I know all the Officers are. In the middle of writing this, the papers with Lloyd George's speech have come in, he was generous to Clan, though I think he must at first have ruefully misunderstood Clan's letter, but I hope all will remember that Clan's letter was published on the 29th of Nov & Wilson's speech was the 4th of Dec, so Clan was the first to suggest these ideas, & <u>Wilson's</u> speech agreed with them, not as Lloyd George says that Clan's letter agreed with Wilson's ideas.[43]

Lord Kerry disapproved of his father's letter but, at a British war aims meeting on 15 December, said:

Every one conversant with public affairs knows that the written as well as the spoken word is always liable to misconstruction. Lord Lansdowne's letter has been so construed by a large portion of the Press and public that meanings have been read into his words which they were certainly not intended to convey. At the same time I must admit that his views, as I first read them, did not commend themselves to me. Of this I have made no secret. A few days after the publication of Lord Lansdowne's letter there appeared in the Press a report of a speech delivered by President Wilson in America, and a great deal of the discussion on this matter has centred on the extent to which the aims and objects of these two pronouncements might be held to agree or to differ. There was much which was identical in both, notably five points enumerated towards the end of my father's letter which are to be found expressed in different language, but with the same purpose, in the speech of the American President. There were, however, some notable passages in the speech which I should like to have seen, but did not find, in my father's letter. I refer particularly to those which dealt with the determination of the Allies to secure the objects for which we originally entered the war – a determination which was forcibly expressed by Mr Asquith a few days ago and again by the Prime Minister on Friday night. Speaking generally, I think it will be agreed that the two utterances differed considerably in tone, and that this difference in tone was mainly responsible for the difference in intention which was generally held to underlie them. Lord Lansdowne's critics must, I think, admit that he himself is the best judge of his own intentions, and, as far as these are concerned, this question has been publicly disposed of by a statement which he made to the representative of the *New York Times*. Lord Lansdowne said – 'I have read the President's address with warm admiration. I am in agreement with the policy which he has so eloquently described, and I notice with much pleasure that his speech contains passages which completely support the views which I have endeavoured to express.' I may add that I have myself discussed these matters at length with my father, and he has assured me that nothing was further from his object than to suggest a line of action differing in any way from that advocated by President Wilson.[44]

Lansdowne believed that the close correspondence between his letter and Wilson's speech showed that the critics had argued their case by wilfully and recklessly distorting both documents, without allowing for the different circumstances of their origins.[45] Kerry never concealed that he fundamentally disagreed with his father's line. At no stage in the war did he see any other course than to fight to the finish. He even wanted the Kaiser shot, which was certainly not Lansdowne's policy.

He dissociated himself from his father's views very strongly in a letter to Mr Green-Smith, one of his constituents. It was published, which he regretted, and acclaimed by Lansdowne's opponents.[46] That Kerry forgot to mark it private and 'disremembered' it so completely allowed Lansdowne to write a severe snub to Mr Green-Smith, who must have relished the contradiction between the letters.[47]

The political fallout from Lansdowne's letter held public attention for weeks, while Lloyd George distanced himself and the government completely from it. As pressure mounted, on 5 January 1918 Lloyd George made his most definitive statement of Britain's war aims to a conference of trade unionists. The speech was less intriguing for its content than for the way observers interpreted it. Lord Newton asked Lansdowne what he considered was the difference between Lloyd George's speech and his letter. Lansdowne replied enigmatically that everyone had been asking him that. Newton thought the speech had been dictated to Lloyd George by the Labour people, who would not support war much longer. However, his speech made clear that talk of a negotiated peace would not be allowed to threaten the political structure in Britain.

Three days later, international attention was caught by President Wilson's famous Fourteen Points. The speech, which reached a wider public than Lansdowne's letter, supported a national and international debate about war aims, and was meant to assure Americans and the Allies that the war was being fought for a moral cause and for peace in Europe. The speech subsequently became the basis of a peace programme and post-war order. In 1929 Colonel House admitted that Lansdowne's proposals had been the inspiration for Wilson's Fourteen Points: 'I well remember how much encouragement Lord Lansdowne's announcement gave me. I had been trying to get an expression from the Allies as a whole upon their war aims, but without success. Lord Lansdowne's courageous statement struck a note that had been strangely lacking up to that time. His party affiliations and his prestige gave weight to what he said. It was certainly one of the contributing causes to the formation of the Fourteen Points.'[48]

Although, in November 1917, Lansdowne had no inkling of how his letter would be received, his courage triggered new departures in the search for a negotiated settlement and notably made war aims central to political debate.

39

THE LANSDOWNE
MOVEMENT

LANSDOWNE'S LETTER NOT only placed him in the political spotlight again but was a proclamation around which diverse groups could rally. It initiated a number of progressive developments, including a peace activist movement. In January 1918 minor 'Asquithian' figures such as Lord Beauchamp, former Governor of New South Wales, and Richard Durning Holt, MP for Hexham, pressed their leaders to do more to support Lansdowne. Margot Asquith mobilised such calls, working with H.A. Gwynne, editor of the *Morning Post*, and William Pringle, radical MP for North West Lanarkshire, in an attempt to create a new coalition.[1] While Lloyd George was negotiating at Versailles, Asquith and Lansdowne met regularly at Lansdowne House[2] and discussed their situation. While neither seriously contemplated returning to office, they became newsworthy figures once more. Although they agreed to differ on certain subjects, they decided they would have to let Lloyd George stay in office.[3] In the months after the letter appeared, Lansdowne's principal object was to support those pursuing revised war aims and a negotiated peace. In his opinion the letter was public property.[4]

In February Arthur Henderson, the former leader of the Labour Party, warned that Labour MPs would vote against Lloyd George if they were dissatisfied with his explanations of what had happened at Versailles, with the sidelining of William Robertson, Chief of Imperial General Staff, and the conferring of executive power on the Supreme War Council. According to Francis Bertie, the ambassador in Paris, 'His [Henderson's] alternatives are, (1) Lansdowne! (2) Asquith, (3) himself!'[5]; 'If the war must continue, Lloyd George had best remain to carry it through: neither a Lansdowne coalition nor an Asquith coalition ministry would last long. The Labour Party do not want to come into office for the present.'[6] Lord Stamfordham (Arthur Bigge) thought a Lansdowne ministry absurd and anyway he would never take the job.[7] Lansdowne would have agreed: he had no desire to re-enter frontline politics. That Lansdowne was even considered for Prime Minister was a remarkable achievement for a man of seventy-three who had recently been savagely attacked by journalists and politicians.

In mid-January 1918, Francis Wrigley Hirst, editor of *Common Sense*, formerly of *The Economist* and an influential anti-war activist and veteran Cobdenite, began a correspondence with Lansdowne. *Common Sense*, a fanatically free trade periodical established in October 1916, decided to promote Lansdowne and the 'Peace Letter' in a movement towards a negotiated peace. Hirst imagined Lansdowne himself taking a leading role in this movement, which had the support of Loreburn, the former Lord Chancellor. On 31 January a deputation of pacifists led by Loreburn went to Lansdowne House to thank him for his letter to the *Daily Telegraph*. Lansdowne, who was impressed by Hirst, met Loreburn and spoke about war aims, the idea of a crushing victory, the duration of the war and territorial agreement.[8] The meeting was well reported in the press and gave impetus to the movement.

At Versailles, the Supreme War Council decided to reject the latest Austro-Hungarian and German peace overtures by Count Czernin, Austro-Hungarian Foreign Minister, and Count Hertling, German Chancellor. Their speeches of 24 January, which were a reply to Wilson's Fourteen Points and Lloyd George's Caxton Hall speech on British war aims,[9] questioned some issues but stressed a genuine desire for peace. On 4 February, boasting that their only task was the vigorous and effective prosecution of the war, the Allied leaders declared their intention to fight on to victory. Hirst was disappointed and immediately sent Lansdowne the notice of a proposed conference to raise awareness of their cause. The notice stated that this decision of the Supreme War Council had created profound uneasiness among those who had hoped to support the present government, believing it would entertain peace overtures by the Central Powers, and the time had come to supersede the government by one pledged to negotiate an honourable and satisfactory peace.[10] As peace-by-negotiation groups rallied to Lansdowne, he replied,

I have come to the conclusion that I had better not be present at the proposed conference. The printed notice which you handed me makes it clear that the meeting is really summoned for the purpose of 'superseding' the present government. I agree with you in deploring the recent pronouncement of the Versailles War Council [4 February] but I am not convinced that as matters now stand the destruction of the government is the best means of obtaining what we desire.[11]

Lansdowne did not believe there was any alternative government.

The first meeting of what Hirst called the 'Lansdowne–Labour movement', on 26 February at the Essex Hall in the Strand, was attended by 360 people, many from the North of England and the Midlands with backgrounds in banking, insurance, manufacturing, the arts and politics. Lord Beauchamp took the chair alongside Loreburn and Lord Parmoor, a former Unionist MP and lawyer who had opposed the war in 1914. Lansdowne, who had very little in common with this group, did not attend and made it known that he had no intention of becoming their leader. Hirst found it difficult to engineer an alliance between Lansdowne and his followers, not least because Lansdowne wanted a negotiated peace to prevent civilisation and humanity from irreparable harm, whereas the radicals and socialists wanted peace to change the world.[12] Nor did the 'Lansdownites', as they were called, imagine he could give effective leadership.[13] However, with the Liberal leadership in a state of inactivity, allying with Lansdowne gave them recognition and credibility at that time.

Wilson was also upset by the Supreme War Council declaration and on 11 February countered it in a speech to Congress. Highlighting the latest German and Austrian speeches, he expanded on his earlier Fourteen Points speech and set our terms on which belligerent nations were to negotiate any potential settlement. While Hirst and other journalists seeking a negotiated peace gave prominence to the speech, Lansdowne was preparing to make another move. On 2 March 1918, he wrote a second letter, published in the *Daily Telegraph* three days later, 'to keep the sounder view in evidence'.[14] Taking Count Hertling's recent speech to the Reichstag of 25 February in reply to Wilson's speech to Congress, 'which had not been done justice',[15] Lansdowne noted four important points:

(1) The distinct expression of a wish that, in order to remove misunderstandings, and in the hope of reaching 'a compromise of the existing contradictions,' responsible representatives of the belligerent Powers should come together 'in an intimate meeting' for discussion.

(2) An admission that 'a general peace is discussable,' on the basis of the four principles laid down in President Wilson's Message of February 11, if recognised definitely by all States and nations.

(3) An assurance that the Chancellor would 'joyfully greet' an impartial Court of International Arbitration, and 'gladly co-operate to realise such ideals.'

(4) An intimation that Germany does not think of retaining Belgium or making the Belgian State a component part of the German Empire.[16]

Lansdowne implored Britons not to remain unyieldingly militant.

He also urged Hertling to clarify his statement on Belgium without equivocation.[17] Lansdowne wished to see public dialogue between Wilson, Hertling and Czernin continue, believing this would lead towards an informal meeting of representatives from both sides. His letter also encouraged those in Germany pressing Hertling to go beyond his statements of 24 January and 25 February to disclaim a policy of conquest and annexation.[18]

The reaction to Lansdowne's second letter was less sensational than the first, although its circulation in the foreign press was wider, particularly in North America and France. Walter Page, the American ambassador, who was strongly attached to the British cause and a supporter of Lloyd George, told Wilson that

> Lansdowne and his friends (how numerous they are nobody knows) are the loudest spokesmen of such a peace as might be made now, especially if Belgium can be restored and an agreement reached about Alsace-Lorraine. But it is talked much of in Asquith's circle that the time may come when this policy (its boldness is somewhat modified) may be led by Mr Asquith.[19]

Selborne, Lansdowne's Unionist colleague, commented that the letter 'could be of no advantage to anybody except the German military party'.[20] Parmoor noted, 'this is the letter of a wise statesman of life experience who refuses to follow blindly the dictates of a military press [in Britain] which does much to help the war party in Germany.'[21]

In Germany it also resonated with moderates. A circle around Prince Max von Baden, a liberal-minded soldier and politician, including Kurt Hahn, a German Foreign Office specialist, tried vainly to persuade Hertling to reply publicly to the questions raised by Lansdowne's second letter. One can speculate that if Hertling had had more courage and political power, Lansdowne's peace initiative would have been transformative. However, Hertling made no reply and the Kaiser spoke angrily of Lansdowne and his clique.[22] Francis Bertie, reading the letter in Paris, believed it had 'not done so much here as might have been expected',[23] although a Leftist organisation called the Republican Coalition emerged as a voice against annexations and penal indemnities.

Lansdowne's second intervention was intended to keep the dialogue alive, but the damage done by the 4 February Versailles declaration was unstoppable. Two days before Lansdowne's second letter was published, the Bolsheviks made a separate peace with the Germans at Brest-Litovsk. Unlike previous Russian political initiatives, which had given support to the peace movement in Britain, this event weakened it, mainly by ending the war in the East and allowing Germany to focus the war on the West. Even if any chance of reform in Germany was dampened by Brest-Litovsk, Lansdowne and Hirst remained undeterred. On 6 March Hirst organised a second Lansdowne–Labour conference. The meeting, more crowded and successful than the first, was timed to coincide with Lansdowne's second letter. As on the previous occasion, Lansdowne decided against attending; in his absence, a Lansdowne committee was formed, with Lord Beauchamp as chairman.

Raising awareness of their cause in Parliament, on 19 March Lord Parmoor moved a resolution that 'this House approve the principle of a League of Nations and the constitution of a Tribunal whose orders should be enforceable by an adequate sanction'. Lansdowne spoke, in the debate, of his belief in a great peace conference which would ripen into a League of Nations, and that 'a military victory and the imposition of crushing terms would be very unlikely to yield that security which to many is the chief argument for going on with the war'.[24] He began by saying,

what I certainly do not mean when I talk of a League of Nations. I do not mean a coalition of Powers against another coalition. That would only be a perpetuation of the condition of things which we desire to see ended. Nor, again, do I mean merely an increased resort to arbitration. I venture to think that a League of Nations has two essential features. The first of them is this. I think it must be open to all, and must, if possible, comprise all the important Powers. The second essential is, I think, this, that your League must be armed with executive powers – powers sufficient to secure unquestioning obedience to its decisions.

He concluded:

My Lords, this war has taught the world something of the cost – I do not mean the money cost – which these internecine struggles involve, and of their difficulty, and there may be another revelation in store for the world. If we are simply to revert to the old order of things, may the victors in this war not find that when they have beaten their foe to his knees they are still very far from the accomplishment of the object with which they have set out? – I mean the object of saving their children and grandchildren from a recurrence of the catastrophe which has fallen upon us in our time. I should like your Lordships to consider from that point of view whether any crushing of an adversary can be regarded as a final crushing, and I would like, in order to illustrate my meaning, to remind the House of a very well-known episode in the History of Europe. After the battle of Jena, Prussia was crushed by her adversary; she was deserted by her allies; she had accepted at Tilsit the terms imposed upon her by the two

Emperors; she had been compelled to surrender territory and to pay a large indemnity; she had been disarmed; and she was treated with every possible contumely during the years that followed. But in 1814 Blücher was marching into Paris. That is a good illustration of the absence of finality in these crushing defeats. The moral of all this is that success in the field is not a guarantee, cannot be a guarantee, of permanence. It may give you a breathing space, but it cannot give the world a permanent and secured relief from the ills from which we have been suffering. I believe myself that there is only one way in which you can obtain such a permanent relief. It is the way to which my noble and learned friend [Parmoor] has pointed in his speech to-night. This is not, as some people would have you believe, the baseless fabric of a vision. It is not a mere mirage which will fade as you advance towards it. I believe that what some of us think we see in the distance is the outline of a real Promised Land. I earnestly hope that we shall see to it we get there.[25]

Two days later, news of the long-expected German Spring Offensive halted any further attempt at diplomacy and broke much of the momentum the Lansdowne movement had gathered. Lansdowne admitted it was difficult to think of anything except the events on the Western Front[26] but, as Germany's massive onslaught lost its initial impetus, he continued his crusade for a secure future and a negotiated peace.

40

THE END OF THE WAR

DURING APRIL AND May 1918, as Germany continued its bid for victory in the West, Lloyd George reshuffled his ministry. The changes prompted Lansdowne to write to Evie:

> I wonder what you think of the reconstruction. I cannot help believing that when the great battle now raging dies down, there may be an opportunity once more of talking about Peace. Unless I am much mistaken the country is losing all confidence in this govt. – I am being constantly pestered to take part in various conspiracies to turn them out, but until I see the makings of an alternative administration I prefer limiting myself to doing what I can to inoculate the present people with a spirit of reasonableness & courage. By the latter I do not mean the courage which finds expression in bluster and a refusal to look facts in the face.[1]

Although dissent in Britain at this time was not entirely motivated by pacifism, any organised criticism of the government and their task of managing the war was generally labelled as such. As dissent gained traction, critics claimed that such movements had no right to participate in public life and discussion.

On 8 May Lord Denbigh, a Roman Catholic peer, introduced a motion in the House of Lords asking the government to suppress pacifism, and read out a long list of religious sects and other 'mischievous' organisations in favour of simple peace by surrender. After Beauchamp urged that it was scarcely fair to indiscriminately condemn everyone in the country who had ever spoken in favour of peace by negotiation, Lansdowne remarked:

I do not know if I am included among the defendants in this action which the noble Earl is bringing. I think I am. May I say half a dozen words for the defence. In the first place let me clear the ground upon one point. I have had no part in the meetings, or as they have sometimes been called the secret conferences, which have lately taken place in connection with this question. I have not been present at them, I have not helped to convene them, I have not authorised the use of my name in connection with them; but I hope the noble Earl [Denbigh] will not think, because I say this as a matter of fact, that I desire to dissociate myself from what has been said, for example, by my noble friend Lord Beauchamp, who has already addressed the House. It seems to me that he and some of those who have been acting with him have shown much common sense and much appreciation of the realities of the case.

Let me then add that my own participation, so far as there has been any, has been strictly limited to the letters which I wrote to the public Press. I have nothing to withdraw, nothing to apologise for so far as those letters are concerned and if the noble Earl chooses to challenge any statement which they contain I should be very glad to meet him here or anywhere else. My creed is to be found in those letters.

Then I come back to what appears to be the principal article of faith which the noble Earl professes. There is to be no 'peace by negotiation.' That is the catchword in all the documents and speeches which are delivered in this connection. If there is to be no peace by negotiation, how does the noble Earl expect peace ever to come to us? Does he expect it to drop from the clouds? No; the noble Earl does not leave us in the dark. He thinks there is only one way of obtaining peace. It is by the process generally described as the 'knock-out blow.' He and his friends never tell us how the 'knock-out blow' is to be delivered, when it is to be delivered, how soon it is to be delivered, and at what cost it is to be delivered; and meanwhile the war, which the noble Earl himself has described as a ghastly war which he would not himself prolong for an hour beyond the hour at which it could be honourably ended,[2] goes on taking its toll of the resources of this country, of the manhood of this country, adding to the number of those maimed and pathetic figures whom we meet at every turn of the road, adding to the number of those men and women who, all over the British Empire, have had their hearts broken by the loss of those whom they most love.

Not only does the noble Earl disbelieve in peace by negotiation, but he, and those who think with him, positively go the length of warning negotiators or those who desire to negotiate off the political field. The moment there is any talk of negotiation we are told that this is what is called a 'peace-offensive' or a 'peace-trap.' The overture is turned down before it is made. I must say that those tactics are to me quite unintelligible.

I should have thought that if you were afraid of an insincere overture the best thing to be done was to exhibit its insincerity, and you cannot do that until it has been made.[3]

Shortly afterwards, Lansdowne received a letter from Hahn, saying that he and his circle of German moderates had believed that a negotiated peace was possible before the Spring Offensive, but the 'knock-out blow' politicians in Britain and France had dashed all hopes of it: 'There is no doubt that Graf Hertling was ready for a just peace in February and March and that he was strong enough to carry it – if there had been a response from the other side.'[4]

Some radical groups continued to campaign for a negotiated peace. Among the more popular pressure groups to contribute personnel and propaganda to the Lansdowne–Labour movement was the Union of Democratic Control, even though there was no formal connection and it differed slightly in ideology. Its leaders, both Liberals – Charles Trevelyan, a former government minister, and Arthur Ponsonby MP – hoped Lansdowne might lead a political movement based on peace by negotiation. During the summer, Ponsonby approached Lansdowne, reporting later that Lansdowne was sympathetic but unresponsive.[5] Another group to approach him was the Women's Peace Crusade, whose members, spurred on by Ethel Snowden, collected over '33,000 signatures for a petition' to Lansdowne, urging him 'to make a further public pronouncement, and place [himself] at the head of a movement which, we believe, has the support of a large section of the people of all classes'.[6] Lansdowne replied that his health and deafness prevented him; at that time he was undergoing operations for neuritis in his left arm and hip.

Despite Lansdowne's efforts to avoid taking a prominent role in the movement for a negotiated peace, people continued to use his name. On 31 July Hirst organised a third Lansdowne–Labour conference at Essex Hall. The platform included Lord Parmoor, the Dean of St Paul's Cathedral (Revd William Inge), Philip Snowden, Ramsay MacDonald and two more MPs. Unwilling to attend, Lansdowne sent a third and final letter to the conference. With careful phrasing and drawing on ideas aired on 17 May by Jan Smuts, a member of the Imperial War Cabinet, who had suggested that the 'knock-out blow' favoured by Lloyd George was not necessarily the best way to bring the war to an end, Lansdowne began his letter,

We are about to commence the fifth year of the great struggle for liberty, and next week we shall reaffirm a solemn resolve not to desist from the effort until peace with honour is in sight. Meanwhile, with every month that passes, the toll which the war is claiming becomes heavier and heavier. The civilized world is being drained of its resources, and is spending its energies in purely destructive efforts, each of which involves a further diminution of its reserves of power and a further mutilation of the machinery of production. I have seen estimates which put the casualties sustained by the belligerent nations at 30,000,000 of which no fewer than 7,000,000 have been killed, while 6,000,000 are prisoners or missing. I will not dwell here upon the sacrifices which our own country is making, upon the exhaustion of our national wealth, upon our losses in tonnage, and our infinitely more lamentable losses in human lives.

A few weeks ago the Registrar-General, in a striking paper read at the Royal Institute of Public Health, dwelt upon the enormous decline in the birth-rate. He believes that the present war is costing the belligerent countries of Europe not fewer than $12\frac{1}{2}$ millions of 'potential lives'. Up to the present we had 'lost in England and Wales in potential lives, on the standard of 1913, 650,000.' Every day that the war continues means, he says, a loss of 7,000 'potential lives' to the United Kingdom, France, Italy, and the Central Empires – 'while the war has filled the graves, it has emptied the cradles.' Sooner than accept a dishonourable peace, we are all of us ready to fight on to the bitter end, but there is not a man or woman in the country who does not realize the tragedy of these figures, and indeed there is probably not a Minister who has not, at one time or another, said that it would be criminal to continue the war after an honourable peace had come within our reach.

The desire for peace is, so far as it is possible to judge, widespread among the enemy nations. How can it be otherwise? Upon no other assumption is it possible to explain the language of those Germans and Austrians who are in a position to speak their minds freely or the constant 'feelers' which are launched by the Governments of the Central Powers. But we are, apparently, as far as ever from the end. The tide of carnage and destruction continues to flow, and carries all before it. From time to time a ray of reasonableness illuminates the gloom, only to be followed by a relapse into recriminations and controversies in which each side, instead of searching for points of agreement, is apparently content with dialectic successes. What is it that stands in the way? It is with no desire to embarrass His Majesty's Government that I ask the question. But many of us are sorely perplexed, and feel it our duty to give them a chance of affording us some measure of reassurance and enlightenment.[7]

A number of letters disagreeing with Lansdowne were published in *The Times*, which he felt obliged to argue against. Henry Cabot Lodge, a Republican Senator and critic of Wilson's Fourteen Points, who had great respect for Lansdowne as well as strong personal regard for him, thought that his policy was fundamentally wrong. He noted that his ideas had not produced a good effect in America. The general feeling there was that the time had not come to discuss the details of peace negotiation. Referring to the original 'Peace Letter', he said,

Lord Lansdowne's five points belong to a past era. They contemplate a settlement like that of 1815. They would settle nothing and give no guarantees for the future. After such a war as this I believe a compromise negotiation of that character would be impossible, and his points entirely omit the really vital thing which are the establishment of the small nationalities, the return of territory which Germany has seized by force and the establishment of certain new states which shall block her attempts at further world domination. To us here, if I may judge from the general expressions of feeling, Lord Lansdowne's last utterance particularly is regarded as simply injurious.[8]

Diana Manners, the Duke of Rutland's daughter, wrote about Lansdowne's third letter to her future husband, Duff Cooper, who was at the front:

I thought it excellent and sensible and written in the grand manner. There have been replies to it which mean nothing. I feel so strongly sometimes about politics. I'm afraid you never do. And I don't find myself in agreement with anybody. Lord Lansdowne is the man for me. Do you know him? I like his appearance but I have never spoken to him. He had an ancestor at the end of the eighteenth century whom everybody hated and who was always right.[9]

The first day of the Battle of Amiens, 8 August 1918, described by Erich Ludendorff as 'the black day of the German army', saw General Henry Rawlinson lead a successful Anglo-French attack. From 21 August to 25 September the British advanced along the Somme and victory followed victory. Ferdinand Foch, the Allied Generalissimo, called 'everyone to battle!' and British, French, Belgian and US troops pushed home their advantage. Enemy soldiers began to surrender. This Allied resurgence doomed any prospect of immediate peace negotiation and weakened the peace movement. As the Lansdowne–Labour movement lost momentum and fell into obscurity, many of its members pinned their hopes on the proposed League of Nations. The Allied advance also convinced the German High Command that the war could not be won. Having excluded civilians from directing the war, they now wanted to make them responsible for losing it. On 2 October they told the Kaiser that the government must ask for an immediate ceasefire while making itself more democratic by including leading political parties.

On 3 October the Chancellor, Hertling, resigned to be replaced by Max von Baden, whose government for the first time included social democrats. The new government sent a telegram to Wilson requesting an armistice and asking him to organise peace negotiations based on the Fourteen Points. Wilson replied positively. On 9 October Lansdowne, interviewed by Hirst for *Common Sense*, said he regarded von Baden's peace proposal as the most substantial advance yet made by the Central Powers. He understood Wilson's reply to mean that he would discuss the questions at issue if Germany were willing to satisfy his demands.[10] On 20 October von Baden threw Germany on Wilson's mercy, trusting he would not allow any demand that damaged the honour of the German people or hopes of a just peace. The Germans undertook to stop submarine attacks on passenger ships. On 30 October Turkey signed an armistice with the allies, becoming the second of the Central Powers to do so. [Bulgaria signed an armistice on 29 September.] Four days later the armistice with Austria-Hungary was signed.

Although few on the Allied side realised it at the time, Germany was no longer capable of organised resistance. On 5 November, in Berlin, revolutionary socialists marched, demanding the Kaiser's abdication. He refused, but on 9 November his government announced it anyway, von Baden resigned and Friedrich Ebert became Chancellor, proclaiming a German Republic. On 11 November the Germans signed the armistice. The Great War left about 16 million people dead and 21 million wounded. The financial cost to the Allies was calculated at $125,690,477,000; the cost to the Central Powers was $60,643,160,000. Hirst invited Lansdowne to publicise his views. He declined, remarking:

> It may be that, as time goes on, people will come to see that an honourable but less dramatic peace, made a year or two years ago, would have been better for this country and for the civilized world, than the catastrophic denouement which we are witnessing, but for the moment articulate public opinion is unanimously in favour of the dramatic conclusion which has been reached now, but could not have been reached then, and it is of no use to urge the contrary view. The tide of passion is running too strongly.[11]

When the armistice was signed on 11 November 1918, it was agreed there would be a peace conference in Paris. One effect of Lansdowne's 'Peace Letter' was that he was not invited to take part. On 29 October Moreton Frewen, the Anglo-Irish author, had sent him the draft of a letter defending his cause. Unless Lansdowne disapproved, Frewen offered to give it to Burnham for publication in the *Daily Telegraph*.

Lansdowne replied:

> While I am cordially grateful to you for espousal of my cause, I feel that
> I ought not to encourage you to write such a letter. It mentions me as a
> candidate for appointment to the final Peace Conference, on which I am
> not at all likely to be asked to serve.[12]

The Paris Peace Conference began on 18 January 1919, without
Lansdowne. This was Europe's loss. Bridging the generations from the
mid-nineteenth century to the early twentieth century, Lansdowne's
long experience and achievements in foreign affairs ideally qualified
him to appreciate the complexity of the negotiations and contribute
to their success.

Twenty-four hours after the armistice was signed Lloyd George,
concerned by the growing tension in the Liberal party between his own
supporters and Asquith's, announced his decision to hold a General
Election in alliance with his coalition partners. The decision ended the
eight-year Parliament, which had been extended by emergency wartime
action. Partly because of the success of the coalition as an example
of national unity, Lloyd George and Bonar Law were determined to
extend it in peacetime. To safeguard their position, Lloyd George and
Bonar Law issued each official coalition candidate with a letter of
endorsement, known as a 'coupon'. The fate of those Liberals without
a coupon was sealed. They were effectively defenceless against the
coalition candidates. In the 1918 'coupon' General Election, for the first
time, most men over twenty-one and women over thirty could vote, and
more than 10 million did so on 14 December. The result was a victory
for the coalition government, although not all coupon candidates were
successful. Lansdowne's son Kerry, standing as a coalition Unionist, lost
his West Derbyshire seat. As the party attempted to explain his defeat,
Lansdowne commented, 'it is quite plain that an attempt is being made
to attribute the disaster wholly to the fact you are your father's son and,
as such, suspected of unsoundness in your opinions as to the war'.[13] The
suddenness and completeness of the Allied victory seemed to represent
the 'knock-out blow' so long promised by the Supreme War Council and
to justify their policy of a fight to the finish. The brilliance of this belated
success dazzled the nation, and the coalition was bathed in reflected
glory. Those who had questioned the policy were seen as profoundly
mistaken and – like Lansdowne, and even Kerry – found themselves on
the wrong side of history.

Yet Lansdowne's own contribution during the war and in its aftermath
was vast. While his 'Peace Letter' was not itself enough to bring about
a negotiated peace in 1917 or 1918, it triggered a number of important

developments that led to that goal. Lloyd George was forced to revise the Allied war aims and later to embrace the vision of a League of Nations. The British Labour Party was inspired to challenge the government in pursuit of a Wilsonian policy, and the Lansdowne–Labour conferences emerged as a powerful voice in the peace movement. German moderates were given an immense stimulus to challenge the annexationists in their country. President Wilson was clearly mindful of Lansdowne's ideas when drafting his Fourteen Points, as Colonel House acknowledged. With the benefit of hindsight, I believe that Lansdowne was correct in supporting a revision of the war aims to include a negotiated peace as a means of achieving lasting stability in the world and not merely an absence of war. Appealing to moderate minds of all countries, Lansdowne displayed the highest moral courage and keen political foresight. No period in history can be more suggestive of might-have-beens than the months following Lansdowne's letter and the end of the First World War.

SECTION 4

LEGACY

41

THE FINAL YEARS

THE WAR ALTERED Lansdowne's world. He lost a son and his political reputation. His perception of the world and its hierarchy was undone. The war had brought extreme political, cultural and social change across Europe, Asia and Africa. Four empires had collapsed, old countries were abolished, new ones were formed, boundaries were redrawn and international organisations were established. In Britain a limited number of women were allowed to vote for the first time, and a severe economic recession had taken hold. Living for another nine years, Lansdowne adjusted to the changing situation with his usual caution and wisdom. He maintained his sense of duty and his integrity, meeting the challenges facing his class with common sense. He remained pragmatic and realistic.

With higher rates of tax, falling agricultural income and changing social attitudes to employment Lansdowne was unable to manage his estates and households as before the war. He was forced into retrenchment. Land was sold and staff laid off. On 21 April 1920, Lansdowne organised his final reception at Lansdowne House for the wedding of his granddaughter Dorothy Cavendish and Harold Macmillan, the future Prime Minister. Among the guests were Queen Alexandra, 'Bertie' Duke of York and the author Thomas Hardy.[1] Later he explained his predicament:

> Taxes and rates continue to increase and are submerging us all – apart from this L. House does not pull its weight unless the occupants can afford to be hospitable and I see no prospect of our being able to open the mahogany doors during the remainder of my time. It is not an easy house to let, and a sale is inevitable. But all this makes me abominably sad for

I had set my heart on ending my days in the Square, and but for the war I should have been able to leave K. [Kerry, his son] quite fairly well off.[2]

He made the property over to Kerry, knowing he could not keep it going either. Maud noted,

Clan is very miserable. I fear he simply loves this house and he has struggled all his life to economise so as to be able to preserve it for his successors, and denied himself a great many things, that most factors would not have hesitated to have (for the same reason).[3]

In 1921 the house was let for £5,000 a year to Gordon Selfridge, 'undoubtedly a figure for the highlights of modern romance, the only qualification he misses being that he was not born poor. He entertains a great deal and is a considerable figure in London society where he is very liked. Yet he is at his office nearly every day from half-past eight in the morning until seven at night.'[4] His parties were grand affairs, regularly attended by royalty. The Wyatt ballroom at Lansdowne House was reinvigorated and the waltz of pre-war years surrendered to the wild music of the Charleston and the Black Bottom.[5] Selfridge stayed until 1929.

Lansdowne did not live to see his son sell Lansdowne House in 1929 for £750,000 to Benson Greenall, an American with a large portfolio of property. Meikleour and the other Scottish estates remained in trust for his grandson George Mercer Nairne, who in November 1918 was six years old. Bowood remained under Lansdowne's management until his death. Supervised by a resident agent, it had huge maintenance costs. Lansdowne was forced to sell land and paintings to support it. He was not alone: it is estimated that between 1918 and 1922 a quarter of all privately owned agricultural land in England changed hands. The costs of war, death duties and income tax forced the aristocracy into rapid decline.

During 1919, while the Allied victors were setting the peace terms for the defeated Central Powers in Paris, Lansdowne suffered an appendix-related disease, complicated by crippling rheumatism.[6] Pain kept him awake at night and he became very disheartened. His doctor thought he had intestinal poisoning and gout. As the disease worsened his whole body was affected; his muscles became extraordinarily painful and both knees badly inflamed. He could not move without assistance.[7] For such an active man it was frustrating. In August he fled from London to Bowood, where political friends, including Curzon, Long, Bryce, Midleton and Salisbury, visited him and briefed him on current affairs. He accepted that he would be unable to do much, if any, public work for some time.[8] He resigned as Lord Lieutenant of Wiltshire in March 1920 and as chairman of the Red Cross a month later. Among the few appointments he kept was that at the National Gallery: in January 1919 he was appointed chairman of the board of trustees and negotiated the Lane and Mond bequests for the nation before stepping down in December 1923, by which time he felt unfit to preside.[9]

Maud kept quiet about their golden wedding on 8 November 1919; she did not want a fuss and people giving presents they could not afford. Lady Emma Louise Rothschild, however, sent her gardener from Tring with orchids in a silver-gilt basket, so the servants discovered. The *Devizes Gazette* got the date wrong, with the result that many telegrams arrived on the 15th.[10] A week later, Lansdowne was in better health. He had put on 8½lb, although his hands and feet were still bad; he suffered fits of depression and needed a night nurse.[11] On 2 January 1920, Maud told Evie that he was walking with two sticks, but had to be carried downstairs. He ventured to London every three weeks to see his doctor, but attended no debates in the Lords. Friends continued to visit him and update him on proceedings, although with little cheerful to tell.[12]

On 21 January 1919, the Dáil, an independent legislature, met for the first time at the Mansion House in Dublin. It adopted a provisional constitution, approved a declaration of independence and proclaimed that a state of war existed between the Irish and English. The Irish War of Independence, which lasted until July 1921, resulted in the murders of hundreds of people, including members of the Royal Irish Constabulary (RIC), the Irish Republican Army (IRA), British Army soldiers and Irish civilians. In May 1921, Ireland was partitioned by an Act of Parliament, which created the six-county Northern Ireland polity. Opening Stormont on 22 June 1921, King George V called on 'all Irish men to pause, to stretch out the hand of forbearance and conciliation to forgive and to forget and to join in making for the land they love a new era of peace, contentment and good will'.[13] Following talks with Éamon de Valera, the Sinn Féin leader, violence was suspended by the July truce.

Lansdowne, who had recovered his health by this time, suspected that Sinn Féin intended to look efficient so as to make the Stormont government look inept.[14] In November he told Bryce that

my son [Kerry] has just been over for a few days and gives a very disquieting report – apart from breaches of the truce of which some have been flagrant, there is no such thing as law and order. Plundering goes on wholesale, and the amount of persecution that prevails is deplorable. Many poor devils can stand it no longer and are clearing out. One of the most mischievous fictions that has been circulated is the myth that the country is, for all substantial purposes, being well and peacefully administered under Sinn Fein law. It is a regime of unmitigated tyranny and there is no redress.[15]

Lansdowne worried about the protection of the southern Unionist minority. Although the Dáil debated their protection, the partition in May led to a mass exodus of southern loyalists. By December Lansdowne sensed 'we are only at the beginning of our troubles'.[16] Peace talks resulted in the signing of the Anglo-Irish Treaty on 6 December. British rule in the twenty-six counties came to an end and, one year later, the Irish Free State was born as a self-governing state with Dominion status.

When the Lords debated the Irish Free State (Agreement) Bill in March 1922, no revisions were expected. On 15 March Lansdowne urged the government to give assurances of protection of minorities and compensation for their mistreatment, and questioned whether segregation was a wise policy. 'I believe it is very much better that you should leave a certain admixture of races both in Northern Ireland and in Southern Ireland. The besetting sin of Irishmen is intolerance, and I think that by sorting them carefully and herding them together you will only make them more intolerant than ever. I am one of those who look forward to the ultimate coming together of the whole of Ireland.'[17] But, accepting it as a regrettable necessity, he advised his colleagues against rejecting the bill:

> I remain myself an unrepentant Unionist. But when you come to measures of this kind in which great questions of principle are involved, whether you are dealing with India or with Ireland, when you have gone a certain distance there is no turning back. One can only hope that out of this welter of crime and misery there may emerge a better state of things in Ireland.[18]

The bill completed all stages and received the royal assent on 31 March.

Lansdowne's final effort to influence Irish politics took place during the third reading of the Irish Free State (Constitution) Bill on 4 December 1922. He was especially anxious about the arrangements made for the Senate and protection for the southern Unionists:

> I do not suppose that I misrepresent your Lordships when I say that all of us are Two-Chamber men; that none of us believe in government in a civilised community by a Single Chamber; and I think I may add that we all of us believe that the Second Chamber should be given real and not illusory powers. If ever there was a country in which it was necessary that you should have the protection afforded by an efficient

second chamber, Ireland is that country. We who know Ireland know that it is part of the unwritten law of the Irish jungle that when the top dog gets his teeth firmly embedded in the throat of the other one, the top dog shows very little mercy. That has been the experience of Ireland, and I think it most unfortunate that in this particular matter so little care should have been taken to protect the minority which will always be a minority in Southern Ireland.[19]

Even with his reservations he would not obstruct the bill in any way, but

I will make one prediction only – a negative prediction. I feel deeply convinced that the end of the road will not be found in the Bill. The merit which I discern in it is that it will give to each of the watertight compartments into which we have unfortunately subdivided Ireland, when they have taken stock of the advantages and disadvantages that they have gained, the chance of considering whether, after all, it will not be best for the whole country that they should join hands and make it their common object to create a prosperous, efficient and contented Ireland. That is the aspiration of almost every patriotic Irishman with whom I have discussed this question. It is an aspiration which I share from the bottom of my heart.[20]

It did not happen. As Lansdowne's biographer put it,

Lansdowne's final years found no encouragement for his hope that experience of self-government in both Irish States would create a joint demand for a united Ireland. He saw the steady growth of Border restrictions, the establishment of tariffs, the rejection of conferences on common issues, and other sad proofs that the hatreds of three centuries are not easily abolished.[21]

In spring 1922 disagreement among Republicans over the Anglo-Irish Treaty escalated into civil war. In May Lansdowne told his brother Edmond about the state of his Kerry property:

No rent is being paid, it is impossible to serve leases, the office was broken into and the rentals stolen some time ago. An RC [Roman Catholic] priest was held up close to Kenmare and relieved of £15! I do not expect to see Derreen again. If the situation grows worse it will probably be burned down.[22]

Lansdowne's fear was realised, when at 1 a.m. on 2 September 1922 a gang of masked men locked Derreen's head gardener and his family in their cottage and proceeded to ransack the house. It was utterly wrecked, doors and windows torn out, floors torn up, staircase pulled down, the furniture destroyed or stolen, plantations, shrubs and rare plants wantonly destroyed. Next day the cellar was broken into and the looters carried off what they could not drink. Fortunately none of the staff was hurt. At the same time, the Republicans recaptured Kenmare, and Derreen was cut off. The house was then set on fire, the roof and remaining woodwork burned. Lansdowne felt moral outrage as much as upset,[23] but it was only a minor incident compared with 'the desperate collapse of all our hopes in Ireland'.[24] He wrote to *The Times*:

> Although there have in some places been collisions in the open between the forces of the Irish Free State and those of the Republic, it would be a misuse of the word to describe what has happened in many parts of the South-West of Ireland as in any sense 'warfare'. What is happening, and has happened, is not a conflict in the open between enemies, but the relentless and persistent persecution of a helpless minority, which is obnoxious because it is regarded as of alien origin, because it stands for law and order, because its possessions are coveted, and because it is the settled policy of the conspirators to oust it from the country.[25]

While war had descended on Ireland, England was facing high unemployment, a rising cost of living, a shortage of houses and union-organised strikes. It was a time of anger and anguish. Lansdowne did not enter the controversy over coalition government spending but 'those who plead for economy in these days must expect to be told that they are forcing an open door'. Of course, then as now, 'Economy in the abstract is universally popular' whereas government cuts were the opposite.

> If, however, wars continue, famine will spread, and the cost of the Army and Navy will be more than taxpayers can support. The burden of taxation is already dangerously high. It is to public economy (that is to say to Government) that we must look as the only means of relief. While the war was in progress extravagance had its own way. Things could not be otherwise. There was no time for bargaining or for counting the cost; the war had to be won. Spending departments grew up like mushrooms. It was their business, not so much to regulate and to criticise as to produce results, no matter by what means or at what cost.[26]

Lansdowne believed the Chancellor had a huge task in debt reduction, restoration of the currency and relieving the country of burdens that every class of the community found intolerable. He believed Britain should avoid ambitious ventures, notably commitments abroad. Britain could not afford to act as fairy godmother, and 'Disentanglement should be the watchword'.[27]

On the international stage Lansdowne was a supporter of the League of Nations, which held its first council meeting in Paris on 16 January 1920, six days after the Versailles Treaty came into force. Although he predicted that further wars would be fought, he hoped the machinery of conciliation built into the League of Nations would lessen the likelihood of conflict. Lansdowne's final published article was in *St Martin's Review* on 11 November 1923 – a special armistice issue. He warned,

> Beyond the present turmoil by which all Europe is affected there looms the spectre of a new war of which nothing can be said confidently, except that its horrors, intensified by human ingenuity, will exceed even those of the great conflict we have barely survived. What then is the great lesson which the world has to learn from Christianity at this moment – surely the lesson that the one thing needful is more unselfishness in our conduct. A great beginning has been made in the setting up of the Covenant of the League of Nations. I was one of the first to express my profound belief in the principles of the League, and nothing has happened to shake my faith. We have at any rate now got something which, if it had existed in 1914, might have saved the world from the calamity which then befell it. The existence of a League of Nations in the Autumn of that year would at any rate have given the friends of peace, and we now know how many of those there were, time in which to mobilise their forces.[28]

Although the onset of the Second World War proved the League a failure in the prevention of world wars, the concept re-emerged after that war in the stronger and more comprehensive form of the United Nations, which was more successful in meeting people's hopes and expectations of international involvement in global security.

After the worst of the Irish troubles had ended, the Lansdownes considered the country safe to return to. In September 1923, Lansdowne was making plans for rebuilding his house and garden.[29] Tim Healy, Governor-General of the Irish Free State, said military protection would be provided for reconstruction; Paddy O'Daly, GOC Kerry command considered Lansdowne could safely visit.[30] Lansdowne returned with Maud in June 1924 and, as Maud reported, looked quite young again after catching an 18lb salmon.[31] But, as he told his brother Edmond, Lansdowne was deeply disappointed:

> the journey is in many ways a melancholy one, the shells of the old RIC barracks are not enlivening – one of them just outside the gates – two fine

woods which I had successfully nursed and protected are mangled past recognition – of the house at Derreen I do not dare to write.[32]

Using local carpenters and craftsmen, the house and garden were rebuilt rapidly, the contractor promising to have the roof on within months. He was as good as his word, and in spring 1925 Maud was able to supervise the interior decoration of the house. The following June the Lansdownes settled in, staying until the end of September. Lansdowne remarked,

the country had lost nothing of its charm but after all that had happened the place could never be quite the same, and alas! We too are not what we were. But it is a joy to be home again.[33]

Although Lansdowne was now very infirm, he was able to move around in a bath chair with the assistance of a nurse.[34] During his visit he fished and admired his garden and trees. But much to their dismay the Lansdownes discovered that the newly built house was infected with dry rot. Lansdowne reasoned that 'it looks to me as if the only real solution would be to get the house burned out again – neglectful treatment of the sodden ruins, followed by the use of bad building materials, is I fancy the sum and substance of the indictment'.[35] He began remedial work immediately.

In 1926 Lansdowne and Maud returned to Derreen to find the dry rot removed. Now aged eighty-one, Lansdowne imagined it would be his last visit.[36] It was. On 1 June 1927 he and Maud set off from Bowood, reaching Newton Anmer House, his daughter Bertie's home in Clonmel, Ireland, the following morning. Cosseted by Bertie and her family, he was wonderfully well and hardly tired. But on 3 June he fainted and became very sick; doctors diagnosed an aneurysm of the lung artery. His death that evening, as Maud later noted, was 'most beautiful and painless – just what he wanted, he did not want to go on living, and told me he hoped for a sudden death, he got both his wishes'.[37]

As he wished, Lansdowne was buried in a simple plot at Christ Church, Derry Hill, a village on the edge of the Park at Bowood, for the welfare of which he had done much. Condolences came from friends and politicians, and even from opponents such as William O'Brien.[38] In the House of Lords, Salisbury, Haldane, Beauchamp and Lambourne paid tribute to his career. Lambourne, the peer who had known Lansdowne longest, called him 'a great gentleman, and above all a great Christian, one whom it is an honour to have known and one who leaves behind him in this House a feeling of love and respect which it will be difficult ever to equal'.[39] Haldane's judgement was that he stood for the type of the perfect English gentleman. He was singularly modest and he was also singularly courageous. He was a very wise man. He looked at both sides of every question and he never allowed partisanship to influence him beyond a proper point. As time went on, he became, perhaps, less associated with those with whom he had at one time been associated. That was not because Lord Lansdowne had changed but because the world was moving along. A Whig he was to the end of time, the old type of Whig, and when the times changed he found himself naturally associated with a certain form of Conservatism. Lord Lansdowne was one of those rare figures – they are very rare – who come just at times and make us better by their presence when they are amongst us.[40]

Maud outlived Lansdowne by five years. Soon after the funeral she returned to Derreen and reflected, 'I feel him, I hear him, I see him at every corner of the place, and still feel the most dreadful longing to have him back again.'[41]

42

CONCLUSION: A LIFE OF SERVICE

LANSDOWNE'S OBITUARY IN *The Times* was typical of the notices after his death.[1] He was described as a great noble, the bearer of historic titles who carried the Whig tradition of statesmanship into the twentieth century when the virtual monopoly of the great offices of state by a few noble families had been long since swept away by the advance of democracy. A singularly high ideal of patriotism and of the duties of his rank prompted him to accept the toil and responsibility of office in place of the life of cultivated ease and enjoyment which he might have chosen. While the ink was still drying on such notices, however, Lansdowne's name was already forgotten by the British public. As his 1929 biographer admitted, his merits were largely unrecognised.[2]

The obituaries overflow with polite character assessments but fail to capture any sense of Lansdowne's impact in making the history of his time. This was the price of taking an unpopular course, and memories of the 'Peace Letter' were still fresh in people's minds. It is ironic, of course, that by taking this courageous path he had had the most effect on the history of his time. As his whole career demonstrates, Lansdowne was never afraid of taking tough decisions or of their repercussions as long as he consciously satisfied his own values and Whig principles.

Lansdowne got into politics not simply because his Whig forebears had done so, but because he had a genuine concern for the future of Britain and the Empire, which were threatened by the impersonal forces of history. Lansdowne's education and upbringing impressed on him the need for a secure Empire and a settled pattern in international relations. His political philosophy was built on a desire to make the world around him a better place and preserve the values that he believed in. These values were not simply based on theory but came from personal experience. With the rise of the British middle class, nationalism and competitive global economies, Lansdowne found his own way of life and class under attack. As a Whig aristocrat, Lansdowne was far more accommodating to change than many of his contemporaries, such as Salisbury and Balfour, but on Ireland and the Act of Union, the protection of property and the House of Lords, institutions he valued, he was willing to fight a lifelong struggle.

It is a tribute to his tenacity, political skill and integrity that even his strongest opponents recognised his contribution in these fields. William O'Brien, who unsuccessfully attempted to damage Lansdowne's reputation during the Irish Land War, later praised him as a chivalrous befriender of the Irish cause. It was Lansdowne's wish that Ireland would remain one country and part of the Union. So strongly did he feel on this issue that in 1886 he left the Liberal Party and in 1895 joined the Unionists. Even after Ireland was partitioned by the Liberal Unionist Coalition government of 1920, he hoped that the experience of self-government in the South and the North would result in renewed enthusiasm for a united Ireland. Although his hope now seems unlikely ever to be realised, Lansdowne's commitment to a just settlement for both sides still rings true today.

As with Ireland and the Act of Union, so with the House of Lords, Lansdowne devoted his energy to resisting the forces of change within and without, driven by his concern about the radical tyranny of single-Chamber government. It is ironic that his stand over the People's Budget and the Parliament Bill hastened the Lords' emasculation. In 1911 the power of the Lords as a coordinate member of the legislative was broken, and it never recovered. To blame Lansdowne alone would be ridiculous, but it cannot be denied that his decision to reject the Budget for constitutional reasons was a disastrous error. In the struggle that ensued, his leadership of the House was damaged, but so great was Lansdowne's personal popularity and confidence among his peers while he was Leader in the House for thirteen years that even one of the most outspoken diehards, Lord Selborne, later remarked that Lansdowne had some vision and that he liked and respected him greatly.

If Ireland and the House of Lords were the concerns that carried Lansdowne into public life and sustained him there, they were not his greatest achievements. He occupied what were then the two most important diplomatic posts outside Britain and the two key cabinet posts. Lansdowne was Governor-General of Canada during a turbulent period, when John Macdonald's government faced allegations of corruption over the Canadian Pacific Railway and the economy was entering a recession. The North-West Rebellion of 1885 and the deadlock over fishing rights between Canada and the United States added to the political instability. That Macdonald later remarked that Lansdowne was one of the most perspicacious of the Governors he knew during his nineteen years as Prime Minister was testament to Lansdowne's success in Canada. Likewise, in India, Lansdowne's administration was a success. He strengthened the frontiers of the country against perceived and real threats, and introduced ideas of election and representation to open up the national political arena to Indians. However, his administration suffered grave interference from the growing power of the House of Commons to legislate on Indian affairs, and many of his Whig ideals on social reform had to be surrendered. Queen Victoria offered him a dukedom for his service in India. His refusal was an example of pragmatism rather than self-denial. For all his perceived wealth, he could not afford it.

As Secretary of State for War in Salisbury's 1895 administration, Lansdowne has been accused of weakness. In fact, no part of his legacy has been more widely condemned than his administration of the War Office and the Boer War. Such criticism fails to acknowledge that Lansdowne's decisions were not made in a vacuum, but in consultation with and guided by his military advisers and the cabinet. Under the system of responsible government and the nature of the constitution, the balance of civil and military relations favoured the civilians and Lansdowne could not shake off the political and bureaucratic constraints he inherited. But he was not a mere prisoner of circumstances. Even with the limitations imposed on him, he pushed through subtle reforms that helped to prepare for Haldane, the Liberal Secretary of State for War, and his later, more wholesale, restructuring of the Army and subsequent deployment of the British Expeditionary Force and the Territorial Army during the First World War.

Nowhere did Lansdowne's political nous, practical sense and social standing bring him greater success than at the Foreign Office. His Whig aristocratic values and unemotional approach to foreign policy meant that he felt no affinity for or animus against the various Powers. Flexible, ready to adapt to circumstances, Lansdowne allowed his decisions to be influenced by the logic of developments. Cool in any crisis, he steered clear of war and brought level-headedness to the fractious arena of European politics. Achieving security for Britain's imperial position, Lansdowne formed the special relationship with the United States by recognising their supremacy in Western waters; in concluding the Anglo-Japanese Alliance, he improved security against Russia and relieved pressure on the Royal Navy in the Far East; and, by signing the Entente Cordiale with France, he settled old colonial differences. Lansdowne appreciated that the need to end Britain's isolation would propel her further into European affairs. But he underestimated the long-term consequences of his policy, most notably for Germany. However, the increasing isolation and hardening of Germany after 1905 were not part of Lansdowne's design for the balance of power in Europe.

Lansdowne, as a representative of his class, period and party, epitomised many aspects of late Victorian and Edwardian politics. However, his French appearance and grace combined with his old-fashioned British courtesy distanced him from many of his contemporaries. Cutting his teeth and honing his political skills in the refined atmosphere of House of Lords, he lacked the contempt for opponents typical of his contemporaries in the House of Commons. Had he been a more pushy and less modest man, he might have attained the highest office. Utterly selfless, perfectly genial and with a thoroughly well-balanced mind, he was not without ambition. But his ambition was completely under the control of his judgement. His altruism, which in public life manifested itself as moderation, showed itself in private as genuine kindliness of nature. It was entirely in keeping with his character that he preferred a simple burial in the local churchyard than a grand sculpted tomb in the family mausoleum designed by Robert Adam at Bowood. A cynic might argue that it is much easier for those at the top, cushioned by wealth, rank and patronage, to break with tradition, but in Lansdowne's case he was proud of his lineage and position and never hid from it. His decision was entirely noble. He was, as a Whig, as comfortable among normal people as among the exalted.

Outside politics, Lansdowne's other passions in life were his family and the outdoors. Lansdowne was the adored central figure of an affectionate family circle. His marriage to Maud was a constant source of happiness. The death of his youngest son Charlie in 1914 nearly broke his heart and the suffering he experienced was never properly acknowledged. He left the estates at Bowood, Meikleour and Derreen in good working condition and largely unburdened by debt. Any claims that he exhibited an aloofness and disinterestedness that was supposed to go with independent fortune should be dismissed. To pay off his inherited debts he spent most of his life worrying about money and selling land and chattels. Under his will, Maud and his surviving children were well provided for. However, the ongoing exorbitant costs of maintaining the estates forced the 6th Marquess to sell Lansdowne House and its 4-acre garden in Berkeley Square in 1929. The break-up of Robert Adam's London masterpiece can be seen as a metaphor for the passing of one of the great Whig houses. In memory of his father, the 6th Marquess presented Salvator Rosa's painting *Philosophy* to the National Gallery in London. The Latin inscription included in the painting, when translated, reads: 'Be quiet, unless your speech be better than silence'.

Lansdowne wrote his famous 'Peace Letter' because he could no longer keep quiet. He feared that the First World War would spell ruin to the civilised world and add to the load of human suffering. In his letter Lansdowne should be credited with being the first senior British statesman to publicly call for a revision of Allied war aims, to bring a negotiated peace nearer and by that produce collective security for future generations. Such a display of courage was natural to Lansdowne, who had spent a lifetime doing the right thing irrespective of himself. Although Allied victory seemed inevitable, no one in 1917 could predict when such a moment might come. Some estimated it would not be before 1920. His intervention must be seen in this light. We cannot know whether a negotiated peace during the winter of 1917 might have been possible, but would not a peace settlement at that point have been better than another year of misery and unnecessary tragedy inflicted upon millions of people, followed by the collapse of the German economy, the rise to power of Hitler and another horrifying war? The First World War was decisive in shaping the structures of modern politics. Lansdowne's letter played a meaningful part in the failed attempts at compromise. His letter has something to say to all ages, not just his own. It is as relevant today as it was then.

Lansdowne's unsuccessful appeal for lasting peace in 1917, also marked the end of political Whig influence, such as it then was. What was a libertarian tradition, pitted against extremism of all kinds, ended with an honourable but useless appeal for moderation. He was the last and most typical of his generation of great Whig figures. As a statesman and a representative of his class he also illustrated perfectly the challenges of British politics from the late Victorian period through to the interwar years. It is fitting to bring Lansdowne out of obscurity.

ABBREVIATIONS

BC, Lans (4), EL – Papers of Emily 4th Marchioness of Lansdowne at Bowood House

BC, EFm – Papers of Lord Edmond Fitzmaurice at Bowood House

BC, FL – Papers of Georgiana Dowager Marchioness of La Valette at Bowood House

BC, Lans (5) – Papers of the 5th Marquess of Lansdowne at Bowood House

BC, Lans (5), ML – Papers of the 5th Marchioness of Lansdowne at Bowood House

BC, Lans (5), ED – Papers of Everard Digby at Bowood House

BC, Lans (6) – Papers of the 6th Marquess of Lansdowne at Bowood House

BC, Lans, IE – Papers regarding the Lansdowne Irish Estates at Bowood House

BC, Lans, BE – Papers regarding the Bowood Estate at Bowood House

BL – British Library

BL 88906 – Bowood Papers of the Lansdowne Family c.1700–1930 of the Western Manuscripts Collection at the British Library

CAB – Cabinet Office Files at the National Archives, Kew

FO – Foreign Office Papers at the National Archives, Kew

GVD – King George V's Diary at the Royal Archives, Windsor

MS. Eng. hist. – Manuscripts of English History at the Bodleian Library

Mss. Eur. – Private papers (European Manuscripts) of the OIOC at the BL

Mss. Eur. D558 – 5th Marquess of Lansdowne's papers of the OIOC at the BL

NG – National Gallery, London

OIOC – Oriental and India Office Collection at the BL

PRO – Public Record Office at Kew (The PRO is now known as The National Archives)

PRONI – Public Record Office of Northern Ireland at Belfast

PP – Parliamentary Papers

QVJ – Queen Victoria's Diary at the Royal Archives, Windsor

RA – Royal Archives at Windsor Castle

RC – Royal Commission

BIBLIOGRAPHY

ARCHIVAL SOURCES

Lord Astor of Hever Collection
Minto Papers

Balliol College, Oxford
Jowett, Benjamin
Morier, Sir Robert

The Baring Archive, ING Bank, London
Revelstoke, 2nd Baron

Birmingham University Library, Special Collections
Chamberlain, Austen
Chamberlain, Joseph

Bodleian Library, Oxford
Asquith, 1st Earl of Oxford and
Asquith, 1st Countess of Oxford and
Birrell, Sir Augustine
Bryce, 1st Viscount
Dawson, Geoffrey
Forrest, George William
Fraser, Sir John Malcolm
Harcourt, Sir William Vernon
Hirst, Francis Wrigley
Kimberley, 1st Earl
Lincolnshire, 1st Marquess
MacDonnell, 1st Baron
Milner, 1st Viscount
Monk Bretton, 2nd Baron
Monson, Sir Edmund
Ponsonby of Shulbrede, 1st Baron
Sandars, John Satterfield
Selborne, 2nd Earl
Selborne, 3rd Earl
Simon, 1st Viscount

Bowood Collection, Bowood House (by kind permission of the Marquess of Lansdowne)
Bowood Estate
Digby, Everard
Fitzmaurice, Lord Edmond
Lansdowne, 4th Marchioness
Lansdowne, 4th Marquess
Lansdowne, 5th Marchioness
Lansdowne, 5th Marquess
Lansdowne, 6th Marquess
Lansdowne Estates in Ireland

British Library, Oriental and India Office Collections of the African and Asian Department
Brackenbury, General Sir Henry
Cross, 1st Viscount
Curzon, 1st Marquess
Durand, Sir Henry Mortimer
Elgin, 9th Earl
Grant Duff, Sir Mountstuart
Hamilton, Lord George
Harris, 4th Baron
Ilbert, Sir Courtenay Peregrine
Kimberley, 1st Earl
Lansdowne, 5th Marquess
Lyall, Sir Alfred Comyn
Northbrook, 1st Earl
Reay, 11th Lord
Wenlock, 3rd Baron
White, Field Marshal Sir George
Younghusband, Sir Francis Edward

British Library, Western Manuscripts Department
Arnold-Forster, Hugh Oakeley
Balfour, 1st Earl
Bertie, 1st Viscount
Campbell-Bannerman, Henry
Cecil of Chelwood, 1st Viscount
Cross, 1st Viscount
Dilke, Charles Wentworth

Gladstone, William Ewart
Hamilton, Sir Edward Walter
Lansdowne, 5th Marquess
Long, 1st Viscount
Nightingale, Florence
Ponsonby, Sir Henry Frederick
Scott, Sir Charles
Strachey, John St Loe
Wilkinson, Henry Spenser

British Library, National Sound Archive
Lyttleton, Lady Moira

British Library, Newspaper Archive
Various publications

British Red Cross Museum and Archives, London
Wantage, 1st Baron
Miscellaneous papers

Cambridge University Library Manuscripts
Crewe, 1st Marquess
Hardinge of Penshurst, 1st Baron

Centre Historique des Archives Nationales, Paris
de Flahaut, Charles

Churchill College Archive Centre, Cambridge
Amery, Leo
Churchill, Sir Winston
McKenna, Reginald
Spring Rice, Sir Cecil

Devon Record Office
Buller, General Sir Redvers
Fortescue Family of Castle Hill

The Devonshire Collection, Chatsworth House (by kind permission of the Duke of Devonshire)
Devonshire, 8th Duke
Devonshire, 9th Duke

David M. Rubenstein Rare Book & Manuscript Library, Duke University, North Carolina
Wolseley, 1st Viscount

Eton College Library
Miscellaneous Papers

Gloucestershire Record Office
St Aldwyn, 1st Earl

Hatfield Library, Hatfield House (by kind permission of Lord Salisbury)
Salisbury, 3rd Marquess
Salisbury, 4th Marquess

Hertfordshire Archives
Desborough, 1st Baron
Lytton, 1st Earl

Hove Central Library, Special Collections
Wolseley, 1st Viscount

King's College London, Liddell Hart Centre for Military Archives
Maurice, Major-General Sir
  Frederick Barton

Library and Archives Canada, Ottawa
Griffin, May Elizabeth
Irvine, Matthew Bell
Traill family

Liverpool City Council,
Liverpool Record Office
Derby, 15th Earl

London Metropolitan Archives
Maycock Collection

National Archives of Ireland,
Dublin
Wolseley, 1st Viscount

National Army Museum,
Templer Study Centre, London
Roberts, 1st Earl

National Gallery of Art Archive,
London
Lansdowne, 5th Marquess
Board of Trustees Meeting Minutes

National Library of Scotland
Haldane, 1st Viscount
Minto, 4th Earl
Rosebery, 5th Earl

Österreichisches Staatsarchiv
Mensdorff, Count

Parliamentary Archives
Ashbourne, 1st Baron
Bonar Law, Andrew
Ilbert, Sir Courtenay Peregrine
Lloyd George, 1st Earl
Willoughby de Broke, 19th Baron
Political Journal Papers

Public Record Office, Kew
Cabinet Records (CAB)
CAB 9 Colonial Defence Committee
and Committee of Imperial
Defence and Colonial Defence
Committee
CAB 11 Colonial Defence

Committee and Committee of
Imperial Defence and Colonial
Defence Committee. Defence
Schemes
CAB 37 Photographic Copies of
Cabinet Letters
CAB 41 Photographic Copies of
Cabinet Letters in the Royal
Archives

War Office (WO)
WO 24 Establishment War Office
WO 32 Registered files of the War
Office dealing with all aspects
of the administration of the
departments and the armed forces
WO 33 Confidential printed reports
and memoranda dealing with all
aspects of the administration of
the departments of the armed
forces
WO 105 Field Marshal Lord Roberts
WO 106 Directorate of Military
Operations and Military
Intelligence
WO 108 South Africa
correspondence
WO 132 General Sir Redvers Buller
WO 163 War Office Council, later
War Office Consultative Council,
Army Council, Army Board and
their various committees

Foreign Office (FO)
FO 17 China correspondence
FO 32 Greece correspondence
FO 72 Spain correspondence
FO 633 Evelyn Baring, 1st Earl of
Cromer
FO 800 Private Office Papers of
Secretaries of State between 1900
and 1935 and of many Under-
Secretaries of State from 1886

Treasury (T)

T1 Original Board of Treasury correspondence and letters to the Treasury

T2 Brief entries of Treasury letters and papers, their subject matter, date and disposal

T3 The Skeleton Registers

Colonial Office (CO)

CO 179 Despatches (letters of the Governors), Offices (letters of Government Departments) and Individuals

CO 417 High Commission for South Africa correspondence

CO 537 Secret despatches and telegrams

CO 694 Registers of secret correspondence

CO 879 Africa correspondence

Domestic Records

Ardagh, Major-General Sir John Charles

Cardwell, 1st Viscount

Granville, 2nd Earl

Kitchener of Khartoum, 1st Earl

Midleton, 1st Earl

Public Record Office of Northern Ireland

Bury, Charles Kenneth Howard

Londonderry, 6th Marquess

Rothschild Archive, London

Rothschild, Alfred Charles de

Rothschild, Nathan Mayer

Royal Archives, Windsor Castle

King Edward VII

King George V

Queen Victoria

Royal United Services Institute Library

Miscellaneous Papers

School of Oriental and Asian Studies Library, London

Durand, Sir Henry Mortimer

Shropshire County Council

Bridgeman, 1st Viscount

Surrey History Centre, Surrey

Onslow, 4th Earl

United States Library of Congress, Washington

Choate, Joseph Hodges

Frewen, Moreton

Wiltshire and Swindon Record Office, Wiltshire

Long, 1st Viscount

Money-Kyrle family

Storey-Maskelyne family

Online Collections

Edgar Dewdney, The Glenbow Archives: www.glenbow.org/collections

William Henry Fox Talbot, The Correspondence of William Henry Fox Talbot Project: foxtalbot.dmu.ac.uk

SECONDARY SOURCES

Details of secondary sources are given in the relevant footnotes.

ILLUSTRATION CREDITS

1, 2, 3, 4, 5, 6, 7, 8, 9, 10, 11, 12, 13, 14, 15, 16, 18, 19, 20, 21, 22, 23, 24, 25, 26, 27, 29, 30, 31, 32, 33, 34, 36, 37, 38, 39, 41, 42, 48, 49, 50, 51, 53, 54, 55, 56, 60, 63, 64, 67, 69, 70 from the Bowood Collection. Reproduced with permission.

40, 44 from the Derreen Collection. Reproduced with permission.

71 from the Meikleour Collection. Reproduced with permission.

65 © The Keasbury-Gordon Photographic Archive.

28, 68 Classic Images/Alamy Stock Photo.

52, 57, 58, 59, 61, 62 photographed by Marcus Dawkins in 1914. Reproduced with permission of Mike Hardy.

17 © The British Library Board (Maps.70619.(2)).

35 © The British Library Board (Maps.32.a.49).

43 © The British Library Board (T00027-42, 12332.ff. 15).

45, 46, 47 reproduced with permission of Punch Ltd.

66 from the Collection of the National Gallery of Art, Washington DC.

ENDNOTES

Chapter 1: Early Life and School

1   The name 'Whig' was originally a term of abuse used for Scottish Presbyterians in the seventeenth century. It appears to be a shortened form of 'whiggamor' (cattle driver).

2   So called from Gerald FitzWalter, the Castellan of Windsor under William I, whose son Maurice participated in the Norman invasion of Ireland in 1169.

3   Or eighteen; sources disagree.

4   P.G. Dale, *Sir William Petty of Romsey* (Romsey 1987), p. 58.

5   J. Swift, *A Journal to Stella*, quoted in 6th Marquess of Lansdowne, *Glanerought and the Petty-Fitzmaurices* (London 1937), p. 225.

6   Punch, vol. 33 (Oct. 1857), p. 144.

7   F. de Bernardy, *Son of Talleyrand: The Life of Comte Charles de Flahaut, 1785–1870* (London 1956), p. 251.

8   Holland House papers, 52156, f. 37, 13 Mar. 1845.

9   G. Lyster (ed.), *A Family Chronicle, derived from notes and letters selected by Barbarina, the Hon. Lady Grey* (London 1908), p. 243.

10   BL 88906/12/1, 2 Jul. 1857.

11   Ibid., 25 Mar. 1858.

12   BC, Lans (4), EL, n.d. [*c*.1858].

13   The future Prime Minister.

14   A fag was required to act as a personal servant, running errands and doing chores, for a senior boy.

15   BC, Lans (4), EL, n.d. [1859].

16   BL 88906/12/1, 13 Dec. 1861.

17   Ibid., 11 Apr. 1862.

18   Ibid., Aug. 1862.

19   BC, Lans (4), EL, undated, 1861.

20   *The Gentleman's Magazine*, vol. 235 (Oct. 1874), p. 443.

21   BL 88906/20/9, 17 Nov. 1868.

22   BC, Lans (4), EL, 4 Apr. 1892.

23   T. Card, *Eton Renewed: A History from 1860 to the Present Day* (London 1994), p. 20. Although there is some difference of opinion as to the origin of the name 'check nights', one explanation is that rowing faults were checked and another that the boys wore checked shirts on such occasions.

24   BL 88906/12/1, 3 Sep. 1862.

25   Choate papers, 15768 box 15, 21 Oct. 1904.

26   BC, Lans (4), EL, 17 Jul. 1862.

27   BL 88906/20/9, 2 Jan. 1876.

28   Lord Newton, *Lord Lansdowne: A Biography* (London 1929), p. 6.

Chapter 2: Oxford

1   BC, FL, 17 Feb. 1863.
2   Ibid.
3   Fox Talbot papers, 21742/8672.
4   BC, Lans (4), EL, 19 Oct. 1863.
5   BC, Lans (4), EL, 17 Oct. 1863.
6   BC, Lans (4), EL, Oct. 1863.
7   BC, Lans (4), EL, 8 Nov. 1863.
8   BC, Lans (4), EL, 6 Oct. 1893.
9   Nightingale papers, 45785, f. 179, 14 Dec. 1891.
10 BC, Lans (4), EL, 1 May 1864.
11 The Torpids is the Oxford Easter-term boat race between Second Eight rowing boats.
12 BC, Lans (4), EL, 14 Feb. 1864.
13 BC, Lans (4), EL, 5 Nov. 1864.
14 Ibid.
15 D.R. Barker, *Prominent Edwardians* (London 1969), p. 144.
16 Ibid.
17 BL 88906/20/9, 7 Aug. 1865.
18 BC, Lans (4), EL, 1 Mar. 1866.
19 Newton, *Lansdowne*, pp. 506–11.
20 BC, Lans (4), EL, 2 Aug. 1884.
21 J. Bateman, *The Acre-ocracy of England. A list of all owners of three thousand acres and upwards, with their possession and incomes arranged under their various counties and also their colleges and clubs* (London 1876), p. 259.
22 BL 88906/20/9, 9 Jul. 1866.
23 BC, Lans (4), EL, 30 Oct. 1866.
24 BL 88906/20/9, 2 Apr. 1867.
25 BC, Lans (4), EL, 28 Jul. 1867.
26 Jowett papers, II/N/163, 15 Sep. 1867.
27 BC, Lans (4), EL, 28 Nov. 1867.
28 BC, Lans (4), EL, 8 Dec. 1867.
29 BL 88906/20/9, 15–22 Jan. 1868.

Chapter 3: A Year Off

1   BC, Lans (4), EL, 8 Jun. 1873.
2   BC, Lans (4), EL, 27 May 1873.
3   The present-day monetary values are approximately fifty times what they were then.
4   BC, Lans (4), EL, 11 Nov. 1882.
5   BC, Lans (4), EL, 28 Jul. 1883.
6   BC, Lans (4), EL, 5 Jan. 1888.
7   BC, Lans (4), EL, 23 Mar. 1890.

8   BC, Lans (4), EL, 7 Apr. 1893.

9   BC, Lans (4), EL, 31 Jan. 1893.

10   BC, Lans (4), EL, 21 Aug. 1887.

11   BC, Lans (4), EL, 8 Dec. 1887.

12   BC, Lans (4), EL, 14 Oct. 1889.

13   Ibid.

14   BC, Lans (4), EL, 7 Apr. 1893.

15   BC, Lans (4), EL, 9 Feb. 1886.

16   BC, Lans (4), EL, 31 Jul. 1879.

17   BC, Lans (4), EL, 27 Jul. 1894.

18   BC, Lans (4), EL, 30 Oct. 1893.

19   BC, Lans (4), EL, 9 Feb. 1886.

20   It is interesting, however, that with the exception of his sale of
     Rembrandt's painting *The Mill* in 1911 to the Widener family in
     Pennsylvania, public attention was largely uninterested in his financial
     affairs.

21   Hansard 3, vol. 190, c. 689.

22   BC, Lans (4), EL, 27 Feb. 1868.

23   M. Parsons (ed.), *Alice Catherine Miles. Every Girl's Duty: The Diary of a
     Victorian Debutante* (London 1992), p. 14.

24   Ibid., p. 23.

25   BC, Lans (4), EL, 5 Nov. 1868.

26   D. Seward, *Eugénie: The Empress and her Empire* (Stroud 2004), p. 64.

27   BC, Lans (4), EL, 19 Nov. 1868.

28   D. Seward, *Eugénie*, p. 65.

29   BC, Lans (4), EL, 19 Nov. 1868.

30   Ibid.

31   Holland House papers, 52155, f. 83, 27 Dec. 1868.

32   Ibid.

33   BC, Lans (4), EL, 22 Nov. 1868.

34   BC, Lans (4), EL, 19 Nov. 1868.

Chapter 4: Getting Started

1   BC, Lans (4), EL, 20 Sep. 1868.

2   BC, Lans (4), EL, 3 Oct. 1870.

3   6th Marquess of Lansdowne, *Glanerought*, p. 136.

4   BC, Lans (5), ED, 6 Jun. 1890.

5   BC, Lans, BE, 11 Sep. 1868.

6   BC, Lans (4), EL, 20 Sep. 1868.

7   BC, Lans (4), EL, 20 Oct. 1868.

8   M.E. Griffin papers, MG30-D37 (reel A-1086), 12 Dec. 1900.

9   BL 88906/20/9, 17 Nov. 1868.

10   The Glorious Revolution of 1688–89 replaced King James II with

the joint monarchy of his Protestant daughter Mary and her Dutch husband, William of Orange. The revolution was largely bloodless and it established the supremacy of Parliament over the Crown, setting Britain on the path towards constitutional monarchy and parliamentary democracy. The causes of the revolution were as much religious as political. Restoration England was afflicted by religious conflict. In the 1670s and 80s public fear of 'popery' in England escalated. Against such a Catholic tyranny and fearing the danger posed to the Protestant succession and the Anglican establishment, seven peers wrote to William on 30 June 1688, pledging their support to the Prince if he brought a force into England against James. With an armada four times the size of that launched by the Spanish in 1588, William landed at Torbay on 5 November 1688. In declining health and with notable betrayals among his close circle, James fled the country.

11   H. Macmillan, *The Past Masters: Politics and Politicians 1906–1939* (London 1975), p. 186.

12   L.G. Mitchell, 'The Whigs, People and Reform', *Proceedings of the British Academy*, eds T.C.W. Blanning and P. Wende, 100 (1999), p. 29.

13   Ibid., p. 34.

14   L.G. Mitchell, *The Whig World: 1760–1837* (London 2005), p. 178.

15   Ibid., p. 29.

16   D. Cannadine, *The Decline and Fall of the British Aristocracy* (London 1996), p. 507.

17   R. Douglas, 'The Riddle of the Whigs', *The Times Higher Education Supplement*, 10 Jun. 1988, p. 29.

18   Ibid., p. 505.

19   W. Bagehot, *The National Review*, vol. 1, no. 2 (1855), p. 262.

20   Ibid., p. 184.

21   L.G. Mitchell, *The Whig World*, p. 5.

22   A. Sykes, *The Rise and Fall of British Liberalism, 1776–1988* (London 1997), p. 108.

23   BL 88906/21/3, 20 Dec. 1868.

24   M.A. Patchett (ed.), *The Life and Letters of the Right Hon. Robert Lowe, 1st Viscount Sherbrooke* (London 1893), p. 360.

25   BL 88906/21/4, 25 Nov. 1868.

26   BC, Lans (4), EL, 27 Mar. 1870.

27   BC, Lans (4), EL, 21 May 1870.

28   BL 88906/20/9, 11 Mar. 1869.

29   BL 88906/12/5/3, 24 Nov. 1883.

30   Holland House papers, 52155, f. 90, 26 Oct. 1869.

31   BC, Lans (4), EL, 9 Nov. 1869.

32   *The Devizes and Wiltshire Gazette*, 11 Nov. 1869.

33   BC, Lans (4), EL, 8 Nov. 1869.

34 BL 88906/19/14, 21 Nov. 1869.

35 BC, Lans (4), EL, 8 Nov. 1869.

36 Fox Talbot papers, 9574, 19 Sep. 1869.

37 BC, Lans (4), EL, 20 Mar. 1870.

38 Jowett papers, IV/N/351, 16 Mar. 1872.

39 BC, Lans (4), EL, 24 Apr. 1872.

40 Ibid.

41 E.M. Spiers, *The Army and Society, 1815–1914* (London 1980), p. 178.

42 Ibid., p. 179.

43 BC, Lans (4), EL, 24 Apr. 1872.

44 Jowett papers, IF/2/30, 27 Apr. 1872.

45 BC, Lans (4), EL, 24 Apr. 1872.

46 BL 88906/13/6, 1873.

47 Ibid., 29 Jan. 1874.

48 BC, Lans (4), EL, 20 Nov. 1872.

49 Jowett papers, V/N/433, 5 Jul. 1874.

50 Jowett papers, V/N/471, 31 Dec. 1875.

51 BL 88906/20/9, 2 Jan. 1876.

52 J.R. Vincent, *The Formation of the British Liberal Party, 1857–1868* (London 1972), p. 34.

53 BC, Lans (4), EL, 20 Aug. 1892.

54 BC, Lans (4), EL, 18 Apr. 1880.

55 L. McKinstry, *Rosebery: Statesman in Turmoil* (London 2005), p. 89, n. 34.

56 BC, EFm, n.d. [*c*.1880].

Chapter 5: A Matter of Principle

1 BL 88906/20/9, 28 Jun. 1880.

2 A. Ramm (ed.), *The Political Correspondence of Mr. Gladstone and Lord Granville, 1876–1886* (Oxford 1962), vol. 1 (1876–82), p. 142.

3 BL 88906/20/9, 3 Jul. 1880.

4 Gladstone papers, 44438, f. 57, 4 Jul. 1880.

5 Ripon papers, 43626, f. 176, 7 Jul. 1880.

6 R. Douglas, *Land, People and Politics: A History of the Land Question in the United Kingdom, 1878–1952* (London 1976), p. 50.

7 RA VIC/QVJ, 9 Jul. 1880.

8 RA VIC/D29/24, 9 Jul. 1880.

9 RA VIC/D29/26, 10 Jul. 1880.

10 A. Adonis, 'Fitzmaurice, Henry Charles Keith Petty-, fifth marquess of Lansdowne (1845–1927)' in *Oxford Dictionary of National Biography*, eds H.C.G. Matthew and B. Harrison (Oxford 2004).

11 D. Southgate, *Passing of the Whigs, 1832–1886* (London 1965), p. 372.

12 D.W.R. Bahlman (ed.), *The Diary of Sir Edward Walter Hamilton* (Oxford 1972), vol. 1 (1880–1885), p. 32.

13 The Earl of Oxford and Asquith, *Fifty Years of Parliament* (London 1926), vol. 1, p. 50.

14 I.F. Eagar, *The Nun of Kenmare* (Cork 1970), p. 93.

15 BC, Lans (4), EL, 23 Sep. 1880.

16 Ibid.

17 Ibid.

18 BC, Lans (4), EL, 11 Nov. 1880.

19 C. Russell, *New Views on Ireland, or Irish Land: Grievances: Remedies* (London 1880), p. 63.

20 BC, EFm, 14 Nov. 1880.

21 C. Russell, *New Views*, p. vi.

22 PP, 1881, XVIII, C. 2779, 'Royal Commission of Inquiry into Working of Landlord and Tenant (Ireland) Acts. Report, Digest and Minutes of Evidence, Appendices, Index', pp. 37601–3.

23 J.L. Garvin, *The Life of Joseph Chamberlain* (London 1932–34), vol. 1, p. 317.

24 BL 88906/27/2, 1 Aug. 1881; Hansard 3, vol. 264, c. 291.

25 BC, EFm, 20 Aug. 1881.

26 BC, Lans (4), EL, 8 May 1882.

27 BC, Lans (4), EL, 16 Nov. 1882.

28 Jowett papers, IF/12/30/37, 23 July 1882.

29 BL 88906/23/1, 10 Jul. 1883.

30 D.W.R. Bahlman (ed.), *Diary*, vol. 1, p. 460.

31 BL 88906/12, Aug. 1883.

32 BC, Lans (4), EL, 29 Jan. 1881.

33 Gladstone papers, 44481, f. 204, 15 Jun. 1883.

34 Rosebery papers, 10080, f. 195, 25 May 1883.

35 BC, EFm, 30 Sep. 1883.

Chapter 6: Canada – Settling In

1 BC, Lans (4), EL, 23 Oct. 1883.

2 F. Hamilton, *The Days Before Yesterday* (London 1920), p. 254.

3 Rosebery papers, 10081, f. 42, 30 Mar. 1884.

4 BC, Lans (4), EL, 26 Oct. 1883.

5 Rosebery papers, 10081, f. 42, 30 Mar. 1884.

6 C. Miller, *The Canadian Career of the Fourth Earl of Minto: The Education of a Viceroy* (Ontario 1980), p. 8.

7 Ibid., p. 194.

8 Ibid., p. 26.

9 BL 88906/19/19, 25 Nov. 1883.

10 Ibid.

11 *Blackwoods Magazine*, vol. 208, p. 613.

12 BL 88906/19/19, 25 Nov. 1883.

13 BC, Lans (4), EL, 13 Dec. 1883.
14 BC, Lans (4), EL, 9 Feb. 1884.
15 BL 88906/18/1, 11 Nov. 1883.
16 BL 88906/12/5/3, 24 Nov. 1883.
17 BC, Lans (4), EL, 4 Dec. 1883.
18 BL 88906/19/14, 21 Nov. 1869.
19 In 1846 the Oregon Treaty permanently established the 49th parallel as the boundary between the United States and British North America.
20 The previous Governor-Generals were The Viscount Monck, Lord Lisgar, The Earl of Dufferin and The Marquess of Lorne.
21 D. Creighton, *John A. Macdonald: The Old Chieftain* (Boston 1955), p. 501.
22 D. Cannadine, *Decline*, p. 588.
23 D. Creighton, *Macdonald*, p. 354.
24 BL 88906/14/1, 24 Feb. 1884.
25 BL 88906/18/1, 11 Nov. 1883.
26 Ibid.
27 C.H. Tupper, *Recollections of Sixty Years* (London 1914), p. 174.
28 The date of expiry was 1 July 1885.
29 BL 88906/14/1, 8 Dec. 1883.
30 Ibid., 2 May 1884.
31 BC, Lans (4), EL, 25 May 1884.
32 Ibid., 13 Aug. 1884.
33 Ibid., 5 Jun. 1884.
34 BL 88906/14/6, 10 Jul. 1884.
35 BL 88906/14/1, 9 Aug. 1884.
36 Ibid.
37 BC, Lans (4), EL, 9 Dec. 1884.
38 BL 88906/19/14, 30 Nov. 1884.
39 BC, Lans (4), EL, 17 Jan. 1885.
40 BL 88906/14/2, 27 Apr. 1885.

Chapter 7: The North-West

1   G.F.G. Stanley, *The Birth of Western Canada: A History of the Riel Rebellions* (Toronto 1961), p. 323.
2   Minto papers, 12550, f. 76, 10 Apr. 1885.
3   J. Mason, *The North-West Rebellion of 1885* (Toronto 1899), p. 529.
4   BC, Lans (4), EL, 26 Apr. 1885.
5   BC, Lans (4), EL, 17 May 1885.
6   BL 88906/14/7, 12 Jun. 1885.
7   D. Creighton, *Macdonald*, p. 438.
8   BL 88906/18/4, 12 Nov. 1885.
9   Minto papers, 12507, Journal, 16 Oct. 1885.
10 Minto papers, 12550, f. 74, 6 Apr. 1885.

11 G.F.G. Stanley, *Birth*, p. 378.

12 BC, Lans (4), EL, 13 Aug. 1885.

13 Lincolnshire papers, Microfilm 1137, 10 Feb. 1886.

14 Minto papers, 12378, f. 52, 8 Feb. 1886.

15 BL 88906/14/14/1, 20 Sep. 1885.

16 BC, Lans (4), EL, 1 Oct. 1885.

17 Ibid.

18 Ibid.

19 BL 88906/14/14/1, 30 Sep. 1885.

20 BC, Lans (4), EL, 1 Oct. 1885.

21 P.B. Waite, *Canada: 1874–1896: Arduous Journey* (Toronto 1971), p. 144.

22 BC, Lans (4), EL, 10 Oct. 1885.

23 5th Marquess of Lansdowne, *Canadian North-West and British Columbia: Two Speeches* (Ottawa 1886).

Chapter 8: A Tempting Offer

1 Rosebery papers, 10085, f. 83, 22 Feb. 1885.

2 BC, EFm, 8 Mar. 1886.

3 BL 88906/14/3, 2 Apr. 1886.

4 Minto papers, 12378, f. 56, 6 Apr. 1886.

5 BL 88906/14/3, 11 May 1886.

6 BL 88906/14/3, 13 May 1886.

7 Ibid.

8 Ibid., 18 May 1886.

9 BC, Lans (4), EL, 7 Mar. 1885.

10 BL 88906/14/3, 5 Sep. 1886.

11 Minto papers, 12378, f. 66, 28 Aug. 1886.

12 BC, Lans (4), EL, 6 Mar. 1887.

13 Devonshire papers, Cal F6 2517, 2 Jul. 1917.

14 BC, Lans (4), EL, 6 Mar. 1887.

15 BL 88906/12/4/3, 3 Jan. 1887.

16 Ibid.

17 Ibid., 4 Jan. 1887.

18 BC, Lans (4), EL, 6 Jan. 1887.

19 BL 88906/12/4/3, 4 Jan. 1887.

20 BC, Lans (4), EL, 6 Jan. 1887.

21 BL 88906/19/14, 6 Jan. 1887.

22 BC, Lans (4), EL, 6 Jan. 1887.

23 BL 88906/12/4/3, 7 Jan. 1887.

24 Newton, *Lansdowne*, p. 44.

25 BL 88906/14/14/1, 11 Jul. 1886.

26 BL 88906/19/14, 31 Mar. 1886.

27 BC, Lans (4), EL, 18 Oct. 1885.

28   BL 88906/18/5, 8 Jun. 1887.

29   BC, Lans (4), EL, 30 Mar. 1887.

30   Hansard 4, vol. 48, c. 494.

31   Newton, *Lansdowne*, p. 493.

32   *Evening Gazette Pittston*, 28 Apr. 1887.

33   BL 88906/14/4, 7 May 1887.

34   Ibid.

35   Ibid., 17 May 1887; BL 88906/14/9, 12 May 1887.

36   BC, Lans (4), EL, 29 May 1887.

37   BL 88906/14/4, 30 May 1887.

38   BL 88906/14/4, 19 Sep. 1887.

39   C.H. Tupper, *Supplement to the Life and Letters of the Rt. Hon. Sir Charles Tupper* (Toronto 1926), p. 108.

40   P.B. Waite, *The Man from Halifax: Sir John Thompson, Prime Minister* (London 1985), p. 210.

41   BL 88906/14/4, 12 Dec. 1887.

42   BC, Lans (4), EL, 7 Dec. 1885.

43   BC, Lans (4), EL, 16 Oct. 1887.

44   BC, Lans (4), EL, 28 Dec. 1888.

45   BL 88906/19/14, 4 Jan. 1888.

46   BL 88906/19/8, 18 Feb. 1888.

47   BL 88906/12/4/4, 31 Dec. 1887.

48   BL 88906/18/1, 15 Mar. 1888.

49   Granville papers, PRO 30/29/28, 9 Feb. 1888.

50   BL 88906/12/4/4, 14 Jan. 1888.

51   *The Times*, 9 Feb. 1888.

52   BC, Lans (4), EL, 8 Feb. 1888.

53   *Montreal Gazette*, 18 May 1888.

54   *The Mail*, 18 May 1888.

55   P.B. Waite, 'Petty-Fitzmaurice, Henry Charles Keith, 5th Marquess of Lansdowne' in *Dictionary of Canadian Biography*, vol. 15, ed. John Richard English (Toronto 2005).

56   D. Creighton, *Macdonald*, p. 506.

57   J. Pope (ed.), *Correspondence of Sir John Macdonald* (Toronto 1921), p. 328.

Chapter 9: The Viceroyalty

1   Newton, *Lansdowne*, p. 56.

2   BC, Lans (4), EL, 26 Nov. 1888.

3   Mss. Eur. D558/59, 3 Dec. 1888.

4   Newton, *Lansdowne*, p. 56.

5   BC, Lans (4), EL, 3 Dec. 1888.

6   Newton, *Lansdowne*, p. 58.

7   BC, Lans (4), EL, 10 Dec. 1888.

8   BC, Lans (4), EL, 17 Dec. 1888.

9   BL 88906/19/19, 13 Dec. 1888.

10   P. Beaumont and R. Beaumont, *Imperial Divas: The Vicerines of India* (London 2010), p. 35.

11   BL 88906/19/19, 13 Dec. 1888.

12   BC, Lans (4), EL, 10 Dec. 1888.

13   BC, Lans (4), EL, 3 Mar. 1889.

14   BC, Lans (5), n.d. [*c*.1889].

15   Captain Henry Streatfeild and Lieutenant Hercules Pakenham were retained from his Canadian staff, and Captain the Hon. Charles Harbord and Major Frederick Rowan-Hamilton, Dufferin's brother-in-law, were added.

16   Elgin papers, Mss. Eur. F84/137, 18 Oct. 1893.

17   J. Cannon, 'Petty, William, 2nd Earl of Shelburne and 1st Marquess of Lansdowne' in *Oxford Dictionary of National Biography*, eds H.C.G. Matthew and B. Harrison (Oxford 2004).

18   J.P. Misra, *The Administration of India under Lord Lansdowne, 1888–1894* (New Delhi 1975), p. 7.

19   BL 88906/14/19, 15 Jun. 1888.

20   R. Symonds, *Oxford and Empire: The Last Lost Cause?* (Oxford 1991), p. 27.

21   Nightingale papers, 45778, f. 192, 6 Nov. 1888.

22   Ibid., f. 188, 28 Oct. 1888.

23   Mss. Eur. D558/11, 23 Nov. 1888.

24   Lincolnshire papers, Microfilm 1121, 15 Jun. 1888.

25   BL 88906/15/34, 15 Feb. 1888; BL 88906/21/5, 26 Apr. 1888; Jowett papers, IF/2/39, 20 Feb. 1888.

26   BL 88906/15/37, 10 Feb. 1888.

27   Ibid., 28 Apr. 1888.

28   Newton, *Lansdowne*, p. 57.

29   RA VIC/N45/103, 3 Nov. 1888.

30   BL 88906/19/14, 20 Jan. 1889.

31   BC, Lans (4), EL, 6 Apr. 1890.

32   Cross papers, Mss. Eur. E243/27, 5 Jul. 1889.

33   BC, Lans (4), EL, 20 Jun. 1894.

34   BC, Lans (4), EL, 17 Apr. 1889.

35   Fifteen years older than Lansdowne.

36   A.C. Lyall papers, Mss. Eur. F132/164, 1 Sep. 1892.

37   Ibid., 9 Sep. 1891.

38   BC, EFm, 13 Jan. 1889.

39   D. Gilmour, *Curzon* (London 1994), p. 151.

40   D. James, *Lord Roberts* (London 1954), p. 199.

41   Ibid.

42   M. Durand papers, Mss. Eur. D727/3, 14 Feb. 1890.

Chapter 10: A Fighting Viceroy

1 R.J. Moore, 'The Twilight of the Whigs and the Reform of the Indian Councils, 1886–1892', *The Historical Journal*, vol. 10, issue 3 (1967), p. 414.
2 BL 88906/19/14, 20 Jan. 1889.
3 Indian National Congress, *Report of the Indian National Congress* (Madras 1885).
4 Mss. Eur. D558/16, 1 May 1889.
5 Cross papers, Mss. Eur. E243/26, 1 Jan. 1889.
6 Cross papers, Mss. Eur. E243/19, 18 Jan. 1889.
7 Mss. Eur. D558/2, 30 Jan. 1889.
8 Cross papers, Mss. Eur. E243/26, 20 Apr. 1889.
9 Ibid., 24 Mar. 1889.
10 Mss. Eur. D558/16, 1 May 1889.
11 Cross papers, Mss. Eur. E243/26, 4 May 1889.
12 Cross papers, Mss. Eur. E243/27, 5 Jul. 1889.
13 P. Duckers, *The British-Indian Army 1860–1914* (Princes Risborough 2003), p. 36.
14 BC, Lans (4), EL, 30 Dec. 1888.
15 Mss. Eur. D558/25, 16 Jan. 1894.
16 Mss. Eur. D558/14, 1 Apr. 1892.
17 BL 88906/18/2, 29 Jan. 1889.
18 Cross papers, Mss. Eur. E243/26, 2 Apr. 1889.
19 Ibid., 27 Mar. 1889.
20 Cross papers, Mss. Eur. E243/30, 25 Feb. 1891.
21 P. and R. Beaumont, *Imperial Divas*, p. 51.
22 Mss. Eur. D558/20, 24 Jun. 1891.
23 P. Kanwar, *Imperial Simla: The Political Culture of the Raj* (Oxford 1990), p. 97.
24 Mss. Eur. D558/20, 24 Jun. 1891.
25 BL 88906/19/14, 25 May 1889.
26 BC, Lans (5), ED, 14 Apr. 1889.
27 Mss. Eur. D558/16, 23 Jun. 1889.
28 BL 88906/19/14, 25 May 1889.
29 Cross papers, Mss. Eur. E243/26, 8 Jan. 1889.
30 Devonshire papers, DF15/3/1/3/3, 12 Oct. 1890.
31 BL 88906/19/14, 25 May 1889.
32 BC, Lans (4), EL, 17 May 1889.
33 Mss. Eur. D558/14, 1 Apr. 1892.
34 Mss. Eur. D558/21, 11 Aug. 1891.
35 BC, Lans (4), EL, 26 Oct. 1889.

Chapter 11: People and Policy in India

1 BL 88906/18/2, 6 Jan. 1890.
2 BC, Lans (4), EL, 5 Jan. 1890.

3   BC, Lans (4), EL, 1 Jan. 1891.
4   The falling value of silver was a result of it being demonetised by major countries and a massive increase in silver production between 1860 and 1890.
5   Mss. Eur. D558/59, 4 Dec. 1888.
6   Mss. Eur. D558/5, 21 Nov. 1892.
7   Mss. Eur. D558/13, 3/9 Sep. 1891.
8   Cross papers, Mss. Eur. E243/27, 23 Aug. 1889.
9   Cross papers, Mss. Eur. E243/26, 14 Jun. 1889.
10 R.K. Perti, *South Asia: Frontier Policies, Administrative Problems and Lord Lansdowne* (New Delhi 1976), p. 267.
11 Mss. Eur. D558/58, 15 Sep. 1890.
12 Mss. Eur. D558/12, 11 Jul. 1890.
13 Northbrook papers, Mss. Eur. C144/5, 6 Sep. 1890.
14 Mss. Eur. D558/13, 3 Feb. 1891.
15 Mss. Eur. D558/59, 19 Mar. 1891.
16 Ibid.
17 Mss. Eur. D558/3, 9 Jun. 1890.
18 Cross papers, Mss. Eur. E243/19, 18 Apr. 1890.
19 Harris papers, Mss. Eur. E256/6, 20 Jun. 1890.
20 Cross papers, Mss. Eur. E243/28, 16 Jun. 1890.
21 Cross papers, Mss. Eur. E243/19, 9 Oct. 1890.
22 Morier papers, Box 2 (file 1), 28 Nov. 1890.
23 Cross papers, Mss. Eur. E243/20, 12 Nov. 1891.
24 Cross papers, Mss. Eur. E243/30, 7 Jan. 1891.
25 Cross papers, Mss. Eur. E243/29, 31 Dec. 1890.
26 Morier papers, Box 2 (file 1), 13 Jan. 1891.
27 Mss. Eur. D558/20, 30 Jan. 1891.
28 Cross papers, Mss. Eur. E243/30, 21 Jan. 1891.
29 Mss. Eur. D558/13, 1 Feb. 1891.
30 Morier papers, Box 2 (file 1), 16 Feb. 1891.
31 Cross papers, Mss. Eur. E243/30, 11 Mar. 1891.

Chapter 12: Manipur and Maharajas

1   J.P. Misra, *Lord Lansdowne*, p. 174.
2   Ibid., p. 176.
3   Cross papers, Mss. Eur. E243/20, 1 Jan. 1891.
4   J.P. Misra, *Lord Lansdowne*, p. 178.
5   Cross papers, Mss. Eur. E243/30, 25 Feb. 1891.
6   R.K. Perti, *South Asia*, p. 294.
7   J.P. Misra, *Lord Lansdowne*, p. 179.
8   Cross papers, Mss. Eur. E243/30, 24 Mar. 1891.
9   BC, Lans (4), EL, 18 Apr. 1891.

10   BC, Lans (4), EL, 28 Apr. 1891.

11   Cross papers, Mss. Eur. E243/20, 21 May 1891.

12   Mss. Eur. D558/58, 18 Apr. 1891.

13   Cross papers, Mss. Eur. E243/20, 24 Apr. 1891.

14   Mss. Eur. D558/13, 24 Apr. 1891.

15   BL 88906/18/2, 18 Apr. 1891.

16   Ibid.

17   Cross papers, Mss. Eur. E243/31, 15 Sep. 1891.

18   Cross papers, Mss. Eur. E243/20, 28 May 1891.

19   Mss. Eur. D558/8, 30 May 1891.

20   Cross papers, Mss. Eur. E243/20, 19 Jun. 1891.

21   Cross papers, Mss. Eur. E243/30, 23 Jun. 1891.

22   Cross papers, Mss. Eur. E243/31, 14 Jul. 1891.

23   Harris papers, Mss. Eur. E256/5, 6 Jul. 1891.

24   Wenlock papers, Mss. Eur. D592, 9 May 1891.

25   Mss. Eur. D558/13, 12 Jun. 1891.

26   Mss. Eur. D558/8, 3 Aug. 1891.

27   Cross papers, Mss. Eur. E243/31, 11 Aug. 1891.

28   Mss. Eur. D558/13, 23 Aug. 1891.

29   Mss. Eur. D558/21, 1 Aug. 1891.

30   Cross papers, Mss. Eur. E243/31, 4 Aug. 1891.

31   Mss. Eur. D558/13, 23 Aug. 1891.

32   Ibid., 17 Sep. 1891.

33   Ibid., 27 Aug. 1891.

34   Cross papers, Mss. Eur. E243/31, 1 Sep. 1891.

35   Ibid., 17 Sep. 1891.

36   BL 88906/19/19, 10 Oct. 1891.

37   BL 88906/18/2, 2 Dec. 1891.

38   Jowett papers, II/12/7, 2 Nov. 1889.

39   Mss. Eur. D558/20, 26 Oct. 1891.

40   Cross papers, Mss. Eur. E243/26, 31 Oct. 1891.

41   One lakh, which was worth 100,000 rupees, was equivalent to £6,667.
     This would be about £400,000 today.

42   Mss. Eur. D558/8, 7 Nov. 1891.

43   BC, Lans (4), EL, 7 Oct. 1891.

44   BC, Lans (4), EL, 22 Nov. 1891. The letter was started on 22 November
and sent on 26 November.

45   Ibid.

46   Ibid.

Chapter 13: A Year of Change

1   R.K. Perti, *South Asia*, p. 51.

2   Cross papers, Mss. Eur. E243/26, 8 Jan. 1889.

3   Mss. Eur. D558/20, 30 Jun. 1891.

4   Ibid.

5   Cross papers, Mss. Eur. E243/32, 23 Mar. 1892.

6   Mss. Eur. D558/19, 30 Jun. 1891.

7   Kimberley papers, MS. Eng. hist. c. 4325, f. 1, 17 Jul. 1892.

8   BC, Lans (4), EL, 1 Apr. 1892.

9   Ibid.

10   BC, Lans (4), EL, 2 Sep. 1892.

11   BC, Lans (4), EL, 26 Jun. 1892.

12   BC, Lans (4), EL, 3 Jun. 1892.

13   Devonshire papers, DF15/3/1/3/3, 28 May 1892.

14   BC, Lans (4), EL, 29 May 1892.

15   Devonshire papers, DF15/3/1/3/3, 12 Oct. 1890.

16   BC, Lans (4), EL, 15 May 1892.

17   Cross papers, Mss. Eur. E243/32, 13 Jan. 1892.

18   Cross papers, Mss. Eur. E243/30, 23 Jun. 1891.

19   Cross papers, Mss. Eur. E243/32, 19 Jul. 1892.

20   Ibid., 16 Aug. 1892.

21   Ibid., 19 Jul. 1892.

22   BL 88906/18/2, 12 Aug. 1892.

23   Mss. Eur. D558/14, 19 Aug. 1892.

24   BC, Lans (4), EL, 19 Aug. 1892.

25   BL 88906/18/3, 26 Aug. 1892.

26   Mss. Eur. D558/14, 19 Aug. 1892.

27   Mss. Eur. D558/5, 21 Dec. 1892.

28   Ibid., 21 Dec. 1892.

29   Ibid., 14 Dec. 1892.

30   Jowett papers, IF/Z/51, 8 May 1892.

31   A.C. Lyall papers, Mss. Eur. F132/164, 29 May 1892.

32   Kimberley papers, MS. Eng. hist. d. 2466, f. 20, 6 Jun. 1892.

33   BL 88906/18/2, 2 Jun. 1892.

34   S. Maccoby (ed.), *English Radicalism, 1886–1914* (London 1953), p. 425.

35   R.J. Moore, 'The Twilight of the Whigs', p. 414.

36   Kimberley papers, MS. Eng. hist. d. 2466, f. 62, 30 Jan. 1892.

37   Mss. Eur. D558/5, 16 Nov. 1892.

38   Mss. Eur. D558/9, 12/24 Dec. 1892.

39   Ibid.

40   Mss. Eur. D558/10, 14 Jan. 1893.

41   BC, Lans (4), EL, 21 Jan. 1893.

42   Kimberley papers, MS. Eng. hist. d. 2466, f. 178, 18 Jan. 1893.

Chapter 14: The End in Sight

1   Mss. Eur. D558/60, 3 Feb. 1893.

2   BC, Lans (4), EL, 31 Jan. 1893.

3   Mss. Eur. D558/22, 25 Mar. 1892.

4   J.F. Riddick, *The History of British India: A Chronology* (London 2006), p. 82.

5   A sovereign was equivalent to a pound; there were 20 shillings to the pound.

6   J.F. Riddick, *The History of British India: A Chronology* (London 2006), p. 82.

7   S.P. Reti, *Silver and Gold: The Political Economy of International Monetary Conferences, 1867–1892* (Westport, Conn. 1998), p. 115.

8   BC, Lans (4), EL, 6 Mar. 1893.

9   R.K. Perti, *South Asia*, p. 248.

10   Mss. Eur. D558/6, 20 Jun. 1893.

11   BC, Lans (4), EL, 25 Jun. 1893.

12   Ardagh papers, PRO 30/40/10, 3 Jul. 1893.

13   Mss. Eur. D558/10, 26 Jun. 1893.

14   BC, EFm, 8 Jul. 1893.

15   Harris papers, Mss. Eur. E256/7, 20 Aug. 1893.

16   Kimberley papers, MS. Eng. hist. d. 2467, f. 237, 9 Aug. 1893.

17   Mss. Eur. D558/6, 22 Aug. 1893.

18   I. Copland, 'What to do about cows? Princely versus British approaches to a South Asian dilemma', *Bulletin of the School of Oriental and African Studies*, vol. 68, no. 1 (2005), pp. 59–76.

19   Kimberley papers, MS. Eng. hist. d. 2467, f. 229, 16 Aug. 1893.

20   Kimberley papers, MS. Eng. hist. d. 2467, f. 237, 9 Aug. 1893.

21   Ibid.

22   Harris papers, Mss. Eur. E256/8, 22 Aug. 1893.

23   Mss. Eur. D558/6, 22 Aug. 1893.

24   R.J. Moore, 'The Twilight of the Whigs', p. 414.

25   Mss. Eur. D558/25, 31 Oct. 1893.

26   Mss. Eur. D558/60, 23 Jan. 1894.

27   Cross papers, Mss. Eur. E243/32, 13 Jan. 1892.

28   M. Durand papers, Mss. Eur. D727/5, 9 Oct. 1893.

29   Mss. Eur. D558/6, 8 Aug. 1893.

30   M. Durand papers, Mss. Eur. D727/4, 8 Dec. 1893.

31   BC, Lans (4), EL, 12 Nov. 1893.

32   RA VIC/N49/42, 12 Nov. 1893.

33   Devonshire papers, DF15/3/1/3/3, 18 Nov. 1893.

34   BC, Lans (4), EL, 25 Apr. 1893.

35   BC, Lans (4), EL, 20 Jun. 1893.

36   BC, Lans (4), EL, 5 Sep. 1893.

37   BL 88906/19/14, 5 Sep. 1893.

38   Devonshire papers, DF15/3/1/3/3, 17 Sep. 1893.

39   BL 88906/18/3, 27 Sep. 1893.

40   Harris papers, Mss. Eur. E256/8, 21 Oct. 1893.

41 M. Durand papers, MS. 55, Box 6 (file 40), 26 Nov. 1893.

42 Cross papers, 51264, f. 105, 31 Oct. 1893.

Chapter 15: Farewell to India

1 This large and comfortable Royal Indian Marine troopship, which was named after the first Governor-General of India, was claimed to be 'practically unsinkable' because of her thirty-three watertight compartments. However, she ran aground on the coast of Reunion Island, in the Indian Ocean, on 14 January 1897.

2 Devonshire papers, DF15/3/1/3/3, 13 Dec. 1893.

3 BC, Lans (4), EL, 14 Jan. 1894.

4 BC, Lans (4), EL, 24 Jan. 1894.

5 BC, Lans (4), EL, 1 Feb. 1894.

6 BC, Lans (4), EL, 14 Jan. 1894.

7 BC, Lans (4), EL, 12 Nov. 1893.

8 Devonshire papers, DF15/3/1/3/3, 27 Nov. 1893.

9 Ardagh papers, PRO 30/40/2, 21 Feb. 1894.

10 Rosebery papers, 10092, f. 128, 12 Mar. 1894.

11 BC, Lans (4), EL, 14 Jan. 1894.

12 BC, Lans (5), Jan. 1894.

13 Lansdowne's equestrian statue stood opposite the equestrian statue of Lord Roberts. Both have since been removed from the Maidan, along with other statues of prominent British officials, to make way for statues of India's nationalist leaders.

14 Curzon papers, Mss. Eur. F111/160, 10 Jan. 1901. When Curzon wrote this in 1901, Campbell-Bannerman was Leader of the opposition Liberal party and Jesse Collings was Under-Secretary of State for the Home department.

15 Mss. Eur. D558/6, 24 Jan. 1894.

Chapter 16: The War Office

1 R. Jenkins, *Gladstone* (London 2002), p. 614.

2 BL 88906/18/3, 19 Feb. 1894.

3 Ibid., 25 Feb. 1894.

4 Mss. Eur. D558/59, 29 Aug. 1889.

5 BC, Lans (4), EL, 23 Apr. 1894.

6 Ibid., 20 Mar. 1894.

7 Ibid., 22 Aug. 1894.

8 Ibid., 20 Jun. 1894.

9 BL 88906/19/14, 26 Jun. 1895.

10 Ardagh papers, PRO 30/40/2, 31 Mar. 1902.

11 On 2 March 1886, in a speech given in Manchester, Randolph Churchill was the first Conservative politician to use the appellation 'Unionist Party' as a means of describing all those who were opposed to Home Rule.

12   D. Steele, *Lord Salisbury: A Political Biography* (London 1999), p. 296.

13   G.R. Searle, *A New England? Peace and War 1886–1918* (Oxford 2004), p. 217.

14   H. Gordon, *The War Office* (London 1935), p. 76.

15   H. Thring, 'Lessons of the War: Place the War Office in Commission', *Nineteenth Century*, vol. 48, no. 285 (1900), p. 697.

16   PP, 1896, (310), X, 'Report from the Select Committee on government offices (appropriation of sites); together with the proceedings of the committee, minutes of evidence, and appendix', p. 14; *The Times*, 10 Jul. 1896; T. Wintringham, 'The War Office', *The Political Quarterly*, vol. 13, no. 2 (1942), pp. 117–29.

17   *The Broad Arrow, The Naval and Military Gazette*, vol. 55, no. 1414 (1895), p. 130.

18   PP 1896 X (310), p. 14; *The Times*, 10 Jul. 1896.

19   J. Wilson, *CB: A Life of Sir Henry Campbell-Bannerman* (London 1973), p. 175.

20   E.M. Spiers, *The Late Victorian Army, 1868–1902* (Manchester 1992), p. 48.

21   Earl of Midleton, *Records and Reaction, 1856–1939* (London 1939), p. 49.

22   Hansard 4, vol. 176, c. 1344.

23   Midleton, *Records*, p. 92.

24   The pre-Cardwellian army that Prince Albert, the Duke of Cambridge and other royals were involved with was controlled by soldiers who had sworn an allegiance to the Crown. Officers or men of other ranks were enlisted for twenty-one years in a particular regiment which had its own traditions and separate identity. Owing to their lineage and connections with the Crown, a marked social hierarchy developed in these regiments, often giving rise to a culture of gentlemanly amateurism.

25   E.M. Spiers, *Late Victorian Army*, p. 30.

26   *Army and Navy Gazette*, vol. 44, no. 2281 (1903), p. 961.

27   Salisbury papers, 3M/E/Lansdowne, f. 83, 1 Jul. 1895.

28   A.H. Page, 'The Supply Services of the British Army in the South Africa War 1899–1902', PhD thesis (Oxford 1976), p. 35.

29   A.H. Atteridge, 'The War Office: Its Work and Personnel', *The Windsor Magazine: An Illustrated Monthly for Men and Women*, 7 (1897), p. 550; Midleton, *Records*, p. 74.

30   *Army and Navy Gazette*, vol. 56, no. 1454 (1896), p. 555.

31   O. Wheeler, *The War Office Past and Present* (London 1914), p. 129.

32   PP, 1901, XL, Cd. 581, 'Minutes of evidence taken before the committee to enquire into War Office organisation together with appendices, digest and index', Appendix 1, p. 409.

33   Salisbury papers, 3M/E/Lansdowne, f. 83, 1 Jul. 1895.

34   His retirement date was subsequently postponed until November.

35   Ardagh papers, PRO 30/40/12, 19 Jul. 1892.

36 Viscount Wolseley, 'The Standing Army of Great Britain' in Various Authors, *The Armies of To-day: A Description of the Armies of the Leading Nations at the Present Time* (New York 1893), p. 93.

37 M. Roper, *The Records of the War Office and Related Departments, 1660–1964* (Kew 1998), p. 103.

38 BL 88906/19/6, 19 May 1897.

39 Forrest papers, MS. Eng. hist. d. 275, f. 57, 3 Dec. 1895.

40 Hansard 4, vol. 90, c. 356.

41 PP, 1887, XIX, C. 5226, 'Report of the Royal Commission appointed to inquire into the civil establishments of the different offices of state at home and abroad, with minutes of evidence, appendix', 5160, p. 192.

42 PP, 1904, XLI, Cd. 1791, 'Minutes of evidence taken before the Royal Commission on the War in South Africa', 21438, p. 531.

43 *The Times*, 14 Jul. 1898.

44 Hansard 4, vol. 55, c. 726.

45 Ibid., vol. 87, c. 602.

46 PP, 1904, XLI, Cd. 1791, RC, 21489, p. 534.

47 Hansard 4, vol. 188, c. 1581.

48 CAB 37/42/32, 10 Jul. 1896.

49 I.F.W. Beckett, 'Edward Stanhope at the War Office 1887–1892', *Journal of Strategic Studies*, 5 (1982), p. 245.

50 PP, 1904, XLI, Cd. 1791, RC, 21438, p. 531.

51 Salisbury papers, 3M/E/Lansdowne, f. 695, 11 Jul. 1902.

52 'I am astounded at reading the recommendations of Sir J. Ardagh. I suppose he reflects the dominant view of the Horse Guards.' FO 800/145, 21 Apr. 1897.

53 Hansard 4, vol. 90, c. 545.

54 J. Parry, 'Cavendish, Spencer Compton, Marquess of Hartington and Eighth Duke of Devonshire' in *Oxford Dictionary of National Biography*, eds H.C.G. Matthew and B. Harrison (Oxford 2004).

55 *The Times*, 21 May 1896.

56 P.T. Marsh, *Joseph Chamberlain: Entrepreneur in Politics* (New Haven, Conn. 1994), p. 470.

57 *The Times*, 14 Nov. 1896.

58 T.H. O'Brien, *Milner: Viscount Milner of St James's and Cape Town, 1854–1925* (London 1979), p. 122.

59 *The Times*, 14 Nov. 1896.

60 Viscount Morley, *Recollections* (London 1917), vol. 2, pp. 201–02.

61 C.I. Hamilton, *The Making of the Modern Admiralty: British Naval Policy 1805–1927* (Cambridge 2011), p. 307.

62 A.D. Lambert, 'The Royal Navy and the Defence of Empire, 1856–1918' in *Imperial Defence: The Old World Order 1856–1956*, ed. G. Kennedy (London 2007), p. 120.

63 Ibid., p. 124.

64 G. Hamilton, *Parliamentary Reminiscences and Reflections* (London 1917), vol. 1, p. 276.

65 RA VIC/C40/62, 28 Jun. 1895.

66 BL 88906/18/1, 15 Mar. 1888.

67 Hansard 4, vol. 36, c. 1382.

68 Ibid., vol. 67, c. 1306.

69 *The Times*, 14 Nov. 1896.

70 L.S. Amery, *The Problem of the Army: A Series of Articles Reprinted from The Times* (London 1903), p. 57.

71 E.M. Spiers, *Army and Society*, p. 258.

72 Hansard 4, vol. 85, c. 1100; BL 88906/16/28/3, 3 Jul. 1899.

73 Hansard 4, vol. 45, c. 1612.

74 H.S. Wilkinson, *The Command of the Sea* (London 1894), p. 66.

75 J.B. Atlay, *Lord Haliburton: A Memoir of his Public Service* (London 1909), p. 211.

76 S.E. Koss, *The Rise and Fall of the Political Press in Britain* (London 1990), p. 5.

Chapter 17: Reform of the War Office

1   Hansard 4, vol. 141, c. 35.

2   Wolseley papers, 24/87/2, 9 Aug. 1895.

3   Hansard 4, vol. 34, c. 1677.

4   O. Wheeler, *War Office*, p. 128; Hansard 4, vol. 90, c. 335.

5   Hansard 4, vol. 36, c. 774.

6   Lansdowne, in contrast to Wolseley, believed that Stanhope's 1888 Order in Council had created 'stupendous centralisation' in the office of the Commander-in-Chief; Hansard 4, vol. 90, c. 347.

7   Hansard 4, vol. 36, cc. 769–770.

8   BL 88906/22/11, 3 Nov. 1903.

9   Ibid.

10 Hansard 4, vol. 36, c. 771.

11 *The Times*, 27 Aug. 1895.

12 Hansard 4, vol. 36, c. 771.

13 Ibid., cc. 771–72.

14 PP, 1904, XLI, Cd. 1791, RC, 21436, p. 531.

15 BL 88906/18/4, 26 Aug. 1895.

16 PP, 1904, XL, Cd. 1790, 'Minutes of evidence taken before the Royal Commission on the War in South Africa', 1140, p. 53.

17 Hansard 4, vol. 36, c. 772.

18 Campbell-Bannerman papers, 41221, f. 239, 26 Dec. 1896.

19 Hansard 4, vol. 36, c. 773.

20 Ibid., c. 774.

21   PP, 1904, XLI, Cd. 1791, RC, 21425, p. 528.

22   BL 88906/19/28, 2/3 Oct. 1895.

23   PP, 1904, XLI, Cd. 1791, RC, 21425, p. 528.

24   Ibid.

25   Ibid.

26   PP, 1904, XLI, Cd. 1791, RC, 21425, p. 530.

27   Ibid.

28   PRO, WO 32/6357; PP, 1904, XLI, Cd. 1791, RC, 21425, p. 530.

29   Ibid., 21433, p. 531.

30   Ibid., 21430, p. 531.

31   Ibid., 21431, p. 531.

32   Ibid., 21434, p. 531.

33   Ibid., 21425, p. 530.

34   Ibid., 21427, p. 530.

35   PP, 1890, XIX, C. 5979, 'Royal Commission appointed to enquire
      into the civil and professional administration of the naval and military
      departments and the relation of those departments to each other and to
      the treasury', 20, p. viii.

36   F.A. Johnson, *Defence by Committee: The British Committee of Imperial Defence,
      1885–1959* (Oxford 1960), p. 20.

37   Ibid., p. 29; Hansard 4, vol. 36, cc. 1483–84.

38   Ibid., cc. 1393–97, cc. 1397–1401 and cc. 1472–74.

39   Salisbury papers, 3M/E/Devonshire, f. 517, 5 Dec. 1895.

40   CAB 37/53/71, 2 Nov. 1900.

41   Ibid., 23 Nov. 1900.

42   Wolseley papers, 28/78, 30 Nov. 1899.

43   CAB 37/53/71, 2 Nov. 1900.

44   Ibid., 7 Nov. 1900.

45   Ibid.

46   Hansard 4, vol. 86, c. 1564.

47   H. Kochanski, 'Field Marshal Viscount Wolseley as Commander-in-
      Chief, 1895–1900: A Reassessment', *Journal of Strategic Studies*, vol. 20,
      no. 2 (1997), p. 121.

48   PP, 1904, XLII, Cd. 1792, 'Appendices to the Minutes of evidence taken
      before the Royal Commission on the War in South Africa', Appendix 42,
      no. 12, p. 283.

49   Ibid.

50   O. Wheeler, *War Office*, p. 257.

51   Sir E. Wood, *From Midshipman to Field Marshal* (London 1906), p. 571; PP,
      1904, XLI, Cd. 1791, RC, 21429, p. 531; PP, 1904, XL, Cd. 1790, RC,
      9332-9336, p. 394.

52   Sir E. Wood, *Midshipman*, p. 571.

53   PP, 1904, XLI, Cd. 1791, RC, 21429, p. 531.

54 H. Kochanski, *Sir Garnet Wolseley: Victorian Hero* (London 1999), p. 217.
55 Wolseley papers, 28/64, 4 Oct. 1899.
56 Ibid., 29/7, 19 Jan. 1900.
57 Ibid., 28/83, 21 Dec. 1899.
58 Ibid., 29/65, 2 Oct. 1900.
59 Ibid., 28/82, 18 Dec. 1900.
60 Ibid., 29/81, 2 Dec. 1900.
61 *The Saturday Review of Politics, Literature, Science and Art*, vol. 80, no. 2080 (1896), pp. 305–06.
62 Hansard 4, vol. 91, c. 22.
63 Hansard 4, vol. 90, c. 357.
64 BL 88906/19/6, 21 Oct. 1895.
65 BL 88906/16/17/2, 2 Nov. 1895.
66 J. Gooch, *The Plans of War: The General Staff and British Military Strategy c.1900–1916* (London 1974), p. 20.
67 BL 88906/20/5/2, 2 Jan. 1896.
68 PP, 1904, XLI, Cd. 1791, RC, 21354, p. 525.
69 G.R. Searle, *A New England?*, p. 273.
70 BL 88906/16/10, 9 Apr. 1897.

Chapter 18: Reform of the Army
1 *The Times*, 10 Dec. 1897.
2 Hansard 4, vol. 45, c. 1247.
3 *The Times*, 10 Dec. 1897.
4 PP, 1904, XLII, Cd. 1792, RC, Appendix 42 (II), p. 284.
5 Hansard 4, vol. 176, c. 1332.
6 *The Saturday Review of Politics, Literature, Science and Art*, vol. 85, no. 2212 (1898), p. 396.
7 Ibid., vol. 85, no. 2210 (1898), p. 318.
8 *The Times*, 18 Nov. 1898.
9 BL 88906/19/6, 2 Feb. 1898.
10 M.A. Ramsay, *Command and Cohesion: The Citizen Soldier and Minor Tactics in the British Army, 1870–1918* (Westport, Conn. 1999), p. 45.
11 BL 88906/16/2, 15 Dec. 1897.
12 *The Times*, 7 Jun. 1898.
13 Ibid.
14 Ibid.
15 Ibid., 24 Nov. 1899; ibid., 7 Nov. 1899.
16 H. Kochanski, *Wolseley*, p. 188.
17 PRO, WO 33/48, 8 Jun. 1888; CAB 37/40/64, 2 Dec. 1895; H.H.R. Bailes, 'The Influence of Continental Examples and Colonial Warfare upon the Reform of the Late Victorian Army', PhD thesis (London 1980), p. 26.

18 The Blue Water School was a collective term to describe politicians, political thinkers and servicemen who regarded a strong navy and the command of the sea as essential to the security of the country.

19 *The Times*, 18 Nov. 1898.

20 Ibid., 14 Nov. 1896.

21 J.H. Lehmann, *All Sir Garnet: A Life of Field Marshal Lord Wolseley* (London 1964), p. 380.

22 Viscount Wolseley, 'Standing Army' in *Armies of To-day*, p. 95.

23 *The Times*, 14 Jul. 1898; Lord Wolseley, *The Soldier's Pocket-Book for Field Service* (London 1869), pp. 3–4.

24 *The Times*, 14 Jul. 1898.

25 Hansard 4, vol. 42, c. 1593.

26 *The Times*, 10 Dec. 1897.

27 CAB 37/42/32, 10 Jul. 1896.

28 The Military Works (Money) Act of 1897 raised £5,458,000 and the Military Works Act of 1899 raised £4,000,000.

29 The four bills were for: authorising a military works loan; military manoeuvres; volunteers to equip rifle ranges out of public funds; the reserve to be more readily utilised in small wars.

30 *The Times*, 14 Nov. 1896.

31 Ibid., 5 Feb. 1897.

32 Ardagh papers, PRO 30/40/10, 24 Sep. 1896.

33 Hansard 4, vol. 46, c. 324.

34 PP, 1904, XLI, Cd. 1791, RC, 21159, p. 508; ibid., 21170, p. 509; ibid., 21226, p. 514.

35 E.M. Spiers, *Army and Society*, p. 229.

36 CAB 37/42/32, 10 Jul. 1896.

37 BL 88906/16/10, 23 Jul. 1896.

38 Hansard 4, vol. 45, c. 1247.

39 Ibid., c. 1248.

40 BL 88906/16/18, 29 Dec. 1896.

41 Ibid., 29 Dec. 1896.

42 Ibid., 6 Jan. 1897.

43 By the Aliens Expulsion Act of 1896 the Government of the Transvaal could expel aliens who were considered 'a danger to the public peace and order'. The Aliens Immigration Act of 1896 imposed severe limitations on the entrance of foreigners to the Transvaal, particularly from India.

44 J.L. Garvin, *Chamberlain*, vol. 3, pp. 140–41.

45 BL 88906/16/10, 9 Apr. 1897.

46 Salisbury papers, 3M/E/J Chamberlain, f. 86, 8 Apr. 1897.

47 BL 88906/19/8, 13 Apr. 1897; BL 88906/19/6, 13 Apr. 1897.

48 BL 88906/19/6, 13 Apr. 1897.

49 C. Headlam (ed.), *The Milner Papers: South Africa 1897–1905* (London 1933), vol. 1, p. 561.

50 E. Drus, 'Select documents from the Chamberlain papers concerning Anglo-Transvaal relations, 1896–1899', *Bulletin of the Institute for Historical Research*, 27 (1954), p. 168.

51 C. Headlam (ed.), *Milner Papers*, vol. 1, pp. 114–15.

52 CAB 37/45/73, 6 Oct. 1897.

53 BL 88906/19/2, 28 Oct. 1897.

54 W.W. Gosse, *Aspects and Impressions* (London 1922), p. 289; N. Lyttelton, *Eighty Years: Soldiering, Politics, Games* (London 1927), p. 170.

55 *The Broad Arrow, The Naval and Military Gazette*, vol. 58, no. 1511 (1897), p. 685.

56 Ibid.

57 CAB 37/45/43, 15 Dec. 1897.

58 BL 88906/16/2, 13 Dec. 1898.

59 *The Times*, 24 Sep. 1897.

60 BL 88906/19/4, 4 Oct. 1897.

61 *The Times*, 14 Oct. 1897.

62 RA VIC/QVJ, 2 Dec. 1897.

63 J.B. Atlay, *Haliburton*, p. 145.

64 *The Saturday Review of Politics, Literature, Science and Art*, vol. 85, no. 2211 (1898), p. 362.

65 BL 88906/19/21, 25 Nov. 1897.

66 BL 88906/19/18, 13 Nov. 1897.

67 Ibid., 19 Nov. 1897.

68 CAB 37/45/42, 2 Dec. 1897.

69 PP, 1904, XL, Cd. 1789, 'Report of His Majesty's commissioners appointed to inquire into the military preparations and other matters connected with the War in South Africa', Appendix D, p. 243.

70 CAB 37/45/43, 15 Dec. 1897.

71 *The Times*, 10 Dec. 1897.

72 BL 88906/18/5, 1 Jan. 1898.

73 *The Times*, 22 Dec. 1897.

74 Chamberlain papers, JC51/39, 1 Feb. 1898.

75 Ibid.

76 BL 88906/19/6, 2 Feb. 1898.

77 *The Times*, 27 Jan. 1898.

78 BL 88906/19/6, 2 Feb. 1898.

79 Ibid.

80 FO 800/115, 2 Feb. 1898.

81 PP, 1904, XLI, Cd. 1791, RC, 21318, p. 523,

82 *The Saturday Review of Politics, Literature, Science and Art*, vol. 85, no. 2212 (1898), p. 396.

83   *The Times*, 4 Feb. 1898.

84   Ibid.

85   Ibid., 22 Jan. 1898.

86   PRO, WO 32/6178, 16 Mar. 1898.

87   Hansard 4, vol. 54, c. 55.

88   PP, 1904, XLII, Cd. 1792, RC, Appendix 42 (II), p. 284.

89   Ibid., c. 344.

90   *The Broad Arrow, The Naval and Military Gazette*, vol. 62, no. 1596 (1899), p. 66.

91   *The Times*, 18 Nov. 1898.

92   Hansard 4, vol. 52, c. 77.

93   Ibid., vol. 48, c. 493.

94   *The Times*, 7 Jun. 1898.

95   BL 88906/19/29, 30 Aug. 1897.

96   BL 88906/19/6, 7 Sep. 1898.

97   *The Times*, 18 Nov. 1898.

98   Hansard 4, vol. 61, c. 451.

99   BL 88906/18/5, 24 Apr. 1898.

100 F.B. Maurice and G.C.A. Arthur, *The Life of Lord Wolseley* (London 1924), p. 316.

101 Wolseley papers, 37/96, 6 Oct. 1898.

102 PP, 1904, XLI, Cd. 1791, RC, 21387, p. 526.

103 BL 88906/19/2, 28 May 1898.

104 Ibid.

105 Ibid., 1 Jun. 1898.

106 Ibid.; PP, 1904, XLI, Cd. 1791, RC, 21097, p. 502.

107 BL 88906/19/6, 7 Sep. 1898.

108 BL 88906/16/30, 17 Nov. 1898.

109 E.M. Spiers, *Late Victorian Army*, p. 238.

110 *The Broad Arrow, The Naval and Military Gazette*, vol. 55, no. 1414 (1895), p. 129.

111 Hansard 4, vol. 55, c. 982.

112 PP, 1904, XLI, Cd. 1791, RC, 21396, p. 527.

113 Hansard 4, vol. 55, c. 950.

114 *The Broad Arrow, The Naval and Military Gazette*, vol. 55, no. 1553 (1898), p. 367.

115 Hansard 4, vol. 55, c. 957.

116 BL 88906/16/24, 12 Dec. 1898.

117 BL 88906/16/2, 30 Jan. 1899.

118 BL 88906/18/6, 12 Oct. 1898.

119 Cross papers, 51280, f. 15, 29 Sep. 1898.

120 BL 88906/19/28, 29 Nov. 1898.

121 BL 88906/16/24, 13 Jan. 1899.

122 Ibid.

123 Balfour papers, 49773, f. 158, 2 Feb. 1899.

124 Ibid., 49720, f. 56, 18 Jan. 1899.

125 Ibid.

126 BL 88906/16/24, 30 Jan. 1899.

127 The four commissions were the Stephen Royal Commission on Warlike Stores (1887), the Ridley Royal Commission on Civil Establishments (1887), the Morley Commission on the Organization and Administration of Army Manufacturing Departments (1887) and the Hartington Commission on Civil and Professional Administration of the Naval and Military Departments (1890).

128 Hansard 4, vol. 66, c. 1257.

129 BL 88906/19/13, 16 Dec. 1898.

Chapter 19: Origins of the War in South Africa

1 The Hertford House or Wallace Collection consists of works of art collected in the eighteenth and nineteenth centuries by the first four Marquesses of Hertford and Sir Richard Wallace. Sir Richard Wallace was the illegitimate son of the 4th Marquess.

2 *Manchester Evening News*, 16 Oct. 1897.

3 BC, Lans (5), n.d. [*c*.1915], 5th Marquess of Lansdowne, 'Major Lord Charles Mercer Nairne'.

4 BL 88906/19/19, 1 Jul. 1897.

5 RA GVD, 25 Jun. 1897.

6 The Royal United Services Institute had been founded in 1831 with the support of the Duke of Wellington.

7 WO 32/7847, 12 Jul. 1899.

8 PP, 1904, XLI, Cd. 1791, RC, 21352, p. 525.

9 PP, 1904, XLI, Cd. 1791, RC, 21353-56, p. 525.

10 G. Powell, *Buller a Scapegoat? A Life of General Sir Redvers Buller 1839–1908* (London 1994), p. 119.

11 CAB 37/50/49, 12 Aug. 1899.

12 PP, 1904, XLI, Cd. 1791, RC, 21154, p. 508.

13 A. Roberts, *Salisbury: Victorian Titan* (London 1999), p. 728.

14 Selborne papers, MS. 9, f. 63, 14 Aug. 1899.

15 T. Pakenham, *The Boer War* (London 1979), p. 82.

16 I.R. Smith, *The Origins of the South African War, 1899–1902* (London 1996), p. 345.

17 CAB 37/50/52, 17 Aug. 1899.

18 BL 88906/19/9, 21 Aug. 1899.

19 BL 88906/19/16, 27 Aug. 1899.

20 BL 88906/22/11, 27 Aug. 1899.

21 PP, 1904, XLI, Cd. 1791, RC, 21192, p. 510.

22   BL 88906/19/29, 3 Sep. 1899.

23   G. Powell, *Buller*, pp. 122–25.

24   CAB 37/50/62, 5 Sep. 1899.

25   CAB 37/50/69, 5 Sep. 1899.

26   PP, 1904, XL, Cd. 1790, RC, 8788, p. 369.

27   CAB 37/50/69, 5 Sep. 1899; PP, 1904, XLI, Cd. 1791, RC, 21247-53, p. 515.

28   CAB 37/50/63, 6 Sep. 1899.

29   BL 88906/18/6, 8 Sep. 1899.

30   G. Powell, *Buller*, p. 125.

31   T. Pakenham, *Boer War*, p. 96.

32   PP, 1904, XLI, Cd. 1791, RC, 21202, p. 512.

33   Ibid.

34   Hamilton papers, Mss. Eur. F123/81, 14 Sep. 1899.

35   Louis David Riel was a Canadian politician and leader of two resistance movements against the Canadian government (see chapter 6); BL 88906/19/19, 3 Nov. 1885.

36   BL 88906/19/6, 21 Sep. 1899.

37   The Transvaal and the Orange Free State, or Boer States, were strongly independent, Protestant, self-governed republics established by the Dutch-speaking inhabitants of the Cape Province. The Transvaal, or South African Republic, was recognised as an independent country by Great Britain on 17 January 1852 and the Orange Free State achieved independence from Great Britain on 23 February 1854. The Transvaal and the Orange Free State developed into successful independent countries that were recognised by the Netherlands, France, Germany, Belgium and the US. These countries continued to exist despite the First Boer War of 1880.

38   WO 32/7844, 3 Jun. 1899; WO 32/6369/266/Cape/42, 8 Aug. 1899.

39   CAB 37/51/74.

40   Salisbury papers, 3M/E/Lansdowne, f. 444, 29 Sep. 1899.

41   Ibid., f. 442, 30 Sep. 1899.

42   CAB 37/50/76, 3 Oct. 1899.

43   A. Roberts, *Salisbury*, p. 739.

44   Chamberlain papers, JC51/89, 10 Oct. 1899.

45   Wolseley papers, 28/65, 11 Oct. 1899.

46   K.T. Surridge, *Managing the South African War, 1899–1902: Politicians v. Generals* (Woodbridge 1998), p. 73.

47   *The Times*, 12 Oct. 1899.

48   Hansard 4, vol. 77, c. 71.

Chapter 20: The War in South Africa

1   J.W. Mackail and G. Wyndham, *Life and Letters of George Wyndham* (London 1925), vol. 2, p. 70.

2   J. Adye, *Soldiers and Others I Have Known* (London 1925), p. 166.
3   BL 88906/19/18, 18 Oct. 1899.
4   *The Belfast News-Letter*, 3 Nov. 1899.
5   Hansard 4, vol. 77, c. 418.
6   PP, 1904, XL, Cd. 1789, RC, Appendix D, p. 275.
7   Ibid., Cd. 1790, RC, 9467, p. 401.
8   BL 88906/19/3, 7 Nov. 1899.
9   PP, 1904, XL, Cd. 1789, RC, Appendix D, p. 275.
10 Salisbury papers, 3M/E/Hicks Beach, f. 173, 12 Oct. 1899.
11 W.S. Hamer, *The British Army: Civil-Military Relations, 1885–1905* (Oxford 1970), p. 70.
12 Hansard 4, vol. 77, c. 427.
13 Ibid., c. 430.
14 PP, 1904, XLI, Cd. 1791, RC, Appendix J, p. 619.
15 BL 88906/19/5, 11 Nov. 1899.
16 PP, 1904, XLI, Cd. 1791, RC, Appendix J, p. 621.
17 BL 88906/22/20, 15 Dec. 1899.
18 BL 88906/19/5, 15 Dec. 1899.
19 BL 88906/22/20, 16 Dec. 1899.
20 P. Lewsen (ed.), *Selections from the Correspondence of John X. Merriman* (Cape Town 1966), vol. 3, p. 127.
21 J.L. Garvin, *Chamberlain*, vol. 3, p. 519.
22 H.S. Wilkinson, *Lessons of the War: Being Comments from Week to Week to the Relief of Ladysmith* (London 1900), p. 31.
23 K.O. Morgan, 'The Boer War and the Media (1899–1902)', *Twentieth Century British History*, vol. 13, no. 1 (2002), p. 4.
24 BL 88906/18/9, 15 Oct. 1899.
25 *The Spectator*, 6 Jan. 1900.
26 Balfour papers, 49691, f. 82, 19 Dec. 1899.
27 Wolseley papers, 28/71, 31 Oct. 1899.
28 Ibid., 28/83, 21 Dec. 1899.
29 Ibid., 28/63, 28 Sep. 1900.
30 BL 88906/19/22, 22 Oct. 1899.
31 Ibid., 16 Dec. 1899.
32 Curzon papers, Mss. Eur. F111/405, 12 Dec. 1899.
33 Salisbury papers, 3M/E/Balfour, f. 42, 18 Dec. 1899.
34 Ibid.
35 RA VIC/QVJ, 17 Dec. 1899.
36 T. Pakenham, *Boer War*, p. 245.
37 B.E.C. Dugdale, *Arthur James Balfour: First Earl of Balfour* (London 1936), vol. 1, p. 296.
38 BL 88906/22/20, 18 Dec. 1899.
39 C.H. Melville, *The Life of General the Right Hon. Sir Redvers Buller* (London

1923), vol. 2, p. 128; BL 88906/22/18, 20 Jun. 1900.

40 CAB 37/51/105, 29 Dec. 1899.

41 PP, 1904, XL, Cd. 1789, RC, Appendix D, p. 275.

42 In August 1900 he remarked that he had 'lost interest in my work'; Wolseley papers, 29/49i, 1 Aug. 1900. By October it was his view that 'work grates on me'; ibid., 29/67, 24 Oct. 1900.

43 Ibid., 29/63, 28 Sep. 1900.

44 Ibid., 29/47, 13 Jul. 1900.

45 *The Sheffield and Rotherham Independent*, 19 Dec. 1899.

46 Ibid.

47 *The Times*, 28 May 1900.

48 Hansard 4, vol. 78, c. 1181.

49 PP, 1904, XL, Cd. 1789, RC, Appendix E, p. 278.

50 PP, 1904, XLI, Cd. 1791, RC, 21281, p. 520.

51 Ibid., 21325, p. 523.

52 Ibid., 21396-21420, pp. 527–28.

53 PP, 1904, XLI, Cd. 1791, RC, 21280, p. 520.

54 BL 88906/19/3, 12 May 1900.

55 Ibid., 29 May 1900.

56 PP, 1904, XL, Cd. 1790, RC, 239, p. 12.

57 Hansard 4, vol. 83, c. 202.

58 WO 32/6360/266/283&282&281, 6 Jan. 1900.

59 *The Times*, 18 May 1900.

60 G.R. Searle, *A Quest for National Efficiency: A Study in Politics and Political Thought, 1899–1914* (Oxford 1971), p. 40.

61 BL 88906/16/28/5, 17 Jan. 1900.

62 WO 32/6360/266/280, 9 Jan. 1900; WO 32/6360/266/283, 9 Jan. 1900; WO 32/6360/266/282, 8 Jan. 1900.

63 Hansard 4, vol. 83, c. 1179.

64 *The Times*, 13 Feb. 1900.

65 BL 88906/16/28/5, 17 Jan. 1900.

66 Hansard 4, vol. 83, c. 1262.

67 Ibid., vol. 80, c. 1294.

68 Wolseley papers, 28/7i, 18 Jan. 1900.

69 BL 88906/16/28/5, 11 Feb. 1900.

70 Hansard 4, vol. 80, c. 610.

71 Ibid., vol. 80, c. 627.

72 Ibid., vol. 78. c. 1301.

73 *The Times*, 13 Feb. 1900.

Chapter 21: Fighting the War in South Africa

1   WO 108/109, 26 Jan. 1900.

2   BL 88906/22/20, 27 Oct. 1899.

3   BL 88906/19/22, 5 Jan. 1900.

4   WO 105/30, 28 Jan. 1900.

5   W.E. Cairnes, *An Absent-Minded War: Being some reflections on our reserves and the causes that have led to them* (London 1900).

6   G.R. Searle, *A New England?*, p. 279.

7   K.T. Surridge in *The Boer War: Direction, Experience and Image*, ed. J. Gooch (London 2000), p. 35.

8   BL 88906/19/22, 27 Jan. 1900.

9   WO 32/8098, 11 Feb. 1900.

10   Hansard 4, vol. 78, c. 41.

11   Ibid., c. 42.

12   PP, 1904, XLI, Cd. 1791, RC, 21417, p. 528.

13   BL 88906/19/7, 19 Apr. 1900.

14   Ibid., 27 Apr. 1900.

15   *The Times*, 4 May 1900.

16   BL 88906/19/7, 12 Apr. 1900.

17   Balfour papers, 49727, f. 130, 22 Apr. 1900.

18   BL 88906/18/7, 17 Mar. 1900.

19   Ibid., 9 Apr. 1900.

20   Devonshire papers, DF15/3/1/4/1, 20 Jun. 1900.

21   Hansard 4, vol. 78, c. 725,

22   T. Pinney (ed.), *The Letters of Rudyard Kipling* (Basingstoke 1990–2004), vol. 3 (1900–10), p. 22.

23   J.A. Spender, *Life, Journalism and Politics* (London 1927), vol. 2, p. 93.

24   H.E. Raugh Jnr, *The Victorians at War, 1815–1914: An Encyclopaedia of British Military History* (London 2004), p. 53.

25   Monson papers, MS. Eng. hist. c. 1209, f. 52, 4 Apr. 1900.

26   Hansard 4, vol. 79, c. 1356.

27   Minto papers, 12568, f. 212, 4 Mar. 1900.

28   BL 88906/19/24, 27 Jul. 1900.

29   PP, 1904, XL, Cd. 1790, RC, 10520, p. 446.

30   *The New York Times*, 15 Mar. 1900.

31   BL 88906/19/23, 8 Jun. 1900.

32   Hansard 4, vol. 85, cc. 618–20.

33   Ibid., vol. 86, c. 1581.

34   BL 88906/19/7, 6 Jun. 1900.

35   Salisbury papers, 3M/E/Hicks Beach, f. 222, 1 Oct. 1900.

36   BL 88906/19/3, 7 Sep. 1900.

37   Ibid., 10 Sep. 1900.

38   BL 88906/18/8, 27 Sep. 1900.

39   Devonshire papers, DF15/3/1/4/1, 11 Oct. 1900.

40   BL 88906/19/7, 26 Aug. 1900.

41   Interestingly, the government did refer questions to a committee (The

Committee on the Re-organisation of the War Office, under the chairmanship of Clinton Dawkins) within a few weeks of Lansdowne's departure from the War Office.

42   BL 88906/19/7, 2 Feb. 1900.

43   Salisbury papers, 3M/E/Lansdowne, f. 587, 3 Sep. 1900.

44   FO 800/115, 1 Sep. 1900.

45   MacDonnell papers, MS. Eng. hist. c. 351, f. 33, 24 Dec. 1900.

46   A. Roberts, *Salisbury*, p. 756.

47   Ibid., p. 786.

48   Sandars papers, MS. Eng. hist. c. 732, ff. 70–77, 20 Oct. 1900.

49   Ibid., MS. Eng. hist. c. 733, f. 11, 1 Nov. 1900.

50   BL 88906/19/24, 1 Nov. 1900.

51   BL 88906/18/4, 27 Oct. 1895.

52   RA VIC/B51/104, 28 Oct. 1900.

53   Ardagh papers, PRO 30/40/3, 4 Nov. 1900.

54   BL 88906/12/4/6, 1 Mar. 1900.

55   Minto papers, 12393, f. 91, 8 Feb. 1901.

56   *The Times*, 14 Jul. 1898.

57   Ibid., 11 Nov. 1895.

58   Hansard 4, vol. 45, c. 1247.

59   PP, 1904, XL, Cd. 1789, RC, Appendix D, 10, p. 261.

60   Ibid., 21108, p. 503; and 21347, p. 525.

61   Ibid., 21157, p. 508.

62   PP, 1904, XLI, Cd. 1791, RC, 21285-21286, p. 520.

63   Ibid., 21234, p. 514; 21247, p. 515; and 21489, p. 534.

64   H.S. Wilkinson, *Thirty-Five Years 1874–1909* (London 1933), p. 245.

Chapter 22: The Foreign Office

1   J. Charmley, *Splendid Isolation? Britain and the Balance of Power, 1874–1914* (London 1999), p. 279.

2   G.R. Searle, *A New England?*, p. 260.

3   A. Roberts, *Salisbury*, p. 843.

4   S.J. Lee, *Aspects of European History, 1789–1980* (London 1982), p. 260.

5   Roberts papers, 7101/23/34/428, 16 Nov. 1900.

6   Balfour papers, 49727, f. 73, 14 Oct. 1898.

7   Z.S. Steiner, *The Foreign Office and Foreign Policy, 1898–1914* (Cambridge 1969), p. 58.

8   Viscount Grey of Fallodon, *Twenty-Five Years, 1892–1916* (London 1925), vol. 1, p. 1.

9   The National Archives, 'The Permanent Under-Secretary of State: A Brief History of the Office and its Holders. The Last Super-Clerk, 1894–1906'.

10   Z.S. Steiner, *Foreign Office*, pp. 12–13.

11 G.R. Searle, *A New England?*, p. 262.

12 B.E.C. Dugdale, *Balfour*, vol. 2, p. 292.

13 Z.S. Steiner, *Foreign Office*, p. 172.

14 FO 800/144, f. 437, 7 Dec. 1905.

15 Grey, *Twenty-Five Years*, p. 251.

16 P.G. Richards, *Parliament and Foreign Affairs* (London 1967), Introduction.

17 A. Adonis, *Making Aristocracy Work: The Peerage and Political System in Britain, 1884–1914* (Oxford 1999), p. 72.

18 M.V. Brett (ed.), *Journals and Letters of Reginald, Viscount Esher* (London 1934), vol. 1 (1870–1903), p. 267.

19 J. Charmley, *Splendid Isolation*, p. 279.

20 H. von Eckardstein, *Ten Years at the Court of St James, 1895–1905* (London 1921).

21 G.W. Monger, *The End of Isolation: British Foreign Policy, 1900–1907* (London 1963), p. 75.

22 A. Roberts, *Salisbury*, p. 771.

23 G.R. Searle, *A New England?*, p. 272.

24 P.M. Kennedy, *The Rise and Fall of the Great Powers* (London 1987), p. 242.

25 G.W. Monger, *End of Isolation*, p. 23.

26 J.A.S. Grenville, *Lord Salisbury and Foreign Policy: The Close of the Nineteenth Century* (London 1964), p. 340.

27 Margot Asquith papers, MS. Eng. hist. d. 3207, f. 207, 15 Nov. 1909.

28 G.W. Monger, *End of Isolation*, p. 43.

29 Scott papers, 52297, f. 106, 26 Mar. 1901.

30 Ibid.

31 Ibid., 52304, f. 14, 4 Apr. 1901.

32 G.W. Monger, *End of Isolation*, p. 33.

33 K. Neilson, *Britain and the Last Tsar: British Policy and Russia, 1894–1917* (Oxford 1995), p. 40.

34 J.A.S. Grenville, *Salisbury*, p. 429.

35 Chamberlain papers, JC11/21/6, 16 Mar. 1901.

36 M.B. Hayne, *The French Foreign Office and the Origins of the First World War, 1898–1914* (Oxford 1993), p. 104.

37 G.W. Monger, *End of Isolation*, p. 40.

38 BL 88906/22/21, 30 Sep. 1901.

39 Curzon papers, Mss. Eur. F111/160, 17 Oct. 1901.

40 BL 88906/22/21, 9 Jul. 1901.

41 FO 60/645, 29 Nov. 1901.

42 G.W. Monger, *End of Isolation*, p. 54.

43 Bertie papers, 63014, f. 134, 30 Oct. 1901.

44 Ibid.

45 Ibid.

46 Curzon papers, Mss. Eur. F111/161, 16 Feb. 1902.

47   Ibid.

48   G.W. Monger, *End of Isolation*, p. 51.

Chapter 23: New Impetus at the Foreign Office

1   Z.S. Steiner, 'Great Britain and the creation of the Anglo-Japanese Alliance', *The Journal of Modern History*, vol. 31, no.1 (1959).

2   A.J.P. Taylor, *The Struggle for Mastery in Europe, 1848–1918* (Oxford 1954), p. 399.

3   Selborne papers, MS. Selborne 26, f. 106, 10 Sep. 1901.

4   A. Roberts, *Salisbury*, p. 814.

5   A.M. Pooley (ed.), *Secret Memoirs of Count Tadasu Hayashi* (London 1915), p. 131.

6   Balfour papers, 49727, f. 159, 12 Dec. 1901.

7   Ibid., f. 180, 12 Dec. 1901.

8   BL 88906/17/4, 6 Nov. 1901.

9   G.W. Monger, *End of Isolation*, p. 58.

10   Salisbury papers, 3M/E/Lansdowne, f. 665, 1 Jan. 1902.

11   I. Nish, *The Anglo-Japanese Alliance: The Diplomacy of Two Island Empires, 1894–1907* (London 1985), p. 7.

12   A.M. Pooley (ed.), *Hayashi*, p. 189.

13   Hansard 4, vol. 102, c. 1176.

14   H.W.V. Temperley, 'British Secret Diplomacy from Canning to Grey', *Cambridge Historical Journal*, vol. 6, no. 1 (1938).

15   A.J.P. Taylor, *Struggle*, p. 405.

16   The Monroe Doctrine was a US foreign policy, beginning in 1823, of opposing domination of the American continent. It stipulated that further efforts by European nations to colonise land or interfere with states in North or South America would be viewed as acts of aggression, requiring US intervention.

17   Newton, *Lansdowne*, p. 256.

18   Ardagh papers, PRO 30/40/21, 2 Dec. 1902.

19   Curzon papers, Mss. Eur. F 111/161, 24 Dec. 1902.

20   FO 800/144, 4 Dec. 1902.

21   The USA inherited the boundary defined in the 1825 Anglo-Russian treaty, but it claimed the whole coastline, including fjords; Canada demanded control of the heads of certain fjords, especially the Lynn Canal. The Klondike Gold Rush of 1897 and the subsequent rise in population gave the dispute prominence. Negotiations in 1898–99 failed.

22   Balfour papers, 49728, f. 71, 16 Oct. 1903.

23   Minto papers, 12568, f. 260, 11 Jan. 1904.

24   OIOC L/PS/18b/139, 7 Apr. 1902.

25   Chamberlain papers, JC 18/3/1, 14 Apr. 1903.

26   BL 88906/17/6, 20 Jun. 1903.

27   Balfour papers, 49728, f. 41, 12 Apr. 1903.
28   Hansard 4, vol. 121, c. 1348.
29   A.L. Kennedy, *Old Diplomacy and New 1876–1922: From Salisbury to Lloyd-George* (London 1922), p. 131.
30   BL 88906/22/22, 4 Sep. 1903.
31   Salisbury papers, 4M/53, f. 93, 21 Sep. 1903.
32   BL 88906/17/6, 25 Sep. 1903.
33   BL 88906/18/9, 28 Sep. 1903.
34   BL 88906/22/22, Dec. 1904.
35   A.L. Kennedy, *Diplomacy*, p. 134.
36   BL 88906/17/5, 28 Oct. 1903.
37   K. Neilson, *Britain*, p. 312.
38   BL 88906/21/5, 27 Feb. 1904.
39   Newton, *Lansdowne*, p. 305.
40   BL 88906/22/22, Dec. 1904.
41   BL 88906/17/5, 22 Dec. 1903.
42   A.L. Kennedy, *Diplomacy*, p. 135.
43   Sandars papers, MS. Eng. hist. c. 716, f. 154, 16 Dec. 1904.
44   BL 88906/21/5, 18 May 1905.
45   A.K. Kennedy, *Diplomacy*, p. 136.
46   BL 88906/18/11, 23 Aug. 1902.
47   BL 88906/17/5, 24 Aug. 1902.
48   BL 88906/18/11, 25 Aug. 1902.
49   G.W. Monger, *End of Isolation*, p. 89.
50   BL 88906/18/11, 28 Aug. 1902.
51   Ibid., 25 Oct. 1902.
52   Ibid., 3 Nov. 1902.
53   Ibid.

Chapter 24: Further Changes in Direction

1   BL 88906/12/4/7, 10 Jul. 1902.
2   Ibid., 12 Jul. 1902.
3   Curzon papers, Mss. Eur. F 111/161, 17 Jul. 1902.
4   G.W. Monger, *End of Isolation*, pp. 98-99.
5   Sandars papers, MS. Eng. hist. c. 715, f. 9, 19 Feb. 1903.
6   Newton, *Lansdowne*, p. 272.
7   Sandars papers, MS. Eng. hist. c. 715, f. 9, 19 Feb. 1903.
8   Curzon papers, Mss. Eur. F 111/162, 8 Apr. 1903.
9   A. Lamb, *Britain and Chinese Central Asia: The Road to Lhasa, 1767–1905* (London 1960), p. 298.
10   BL 88906/17/4, 1 Oct. 1903.
11   BL 88906/22/22, 19 Dec. 1903.
12   BL 88906/17/6, 5 May 1904.

13 BL 88906/17/2, 4 Oct. 1904.

14 G.W. Monger, *End of Isolation*, p. 126.

15 Monson papers, MS. Eng. hist. c. 595, f. 75, 11 Mar. 1903.

16 I. Dunlop, *Edward VII and the Entente Cordiale* (London 2004), p. 194.

17 Ibid.

18 Cromer papers, FO 633/6, 17 Nov. 1903.

19 S.R. Williamson, *The Politics of Grand Strategy: Britain and France Prepare for War, 1904–1914* (Cambridge, Mass. 1969), p. 1.

20 I. Dunlop, *Edward VII*, p. 224.

21 BL 88906/18/12, 13 Apr. 1904.

22 BL 88906/12/4/8, 11 Apr. 1904.

23 L. McKinstry, *Rosebery*, p. 463.

24 A.J.P. Taylor, *Struggle*, p. 420.

25 BL 88906/18/12, 15 Apr. 1904.

26 A.J.P. Taylor, *Struggle*, p. 421.

27 The Egyptian Khedivial Decree appended to the Anglo-French Entente Cordiale concerned the administration and liquidation of Egyptian debt. The Decree gave protection to foreign bondholders, and to the Egyptian Government a free hand in the management of its financial affairs so long as punctual payment of interest on its debt was assured.

28 Sandars papers, MS. Eng. hist. c. 716, f. 40, 4 May 1904.

29 Ibid.

30 BL 88906/22/21, 10 May 1904.

31 A.W. FitzRoy, *Memoirs* (London 1925), vol. 1, p. 97.

32 6th Marquess of Lansdowne, *Glanerought*, p. 191.

33 T. Pakenham, *The Scramble for Africa* (London 1991), p. 588.

34 BL 88906/22/1, Jul. 1907.

35 Lord Monkswell, 'The Government and the Congo Free State: A Plea for British Consular Jurisdiction', *Fortnightly Review*, 81 (1907), pp. 476–88.

36 BL 88906/22/1, 4 Jul. 1904.

37 Lord Monkswell, 'Government', *Fortnightly Review*, 81 (1907), pp. 476–88.

38 BL 88906/27/4, 31 Aug. 1902.

39 BL 88906/27/4, 7 Mar. 1905.

40 Balfour papers, 49729, f. 266, 13 Oct. 1906.

41 BL 88906/20/5, 13 Oct. 1906.

42 BL 88906/19/9, 13 Oct. 1906.

Chapter 25: The Transformation of the Foreign Office

1 Minto papers, 12568, f. 260, 11 Jan. 1904.

2 Sandars papers, MS. Eng. hist. c. 744, f. 174, 6 Oct. 1903.

3 BL 88906/22/28/3, 16 Oct. 1903.

4 Sandars papers, MS. Eng. hist. c. 745, f. 30, 7 Oct. 1903.

5 J. Amery, *The Life of Joseph Chamberlain*, vol 5: *1901–1903 Joseph Chamberlain*

and the Tariff Reform Campaign (London 1969), p. 590.

6   The Cobden Club was a political gentlemen's club in London founded in 1866 for believers in free trade. It was named in honour of Richard Cobden, a Liberal statesman and free trade campaigner, who died in 1865.

7   Joseph Chamberlain's fiscal dream was for an imperial federation, based on the model of Bismarckian Germany, to enable Britain to maintain its global role in the thick of the economic challenge of the United States and Germany. He wanted imperial preference in trade with the Empire and tariffs on foreign imports. He believed that such tariffs would secure finance for social welfare improvements. With a certain degree of self-interest he also believed his programme would help maintain the Unionists' hold on the West Midlands, and further enhance his power within the government.

8   Curzon papers, Mss. Eur. F 111/62, 1 Feb. 1904.

9   BL 88906/17/5, 20 Dec. 1904.

10 G.P. Gooch and H.W.V. Temperley, *British Documents on the Origins of the War 1898–1914*, vol. 2: *The Anglo-Japanese Alliance and the Franco-British Entente* (London 1927), no. 259.

11 Balfour papers, 49728, f. 109, 22 Dec. 1903.

12 BL 88906/22/15, 22 Dec. 1903.

13 BL 88906/17/5, 22 Dec. 1903.

14 BL 88906/17/6, 1 Jan. 1904.

15 A.S.T. Griffith-Boscawen, *Fourteen Years in Parliament* (London 1907), p. 321.

16 Newton, *Lansdowne*, p. 315.

17 R.K. Massie, *Nicholas and Alexandra: An Intimate Account of the Last of the Romanovs and the Fall of Imperial Russia* (London 1968), p. 89.

18 BL 88906/18/12, 26 Oct. 1904.

19 Ibid., 28 Oct. 1904.

20 Bertie papers, 63016, f. 142, 27 Oct. 1904.

21 Newton, *Lansdowne*, p. 316.

22 FO 800/134/229, 2 Feb. 1905.

23 BL 88906/22/26, 12 Feb. 1905.

24 M. Durand papers, MS. 55, Box 6 (file 42), 17 Mar. 1905.

25 D. Steeds, 'The Second Anglo-Japanese Alliance and the Russo-Japanese War', *The Suntory and Toyota International Centres for Economics and Related Disciplines*, Discussion Papers, no. IS/02/432, 2002, p. 20.

26 BL 88906/22/26, 24 Mar. 1905.

27 FO 800/144, 25 Jan. 1905.

28 D. Steeds, 'The Second Anglo-Japanese Alliance', p. 21; G.P. Gooch and H.W.V. Temperley, *British Documents*, vol 4: *The Anglo-Russian Rapprochement, 1903–1907* (London 1953), no. 155.

29 M. Paléologue, *The Turning Point: Three Critical Years, 1904–1906* (London 1935), p. 301.

30 S. Gwynn (ed.), *The Letters and Friendships of Sir Cecil Spring Rice: A Record* (London 1929), vol. 1, p. 486.

31 Newton, *Lansdowne*, p. 338.

32 Balfour papers, 49729, f. 77, 18 Jan. 1905.

33 G.W. Monger, *End of Isolation*, p. 186.

34 E.N. Anderson, *The First Moroccan Crisis, 1904–1906* (London 1966), p. 209.

35 BL 88906/22/23, 25 May 1905.

36 Newton, *Lansdowne*, p. 341.

37 BL 88906/17/5, 23 Aug. 1905.

38 E.N. Anderson, *Moroccan Crisis*, p. 292.

39 Balfour papers, 49727, f. 200, 17 Mar. 1902.

40 Lansdowne interviewed by Harold Temperley, 11 July 1926, quoted in H.W.V. Temperley, 'British Secret Diplomacy from Canning to Grey', *Cambridge Historical Journal*, vol. 6, no. 1 (1938), p. 26.

41 BL 88906/17/4, 1 Dec. 1905.

42 Roberts papers, NAM 7101/23/34/458, 5 Dec. 1905.

43 R.J.Q. Adams, *Balfour: The Last Grandee* (London 2007), p. 228.

44 Z.S. Steiner, *Foreign Office*, p. 185.

45 J.A.S. Grenville, *Salisbury*, p. 437.

46 The Committee of Imperial Defence (CID) was established by Balfour after the deliberations of the Elgin Commission were reported in 1904. It was an advisory committee to the government that replaced the cabinet's decrepit Defence Committee. It dealt with matters of military planning and the problems of imperial strategy.

47 Z.S. Steiner, *Foreign Office*, p. 54.

48 *The Times*, 7 Nov. 1905.

49 BL 88906/12/5/8, n.d. [*c*.1918].

50 BL 88906/21/2/2, 1 Dec. 1920. Translated: 'May this agreement persist, because without it I do not see Europe without disorder and confusion.'

Chapter 26: Living with the Liberals

1 Sandars papers, MS. Eng. hist. c. 751, f. 106, 22 Jan. 1906.

2 Ibid.

3 Hansard 4, vol. 176, c. 1429.

4 The Unionist free fooders or free traders were a small group of Cecilian Conservatives and Liberal Unionists totally opposed to protection and Chamberlain's doctrines of tariff reform.

5 Devonshire papers, 318.7a, 25 Jan. 1906.

6 BL 88906/19/13, 28 Jan. 1906.

7 BL 88906/19/1, 28 Jan. 1906.

8 BL 88906/19/1, 4 Feb. 1906.

9 Ibid., 4 Feb. 1906.

10   J. Amery, *The Life of Joseph Chamberlain*, vol 6: *1903–1968 Joseph Chamberlain and the Tariff Reform Campaign* (London 1969), p. 832.

11   BL 88906/19/1, 7 Feb. 1906.

12   The Valentine Letters exchanged between Balfour and Chamberlain were published on 15 February 1906. They got their name as they were written on St Valentine's day.

13   *The Times*, 22 Feb. 1906.

14   C. Jones and D.L. Jones (eds), *Peers, Politics and Power: The House of Lords, 1603–1911* (London 1986), pp. 463–64.

15   A.M. Gollin, *Proconsul in Politics: A Study of Lord Milner in Opposition and in Power* (London 1964), p. 90.

16   H.W. Lucy, *Lords and Commoners* (London 1921), p. 69.

17   A. Adonis, *Making Aristocracy Work*, p. 59.

18   H.W. Lucy, *Lords and Commoners*, p. 70.

19   A. Adonis, *Making Aristocracy Work*, p. 59.

20   M.V. Brett (ed.), *Esher*, vol. 2 (1903–10), p. 154.

21   Newton, *Lansdowne*, p. 353.

22   BL 88906/19/1, 5 Apr. 1906.

23   Balfour papers, 49729, f. 228, 13 Apr. 1906.

24   Hansard 4, vol. 162, cc. 1550–62.

25   Ibid., c. 1551.

26   BL 88906/19/13, 13 Dec. 1906.

27   J.D. Fair, *British Interparty Conferences: A Study of the Procedure of Conciliation in British Politics 1867–1921* (Oxford 1980), p. 265.

28   Hansard 4, vol. 165, c. 1382 and c. 1416.

29   Ibid., vol. 167, c. 1740.

30   R. Douglas, *Liberals: A History of the Liberal and Liberal Democratic Parties* (London 2005), p. 121.

31   *Newcastle Daily Journal*, 6 Dec. 1906.

32   *The Times*, 5 Dec. 1906.

33   Devonshire papers, 340. 3244, 15 Nov. 1906; B.E.C. Dugdale, *Balfour*, vol. 2, p. 39.

Chapter 27: Unionist Blocking

1   The fish were not poisoned for malevolent reasons but for the purpose of capturing the fish and selling them. Lansdowne's pools escaped because of watchful ghillies.

2   Haldane papers, 5907 f. 175, 26 Jul. 1907.

3   Duchess of Devonshire, *The House: A Portrait of Chatsworth* (London 1982), p. 43.

4   Minto papers, Astor of Hever, uncatalogued, 27 Aug. 1908.

5   Ibid, 15 Sep. 1908.

6   M. Countess of Minto, *My Indian Journal*, vol. 4, Diary 1909 (Calcutta,

undated), pp. 10–11, 15 Jan. 1909.

7   A. FitzRoy, *Memoirs*, vol. 1 (London 1925), p. 313.

8   Hansard 4, vol. 169, cc. 18–31.

9   D. Cannadine, *Decline*, p. 462.

10   C.T. King, *The Asquith Parliament (1906–1909): A Popular History of its Men and its Measures* (London 1910), p. 160.

11   Rosebery papers, 10020, f. 159. 14 May 1907.

12   D. Cannadine, *Decline*, p. 463.

13   R. Jenkins, *Mr Balfour's Poodle: People vs Peers* (London 1999), p. 52.

14   Hansard 4, vol. 176, c. 909.

15   Selborne papers, MS. 79, f. 20, 4 Jul. 1907.

16   Hansard 4, vol. 176, c. 926.

17   N. Blewett, *The Peers, the Parties and the People: The General Elections of 1910* (Toronto 1972), p. 48.

18   *Birmingham Post*, 12 Dec. 1907.

19   *Scotsman*, 14 Dec. 1907.

20   R.A. Rempel, *Unionists Divided, Arthur Balfour, Joseph Chamberlain and the Unionist Free Traders* (London 1972), p. 181.

21   Ibid.

22   Newton, *Lansdowne*, p. 366.

23   J. Pope-Hennessy, *Lord Crewe, 1858–1945: The Likeness of a Liberal* (London 1955), p. 54.

24   BC, EFm, 12 Dec. 1908.

25   Hansard 4, vol. 192, c. 1421.

26   Ibid.

27   On 27 May 1907 the government announced the Evicted Irish Tenants Bill, by which the Estates Commissioners could compel landowners to sell to them land required for evicted tenants. Lansdowne advised the Lords on passing the measure after making amendments. It was introduced on 27 June and passed its third reading the following August by 228 votes to 49.

28   B. Tuchman, *The Proud Tower: A Portrait of the World Before the War, 1890–1914* (London 1966), p. 443.

29   J. Grigg, *Lloyd George: The People's Champion, 1902–11* (London 1978), p. 173.

30   A. FitzRoy, *Memoirs*, vol. 1, p. 368.

31   Newton, *Lansdowne*, p. 369.

32   *Sunday Chronicle*, 29 Nov. 1908.

Chapter 28: The People's Budget

1   RA GVD, 16 Feb. 1909.

2   BL 88906/21/5, 9 Jan. 1909.

3   Minto papers, 12775, f. 120, 30 Dec. 1908.

4   BL 88906/22/3, 21 Jan. 1909.

5   Ibid., 18 Mar. 1903.

6   D. Cannadine, *Decline*, p. 48.

7   B. Tuchman, *Proud Tower*, p. 386.

8   B.K. Murray, *The People's Budget 1909/10: Lloyd George and Liberal Politics* (Oxford 1980), p. 13.

9   Between 3 May and 16 July Lansdowne made no public speeches. From 21 May until 27 July Balfour made no public speeches regarding the Budget.

10   *Guardian*, 20 Jul. 1909.

11   Sandars papers, MS. Eng. hist. c. 759, f. 57, 4 Aug. 1909.

12   Ibid., c. 758, f. 99, 11 Aug. 1909.

13   Lady V. A. Hicks Beach, *Life of Sir Michael Hicks Beach (Earl St Aldwyn)* (London, 1932), vol. 2, p. 260.

14   G. Lee, *The People's Budget: An Edwardian Tragedy* (London 2008), p. 54.

15   *The Times*, 9 Aug. 1909.

16   Curzon papers, Mss. Eur. F112/16, 6 Sep. 1909.

17   G. Lee, *People's Budget*, pp. 54–56.

18   D. Cannadine, *Decline*, p. 49.

19   B. Tuchman, *Proud Tower*, p. 388.

20   Hansard 5, vol. 4, c. 589.

21   A. FitzRoy, *Memoirs*, vol. 1, p. 386.

22   W.S. Blunt, *My Diaries: Being a Personal Narrative of Events 1888–1914* (London 1920), vol. 2 (1900–14), p. 293.

23   J. Grigg, *People's Champion*, p. 232.

24   D. Cannadine, *Decline*, p. 50.

25   *The Times*, 4 Dec. 1909.

26   Ibid., 6 Dec. 1909.

Chapter 29: The 1910 General Elections

1   *The Times*, 4 Dec. 1909.

2   N. Blewett, *Peers*, p. 103.

3   Balfour papers, 49730, f. 56, 1 Feb. 1910.

4   *The Times*, 6 Jan. 1910.

5   A. Adonis, *Making Aristocracy Work*, p. 267.

6   Chamberlain papers, AC8/5/4, 31 Jan. 1910.

7   A. FitzRoy, *Memoirs*, vol. 1, p. 397.

8   Chamberlain papers, AC8/5/4, 31 Jan. 1910.

9   BL 88906/24/3, 15 Feb. 1910.

10   R. Jenkins, *Mr Balfour's Poodle*, p. 130.

11   'Guillotine' or time motions were used to limit the amount of time that MPs could spend debating a particular stage of a bill in the House of Commons.

12   Selborne papers, MS. Selborne 74, f. 7, 23 Mar. 1910.

13   A. Chamberlain, *Politics From Inside: An Epistolary Chronicle, 1906–1914*

(London 1936), p. 233.

14 BL 88906/24/2, 17 Mar. 1910.

15 BL 88906/24/3, 22 Mar. 1910.

16 That is, 'hasten the outcome'.

17 A. Chamberlain, *Politics From Inside*, p. 261.

18 BL 88906/24/3, 13 May. 1910.

19 G. Lewis, *Carson: The Man Who Divided Ireland* (London 2005), p. 72.

20 BL 88906/24/2, 2 Aug. 1910.

21 Ibid.

22 Ibid., 29 Aug. 1910.

23 *Daily Mail*, 16 Nov. 1910.

24 Bryce papers, MS. Bryce 250, 28 Sep. 1917.

25 BL 88906/24/5, 25 Oct. 1910.

26 Strachey papers, S/9/7/2, 26 Nov. 1910.

27 BL 88906/24/2, 14 Dec. 1910.

28 Ibid.

29 Sandars papers, MS. Eng. hist. c. 763, f. 162, 12 Aug. 1911.

30 Strachey papers, S/9/7/3, 8 Jan. 1911.

Chapter 30: The King

1   RA GVD, 27 Jan. 1911.

2   Newton, *Lansdowne*, pp. 409–10.

3   Ibid.

4   Ibid.

5   *The Times*, 6 Feb. 1911.

6   British Library Sound Archive, c. 707/395/1-3, Disc 4, Track 4.

7   Balfour papers, 49730, f. 203, 19 Mar. 1911.

8   Ibid., 49730, f. 196, 19 Mar. 1911.

9   Salisbury papers, 4M 70 f. 10, 13 Apr. 1911.

10 BL 88906/24/12, 15 Jan. 1918.

11 Newton, *Lansdowne*, p. 415.

12 A. Chamberlain, *Politics From Inside*, p. 338.

13 M. Bonham Carter and M. Pottle (eds), *Lantern Slides: The Diaries and Letters of Violet Bonham Carter 1904–1914* (London 1997), p. 272.

14 Roberts papers, 7101/23/34/493, 12 May 1911.

15 E. Allyn, *Lords versus Commons: A Century of Conflict and Compromise, 1830–1930* (Philadelphia, Penn. 1931), p. 207.

16 W.S. Blunt, *Diaries*, vol. 2 (1900–14), p. 363.

17 BL 88906/12/5/12, 5th Marquess of Lansdowne, 'The Marquis and the Beetle'.

18 *The Standard*, 19 May 1911.

19 E.T.S. Dugdale (ed.), *German Diplomatic Documents, 1871–1914*, vol. 3: *The Growing Antagonism, 1898–1910* (London 1930), p. 414.

20   Lansdowne's amendment excluded from the Parliament Bill's provisions any Bills affecting the Crown, devolution and any 'issue of great gravity upon which the judgment of the country has not been sufficiently ascertained', and to subject them to the Referendum. Hansard 5, vol. 9, cc. 100–101.

21   J.A. Spender and C. Asquith, *Life of Henry Herbert Asquith, Lord Oxford and Asquith* (London 1932), vol. 1, p. 309.

22   G.D. Phillips, 'Lord Willoughby de Broke and the Politics of Radical Toryism, 1909–1914', *Journal of British Studies*, vol. 20, no. 1 (1980), pp. 209–11.

23   BL 88906/24/6, 19 Jul. 1911.

24   L. Masterman, *C.F.G. Masterman: A Biography* (London 1939), p. 200.

25   BL 88906/24/6, 19 Jul. 1911.

Chapter 31: The Final Stages of the Parliament Bill

1   Willoughby de Broke papers, WB2/123, 17 Jun. 1911.

2   J.A. Spender and C. Asquith, *Asquith*, vol. 1, p. 309.

3   Hansard 5, vol. 9, c. 585.

4   BL 88906/24/5, 20 Jul. 1911.

5   BL 88906/24/6, 23 Jul. 1911.

6   Curzon papers, Mss. Eur. F112/89, n.d. [*c*.1910s].

7   Devonshire papers, A5 348, n.d. [*c*.1910s].

8   Newton, *Lansdowne*, p. 425.

9   Strachey papers, S/5/5/21, 26 Jul. 1911.

10   Sandars papers, MS. Eng. hist. c. 763, f. 162, 12 Aug. 1911.

11   Ibid., MS. Eng. hist. c. 763, f. 122, 29 Jul. 1911.

12   Ibid., MS. Eng. hist. c. 763, f. 162, 12 Aug. 1911.

13   Curzon papers, Mss. Eur. F112/89, 10 Aug. 1911.

14   Strachey papers, S/2/4/34, 2 Aug. 1911.

15   Sandars papers, MS. Eng. hist. c. 763, f. 162, 12 Aug. 1911.

16   Viscount Simon, *Retrospect: the memoirs of the Rt. Hon. Viscount Simon* (London 1952), p. 83.

17   R. Jenkins, *Mr Balfour's Poodle*, p. 254.

18   A. FitzRoy, *Memoirs*, vol. 2, p. 458.

19   R.J.Q. Adams, *Balfour*, p. 254.

20   R. Jenkins, *Mr Balfour's Poodle*, p. 243.

21   M. Bonham Carter and M. Pottle (eds), *Lantern Slides*, p. 277.

22   G. Lee, *People's Budget*, p. 70.

23   W.S. Blunt, *Diaries*, vol. 2 (1900–14), p. 376.

24   D. Cannadine, *Decline*, p. 525.

25   M. Egremont, *The Cousins: The Friendship, Opinions and Activities of Wilfrid Scawen Blunt and George Wyndham* (London 1977), p. 279. The Harmsworth Press refers to *The Times, Daily Mail, Daily Mirror* and regional newspapers

owned by Lord Northcliffe (formerly Alfred Harmsworth).

26 Roberts papers, 7101/23/34/494, 12 Aug. 1911.

27 BL 88906/24/6, 19 Aug. 1911.

28 Newton, *Lansdowne*, p. 431.

29 The dockers' strike began in May at Newport and the merchant seamen's and firemen's strikes began in mid-June.

30 Newton, *Lansdowne*, p. 431.

31 Devonshire papers, C8 1365, 22 Aug. 1911.

32 Ibid., C8 1367, 11 Aug. 1911.

33 Ibid.

Chapter 32: New Direction

1 Willoughby de Broke papers, WB/3/74, 7 Oct. 1911.

2 Balfour papers, 49730, f. 4, 17 Oct. 1911.

3 Devonshire papers, C8 1362, 14 Oct. 1911.

4 Balfour papers, 49730, f. 252, 2 Nov. 1911.

5 J. Vincent (ed.), *The Crawford Papers: The Journals of David Lindsay, 27th Earl of Crawford and 10th Earl of Balcarres, 1871–1940, during the years 1892–1940* (Manchester 1984), p. 239.

6 Bonar Law papers, 24/3/13, 12 Nov. 1911.

7 Devonshire papers, C9 1389, 12 Nov. 1911.

8 Ibid., C9 1391, 23 Nov. 1911.

9 Ibid.

10 Curzon papers, Mss. Eur. F112/18, 25 Sep. 1911.

11 R. Blake, *The Unknown Prime Minister: The Life and Times of Andrew Bonar Law, 1858–1923* (London 1955), p. 102.

12 BL 88906/23/22/1, 7 Feb. 1911.

13 A. Chamberlain, *Politics From Inside*, p. 475.

14 A. Taylor, *Bonar Law* (London 2006), p. 46.

15 J. Vincent (ed.), *The Crawford Papers*, p. 264.

16 Bonar Law papers, 28/3/28, 10 Oct. 1912.

17 Ibid.

18 George Wyndham's 1903 Irish Land (Purchase) Act: the basis was that the sale of land was made not compulsory but attractive to both parties, based on the government paying the difference between the price offered by tenants and that demanded by landlords.

19 Home Rule All Round meant a system of partial autonomy within the British Empire for all those who wanted it (i.e. Home Rule for Scotland and Wales as well as Ireland).

20 Curzon papers, Mss. Eur. F112/18, 25 Sep. 1911.

21 *Daily Telegraph*, 2 Dec. 1911.

22 A. Jackson, *Home Rule: An Irish History 1800–2000* (Oxford 2004), p. 128.

23 Newton, *Lansdowne*, p. 504.

24   Chamberlain papers, AC10/2/21, 22 Aug. 1912.

25   Long papers, 947, f. 439, 13 Apr. 1913.

26   *Birmingham Daily Post*, 25 Jul. 1912.

27   *The Times*, 14 Nov. 1912.

28   R.J.Q. Adams, *Bonar Law* (London 1999), p. 84.

29   Devonshire papers, C8 1380, 11 Jan. 1913.

30   BC, EFm, 11 Jan. 1913.

31   Milner papers, MS. Milner 39, f. 42, 14 Dec. 1912

32   G. Lewis, *Carson*, p. 110.

33   *The Times*, 31 Jan. 1913.

34   Ibid., 9 Dec. 1912.

35   A. O'Day, *Irish Home Rule*, p. 254.

Chapter 33: Home Rule Progresses

1   Hansard 5, vol. 55, c. 802.

2   Howard Bury papers, T/3069/Q/5, 31 Jul. 1913.

3   *Daily Telegraph*, 15 Jul. 1913.

4   Ibid.

5   H. Nicolson, *King George the Fifth: His Life and Reign* (London 1952), p. 220.

6   BL 88906/27/6, 10 Sep. 1913.

7   Ibid.

8   D.H. Parker, *The Story of My Life in Gentleman's Service* (privately printed, May 1978), p. 6.

9   *The Evening News*, 15 Sep. 1913.

10   *The Times*, 11 Sep. 1913.

11   J. Kendle, *Ireland and the Federal Solution: The Debate over the United Kingdom Constitution, 1870–1921* (Quebec 1989), p. 160.

12   BL 88906/27/7, 11 Sep. 1913.

13   BL 88906/19/20, 26 Sep. 1913.

14   Bonar Law papers, 33/5/56, 18 Sep. 1913.

15   Ibid., 30/2/17, 20 Sep. 1913.

16   Ibid., 30/3/3, 2 Oct. 1913.

17   BL 88906/27/7, 8 Oct. 1913.

18   *The Times*, 27 Oct. 1913.

19   Bonar Law papers, 30/3/56, 27 Oct. 1913.

20   *The Times*, 19 Nov. 1913.

21   Bonar Law papers, 33/6/109, 8 Dec. 1913.

22   R. Blake, *Bonar Law*, p. 166.

23   Bonar Law papers, 31/1/25, 11 Dec. 1913.

24   Ibid., 31/1/63, 29 Dec. 1913.

25   A. O'Day, *Irish Home Rule*, p. 258.

26   Bonar Law papers, 31/1/15, 23 Dec. 1913.

Chapter 34: Rising Militancy

1   Devonshire papers, C8 1364, 22 Jun. 1913.

2   *Morning Post*, 10 Jul. 1913.

3   R. Douglas, *Land, People and Politics*, p. 165.

4   A. Sykes, *Tariff Reform in British Politics, 1903–1913* (London 1979), p. 279.

5   J. Grigg, *Lloyd George: From Peace to War, 1912–1916* (London [1985] 1997), p. 98.

6   Bonar Law papers, 30/3/47, 23 Oct. 1913.

7   Catherine Marshall papers, D/Mar 3/22, 9 Aug. 1913.

8   Ibid.

9   Willoughby de Broke papers, WB8/12, 5 Feb. 1914.

10 Hansard 5, vol. 15 cc. 56–144.

11 Willoughby de Broke papers, WB/8/26, 7 Feb. 1914.

12 Ibid., WB 8/47, 8 Feb. 1914.

13 J. Grigg, *Lloyd George: From Peace to War*, p. 118.

14 R.J.Q. Adams, *Balfour*, p. 280.

15 A. Jackson, *Home Rule*, p. 151.

16 *The Times*, 24 Mar. 1914.

17 F. Partridge, *T.A.B.: A Memoir of Thomas Allnutt, Second Earl Brassey* (London 1921), p. 218.

18 *The Times*, 2 May 1914.

19 Ibid.

20 Willoughby de Broke papers, WB/10/9, 10 May 1913.

21 A.M. Gollin, *'The Observer' and J.L. Garvin, 1908–1914: A Study in a Great Editorship* (Oxford 1960), p. 218.

22 BL 88906/27/8, 8 Jun. 1914.

23 *The Irish Times*, 25 May 1914.

24 Long papers, 62403, f. 168, 26 May 1914.

25 Bonar Law papers, 32/3/55, 27 May 1914.

26 BL 88906/27/8, 31 May 1914.

27 Bonar Law papers, 32/3/57, 29 May 1914.

28 *The Times*, 16 Jun. 1914.

29 *The Tablet*, 27 Jun. 1914.

30 R.J.Q. Adams, *Balfour*, p. 284.

31 Mensdorff papers, AT-OeSta/HHStA SB NI Mensdorff, 11-9, 28 Jun. 1914.

32 Hansard 5, vol. 16, c. 540.

33 Ibid.

34 A. Jackson, *Home Rule*, p. 159.

35 E. David (ed.), *Inside Asquith's Cabinet: From the Diaries of Charles Hobhouse* (London 1977), p. 175.

36 G.R. Searle, *A New England?*, p. 433.

Chapter 35: The Outbreak of the First World War

1   S. Gwynn (ed.), *Spring Rice*, vol. 2, p. 210.

2   D.H. Parker, *The Story of My Life*, p. 9.

3   Chamberlain papers, AC14/2/2, n.d. [*c*.1914].

4   BL 88906/25/21/1, 2 Aug. 1914.

5   J.W. Young, 'Conservative Leaders, Coalition, and Britain's Decision for War in 1914', *Diplomacy and Statecraft*, vol. 25, no. 2 (2014), p. 231.

6   Ibid., 1/2 Aug. 1914.

7   Ibid., 4 Aug. 1914.

8   *Glasgow Evening Citizen*, 6 Aug. 1914.

9   Ibid.

10   *The Times*, 7 Aug. 1914.

11   M. Brock and E. Brock (eds), *H H Asquith: Letters to Venetia Stanley* (Oxford 1985), p. 160.

12   BL 88906/20/4, 21 Aug. 1914.

13   Hansard 5, vol. 17, c. 612.

14   M. Brock and E. Brock (eds), *Letters*, p. 235.

15   *Nottingham Post*, 18 Sep. 1914.

16   *Queen*, 26 Nov. 1914.

17   *Westminster Gazette*, 22 Sep. 1914.

18   Selborne papers, MS. Selborne 92, f. 214, 22 Oct. 1914.

19   Sandars papers, MS. Eng. hist. c. 767, f. 85, 5 Nov. 1914.

20   Curzon papers, Mss. Eur. F112/96, 2 Nov. 1914.

21   BC, Lans (5), n.d. [*c*.1915], 5th Marquess of Lansdowne, 'Major Lord Charles Mercer Nairne'.

22   *Sheffield Daily Telegraph*, 12 Nov. 1914.

23   MS. Bonham Carter 737, ff. 4–7, 11 Nov. 1914.

24   The 'pranks' refers to action taken by Winston Churchill, then First Lord of the Admiralty, to take matters into his own hands after King Albert and the Belgian government decided to evacuate the fortified city of Antwerp and to withdraw to Ostend.

25   Selborne papers, MS. Selborne 92, f. 214, 22 Oct. 1914.

26   Bonar Law papers, 35/5/52, 20 Dec. 1914.

27   Ibid., 23 Dec. 1914.

28   Curzon papers, Mss. Eur. F112/96, 15 Dec. 1914.

29   Ibid., 7 Jan. 1915.

30   C. Hazlehurst, *Politicians at War, July 1914 to May 1915: A Prologue to the Triumph of Lloyd George* (London 1974), p. 154.

31   M. Brock and E. Brock (eds), *Letters*, p. 364.

32   *Daily Sketch*, 2 Feb. 1915.

33   Hansard 5, vol. 18, c. 416.

34   R.J.Q. Adams, *Bonar Law*, p. 178.

35   Lord Hankey, *The Supreme Command, 1914–1918* (London 1961), vol. 1, p. 289.

36   S.W. Roskill, *Hankey: Man of Secrets, 1877–1918* (London 1970), vol. 1, p. 161.

37   R.J.Q. Adams and P.P. Poirier, *The Conscription Controversy in Great Britain, 1900–1918* (Basingstoke 1987), p. 75.

38   BC, EFm, 20 May 1915.

39   G.R. Searle, *A New England?*, p. 678.

40   Lloyd George papers, LG/C/6/12/17, 22 May 1915.

41   Grey had been suffering from failing eyesight and fatigue.

42   Lloyd George papers, LG/C/6/12/17, 22 May 1915.

43   Fraser papers, MS. Eng. hist. c. 4790, f. 148, 26 May 1915.

44   *Liverpool Post*, 29 May 1915.

45   E. David (ed.), *Inside Asquith's Cabinet*, p. 249.

46   J. Grigg, *From Peace to War*, p. 308.

47   BL 88906/20/11/1, 9 Nov. 1915.

48   J. Grigg, *From Peace to War*, p. 320.

49   Lord Hankey, *Supreme Command*, p. 444.

50   M. Gilbert (ed.), *Winston S. Churchill*, vol 3: *The Challenge of War, 1914–1916* (London 1966), p. 587.

51   Sir G. Arthur, *Life of Lord Kitchener* (London 1920), vol. 3, p. 307.

52   Lloyd George papers, LG/D/24/10/7, 12 Jun. 1915.

53   Bonar Law papers, 51/2/8, 7 Aug. 1915; Balfour papers, 49730, f. 283, 5 Aug. 1915.

54   Lloyd George papers, LG/D/24/10/K, 8 Oct. 1915.

55   Ibid., LG/D/24/10/13, 29 Sep. 1915.

56   They were promised that only entire groups would be called for active service and that they would have fourteen days' advance notice. It was intended that single men's groups would be called before married ones and that anyone who married after the first day that the scheme came into operation would be classified as single. Married men were promised that their groups would not be called should sufficient single men attest, unless conscription was introduced.

57   Lloyd George papers, LG/D/24/10/15, 8 Oct. 1915.

58   R.J.Q. Adams and P.P. Poirier, *Conscription Controversy*, p. 255.

59   BL 88906/25/16, 23 Nov. 1915.

60   *Morning Post*, 26 Jan. 1916.

61   *The Times*, 26 Jan. 1916.

62   R.J.Q. Adams and P.P. Poirier, *Conscription Controversy*, p. 120.

63   A.J.P. Taylor (ed.), *Lloyd George: A Diary by Frances Stevenson* (London 1971), p. 105.

64   Ibid., p. 168.

Chapter 36: The Fall of the Asquith Coalition

1   BC, Lans (5), ML, 26 Apr. 1916.

2   *The Times*, 27 Apr. 1916.

3   The Easter Rising was an armed insurrection in Ireland during Easter Week of April 1916. It was started by a group of Irish republicans intent on ending British rule in Ireland and establishing an independent Irish Republic. It was the most important uprising in Ireland since the rebellion of 1798, and the first armed action of the Irish revolutionary period.

4   G. Lewis, *Carson*, p. 188.

5   Lloyd George papers, LG/D/15/1/10, 2 Jun. 1916.

6   Ibid.

7   Margot Asquith papers, MS. Eng. hist. c. 6680, f. 150, 9 Jun. 1916.

8   The other Unionist ministers were Austen Chamberlain, Lord Selborne and Walter Long.

9   Lloyd George papers, LG/D/14/3/34, 22 Jun. 1916.

10   A. O'Day, *Irish Home Rule*, p. 272.

11   Selborne papers, MS. Selborne 80, f. 209, 23 Jun. 1916.

12   Asquith papers, MS. Asquith 8, ff. 171–78, 27 Jun. 1916.

13   Crewe papers, C/30, 25 Jun. 1916.

14   Long papers, 947/268, 26 Jun. 1916.

15   BC, EFm, 1 Jul. 1916.

16   Selborne papers, MS. Selborne 80, f. 224, 1 Sep. 1916.

17   BC, EFm, 1 Jul. 1916.

18   F.S.L. Lyons, *John Dillon: A Biography* (London 1968), p. 399.

19   W.A.S. Hewins, *The Apologia of an Imperialist: Forty years of Empire Policy* (London 1929), vol. 2, p. 83.

20   A. Jackson, *Home Rule*, p. 195.

21   *The Times*, 12 Jul. 1916.

22   *Guardian*, 13 Jul. 1916.

23   *The Times*, 14 Jul. 1916.

24   Selborne papers, MS. Selborne 84, f. 1, 24 Jul. 1916.

25   On 1 June the British and German fleets met at the Battle of Jutland, which lasted only twenty minutes but confirmed the Royal Navy's control of the seas. Britain lost three battle cruisers, four armoured cruisers, eight destroyers and 6,094 dead, whereas Germany lost one battle cruiser, an outdated battleship, four light cruisers, five destroyers and 2,551 dead. As a result, it did not seem like a British victory. Four days later, HMS *Hampshire* – on its way to Russia with Lord Kitchener on board – was sunk by a mine off the Orkneys. Public confidence in the Admiralty sank with it. G.R. Searle, *A New England?* p. 689.

26   Margot Asquith papers, MS. Eng. hist. c. 6680, f. 150, 9 Jun. 1916.

27   BL 88906/26/5, 26 May 1916.

28   Esher (3rd Viscount) (ed.), *Journals and Letters of Reginald, Viscount Esher*

(London 1938), vol. 4 (1916–30), p. 18.

29 A.J.P. Taylor, *Struggle*, p. 552.

30 The first offer of peace was made when an emissary was employed by the Germans to sound out the French and to try to discover the terms upon which an armistice might be granted with a view of subsequently discussing terms of peace.

31 Esher (ed.), *Journals*, vol. 4, p. 35.

32 BL 88906/26/3/1, 13 Nov. 1916.

33 Ibid.

34 Ibid.

35 D.R. Woodward (ed.), *The Military Correspondence of Field-Marshal Sir William Robertson, Chief of the Imperial General Staff, December 1915–February 1918* (London 1989), p. 21.

36 BL 88906/26/3/1, 24 Nov. 1916.

37 J. Grigg, *From Peace to War*, p. 425.

38 Lloyd George papers, LG/E/8/4/2/(e), 27 Nov. 1916.

39 A.J.P. Taylor (ed.), *Lloyd George: A Diary* p. 127.

40 A. Chamberlain, *Down the Years* (London 1937), p. 112.

41 BC, EFm, 24 Nov. 1916.

42 Bonar Law papers, 117/1/29, 1 Dec. 1916.

43 Beaverbrook papers, BBK/G/2/12, 1 Dec. 1916.

44 BL 88906/25/21/2, 3 Dec. 1916.

45 D. Gilmour, *Curzon*, p. 456.

46 J. Vincent (ed.), *The Crawford Papers*, pp. 372–73.

47 Devonshire papers, N15 6269, 5 Dec. 1916.

48 R.J.Q. Adams, *Bonar Law*, p. 23.

49 BC, Lans (5), ML, 6 Dec. 1916.

50 Ibid., 7 Dec. 1916.

51 Devonshire papers, N15 6268, 15 Dec. 1916.

52 BL 88906/22/7, 16 Dec. 1916.

53 BC, EFm, 13 Dec. 1916.

54 Criss-crossing.

55 BC, EFm, 13 Dec. 1916.

Chapter 37: Out of Office

1 Devonshire papers, O19 6996, 19 Jan. 1917.

2 The Speaker's Conference on Electoral Reform unanimously recommended, in January 1917, a mix of Alternative Vote and Single Transferable Vote for elections to the House of Commons.

3 Devonshire papers, N15 6275, 22 Jul. 1917.

4 Chamberlain papers, AC 12/116, 22 Jul. 1917.

5 *The Times*, 25 Apr. 1918.

6 The Dardanelles Commission was an investigation into the disastrous

1915 Dardanelles Campaign.

7   BC, EFm, 13 Mar. 1917.

8   The purpose of the Commission was to inquire into the origin, inception and conduct of operations of the war in Mesopotamia, including the supply of drafts, reinforcements, ammunition and equipment to the troops and fleet, care for the sick and wounded, and the responsibility of those government departments whose duty it was to minister to the wants of the forces employed in the theatre of war.

9   *Daily Chronicle*, 12 Jul. 1917.

10 Chamberlain papers, AC 12/116, 22 Jul. 1917.

11 Hansard 5, vol. 24, cc. 490–91.

12 The Officers' Families Fund was intended to benefit the wives and dependent relatives of officers in the Navy and Army, including the Territorial Forces, ordered on active service, who found themselves in financial or any other difficulty.

13 *Irish Society*, 4 Apr. 1917.

14 BC, EFm, 4 Oct. 1917.

15 Hardinge of Penshurst papers, 72, f. 702, 5 Nov. 1915.

16 *The Times*, 9 Dec. 1915.

17 Ibid., 31 May 1915.

18 Devonshire papers, A2 3985, n.d. [*c*.1915].

19 BC, EFm, 4 Aug. 1915.

20 Money-Kyrle papers, 1720, f. 869, 2 Mar. 1917.

21 Devonshire papers, N3 56504, 23 Feb. 1918.

22 Ibid., N3 5656, 22 Apr. 1917.

23 Ibid., N3 5650, 13 Dec. 1917.

24 The measure was divided into five parts: a minimum price for wheat and oats, a minimum agricultural wage, restriction on raising agricultural rents, power to enforce proper cultivation and a general schedule. In part it deprived landlords control over their own land. It was a relief to 'arable farmers, because it guaranteed them a minimum price for wheat and oats until 1922 and fixed their rents at a level that fell well below inflation'. G.R. Searle, *A New England?*, p. 798.

25 *Manchester Guardian*, 24 Feb. 1917.

26 Hansard 5, vol. 25, c. 559.

27 Devonshire papers, F6 2518, 2 Jul. 1917.

28 BC, EFm, 30 Aug. 1917.

29 *The Times*, 4 Oct. 1917.

Chapter 38: Moves towards Peace

1   A. Chamberlain, *Down the Years*, p. 112.

2   J. Turner, *British Politics and the Great War: Coalition and Conflict, 1915–1918* (London 1992), p. 205.

3   Devonshire papers, F6 2517, 2 Jul. 1917.

4   V.H. Rothwell, *British War Aims and Peace Diplomacy 1914–1918* (Oxford 1971), p. 75.

5   6th Marquess of Lansdowne, 'The Peace Letter of 1917', *The Nineteenth Century and After*, vol. 115 (1934), p. 370.

6   BL 88906/26/3/2, 16 Nov. 1917.

7   C. Seymour (ed.), *The Intimate Papers of Colonel House*, vol. 3: *Into the World War, April 1917–June 1918* (London 1926), p. 237.

8   BL 88906/26/3/2, 22 Nov. 1917.

9   Balfour and Lansdowne met outside St Margaret's Church, Westminster Abbey, on 26 November, after the memorial service for Neil James Archibald Primrose, the second son and youngest child of Lord Rosebery.

10   BL 88906/26/4, n.d. [*c*.1918].

11   Ibid., n.d. [*c*.1918].

12   Ibid., 28 Nov. 1917.

13   6th Marquess of Lansdowne, 'The Peace Letter of 1917', *The Nineteenth Century and After*, vol. 115 (1934), p. 370.

14   Lloyd George papers, LG/F/160/1/9, 30 Nov. 1917.

15   *Daily Mail*, 30 Nov. 1917.

16   *Daily Express*, 30 Nov. 1917.

17   *Morning Post*, 1 Dec. 1917.

18   RA GV/Q1085/39, 7 Dec. 1917.

19   J.L. Thompson, *Politicians, The Press, and Propaganda: Lord Northcliffe and the Great War, 1914–1919* (Kent, Ohio 1999), p. 177.

20   D. Rossini (ed.), *From Theodore Roosevelt to FDR: Internationalism and Isolationism in American Foreign Policy* (Keele 1995), p. 31.

21   Lloyd George papers, LG/F/160/1/9, *Daily Chronicle*, 30 Nov. 1917.

22   J. Grigg, *Lloyd George: War Leader, 1916–1918* (London 2002), p. 327.

23   V.H. Rothwell, *War Aims*, p. 75.

24   D. Newton, 'The Lansdowne "Peace Letter" of 1917 and the Prospect of Peace by Negotiation with Germany', *Australian Journal of Politics and History*, vol. 48, no. 1 (2002), p. 20.

25   *The Times*, 1 Dec. 1917.

26   RA GV/Q1085 /48, 4 Dec 1917; 'the following correspondence' was Lansdowne to Balfour (16 Nov. 1917) and Balfour to Lansdowne (22 Nov. 1917).

27   BL 88906/26/5, 1 Aug. 1933.

28   J. Grigg, *War Leader*, p. 330.

29   R. Blake, *Bonar Law*, p. 363.

30   R.J.Q. Adams, *Bonar Law*, p. 263.

31   T. Pinney (ed.), *The Letters of Rudyard Kipling*, vol. 4 (1911–19), p. 474.

32   BL 89906/25/21/3, 3 Dec. 1917.

33   H. Cecil, *Lord Lansdowne: From the Entente Cordiale of 1904 to the 'Peace Letter'*

of 1917: A European Statesman Assessed (London 2004), p. 27.
34 M. Bentley, *The Liberal Mind 1914–1929* (Cambridge 1977), p. 60.
35 Devonshire papers, CS9 AA4 11862A, 3 Feb. 1918.
36 Lloyd George papers, LG/F/160/1/9, 3 Dec. 1917.
37 G.M. Trevelyan, *Grey of Fallodon: Being the Life of Sir Edward Grey, afterwards Viscount Grey of Fallodon* (London 1937), p. 444.
38 Lloyd George papers, LG/F/160/1/9, *Daily News*, 30 Nov. 1917.
39 H. Kurtz, 'The Lansdowne Letter', *History Today*, 18 (1968), p. 87.
40 *The Times*, 5 Dec. 1917.
41 Lloyd George papers, LG/F/6/5/10, 5 Dec. 1917.
42 *The Times*, 15 Dec. 1917.
43 Devonshire papers, N3 5650, 13/14 Dec. 1917.
44 BC, Lans (6), 17 Dec. 1917.
45 BL 88906/26/4, 14 Dec. 1917.
46 BC, Lans (6), 15 Jan. 1918.
47 BL 88906/22/7, 22 Dec. 1917.
48 D. Rossini (ed.), *Internationalism*, p. 31.

Chapter 39: The Lansdowne Movement
1 J. Turner, *British Politics*, p. 258.
2 Lloyd George papers, LG/F/23/2/14, 13 Feb. 1918.
3 Ibid., LG/F/23/2/15, 15 Mar. 1918.
4 BL 88906/25/21/3, 14 Dec. 1917.
5 Lady A. Gordon-Lennox (ed.), *The Diary of Lord Bertie of Thame, 1914–1918* (London 1924), vol. 2, p. 263.
6 Ibid., p. 264.
7 J. Turner, *British Politics*, p. 258.
8 *Common Sense*, 1 Jun. 1918.
9 On 5 January 1918 Lloyd George spoke at Caxton Hall in Westminster to the Trades Union Congress on the subject of Allied war aims. He called for Germany to be divested of her colonies and Alsace-Lorraine, and that Belgium should be restored to independence. He hinted at reparations and a new international order. The speech increased his support from the Trade Unions and the Labour party.
10 BL 88906/26/4, n.d. [*c*.1918].
11 Ibid., 15 Feb. 1918.
12 K. Robbins, *The Abolition of War: The 'Peace Movement' in Britain, 1914–1919* (Cardiff 1976), p. 151.
13 D. Newton, 'The Lansdowne "Peace Letter"', *Australian Journal of Politics and History*, vol. 48, no. 1 (2002), p. 35.
14 F.W. Hirst papers, ex-cat prelim box A, n.d. [*c*.1918].
15 Ibid.
16 *Common Sense*, 1 Jun. 1918.

17 G. Ritter, *The Sword and the Sceptre: The Problem of Militarism in Germany.
    The Reign of Militarism and the Disaster of 1918* Translated by H. Norden
    (London 1972–73), vol. 4, p. 205.

18 D. Newton, 'The Lansdowne "Peace Letter"', *Australian Journal of Politics
    and History*, vol. 48, no. 1 (2002), p. 35.

19 Lord Beaverbrook, *Men and Power, 1917–1918* (London 1956), p. 35.

20 Bryce papers, MS. Bryce 251, f. 63, 8 Mar. 1918.

21 F.W. Hirst papers, ex-cat prelim box A, 5 Jun. 1918.

22 K. Robbins, *Abolition*, p. 205.

23 Lady A. Gordon-Lennox (ed.), *Diary*, p. 276.

24 Hansard 5, vol. 29, c. 499.

25 Ibid.

26 F.W. Hirst papers, ex-cat prelim box A, 25 Mar. 1918.

Chapter 40: The End of the War

1   Devonshire papers, F6 2520, 21 Apr. 1918.

2   Hansard 5, vol. 29, c. 1039.

3   *Common Sense*, 1 Jun. 1918.

4   BL 88906/26/4, 17 May 1918.

5   M. Swartz, *The Union of Democratic Control in British Politics During the First
    World War* (Oxford 1971), p. 193.

6   *Labour Leader*, 6 Jun. 1918, p. 7; ibid., 12 Sep. 1918, p. 7.

7   *The Times*, 1 Aug. 1918.

8   Bryce papers, MS. Bryce USA 7, f. 144, 2 Aug. 1918.

9   D. Cooper, *Autobiography: The Rainbow Comes and Goes* (London 1958),
    p. 191.

10 F.W. Hirst papers, ex-cat prelim box A, 9 Oct. 1918.

11 Ibid., 24 Nov. 1918.

12 Moreton Frewen papers, Box 22, 29 Oct. 1918.

13 BC, Lans (6), 15 Jan. 1919.

Chapter 41: The Final Years

1   M. Perry, *The House in Berkeley Square: A History of the Lansdowne Club*
    (London 2003), p. 109.

2   Devonshire papers, Q1 8420, 7 Dec. 1920.

3   Ibid., F6 5693, 10 Apr. 1921.

4   *Public Opinion*, 7 Jan. 1921.

5   M. Perry, *House*, p. 114.

6   BC, EFm, 11 May 1919.

7   Devonshire papers, F6 5672, 12 Jun. 1919.

8   Long papers, 62403, f. 149, 2 Oct. 1919.

9   Lansdowne NG 26/60, 10 Dec. 1923.

10 Devonshire papers, F6 5679, 20 Nov. 1919.

11 Ibid., A 22 898, 23 Nov. 1919.
12 Ibid., F6 5816, 1 Sep. 1921.
13 *The Times*, 23 Jun. 1921.
14 Devonshire papers, N4 5816, 1 Sep. 1921.
15 Bryce papers, MS. Bryce 199, f. 165, 2 Nov. 1921.
16 Devonshire papers, F6 5820, 20 Dec. 1921.
17 Hansard 5, vol. 49, c. 549.
18 Ibid., vol. 49, c. 549.
19 Ibid., vol. 52, c. 213.
20 Ibid., vol. 52, c. 217.
21 Newton, *Lansdowne*, p. 505.
22 BC, EFm, 2 May 1922.
23 Curzon papers, Mss. Eur. F112/226a, 29 Sep. 1922.
24 MacDonnell of Swinford papers, MS. MacDonnell 33, f. 41, 27 Sep. 1922.
25 *The Times*, 26 Sep. 1922.
26 *Common Sense*, 29 May 1920.
27 Ibid.
28 *St Martin's Review*, 11 Nov. 1923.
29 Devonshire papers, G17 3557, 20 Sep. 1923.
30 BC, Lans IE, 2 Nov. 1923.
31 BC, Lans BE, 13 Sep. 1924.
32 BC, EFm, 12 Jun. 1924.
33 MacDonnell of Swinford papers, MS. MacDonnell D 238, f. 48, 14 Jun. 1925.
34 BC, EFm, f. 223, 13 Jun. 1925.
35 Ibid., f. 225, 22 Aug. 1925.
36 Ibid., f. 245, 13 Aug. 1926.
37 Devonshire papers, Z 5, 10 Jun. 1927.
38 BL 88906/21/5, 18 Jun. 1927.
39 Hansard 5, vol. 67, c. 717.
40 Ibid., vol. 67, c. 716.
41 Grenfell papers, D/ERv C 829/1, 19 Aug. 1927.

Chapter 42: Conclusion: A Life of Service
1 *The Times*, 6 Jun. 1927.
2 Newton, *Lansdowne* p. 496.

INDEX

Abdul Hamid II, Sultan of Turkey, 160

Abercorn, James, 1st Duke of, (father-in-law), 19

Abyssinia, 115, 167

Adam, Robert, 3, 327

Afghanistan, xiv, 58, 65, 67, 81–2, 88, 92, 153, 154, 164

Agadir Crisis (1911), 221

Akers-Douglas, Aretas (later 1st Viscount Chilston), 119

Alaska Boundary Dispute (1903), 157–8

Albert I, King of Belgium, 380

Albert, Duke of Schleswig-Holstein, 276

Albert, Prince, 352

Albert Edward, Prince of Wales, see: Edward VII, King

Albert Victor, Prince of Wales, 68

Alexandra Feodorovna, Empress of Russia, 263

Alexandra, Queen, 151, 168, 191, 315

Alfonso XII, King of Spain, 168

Aliens Expulsion Act (1896), 116, 357

Aliens Immigration Act (1896), 116, 357

Allied War Council, see: Supreme War Council

Alsace-Lorraine, 281, 283, 301, 386

Alverstone, 1st Viscount, 158

America, see: United States of America

Amery, Leo, 132

Amiens, Battle of (1918), 308

Anglo-Ashanti War (1873–74), 24

Anglo-French Agreement (1904), xv, 165–7, 175, 178–9, 180–1, 182, 245, 326, 369

Anglo-German China agreement (1900), 150–1

Anglo-Japanese Alliance (1902), xv, 155–7, 175, 326

Anglo-Japanese Alliance (1905), 177–8, 180, 182

Anson, Florence, 34

Anson, Henry, 34

Ardagh, John, 58, 86, 117, 142, 353

Army Board, 106, 107–8, 111, 117, 118, 131, 143

Army Nursing Reserve, 140

Arnold-Forster, Hugh Oakeley, 104, 109, 110, 118, 120

Ashbourne, 1st Baron, 171

Asquith, Arthur, 211

Asquith, Herbert, Henry (later 1st Earl of Oxford and Asquith), xiv, vi, 28, 131, 189, 193, 194, 199, 202, 203, 205–7, 213, 214–5, 216, 217, 219, 220, 221, 227, 230, 232, 235–6, 238, 240–3, 244–6, 248–9, 250–6, 257, 259, 260–3, 265, 266–8, 276, 285, 287, 293, 296, 298, 301, 310

Asquith, Margot (later 1st Countess of Oxford and Asquith), 194, 201, 212, 219, 251, 259, 261, 291, 298

Asquith, Raymond, 263

Asquith, Violet, 220

Assam, 64, 73, 74, 84

Astor, Violet, see: Petty-Fitzmaurice, Violet

Astor, William Waldorf, 124, 259

Augusta Victoria, German Empress Consort, 213

Austria-Hungary, 160, 167, 211, 220, 244, 263, 276, 280, 283, 286, 288, 300, 307, 309

Austria, see: Austria-Hungary

Backwoodsmen, 195, 212

Baden-Powell, Robert, 131

Baden, Prince Max von, 301, 309

Baghdad Railway, 158–9

Bainbridge, Edmond, 123

Baldwin, Stanley (later 1st Earl Baldwin of Bewdley), 291

Balfour of Burleigh, 6th Lord, 200

Balfour, Arthur James (later 1st Earl of Balfour), xiv–xv, 7, 102, 109, 111, 116, 126, 128, 132, 138, 148, 156, 158–9, 160–1, 162–3, 164, 166, 171, 172, 173, 174, 176, 179, 180, 183–4, 187–8, 190, 193, 196, 198–9, 200–1, 203–5, 206–10, 212, 214–20, 223–5, 226, 248, 252, 259–61, 266, 268, 281–2, 284, 286, 290, 325, 372

Balliol College, Oxford, 8–11, 12

Barrackpore, 59, 65

Barrington, Eric, 147

Bayard, Thomas, 40, 46, 51

Beauchamp, 7th Earl, 298, 300, 302, 304, 322

Bedford, 11th Duke of, 191

Belgium, 170, 180, 211, 246, 248, 287, 300, 361, 386

Benckendorff, Count Alexander, 164–5, 167

Bengal, 70, 71, 83, 84, 87, 225

Beresford, Lord William, 56, 59

Bertie, 1st Viscount Bertie of Thame, 153, 176, 179, 298, 301

Bethmann-Hollweg, Theobald von, 213, 263

Bigge, Arthur, see: Stamfordham, 1st Baron

Birch, Augustus, Revd, 6, 7, 8

Birrell, Augustine, 189, 206

Björkö, Treaty of (1905), 180

Black Week, 131–2

Blandford, Albertha Marchioness of, 22, 151

Blandford, Marquess of, (later 8th Duke of Marlborough), 22

Bloemfontein Conference (1899), 125

Blücher, Gebhard Leberecht von, 303

Blue Water School, 114, 357

Blunt, Wilfrid Scawen, 212, 220

Boer War, see: War in South Africa

Boers, 111, 112, 115, 117, 129, 138–9, 143, 152

Bolshevik, 280, 281, 301

Bombay, 54–5, 61, 64, 70–1, 80, 83, 84, 87, 88

Bonar Law, Andrew, xv, 224–5, 226, 228–9, 230, 234–5, 236, 237–41, 243, 244–5, 251, 252–3, 255, 256, 258, 259, 260–1, 263, 265–8, 275, 280, 291, 310

Borden, Robert, 280

Bowood, vii, xi, xii, 3–4, 6, 11, 13–5, 16, 22, 24–5,

253, 254, 260, 269, 270

Cromer, 1st Earl of, 165, 193

Cross, 1st Viscount, 60, 63, 70, 72–3, 74, 75, 79, 82, 83

Crowfoot, Chief, 41, 44

Curragh incident (1914), 239

Curzon, George (later 1st Marquess Curzon of Kedleston), 74, 83, 91, 127, 153–4, 159, 163, 164–5, 199, 208, 211, 216–7, 218, 219, 220, 224, 226, 249, 250, 252–3, 255, 262, 263, 267, 268, 270, 275, 316, 351

Czernin, Count Ottokar, 280, 286, 299, 301

Damrong, Prince of Siam, 79

Dardanelles Campaign (1915–16), 252–3

Dardanelles Inquiry (1916), 276, 383

Davidson, Randall, (Archbishop of Canterbury), 189, 293

Dawkins, Clinton Edward, 365

Dawson, Geoffrey, 284

de Valera, Éamon, 317

Delcassé, Théophile, 152, 165, 167, 179

Delhi Announcement (1911), 225

Denbigh, 9th Earl of, 304–5

Derby Scheme (1915), 255

Derby, 15th Earl of, 35

Derby, 16th Earl of, 142

Derby, 17th Earl of, 255, 262

Derreen, xi, 13, 14, 16, 19, 168, 170, 191, 213, 221, 259, 279, 319, 320–1, 322–3, 327

Devonshire, 8th Duke of, 21, 26–7, 48, 81, 96, 98, 99, 102, 106, 109, 111, 115, 123, 128, 138, 163, 173, 174, 183, 184, 192

Dicey, Albert Venn, 199, 217, 219

Diehards, 212, 214–7, 218, 220, 222, 223, 224, 241, 325

Digby, Lady Everard, see: Petty-Fitzmaurice, Lady Emily

Digby, Lord Everard, 3, 54, 124

Dilke, Charles Wentworth, 104, 111, 120, 131, 136, 169

Dillon, John, 243

Donaldson, 'Hay' Frederick, 122

Doyle, Arthur Conan, 132

Dudley, 2nd Earl of, 171

Dufferin and Ava, 1st Marquess of, 38, 52, 58, 59, 61, 63, 65, 68, 194, 342

Duke, Henry (later 1st Baron Merrivale), 261

Dunraven, 4th Earl of, 170–1, 173

Durand Mission to Kabul (1893), 88–9

Durand, Mortimer, 67, 81, 88–9, 177

Easter Rising (1916), 257, 260, 282

Ebert, Friedrich, 309

Eckardstein, Baron Hermann von, 149, 151

Eden, Lady Anne Clarissa (Dowager Countess of Avon), 211

Education Act (1902), 188

Education Bill (1906), 188–90

Edward VII, King, xiv, 17, 125, 151, 152, 156, 158, 160, 162, 167, 168, 179, 189, 192, 199, 206, 210–1, 213

Edward VIII, King, 249

Egypt, 115, 118, 159, 178, 165, 166, 369

Egyptian Khedivial Decree, 167, 369

Elgin, 9th Earl of, 89, 90

Emmy, see: Petty-Fitzmaurice, Lady Emily

Entente Cordiale, see: Anglo-French Agreement (1904)

Ernst August, Crown Prince of Hanover, 276

Esher, 2nd Viscount, 149, 293

Eton College, xiii, 6–8, 9, 11, 34, 61, 100, 103

Eugénie, Empress, 17

Evicted Irish Tenants Bill (1907), 195, 373

Fawcett, Millicent, 238

Fenian, 15, 27, 31, 34–5, 36, 39

Fisher, 1st Baron, 251, 276

Fitzroy, Almeric, 168, 171, 192, 195, 196, 201, 219

FitzWalter, Gerald, 336

Flahaut, Charles de, (maternal grandfather), 5, 16

Fleuriau, M. de, 263

Foch, Ferdinand, 308

Food taxes, 225, 229

France, 4, 64, 79, 80, 133, 135, 142, 146, 150–1, 152, 156–7, 160, 161, 165, 166–7, 169, 174–5, 178–9, 180, 182, 211, 244–5, 246, 253, 263, 264, 281, 283, 301, 306, 307, 326, 361

Franz Ferdinand, Archduke, 242

Franz Joseph I, Emperor of Austria, 160

Free fooders, 184, 193, 229, 371

Free trade, 52, 168, 173, 174, 193, 199, 208, 275, 299, 370, 371

French, John (later 1st Earl of Ypres), 139, 239, 249

Frewen, Moreton, 309

Garfield, Harry Augustus, 290

Garvin, James Louis, 198

Geddes, Eric Campbell, 288

George V, King, 192, 197, 205, 206, 213, 214, 216, 217, 220, 225, 232–3, 234, 237, 241, 243, 248, 267–8, 269, 276, 317

George VI, King, 315

German Emperor, see: Wilhelm II, Kaiser of Germany

Germany, xv, 145, 146–8, 150–2, 155, 157, 158, 161, 165, 166–7, 168, 176, 178–9, 180–1, 191, 221, 244–6, 262–3, 276, 280–1, 283, 286–8, 300–1, 303, 304, 308–9, 327, 361, 378, 382, 386

Gladstone, William Ewart, xiv, 21, 22–3, 25, 26, 27–9, 30–1, 34, 36, 49, 51, 82–3, 88, 97, 98

Godley, Arthur (later 1st Baron Kilbracken), 82

Goodenough, William, 121

Goodwood Races, 22, 217

Gordon of Khartoum, Charles George, 122

Gore, Charles, 11, 49, 98

Gorst, John Eldon, 57, 60, 64

Goschen, 1st Viscount, 48, 99, 102, 103, 109, 111, 116, 123, 128

Gough, Hubert, 239, 240

Gould, Edward, 79

Government House, Calcutta, 55–6

Granville, George, 2nd Earl, 7, 9, 19, 21, 23, 25,